Federalist Solutions to Pakistan's Political Crises

Federalist Solutions to Pakistan's Political Crises

Sikander Ahmed Shah

LEXINGTON BOOKS
Lanham • Boulder • New York • London

Published by Lexington Books
An imprint of The Rowman & Littlefield Publishing Group, Inc.
4501 Forbes Boulevard, Suite 200, Lanham, Maryland 20706
www.rowman.com

86-90 Paul Street, London EC2A 4NE

British Library Cataloguing in Publication Information Available

Library of Congress Cataloging-in-Publication Data

Names: Shah, Sikander A., author. Title: Federalist solutions to Pakistan's political crises / Sikander Ahmed Shah. Description: Lanham : Lexington Books, 2024. | Includes bibliographical references and index. | Summary: "This book examines the transformative potential of communal democratic norms in Pakistan's political and economic landscape, advocating for a localized centripetalism model to counter prevailing hegemonic trends and address challenges posed by the existing consociational structure" —Provided by publisher. Identifiers: LCCN 2024010751 (print) | LCCN 2024010752 (ebook) | ISBN 9781666955453 (cloth) | ISBN 9781666955460 (epub) Subjects: LCSH: Federal government—Pakistan. | Civil-military relations—Pakistan. | Pakistan—Politics and government—1988- | Pakistan—Ethnic relations—Political aspects. | Pakistan—Foreign economic relations—China. | China—Foreign economic relations—Pakistan. Classification: LCC JQ629.A38 S867 2024 (print) | LCC JQ629.A38 (ebook) | DDC 320.45491—dc23/eng/20240405
LC record available at https://lccn.loc.gov/2024010751LC ebook record available at https://lccn.loc.gov/2024010752

Contents

Acknowledgments vii

Introduction 1

Chapter 1: Implementing Local Centripetalism in Pakistan: A Federalist Solution for Upholding Distributive Justice, Local Democracy, Collective Protection of Minorities and Multiculturalism to Combat Interethnic Conflict, Civil Military Imbalance, and the Inequalities Exacerbated by Chinese Investments 23

Chapter 2: Ethnic Federalism and Pakistan 71

Chapter 3: Civil-Military Relations 157

Chapter 4: Chinese Expansionism and the Impact of Chinese Investments in Pakistan: Neoliberalism, China's Belt and Road Initiative and Unpacking the Chinese–Pakistan Economic Corridor 227

Conclusion 301

Index 323

About the Author 333

Acknowledgments

This book has evolved from my Ph.D. thesis, fueled by a passion to explore and examine the mechanisms for fostering democracy and advancing human rights in Pakistan. The core of my exploration rests on uncovering solutions to Pakistan's challenges within the transformative potential of communal democratic norms embedded in the country's legal, political, and economic landscape. These norms—comprising distributive justice, grassroots democracy, minority protections, and multiculturalism—bear the promise of ushering in systemic democratic change when integrated into Pakistan's governance structures. Recognizing the limitations of many Western assessments, which often overlook the complex subjectivities and ground realities of post-colonial Pakistan, I endeavor to offer locally relevant and indigenously viable solutions. In doing so, I aim to rectify historical power imbalances that have marginalized specific groups in Pakistan. By placing a principal emphasis on local centripetalism, I propose harnessing centripetal forces to counter prevailing hegemonic trends and cultivate greater sociocultural cohesion within Pakistan's diverse polity. This work delves into Pakistan's civil-military asymmetry, highlighting the influential role of the military establishment and its interwoven relationship with preexisting interethnic tensions. Additionally, it explores how the China-Pakistan Economic Corridor (CPEC) continues to shape Pakistan's federal structure, socioeconomic fabric, and civil-military dynamics.

I extend my sincere gratitude to Abid Rizvi, Sana Afraz, and Anoshay Fazal—remarkable and dedicated individuals—for their unwavering support in providing invaluable research and editorial assistance throughout the entirety of this project. I am equally appreciative of the contributions made by Mirat Sattar, Aima Nisar, and Amna Naqvi, whose research and editorial assistance significantly enriched this work. Moreover, I would like to express my heartfelt thanks to Abdullah Shah, Ibrahim Shah, Hana Shah, Hadi Shah, Uzair Kayani, Asad Farooq, Khalid Mir, Ayesha Malik, Beena Soofi, Lubna Anwar, Anwar Kamal, Zara Zamir, Nadir Shah, Sajida Soofi,

Amjad Soofi, and Hassan Bashir for their indispensable advice and encouragement. I am grateful to Dean Sadaf Aziz (LUMS) for her guidance and for fostering an optimal research environment. Special thanks to professors Hamid Ekbia, Russell Lee Hanson, David Williams, Susan Williams, and William E. Scheuerman for their invaluable support, practical insights, and the opportunities to contextualize my arguments. Additionally, I extend my appreciation to Indiana University, Bloomington, for their support in facilitating seminal secondary research.

The completion of this book would not have been possible without the unwavering support, encouragement, and contributions of these individuals and institutions.

Introduction

As a postcolonial state, Pakistan has consistently grappled with balancing the interplay between historic, indigenous forms of sociocultural, political, and economic ordering, and the forms imposed first by the British colonial regime and—more recently—by contemporary international law and the international trade and commercial framework. The uneven application of political norms throughout the territory of historical Pakistan has further complicated postcolonial efforts to incorporate or indigenize democratic principles of governance; for example, certain areas—such as the country's old Eastern wing (now the independent state of the People's Republic of Bangladesh)—were deliberately excluded from the ambit of governance,[1] resulting in an uneven application of the political norms informing governance mechanisms and arrangements. More recently, preexisting communitarian frictions have fomented extremist and secessionist movements in other, less politically influential provinces of the country, such as the restive provinces of Baluchistan and Khyber-Pakhtunkhwa.[2]

Pakistan inherited a robust military apparatus from the former colonial regime, more forceful and well-entrenched than the civilian infrastructures and governance systems it similarly inherited. This military apparatus—cast in a colonial mold, as it was—turned its attention towards furthering its domestic interests and ambitions. As such, Pakistan has spent much of its postindependence history under intermittent periods of direct military rule, and the military—and its associated industries—continues to wield inordinate influence over the country's politics, economy, foreign relations, and industry.[3] This historical asymmetry between the Pakistani civilian and military establishments has magnified—and, in turn, been magnified by—inter-ethnic differences among the various identity groups within Pakistan.

The Pakistani military has leveraged inter-communal frictions and socioeconomic disenfranchisement to further its political interests, while simultaneously acting—for various geostrategic reasons—as a core contributing factor towards extremism and radicalization in the region. The armed forces also exert significant influence over the country's judiciary and legal system, resulting in the latter's historical legitimization of military excesses.

Instances of armed conflict or national defense have often been used—or even manufactured—by the military to justify greater politico-economic overreach on the institution's part without judicial oversight, in a manner otherwise inconsistent with the country's legal and constitutional framework.

The judiciary has repeatedly been required to rule over explosive political issues and in doing so has frequently seemed to reaffirm the inclinations of the powerful, with some of its jurisprudence reflecting a succumbing to the dominant political and military influences extant in the country.[4] Given this context, it has been difficult for Pakistan to credibly maintain the 'independence' of its judiciary, though the latter does overtly insist to be guided only by the Constitution of Pakistan and the principles of the rule of law.

Furthermore, communitarian strife, often exacerbated by fallout from Pakistan's neoliberal experimentation, has manifested in demonstrably increased religious fundamentalism throughout the country. Much of this can be attributed to the various 'Islamization' processes employed by the political and military leadership throughout the country's history,[5] as well as to the significant political cache religion—i.e., Islam—has within domestic politics. Given the political capital religiosity holds in Pakistan, arguably all political parties have leveraged faith to varying degrees to canvass for support, resulting in a sharpening of religious distinctions within the country and a concomitant increase in the religiosity—perceived or otherwise—of the polity. The increased polarization of Pakistan's political mechanisms—which have continued to deepen over time—have also rendered political discourse in the country an essentially zero-sum proposition, with ethnic federalism propagating historical ethnic and religious differences. These preexisting tensions, arising out of socioeconomic marginalization in Pakistan, become conflated with ethnic or religious differences, fomenting antipathy and occasionally overt violence towards sociocultural minorities.

The patchwork development of the Pakistani economy has also been exacerbated by these inter-ethnic divisions and the marginalization of certain ethnic communities. This marginalization has contributed towards growing extremist and secessionist sentiments in the country's smaller more restive provinces, which, in turn, have prompted violent reprisals and suppression campaigns enacted by the Pakistani federal government and military establishment.[6]

More recently, these inter-ethnic—and inter-provincial—tensions have escalated following the inception of the China-Pakistan Economic Corridor (the "CPEC").[7] Part of China's overall 'Belt and Road Initiative' (the "BRI"), the CPEC is presented by the Pakistani center as an economic 'game-changer,' encompassing ambitious infrastructural projects including transport networks and power generation facilities.[8] Serious concerns have been raised by the smaller provinces, however, regarding the allocation of resources to, and benefits derived from, these projects. The CPEC presents a lightning rod for nationwide critique, with the initiative also generating domestic disquiet regarding Chinese influence over Pakistani governance, and the impact the neoliberal megaprojects under the CPEC have on Pakistani political and economic participation. The impacts of Chinese global investment policies have already raised certain concerns regarding compromised Pakistani workers' labor rights, rendering them more vulnerable to unemployment, as well as to hazards such as occupational illnesses and environmental degradation.[9] Local communities have also expressed their fears over the forcible usurpation of land by the government for the benefit of the project—though these concerns are not novel to the CPEC, with the Pakistani government having previously exercised eminent domain for other major infrastructural projects in the past and leaving the communities so dispossessed with little to no recourse and with inadequate recompense.

Pakistan's federal structure is presently predicated upon distinctly ethnic parameters, with the country attempting to constitutionally address ethnic federalism through consociational means and presenting the country's geopolitical ordering along ethnic lines as a way to ostensibly ensure representation for all extant identity groups in the country. This approach has proved to be seriously flawed as—given Pakistan's sociocultural diversity—it is arguably impossible to ensure adequate political representation—or even participation—for each distinct ethnic or religious group within the country.

This current form of consociationalism in Pakistan has meant that much of the country's socioeconomic development has focused on regions where the dominant ethnic groups reside, such as the province of Punjab, fostering resentment and disenfranchisement among other provinces.[10] On the national stage, this ethnic focus has resulted in the ascendancy of the Punjabi ethnic group, the most numerous such sociocultural bloc, and has seen Punjabis wield inordinate influence over the country's judiciary, its bureaucracy, and its politically significant military.[11] Moreover, instituting quotas for cultural or religious minorities has deepened these communitarian divides, compelling minority candidates to align themselves with political entities representing the dominant groups or else be rendered politically defunct.

During the British Raj (the period of direct British colonial rule from 1858–1947) in what was then the Indian subcontinent, the British Empire employed a 'divide and rule' policy, categorizing communities on the basis of their respective sociocultural 'markers,' such as religion, ethnicity, race, and caste, creating and emphasizing divisions between the various demographic groups indigenous to the region, including Hindus and Muslims.[12] Incidentally, these divisions were also implemented within the army, with control retained with British officers[13] while certain communities—such as the Sikhs or Pashtuns—were considered members of the 'martial races' and thus were overrepresented in the colonial armed forces. This ethnic and racial perception of military acumen persisted following Pakistan's independence, with the British preference for the Punjabi ethnic group and its disfavor for the Bengali ethnic group—the largest ethnic group in the nascent country—resulting in the Punjabis representing approximately 25 percent of the new country's population, and yet representing almost 75 percent of its armed forces.[14]

Under this schema, the British empire often engaged with Muslim elites, offering to safeguard their interests[15] and incentivizing them to demand separate electorates in India. This eventually led to the 1909 Minto-Morley reforms, under which the Muslim demand for separate electorates was first accepted.[16] The British continued to exploit the disaffection between the Hindu-dominated and 'unionist' Congress party and the Jinnah-led 'secessionist' Muslim League, furthering their interest of effecting divisions between the subcontinent's indigenous groups, culminating in the promulgation of Government of India Act, 1935,[17] which—while granting Muslims one-third representation at the center—also accorded extensive control to the British colonial executive, including by barring Indian representatives from legislating on key issues such as the budget, foreign relations, and defense.[18] Subsequently, demands for an independent Muslim homeland intensified, formally introduced through the Lahore Resolution of 1940.[19]

Post-partition, Pakistan inherited much of the same colonial structures instituted by the British regime, with centralized control implemented through the 1935 Act, where the central government enjoyed wide-ranging powers, including the power to dismiss provincial governments and impose governor—i.e., central—rule at the slightest resistance.

In addition to the dismissal of provincial assemblies in the aftermath of independence, the first Constituent Assembly was also subjected to strict executive control.[20] This apex body was constituted with the purpose of drafting a constitution and proposed reforms to the Acts of 1935 and 1947, which were met with significant opposition by the powerful executive seeking to consolidate its own power. The Constituent Assembly was eventually dismissed by the governor-general in 1954, and when the speaker for the Constituent Assembly sought relief from the courts against this executive overreach in the *Maulvi Tamizuddin* case, the Federal Court of Pakistan (now the Supreme Court) validated the governor-general's position on the matter.[21] Very early in the country's history, therefore, the stage was set for its courts to validate the abuse of power by the executive, a pattern that has repeated several times over the course of the country's existence and that has routinely been employed by the military to have the courts essentially 'rubber stamp' coups, which would otherwise be illegal or unconstitutional, on the basis of the 'doctrine of necessity.'[22]

Representatives of Pakistan's minority ethnic communities and the country's Bengali community—the latter of which comprised 53 percent of the entire country and which contained a sizeable Hindu population—in the Constituent Assembly resisted the consolidation of power in the federal executive.[23] These groups feared that a strong form of centripetalism in a diverse multi-ethnic society such as Pakistan would not prove inclusive of many ethnolinguistic and religious groups and would, in turn, increasingly undermine the political and cultural identity of these communities. It must be noted, however, that at this juncture these communities were not arguing for a consociational system of government instead, but merely against the centralization of power within the federal center.

Their concerns were realized, however, when the State made the Objectives Resolution the preamble to the future Constitution of Pakistan, indelibly weaving Islam into the country's constitutional architecture, and in so doing positing the presence of only one form of political identity in Pakistan, that of a Sunni Muslim citizen and subject.[24] Ethnic and religious minorities, particularly the Bengali members in the Assembly—many of them Hindu—saw this as a clear departure from the secular and multicultural state that was promised; in point of fact, the 1949 Objectives Resolution—and the process of its promulgation—was, indeed, a successful attempt by the country's powerful military and bureaucracy to—indirectly impose—a national identity upon a heterogenous and hitherto ecumenical polity by undermining historical multicultural norms. In this process, Urdu, touted as the language of all of India's Muslims, was officially declared as Pakistan's national language, to the dismay of the Bengalis and other ethnic groups, most of whom had their own native languages.

The 1956 formalization of the Constitution demonstrated a sham form of centripetalist federalism in Pakistan; under this framework, the executive continued to retain power at the federal center on key subjects, while the military effectively enjoyed the power to have the Constitution abrogated at its behest, and have the same validated by the courts.[25] Soon after tasting success in its constitutional tinkering, the military emerged openly in the public sphere as the central political entity in Pakistan, with the then–commander in chief of the Pakistan Army, General Ayub Khan, imposing martial law and elevating himself to the rank of field marshal and president of Pakistan. On the pretext of centripetal federalism and grassroots democracy, but with the real objective of diluting the political power of the Bengali community and maintaining a military dictatorship, the military—through Khan—imposed dyadic federalism in Pakistan whereby the country was bisected into only two federating units—i.e., East and West Pakistan—with Bengalis comprising all the former, and all other ethnic communities in the country's western regions clubbed into the latter.

On similar pretexts, General Ayub Khan also framed the "Basic Democracy" system—his attempt to effect greater central control over local and intranational politics—which was based on an electoral college created through non-party elections at the local and municipal levels, which collectively also elected the president of Pakistan. Under this presidential system of government, the 1962 Constitution granted the Pakistani head of state an inordinate amount of power,[26] a position almost purpose-built for military dictatorship. This distorted form of local centripetalism, which was subsequently similarly effected by other proceeding Pakistani military dictators,[27] was essentially veiled attempts by the poltico-military center to cement and extend unconstitutional and undemocratic control over the populace and to extract economic benefits from and exercise political power over. In Khan's case, this warped federal framework eventually precipitated the disintegration of the federation and the secession of East Pakistan following a civil war, during the conduct of which serious and credible allegations of war crimes were levied against the prosecuting Pakistan military.[28]

In addition to the military's misuse of centripetalism and local governance, dyadic federalism has also been criticized by some scholars for having some of the same structural deficiencies experienced by unequally placed ethnic communities in an otherwise divided and multi-ethnic state. This suppression of the Bengalis and their political power through the denial of proportional representation and access to resources is self-explanatory in the context of the reasons for failure of dyadic federations;[29] as Christoph Niessen et al. note:

> federal projects with two major communities can succeed if geographical factors such as the territorial dispersion of the dominant groups play in its favour and when the presence of institutional arrangements (such as a proportional electoral system or a national party system) either ensure fair political representation for both communities or prevent polities from being conceived in exclusively sub-national terms. In the absence of territorial dispersion, other institutional arrangements such as executive inclusiveness and an equal economic distribution between groups appear to be crucial in preventing the breakup of the federation. . . . By contrast, the analysis shows that a bipolar federal project is likely to fail in the absence of stabilizing institutional arrangements (i.e., electoral proportionality and a national party system) and, more particularly, when economic resources are unequally distributed between communities and when these communities are clearly separate territorially speaking.[30]

With the violent breakup of Pakistan, many of its political parties became disillusioned with the efficacy of centripetalist federalism, local governance, and the presidential form of government in promoting political stability and multiculturalism, even though the reasons these political or governance mechanisms failed in Pakistan were not related to any structural or intrinsic defects within them, but instead due to the military's misuse of these systems to its advantage. Consequentially, when his successor, General Yahya Khan, was ousted and a civilian government ushered in, this system was replaced with a parliamentary, consociational system of government based on ethnic federalism under the newly promulgated Constitution of 1973.

The 1973 Constitution reinstated provinces as they existed under the Government of India Act (1935). This formula, paired with the persisting Punjabi hegemony, the country's powerful military, and years of financial mismanagement and internecine divisions, gave rise to persistent ethnic discord in Pakistan. Post-1973, the military has used the ethnic divisions engendered and perpetuated by this federal system with consociationalist tendencies to control political parties and politicians. The military, wielding its inordinate influence over the economy, foreign relations, and Pakistan's various religious factions, manipulated the electoral system to bring the country's politicians into power. During this time, Pakistan's military establishment inextricably involved itself in national political processes—playing its role not only to promote, create, and sustain political parties and leaders, but also to withdraw its support from them and often even indirectly facilitate their ouster, essentially preventing the meaningful realization of national parties, leaders, and grassroots democracy independent of the military influence.[31]

In this era of ethnic federalism, the Pakistani military has leveraged and exploited ethnic divisions and competition between the provinces for power and resources to keep the civilian federal government weak and reliant upon it for support. In doing so, it has increasingly and gradually coopted several areas of competence—such as law enforcement and disaster relief—within its ambit, further entrenching itself within the Pakistani political landscape. The recent statement of the outgoing Chief of the Army Staff Qamar Javed Bajwa that the military had historically interfered in the country's politics over its seventy-odd year history, and that this meddling was unconstitutional, comes as a rare admission of such influence on the part of the country's politically savvy military; Bajwa's protestations that the military had foresworn from intruding in civilian politics since February 2021, however, ring rather hollow given the immense "war chest" of economic and political favors the Pakistani armed forces has garnered for itself over the years.

In Pakistan's post-1973 federal ordering, national political parties were ethnically derived and kept restrained to their respective provinces. The federal government was formed through a coalition between these ethnic parties, with the assent and support of the military. As such, there was no national party capable of challenging the military, which often created new parties and leaders to neutralize other political actors they earlier created and established once the latter became too independent and began to question the military's control over politics, foreign relations, and the economy.[32] During

Pakistan's long periods of military rule, military dictators would often create their own political party and head it as the president of Pakistan;[33] these parties would persist even during periods of civilian rule, during which the military would prop up ethnic and Islamic opposition parties to further weaken and destabilize the civilian government.[34] This set of circumstances persisted from 1973 up until 2017 when, following Prime Minister's Nawaz Sharif's disqualification over the Panama leaks by the Supreme Court,[35] the political landscape and federalism's trajectory in the country has seen a paradigm shift through populist leader Imran Khan's rise to power, effectively presenting a challenge to the military apparatus through his political rhetoric and the positions he adopted.

Khan's election to, and subsequent removal from, the prime minister's office appears to be yet another example of the military's political interventionism. It has been credibly reported that the military establishment supported his party's—the Pakistan *Tehreek-e-Insaaf* ("PTI")—rise to popularity; as Danish Khan describes it, "the military establishment acted as a 'magnet' to first pull the different political actors, such as the electables and allied parties, towards the PTI and then played the role of a 'glue' to keep them together."[36] Similarly, the military's role in PTI's ouster is also an ill-kept secret, though the reasons for this withdrawal of support from the military could be many and varied, such as, for example, that Khan's popularity and broad-based electoral appeal had threatened to expand beyond the military's 'comfort zone.'

Pakistan's military had not predicted that Khan would overtly challenge its political and economic preeminence, though the political positions and actions he took during his tenure, measures that proved immensely popular with the electorate, also proved to be at odds with historical military political 'doctrine.' Directly deciding appointments for the military's top brass and his criticism of and attempts to exercise oversight over the military certainly raised the ire of the institution's leadership. Khan also directly challenged Pakistan's system of consociational federalism, demonstrated most overtly by his attempts to rein in the cartel of ethnic elites by pushing for criminal convictions for fraud and corruption—among senior political representatives from these groups—and by employing rousing rhetoric, such as describing these persons as 'crooks' and 'corrupt politicians' who had promoted internecine conflict and ethnic fragmentation in the country and had looted the national exchequer.

Reforming Pakistan's local government system was also a fundamental part of Khan's political mandate,[37] and he seemed set to effect actual, meaningful devolution of power to the grassroots level—a step that empowered local governments to be more representative and accountable to their local communities—in sharp contrast to the military's own historical attempts at such reforms, which were essentially an eyewash for further centralizing power and control. Khan and his party's preference for managing national issues by way of maximum devolution was evinced by his government's approach to the COVID-19 pandemic; the National Command and Operations Committee (NCOC)—formed exclusively as the primary control center for the national fight against the virus—consisted of representatives from each region of the country, provincial health ministers, and—of course—three-, two-, and one-star senior military officers.[38] Although policymaking was principally done by the federal government, the provinces with local governments were given almost free rein regarding the execution and on-the-ground monitoring and response of these policies, and they were constantly feeding information and responses to the NCOC's central command.[39] Thus, each locality was able to effect quarantines and lockdowns where the spread of the virus crossed certain thresholds, while enabling other regions or neighborhoods not so adversely affected to continue to function under strict standard operating procedures.

Additionally, Khan's well-organized and executed social services programs including the *Sehat* Card—a national health insurance program targeting the country's lower economic strata—made health care affordable and accessible to the most disenfranchised sections of Pakistani society, and his *Naya Pakistan* Housing Program—a program enabling housing ownership for financially underprivileged communities—made serious gains towards effecting meaningful socioeconomic uplift for the country's economically marginalized groups. Khan also instituted the *Kissan* Card program, offering subsidies and cash to poorer agricultural workers to overcome disasters and calamities.[40] In this recognition of the need to bolster small farmers and the agricultural sector—which employs a nontrivial proportion of the Pakistani population—Khan also emphasized the need to reform local government to devolve as much executive and legislative power as was possible to the local level.[41] Khan has also been a proponent of communal alternative dispute mechanisms, such as the *panchayat* and *jirga*, with these forms of tribal councils—in a similar vein as the People's Mediation Committees in China—revived in Azad Jammu and Kashmir.[42]

During his tenure as prime minister, Imran Khan thus sought to secure social justice for the Pakistani polity by providing social services such as health care, housing, and support to small farmers; attempted to strengthen local governance mechanisms through the devolution of powers and funds; and attempted to revive historical and indigenous dispute-resolution mechanisms to effect distributive justice. These—and other—programs instituted by the PTI government underpinned its leadership's rhetoric that the party sought to deliver on its promises to construct a society based on social-welfare principles. These actions, however, and Khan's personal political popularity, were seen as a direct threat to the military's political *status quo*, prompting his government's ouster in April 2022 through an unprecedentedly successful vote of no confidence—the first to succeed in ousting a premier in Pakistan's history—engineered and supported by the country's armed forces.[43]

Following this, Khan responded with strong rhetoric of heading the only truly nationalist party in Pakistan, and to validate these claims he named and blamed senior members of Pakistan's military establishment and his political opposition, tying them all together in an extravagant, foreign-led conspiracy to remove him—the most popular political leader in Pakistan. Subsequently, after surviving a successful assassination attempt, Khan again inculpated certain individuals within Pakistan's Inter-Services Intelligence ("ISI") agency and military's top brass, all in furtherance of instigating a hitherto novel movement in Pakistan where the public was also able to join their voices against these previously unreproachable targets, challenging their narratives as being 'apolitical' national institutions.[44] As touched upon above, these claims were substantiated by outgoing Chief of the Army Staff General Bajwa when he claimed that while the country's military had, in fact, interfered in civilian affairs for over seventy years—and that this was 'unconstitutional'—that it had ceased to do so from February 2021. This confirmation has, however, only added fuel to the fire of the historically unprecedented rhetoric and discourse presently being directed towards Pakistan's military, previously inured from such public critique.

After his ouster from the premiership, Khan demonstrated once again his *fides* as the 'national' leader he claims he is, successfully winning six out of the seven seats he contested in the October 2022 by-elections, conducted to reelect seats vacated by his own party's resignations from the National Assembly.[45] This was the greatest number of seats, contested simultaneously, won by any political leader in the country's history[46] and though this win was politically largely inconsequential, because in Pakistan's current parliamentary system, Khan must chose to retain only one of these six seats in the National Assembly, nonetheless his populist rhetoric as a civilian political leader is far more reminiscent of presidential electioneering—hitherto uncharacteristic of Pakistan. The win also demonstrates his continued appeal across constituencies, regardless of whether or not he eventually will even be representing those electoral divisions. Khan's ability to gain support across geographical regions and ethnicities could thus indicate that Pakistan is ready to gravitate towards a localized centripetalism model with presidential undertones, away from its historical parliamentary and ethnic consociationalist model.

In sum, Imran Khan and his PTI government were able to implement and realize reform through local government with federal support to the satisfaction of many Pakistanis. This form of local centripetalism threatened the military's political and economic might, bolstered by decades of non-trivial influence and consolidation of power over the federal center. Until the PTI and its socioeconomic welfare initiatives, the military were previously providing security, social and health care services, and economic commodities and housing for a fee through its interests in the private sector. However, once Khan was being perceived as providing the same facilities through the realization of social services for free through social and formalized forms of justice, he presented a credible challenge to the military's political interests. Furthermore, his ability to create a national party with a national agenda—due in large part to his own personal popularity—and his rhetoric, which revolved around discussions of the same, and which downplayed provincial identities and consociational competition, was also at odds with the Pakistani armed forces' ability to play political parties against one another if Khan were successfully able to strip Pakistani politics of its ethnic factionalism.

Khan's ouster and its aftereffects have led to poignant observations regarding the interplay between major institutional stakeholders and their ensuing political—or ostensibly 'apolitical'—rhetoric, each attempting to harness national sentiment to promote their narratives. These institutions—the politically emphatic military, the 'apolitical' judiciary, the country's intelligence agencies including most particularly the infamous Inter-Service Intelligence (ISI), and Pakistan's numerous political parties—have each perpetuated narratives historically typical of the role they played in jockeying for the apex of power within the country.

The high-handed way Pakistan's military leverages domestic political events to curate favorable outcomes for itself is evidenced by the—almost transparently orchestrated—events that took place during public protests on the 9th of May, 2023. During the protests—a response to ousted premier Imran Khan's arrest—alleged Khan supporters besieged and damaged key sites with symbolic significance to the military, including the Lahore Corps Commander's residence in Jinnah House, and the Corps Headquarters in Rawalpindi. In response, the military initiated legal proceedings against those allegedly involved; not in the mainstream justice system of Pakistan, however, but in military tribunals set up under sections of the Pakistan Army Act and the Official Secrets Acts instead.

The Jinnah House bore the brunt of the damage, as it was set on fire and allowed to burn for hours, with fire brigades—stationed minutes away from the House—conspicuously absent from the scene. Subsequently, however, media coverage depicted all sections of civil society—political party members, religious leaders, students and academics etc.—visiting the ruined remains of the Jinnah House, effecting a unified scripted narrative of the scale of the damage and by whom it was caused. This media blitz necessitated vociferous protestations of criticism against the demonstrators, made by major governmental organs such as the Parliament and the Judiciary, and stoking public antipathy towards them, and generated an upswell of sympathy for the military. Banners loudly proclaiming support for and arguably public allegiance to the 'victimized' armed forces were visibly installed in urban areas all across the country, and several significant Pakistani corporations took out ads in the print and electronic media declaring their support for the country's armed forces and decrying the protests—and by extension the ostensible motivators behind the demonstrations. This demonization of Khan and his party, which was roundly condemned for the attacks on these symbolic military installations, created an incredibly hostile social and political environment for what is essentially an element of what should otherwise constitute a robust and vibrant political system—i.e., a capable opposition to the incumbent government.

The reality, that has—for the most part—begun to sink in to the Pakistani polity, is that if the military establishment had truly wanted to, it could entirely contain and robustly deter the degree of destruction and infiltration into these sites; this pushback from the armed forces is not unprecedented, as demonstrated in prior protests where heavily armed military personnel—complete with armored personnel carriers—were deployed to restrict protestors' access to military sites including cantonments. In the case of the May protests, however, this forceful resistance to protestors' intrusions into military spaces—the historical norm—was entirely absent, with the military almost deliberately looking the other way to allow, if not encourage outright, the degree of property damage caused. In this context, with Pakistan's armed forces atypically remaining passive observers to civilian incursion into its spaces, it arguably appears as though the underlying reasons were to discredit Khan, smearing him by association with the destructive protests, in the hopes of stymieing his national groundswell of growing support.

It appears as the military is finding it increasingly difficult to concoct and maneuver public sentiment in its favor and where mere emotive, jingoistic sloganeering is falling short, it appears instead to be resorting to more drastic measures of scapegoating some of its own to garner public support and sympathy. However, the fact that the artificially engendered victimhood the military is attempting to draw around itself—something it has employed to a degree of success in the past—is becoming increasingly less convincing is, it appears, testament to the growing strength of opinion within Pakistan's polity that the military's incursions into political spheres are unwelcome, and establishing a healthy balance between the civilian leadership and the military institution is imperative.

Against this backdrop of civil-military imbalance, political disenfranchisement, and decades of ethnic federalism wrought through a consociationalist federal and constitutional architecture, this work will thus propose an alternate form of federal ordering for Pakistan—i.e., localized centripetalism—that will provide a more fertile environment within which to realize and contextualize communal democratic norms, and eventually, it is argued, will engender greater inter-ethnic harmony and promote greater representation of previously disenfranchised groups.

Localized centripetalism seeks to delink ethnic and religious considerations from political participation without disregarding local identities and local government; by incentivizing the participation of multi-ethnic political groups and encouraging identity moderation, centripetalism ensures that inter-communitarian differences—such as ethnicity or religion—are deemphasized in the prosecution of political participation. Rather than, as per a consociationalist framework, organizing political participation along these racialized/communal lines, a centripetalist perspective would provide larger, more prominent groups with tangible reasons to court smaller groups, while providing these smaller units with leverage in the form of their political participation, to help them more effectively advocate for their own interests.

This work will present how local centripetalism will better realize four 'communal democratic norms'—namely: distributive justice; localized, grassroots democracy; collective—as opposed to individual—minority protections; and communitarianism and multiculturalism—which can be implemented to effect positive change by effectively confronting historical and contemporary issues which continue to contribute to internecine frictions and inequity. Pakistan's consociational federal organization has operated to undermine these communal democratic norms, which would otherwise prove to be a net positive in the country's postcolonial context. Specifically, valuing these norms will work towards remedying three key problematic strains found within Pakistan: interethnic conflict, the extant civil-military imbalance, and the inequities brought with China's economic expansionism.

Notions of distributive justice, principally concerned with the equitable distribution of limited resources throughout the polity, can be used to inform governmental decision-making, ensuring that those most economically disenfranchised—and who thus stand the most to gain—have their needs catered to. In this context, given that Pakistan is a developing economy, investing in historically marginalized groups—operating at the economic peripheries of the state—would provide a net increase to national economic productivity.[17] Grassroots democracy would ensure that power and decision-making would devolve to the lowest possible stratum of the country's political architecture, ensuring that political actors are directly accountable, transparent, and responsive to the needs of their constituents.[48] Collective minority rights ostensibly represent a departure from the focus on the rights of the individual, to providing communal, or group, protections. In Pakistan's heterogenous context—where historically the focus on individual rights has hampered minority groups' efforts to exercise them, and where instances of systemic discriminatory practices persist—guaranteeing rights of sociocultural minorities to assert themselves as a group, as opposed to merely a mass of individuals, would not only foster a feeling of belonging (as opposed to secessionist sentiments) amongst these minorities, but would also protect these groups from being assimilated into the larger, more entrenched communities.[49] Finally, a focus on communitarianism or multiculturalism—whereby the tolerance and recognition of distinct sociocultural groups are affected—would engender greater intercommunal harmony; coupled with a deemphasizing of the political value ethnicity presently holds in the Pakistani context, these norms would allow these disparate elements of Pakistan's diverse polity to cohere under shared national values, while retaining their sociocultural uniqueness.[50]

This thesis is organized into four chapters. Chapter 1 discusses the four Communal Democratic Norms crucial to the promotion of sociopolitical stability within Pakistan. After providing a theoretical description of these norms, and discussing the ways in which they are currently undervalued in the Pakistani context, the chapter suggests that the proposed local centripetal framework uses these norms to uplift sociocultural minorities, dilute military supremacy, and empower the polity to push back against damaging economic policies imported from China.

Chapter 2 discusses federalism, and explores the ways in which local centripetalist federalism may potentially offer the means to promote inter-ethnic cohesion and stability and thus foster healthy governance mechanisms that uphold values such as equality, justice, and personal and collective liberty. After examining examples from other postcolonial polities, the chapter analyzes these values specifically in the Pakistani context in an attempt to identify the constitutional modifications required to realize a more equitable and stable form of local centripetalism within the country. The chapter proposes specific prescriptions for reforms to the current federal and electoral framework in Pakistan, which would serve to foster grassroots political engagement by devolving governmental competencies and dilute the disproportionate power wielded by the military establishment, and would operate to blunt the negative impacts of rapacious economic expansion.

Chapter 3 explores the complicated and strained civil-military relationship in Pakistan; it highlights the historical consolidation of inordinate power within the Pakistani military establishment, and how this concentration of power has enabled and exacerbated internecine ethnic conflict. It delineates how democratic communal norms must be realized effectively to effect and sustain political stability in Pakistan, which has instead been deeply impacted by the civil-military imbalance in the country. By outlining the asymmetrical dynamic of increased military power, both in theory and in praxis, this chapter will discuss more specifically how Pakistan's armed forces have consistently exploited historical inter-communal frictions, and consolidated the federation's organization along ethnic lines, all to further its own interests.

Finally, Chapter 4 makes important observations on how the countries involved in the BRI project, including Pakistan, inevitably import Chinese investment policies in the hopes of achieving the high economic growth and rapid development promised under the Initiative; this expansionist experiment, however, regarded by some as a novel form of imperialism under the guise of inclusive growth, is not without its costs and negative implications for local spaces within participant countries. In Pakistan such expansionism has undermined political federalism and distributive justice, and empowered Pakistan's military to appropriate economic resources while undermining the political and human rights of indigenous communities and minorities. The chapter concludes by making certain prescriptions aimed at mitigating the negative consequences of the adoption of such neoliberal policies, focusing instead on sustainable ways in which the state can equip itself to guard against potentially damaging outcomes such as international debt traps, local discontent and alienation, environmental degradation, and unsustainable and inefficient economic investments.

NOTES

1. Shakeeb Asrar and Wajeeha Malik, 'Pakistan's tribal areas: "Neither faith nor union found,"' *Al Jazeera* (2019), accessed on March 24, 2022 <https://interactive.aljazeera.com/aje/2019/pakistans-tribal-areas-fata/index.html>.

2. S. Akbar Zaidi, 'Special report: The Breakup of Pakistan 1969–1971', *DAWN* (Sep 23, 2017), accessed on March 24, 2022 <https://www.dawn.com/news/1359141>; K.M. Shah, "The Baloch and Pashtun nationalist movement in Pakistan: Colonial Legacy and the Failure of State Policy." Quetta: Observer Research Foundation (2019).

3. Ayesha Siddiqa, *Military Inc.: Inside Pakistan's military economy*. Penguin Random House India, 2017.

4. 'Imran Khan asks judiciary to explain why courts opened their doors at midnight prior to his ouster,' *DAWN* (Apr 13, 2022), accessed on April 19, 2022 <https://www.dawn.com/news/1684835>. *See also* James Schwemlein, "The Military Disrupts Pakistan's Democracy Once Again," Carnegie Endowment for International Peace, Commentary (May 10, 2023), accessed August 03, 2023, https://carnegieendowment.org/2023/05/10/military-disrupts-pakistan-s-democracy-once-again-pub-89724.

5. Charles H. Kennedy, "Islamization and legal reform in Pakistan, 1979–1989." *Pacific affairs* (1990): 62–77.

6. *See generally* 'Rising Violence by Separatists Adds to Pakistan's Lethal Instability,' *New York Times* (May 4, 2022), accessed on December 6, 2022, <https://www.nytimes.com/2022/05/04/world/asia/pakistan-baluchistan-violence.html>.

7. Maham Hameed, "The politics of the China—Pakistan economic corridor." *Palgrave Communications* 4.1 (2018): 1–10.

8. 'China Pakistan Economic Corridor is a game-changer,' *Arab News* (Aug 14, 2020), accessed on December 6, 2022, <https://www.arabnews.com/node/1719106/business-economy>.

9. *See supra* note 7.

10. Kriti M. Shah, "The Baloch And Pashtun nationalist movement in Pakistan: Colonial Legacy and The Failure of State Policy." *Quetta: Observer Research Foundation* (2019).

11. Veena Kukreja, "Ethnic diversity, political aspirations and state response: A case study of Pakistan." *Indian Journal of Public Administration* 66.1 (2020): 28–42.

12. 'British Imperialism, Religion, and the Politics of "Divide and Rule" in the Indian-Subcontinent,' *World Financial Review* (Jan 25, 2022), accessed on December 7, 2022, <https://worldfinancialreview.com/british-imperialism-religion-and-the-politics-of-divide-and-rule-in-the-indian-subcontinent/>.

13. *Ibid.*

14. V. Vidya Lakshmi, "Pakistan Army: Martial Race or National Army." *Mantraya* (Jun 1, 2016), accessed on December 8, 2022, <https://mantraya.org/pakistan-army-martial-race-or-national-army/>.

15. *See supra* note 12.

16. *See* Indian Councils Act 1909.

17. Sadaf Aziz, *The Constitution of Pakistan: A Contextual Analysis*. Bloomsbury Publishing, 2018, 17.

18. *Ibid.*

19. *Ibid.* at19. ("..it called for the marking out of territory in which Muslims formed a contiguous majority, particularly in the North West and South East. The former of course contained the provinces of North-West Frontier, Sindh, Balochistan and Punjab, and the latter, the territory now called Bangladesh. This notion of providing faith-denominated populations the cover of political sovereignty introduced the idea of splitting provinces on the same lines.").

20. Following the assassination of then–Prime Minister Liaquat Ali Khan in 1951, his successor, Prime Minister Nazimuddin, was dismissed by the Governor-General Ghulam Muhammad in 1953. *See also Ibid.* at 32. ("the instigators of this dismissal were thought to be many: the military for having had its budget curtailed; the politicians of the Punjab who had been accused of having fomenting hate-based rioting in their province against the Ahmadiyya community; and the cadre of West Pakistani bureaucrats who expressed dislike of the Bengali Nazimuddin's authority").

21. *Federation of Pakistan v Maulvi Tamizuddin Khan* PLD [1955] FC 240. The High Court, relying on powers of writ jurisdiction gained just prior to the dissolution of the Constituent Assembly, granted relief to the dismissed Constituent Assembly. However, on appeal the Federal Court of Pakistan revoked the decision of the High

Court, declaring that the assent of the governor-general was necessary for amendments made to legislation and therefore, the High Court had no power to grant relief.

22. *See generally Nusrat Bhutto v Chief of Army Staff* PLD [1977] SC 657; see also *Zafar Ali Shah v General Pervez Musharraf* PLD [2000] SC 869.

23. *See generally* Richard D. Lambert, "Factors in Bengali regionalism in Pakistan." *Far Eastern Survey* 28.4 (1959): 49–58.

24. *See generally* G. W. Choudhury, "Constitution-making dilemmas in Pakistan." *Western Political Quarterly* 8.4 (1955): 589–600. *See also* supra note 17 at 40: ('Wherein the principles of democracy, freedom, equality, tolerance and social justice as enunciated by Islam shall be fully observed'; and 'Wherein the Muslims shall be enabled to order their lives in the individual and collective spheres in accordance with the teachings and requirements of Islam as set out in the Holy Quran and the Sunnah.').

25. Facing continuous political instability, President Iskander Mirza abrogated the 1956 Constitution and declared martial law, appointing Ayub Khan as chief martial law administrator. The former was deposed three weeks later by General Ayub Khan, assuming direct control. *See also State v Dosso* PLD [1958] SC 533.

26. *See* Basic Democracies Order 1959. Ayub's centralization of power led to growing discontent against him, especially in the Eastern Wing of the country.

27. While both Zia's and Musharraf's dictatorships saw attempts at institutionalizing local government systems, the power remained concentrated with the center in these models (*see* Chapters 1 and 3).

28. 'A leaf from history: After Operation Searchlight,' *DAWN* (Mar 3, 2012), accessed on December 7, 2022, <https://www.dawn.com/news/699975/a-leaf-from-history-after-operation-searchlight>. The military launched 'Operation searchlight' to curb the Bengali nationalist movement.

29. Daniel J. Elazar, "BICOMMUNAL SOCIETIES AND POLITIES-INTRODUCTION." *Publius: The Journal of Federalism* 18.2 (1988): 1–3. *See also* Duchacek, Ivo D. "Dyadic federations and confederations," *Publius: The Journal of Federalism* 18.2 (1988): 5–31.

30. Niessen, Christoph et al., "When have dyadic federations succeeded and when have they failed? A comparative analysis of bipolar federalism around the world." *Federalism and national diversity in the 21st century*. Palgrave Macmillan, Cham, 2020. 41–72, 71.

31. It was Ayub Khan who supported Bhutto's political aspirations and also included him in his cabinet. *See* 'Ayub came to regard Bhutto as a "special protégé": CIA files,' *DAWN* (Jan 30, 2017), accessed on December 8, 2022, <https://www.dawn.com/news/1311058. For instance, Nawaz Sharif was supported by General Zia-ul-Haq in his rise to power within the political sphere. Similarly, Nawaz Sharif was also deposed by military dictator General Pervez Musharraf imposing a coup in October 1999. See 'Political musings: The kingmakers and their prime ministers,' *Express Tribune* (Mar 11, 2016), accessed on December 9, 2022, <https://tribune.com.pk/story/1064066/political-musings-the-kingmakers-and-their-prime-ministers>. ("Soon after General (retd) Pervez Musharraf toppled the PML-N government in the 1999 military coup, a

disgruntled group of the former ruling party emerged as the 'likeminded' faction. The group later turned into the PML-Q, then known as the 'King's party.'")

32. 'A leaf from history: PNA leaders wrangle over ministries,' *DAWN* (Nov 23, 2014), accessed on December 9, 2022, https://www.dawn.com/news/1145733; 'July 5: When Zia toppled Bhutto's government,' *News* (Jul 5, 2016), accessed on December 9, 2022, <https://www.thenews.com.pk/latest/133084-July-5-When-Zia-toppled-Bhuttos-government>. Essentially, the Pakistan National Alliance (PNA) was a consolidated political association, consisting of primarily Islamist parties, who had the overt support of the military in providing robust opposition to the Bhutto-led party, the PPP.

33. 'PML-Q: Musharraf's brainchild fractured, failing,' *Pakistan Today* (Mar 25, 2011), accessed on December 9, 2022, <https://archive.pakistantoday.com.pk/2011/03/25/pml-q-musharrafs-brainchild-fractured-failing/>. Former president General Pervez Musharraf launched his own political party in 2010. 'Musharraf's political party launched,' *DAWN* (Jun 9, 2010), accessed on December 9, 2022, <https://www.dawn.com/news/540513/musharrafaes-political-party-launched>.

34. *See supra* note 31, 'Political musings: The kingmakers and their prime ministers.'

35. 'Pakistan Supreme Court disqualifies Nawaz Sharif,' *Al Jazeera* (Jul 28, 2017), accessed on December 7, 2022, <https://www.aljazeera.com/news/2017/7/28/pakistan-supreme-court-disqualifies-nawaz-sharif>.

36. Danish Khan, 'Is the Military's Political Role Passé? A Dialectic of Change and Continuity in Pakistan,' *Institute of South Asian Studies* (Aug 22, 2022), accessed on December 8, 2022, <https://www.isas.nus.edu.sg/papers/is-the-militarys-political-role-passe-a-dialectic-of-change-and-continuity-in-pakistan/>.

37. It was under his premiership that the Local Government Act, 2019, and the Village Panchayat and Neighborhood Council (VPNC) Act, 2019 were passed, pushing for more power and resources to be directed to this third tier of government. *See* 'Will Imran Khan's new local govt system be a game changer—not just for governance but also for the economy?' *Pakistan Times* (Aug 26, 2019), accessed on December 6, 2022, <https://profit.pakistantoday.com.pk/2019/08/26/will-imran-khans-new-local-govt-system-be-a-game-changer-not-just-for-governance-but-also-for-the-economy/>.

38. 'Inside the NCOC: An eyewitness account,' *DAWN* (Apr 19, 2020), accessed on December 6, 2022, <https://www.dawn.com/news/1550412>.

39. *Ibid.*

40. 'Kisan Card will "transform" Pakistan: PM Imran,' *DAWN* (Apr 26, 2021), accessed on December 7, 2022, <https://www.dawn.com/news/1620494>.

41. *See supra* note 37.

42. 'AJK Govt announces to revive Panchayat, Jirga system in the State soon,' *Daily Times* (Jun 4, 2022), accessed on December 7, 2022, <https://dailytimes.com.pk/946549/ajk-govt-announces-to-revive-panchayat-jirga-system-in-the-state-soon/>. Jiang Heping and Andrew Wei-Min Lee, 'From the Traditional to the Modern: Mediation in China,' *Weinstein International Foundation*, accessed on December 9, 2022, <https://weinsteininternational.org/mediation-in-china/>.

43. 'Imran Khan ousted as Pakistan's PM after vote,' *BBC News* (Apr 10, 2022), accessed on December 6, 2022, <https://www.bbc.com/news/world-asia-61055210>.

44. 'Imran to disclose name of "second officer" monitoring execution of his assassination plot,' *Pakistan Today* (Nov 10, 2022), accessed on December 6, 2022, <https://www.pakistantoday.com.pk/2022/11/10/imran-says-will-reveal-name-of-second-military-officer-involved-in-assassination-attempt/>.

45. 'Imran Khan creates history by winning six seats in the NA,' *Daily Times* (Oct 17, 2022), accessed on December 6, 2022, <https://dailytimes.com.pk/1013495/imran-khan-creates-history-by-winning-six-seats-in-the-na/>.

46. *Ibid.*

47. *See generally* John Rawls, "A theory of justice." *Ethics*. Routledge, 2004, 229–34.

48. Hugh Whalen, "Ideology, Democracy, and the Foundations of Local Self-Government."*Canadian Journal of Economics and Political Science/Revue canadienne de economiques et science politique* 26.3 (1960): 377–95.

49. Zsolt Körtvélyesi, "Transcending the Individual/Collective Minority Rights Divide: A Procedural Solution." *International & Comparative Law Quarterly* 71.1 (2022): 73–106.

50. *See generally* Will Kymlicka, *Multicultural citizenship: A liberal theory of minority rights*. Clarendon Press, 1995.

BIBLIOGRAPHY

"A leaf from history: After Operation Searchlight." *DAWN*, March 3, 2012. https://www.dawn.com/news/699975/a-leaf-from-history-after-operation-searchlight.

"A leaf from history: PNA leaders wrangle over ministries." *DAWN,* November 23, 2014. https://www.dawn.com/news/1145733.

"AJK Govt announces to revive Panchayat, Jirga system in the State soon." *Daily Times*, June 4, 2022. https://dailytimes.com.pk/946549/ajk-govt-announces-to-revive-panchayat-jirga-system-in-the-state-soon/.

"Ayub came to regard Bhutto as a 'special protégé': CIA files." *DAWN*, January 30, 2017. https://www.dawn.com/news/1311058.

"British Imperialism, Religion, and the Politics of 'Divide and Rule' in the Indian-Subcontinent." *World Financial Review*, January 25, 2022. https://worldfinancial-review.com/british-imperialism-religion-and-the-politics-of-divide-and-rule-in-the-indian-subcontinent/.

"China Pakistan Economic Corridor is a game-changer." *Arab News*, August 14, 2020. https://www.arabnews.com/node/1719106/business-economy.

"Imran Khan asks judiciary to explain why courts opened their doors at midnight prior to his ouster." *DAWN*, April 13, 2022. https://www.dawn.com/news/1684835.

"Imran Khan creates history by winning six seats in the NA." *Daily Times*, October 17, 2022. https://dailytimes.com.pk/1013495/imran-khan-creates-history-by-winning-six-seats-in-the-na/.

"Imran Khan ousted as Pakistan's PM after vote." *BBC News*, April 10, 2022. https://www.bbc.com/news/world-asia-61055210.
"Imran to disclose name of 'second officer' monitoring execution of his assassination plot." *Pakistan Today*, November 10, 2022. https://www.pakistantoday.com.pk/2022/11/10/imran-says-will-reveal-name-of-second-military-officer-involved-in-assassination-attempt/.
"Inside the NCOC: An eyewitness account." *DAWN*, April 19, 2020. https://www.dawn.com/news/1550412.
"July 5: When Zia toppled Bhutto's government." *News International*, July 5, 2016. https://www.thenews.com.pk/latest/133084-July-5-When-Zia-toppled-Bhuttos-government.
"Kisan Card will 'transform' Pakistan: PM Imran." *DAWN*, April 26, 2021. https://www.dawn.com/news/1620494.
"Musharraf s political party launched." *DAWN*, June 9, 2010. https://www.dawn.com/news/540513/musharrafaes-political-party-launched.
"Pakistan Supreme Court disqualifies Nawaz Sharif." *Al Jazeera*, July 28, 2017. https://www.aljazeera.com/news/2017/7/28/pakistan-supreme-court-disqualifies-nawaz-sharif.
"PML-Q: Musharraf's brainchild fractured, failing." *Pakistan Today*, March 25, 2011. https://archive.pakistantoday.com.pk/2011/03/25/pml-q-musharrafs-brainchild-fractured-failing/.
"Political musings: The kingmakers and their prime ministers." *Express Tribune*, March 11, 2016. https://tribune.com.pk/story/1064066/political-musings-the-kingmakers-and-their-prime-ministers.
"Rising Violence by Separatists Adds to Pakistan's Lethal Instability." *New York Times*, May 4, 2022. https://www.nytimes.com/2022/05/04/world/asia/pakistan-baluchistan-violence.html.
"Will Imran Khan's new local govt system be a game changer—not just for governance but also for the economy?" *Pakistan Times*, August 26, 2019. https://profit.pakistantoday.com.pk/2019/08/26/will-imran-khans-new-local-govt-system-be-a-game-changer-not-just-for-governance-but-also-for-the-economy/.
Asrar, Shakeeb, and Wajeeha Malik. "Pakistan's tribal areas: 'Neither faith nor union found'." *Al Jazeera*, 2019. https://interactive.aljazeera.com/aje/2019/pakistans-tribal-areas-fata/index.html.
Aziz, Sadaf. *The Constitution of Pakistan: A Contextual Analysis*. Bloomsbury Publishing, 2018.
Basic Democracies Order, 1959.
Begum Nusrat Bhutto v Chief of Army Staff PLD [1977] SC 657.
Choudhury, G. W. "Constitution-making dilemmas in Pakistan." *Western Political Quarterly* 8, no. 4 (1955): 589–600.
Duchacek, Ivo D. "Dyadic federations and confederations." *Publius: The Journal of Federalism* 18, no. 2 (1988): 5–31.
Elazar, Dj. "Bicommunal Societies And Polities-Introduction." *Publius: The Journal of Federalism* 18, No. 2 (1988): 1–3.
Federation of Pakistan v Maulvi Tamizuddin Khan PLD [1955] FC 240.

Hameed, Maham. "The politics of the China—Pakistan economic corridor." *Palgrave Communications* 4, no. 1 (2018): 1–10.

Heping, Jiang and Andrew Wei-Min Lee. "From the Traditional to the Modern: Mediation in China." *Weinstein International Foundation.* https://weinsteininternational.org/mediation-in-china/.

Indian Councils Act, 1909.

Kennedy, Charles H. "Islamization and legal reform in Pakistan, 1979–1989." *Pacific affairs* (1990): 62–77.

Khan, Danish. "Is the Military's Political Role Passé? A Dialectic of Change and Continuity in Pakistan." *Institute of South Asian Studies,* August 22, 2022. https://www.isas.nus.edu.sg/papers/is-the-militarys-political-role-passe-a-dialectic-of-change-and-continuity-in-pakistan/.

Körtvélyesi, Zsolt. "Transcending the Individual/Collective Minority Rights Divide: A Procedural Solution." *International & Comparative Law Quarterly* 71, no. 1 (2022): 73–106.

Kukreja, Veena. "Ethnic diversity, political aspirations and state response: A case study of Pakistan." *Indian Journal of Public Administration* 66, no. 1 (2020): 28–42.

Lakshmi, V. Vidya. "Pakistan Army: Martial Race or National Army." *Mantraya*, June 1, 2016. https://mantraya.org/pakistan-army-martial-race-or-national-army/.

Lambert, Richard D. "Factors in Bengali regionalism in Pakistan." *Far Eastern Survey* 28, no. 4 (1959): 49–58.

Niessen, Christoph, Min Reuchamps, Dejan Stjepanović, and Augustin Habra. "When have dyadic federations succeeded and when have they failed? A comparative analysis of bipolar federalism around the world." In *Federalism and national diversity in the 21st century*, 41–72. Palgrave Macmillan, Cham, 2020.

Rawls, John. "A theory of justice." In *Ethics*, pp. 229–234. Routledge, 2004.

Schwemlein, James. "The Military Disrupts Pakistan's Democracy Once Again." Carnegie Endowment for International Peace, May 10, 2023. https://carnegieendowment.org/2023/05/10/military-disrupts-pakistan-s-democracy-once-again-pub-89724.

Shah, Kriti M. "The Baloch And Pashtun nationalist movement in Pakistan: Colonial Legacy and The Failure of State Policy." *Quetta: Observer Research Foundation* (2019). https://www.orfonline.org/research/the-baloch-and-pashtun-nationalist-movements-in-pakistan-colonial-legacy-and-the-failure-of-state-policy-53691/.

Siddiqa, Ayesha. *Military Inc.: Inside Pakistan's military economy*. Penguin Random House India, 2017.

State v Dosso PLD [1958] SC 533.

Whalen, Hugh. "Ideology, Democracy, and the Foundations of Local Self-Government." *Canadian Journal of Economics and Political Science/Revue canadienne de economiques et science politique* 26.3 (1960): 377–95.

Zafar Ali Shah v General Pervez Musharraf PLD [2000] SC 869.

Zaidi, S. Akbar. "Special report: The Breakup of Pakistan 1969–1971." *DAWN*, September 23, 2017. https://www.dawn.com/news/1359141.

Chapter 1

Implementing Local Centripetalism in Pakistan

A Federalist Solution for Upholding Distributive Justice, Local Democracy, Collective Protection of Minorities and Multiculturalism to Combat Interethnic Conflict, Civil Military Imbalance, and the Inequalities Exacerbated by Chinese Investments

INTRODUCTION

This chapter identifies and examines four seminal and interlinked norms which must be indigenized and realized to effect positive outcomes for Pakistan's diverse polity: these are distributive justice; local or grassroots democracy; collective—as opposed to individual—minority protections; and multiculturalism. These four fundamental norms, which will hereafter collectively be referred to as "Communal Democratic Norms or Values"—if deployed correctly—have the potential to blunt the negative effects of sociocultural factionalism—specifically interethnic conflict, civil-military imbalance of power, and the inequalities exacerbated by China's economic investments in the region—and engender a more favorable context within which to embed this thesis's proposed localized centripetalist federalism framework.[1]

This work, including this chapter in particular, will be exploring these norms in the context of broader discussions of federalism, two principal 'forms' of federalism—namely consociationalism and centripetalism—particularly relevant to this work, and laying the groundwork for the thesis of this work, i.e., the proposed local centripetalist form of federal organization, which this work argues will significantly contribute towards remedying Pakistan's historical internecine frictions.

In the abstract, federalism refers to various modes by which a heterogenous population may be organized to form a coherent national polity, representing forms of national organization enabling pluralistic societies to accommodate internal sociocultural diversity. In the Pakistani context, federalism has been expressed in the form of consociationalism, predicated upon the existence of more robust federating units arranged around a relatively weaker federal center, with each of these units established along ethnic lines. In principle, this move is intended to allow each demographic in a heterogenous society to each enjoy sociopolitical primacy in their 'designated' federal unit. Thus, the provinces of Baluchistan, Khyber-Pakhtunkhwa, Punjab, and Sindh provide spaces within which their respective indigenous Baluchi, Pashtun, Punjabi, and Sindhi each enjoy numerical and political supremacy. As such, each federating unit—being so 'aligned' with a sociocultural group—operates to aggregate and amplify the political power each such group can exercise within the broader federal context. By contrast, centripetalist federalism involves relatively weaker federating units arranged around a strong federal center. Under this model sociocultural groups within the federation are incentivized to collaborate with one another to affect their political goals, with the units—and by extension the federation as a whole—uncoupled from ethnic affiliation.

While the bulk of political theory emanates from western sources, such analyses often leave much to be desired when applied to non-Western contexts. The relative paucity of indigenous scholarship on the matter further compounds the disconnect between doxa and praxis, with Western assumptions on sociopolitical ordering in non-Western contexts taken as gospel, often in the face of ground realities. Of particular note is Pakistan's significant sociocultural diversity, which leaves typical renditions of theories centered around individualism—arguably at the expense of the community—incompatible with, or at least insufficient for, Pakistani culture and political organization. The norms enlisted above, however, are distinct in their particular tolerance of collectivism and—given the culture's emphasis on community over the individual—can as such be successfully indigenized to effect positive outcomes for Pakistan.

This chapter begins with a brief theoretical description of the identified positive values of distributive justice; grassroots democracy through local and self-governance; minority protections; and autochthonous forms of communitarianism/multiculturalism/cosmopolitanism—and will subsequently discuss how these values have been diluted by historical conditions that created and perpetuate the pernicious sociopolitical ills of inter-ethnic conflict, civil-military asymmetry, and economic imbalances actualized by neoliberal forces in Pakistan. This chapter submits that prioritizing these values is essential for progress and stability in Pakistan, as an assimilation of these fundamental values will aid in extirpating these ills from the polity.

Distributive Justice

Distributive justice concerns itself with the ways in which limited resources and goods can be equitably divided amongst the society. Typically, theoretical frameworks organize principles of distributive justice with the aim of codifying an overarching moralistic guidance for states—and their political and social administrative units—to ensure the just dispensation of benefits and burdens in societies.[2] Rawls formalizes his theory of "justice as fairness"[3]—an egalitarian theory which stipulates equality for all in terms of distribution of goods, with "the difference principle"[4] acting as the only exception to this where divergence in equal distribution is possible only when the most disadvantaged sections of society stand to benefit the most materially than they would under strict equality.[5] Similarly, other political philosophers, including John Stuart Mill and Jeremy Bentham, explored utilitarian lines or "welfare-based"[6] principles—targeting an "equality of well-being"[7]; by making welfare the primary good with intrinsic value that needs to be distributed effectively, their theories centered around what qualifies as welfare, and what state policies or programs would maximize the intrinsic value of welfare.[8]

Contemporaneously, distributive justice theory can be used to examine international geopolitical and social interactions: that is to say, "the distributive responsibilities of States, and the extent, if any, to which the institutional structure of the international order should seek to influence the global distribution of resources and wealth."[9] Rawls's distributive justice:

> is concerned with the 'basic structure' of society: the ways in which major social institutions—for example, markets in capital and labor, bequeathable rights to private property—determine the distribution of advantages in society. Reasoning analogously, we might say that a theory of international distributive justice would concern the basic structure of international society, that is the institutions that determine the international distribution of advantages. International transfers (for example, foreign aid programs) certainly have some influence, but by any measure this is insignificant in comparison with other forces that are potentially open to political manipulation, such as private capital flows, the rules of the trade regime, or the system of internationally recognised property rights.[10]

Broadly, theories of distributive justice revolve around two principal tenets: firstly, that all societies must enforce certain universal minimum standards that apply across sociocultural variations and differences—although what specific rights are included in or inform these universal minimum standards is still cause for much debate. Secondly, each government is responsible for ensuring the fulfillment of these rights for its people; international institutions or foreign governments have limited obligations in this regard and should only intervene in the event of extreme deprivation that domestic governments are unable to alleviate, and only insofar as to effectively provide relief without a "morally significant sacrifice."[11]

Localized Self-Government/Grassroots Democracy

Local self-government is a system of democratic administration based on the creation of a system of subordinate authorities, which derive certain authorities and powers by delegation from the central state. Idealistically, "local self-government gives 'community of thought to the whole parliamentary body,' and serves as 'the golden bridge,' which joins state and society into one harmonious whole."[12] Local government can be made to be more representative and accountable when its members are democratically elected and closely tied to the community they represent. Doing so also reinvigorates local politics as a fundamental way for people to participate politically, mobilize, and exert control over their local governments ensuring accountability, transparency, and responsiveness. These arrangements can adopt a variety of forms, from playing a minor administrative role to being critical political companions to the central government.

Democracy is not a necessary political precondition for the existence of local government; however, Professor Herman Finer has put forward a pseudo-empirical hypothesis demonstrating that practically, local-level politics—such as the ones that form local self-governments—are an "inevitable concomitant of political democracy."[13] According to Hugh Whalen's commentary on Finer's hypothesis:

> (g)overnment by its very nature . . . has a tendency toward centralization and the imposition of uniform standards over the largest possible area. When faced with commands based upon average or general considerations—the products of bureaucratic reporting and statistical analysis—the individual, the small group, and the local community respond, naturally and necessarily . . . by demanding and exercising local freedom. Thus, as against the abstract view of people and community's characteristic of central public administration there is a continuing reaction which manifests itself practically in local self-government. According to this view, there must be, in any democratic state, a local authority making the

government 'pliable to the idiosyncrasies and angularities and plastic by reference to peculiar and individual circumstances.'[14]

If local self-government is considered to be an expression of democratic readjustment at the grassroots level for any particular geographical delineation or community, then as a corollary to this realignment the strength and level of authority awarded to such local governments is essential to determining the community's sentiments viz their meaningful political participation and the accountability they can exert over these governance arrangements. This is of particular concern in diverse, heterogenous societies, where certain ethnicities may feel or even be alienated from the political processes, leading to the atomization of the polity.

Political theory also concerns itself with how systems of local governments interact with the center—essentially the way in which political power and administrative functions are shared between local governments and the central government. To this end, polities need to construct organizational relationships between local authorities and the center which demarcate their respective rights and obligations and balance their particular roles in relation to the polity in terms of both the degree of control they exert as well as the execution of responsibilities.

John Stuart Mill's conception of the way in which this relationship can be ordered retains most of the "control" with the center, with the local government acting largely in the execution of administrative responsibilities:

> (t)he executive duties of the locality do indeed require to be divided into departments, for the same reason as those of the State; because they are of diverse kinds, each requiring knowledge peculiar to itself, and needing, for its due performance, the undivided attention of a specially qualified functionary. But the reasons for subdivision which apply to the execution do not apply to the control. The business of the elective body is not to do the work, but to see that it is properly done, and that nothing necessary is left undone. This function can be fulfilled for all departments by the same superintending body; and by a collective and comprehensive far better than by a minute and microscopic view.[15]

Practically, however, certain democracies qualitatively and fundamentally diverge from Mill's model—the political cultures of Switzerland and the United States, for example, accord a significant degree of autonomy to local governments:

> (i)n the former state there are strong local loyalties and much direct democracy; in the latter, particularly in the growing number of states with "home rule" constitutional provisions, localities are sometimes free to choose a wide variety of institutional forms.[16]

> Other countries, such as France and Britain, however, adhere more closely to Mill's conception of governance arrangements, as their "local institutions operate under the active surveillance of, and in close cooperation with, the agents of central authority.[17]

Collective Minority Protections

Perhaps the most universally compatible norms of Western democratic theory in non-Western, socioculturally heterogenous societies are those focused on effecting political compromise and understanding—particularly among such disparate groups—and those which safeguard the interest of these groups at the local level, which is where the government is the most democratic, representative, and accountable. Non-Western societies have had to address intercommunal conflicts and manage the interplay between factions within ecumenical and polyethnic societies throughout their histories; as such, it is entirely possible for them to develop processes negotiating and effecting compromises through group-specific interactions.

Collective—as opposed to individual—minority rights refer to procedures, laws and/or policies that allow minorities to articulate and express their particular cultural, linguistic, or religious identity as a community.[18] These rights accord them equal opportunities for engagement in the broader national context—such as through education and employment—and grants them geopolitical and social space to protect and exercise their historical values and express their communal identity. Further, despite concerns that collective or group rights pose some form of a threat to individual liberties, assimilating collective procedures for implementing such minority rights addresses the roots of inequalities these often-marginalized minorities experience.[19]

Samuel Bagenstos eloquently articulates the need for systems of collective rights, noting:

(b)y focusing on discrete, identifiable acts of wrongdoing undertaken by specific, blameworthy individuals, the law failed to provide a meaningful response to structural or institutional discrimination that cannot be attributed to the fault of a particular racist or sexist.[20] Certain cultural rights—like the official use of one's language—is a systemic right: denial of this right is unlikely to be addressed through strictly individual legal proceedings, and unless it is systemically entrenched, the minority is more likely to be eventually assimilated within the larger polity. Within this context Will Kymlicka calls for new strategies "to revive the flagging political project of diversity in Europe and elsewhere," given the "growing public disenchantment."[21] Asserting collective rights and individual rights are thus not mutually exclusive—the fundamental contention, however, is that unless there exists a robust system guaranteeing collective rights, minorities will not have the means through which to express their identity fully, and to assert their rights.[22]

Minorities without a system of collective protections are not immune from eventual cultural assimilation within the majority, a process that only hurts the minority. From the state's perspective, assimilation is economically, administratively, and politically simpler: the polity is rendered more uniform, dissent is minimized, and ethnic disorder is averted, all without incurring any rolling costs to the state.[23] However, the ethics of assimilation is trumped by the fact that cultural and ethnic diversity are a very tangible element of the sociocultural fabric of many non-Western states, and that meaningful, lasting political stability can only be achieved through the acceptance and recognition of minorities and their cultural identity(ies)—i.e., through an acceptance of multiculturalism. Particularly within contemporary political rhetoric, cultural pluralism and diversity are considered positive attributes of a society,[24] and ironically it can credibly be argued that granting collective minority protections eventually leads to greater assimilation within society—without the negative of eliminating the minority culture—as it rids the polity of a potent source of internal conflict and atomization; a minority community that no longer feels threatened is less likely to pose resistive threats to the majority.[25] A heterogenous federation can thus peacefully coexist as a unified whole, whose constituents are different communities that are permanent and distinct.[26]

The structural solution towards protecting minority rights collectively, while resisting their eventual cultural assimilation, is for the state to actively allow for specific minority protections, such as the right for Canada's French-speaking minority to operate schools in their language. Another such protection is where the minority is granted the autonomy to manage its own distinctiveness—such as the new constitution of Spain allowing autonomous regional parliaments for the country's cultural and linguistic groupings; Canada allowing the territorial Quebecois French population (a majority in Quebec, but a minority in Canada) a provincial government; and the Muslim minority in secular India being granted the right to have their affairs be governed by Islamic legal traditions.[27]

Collective protections must thus include conferred authority for minorities to have the sovereignty to holistically express cultural rights including language, religion, legal norms, and other culturally significant activities.[28] Further, as emphasized earlier, "cultural rights cannot be vindicated solely by upholding individual rights—the rights may well be lost unless the collective is either protected or has the autonomy to protect itself."[29]

Communitarianism and Multiculturalism

Multiculturalism has been steadily gaining traction and recognition since the advent of decolonization policies, resulting in the erosion of the appeal the nation-state enjoyed in the first half of the twentieth century. Even newly formed postcolonial states, most notably South Africa,[30] have—despite years of formalized discriminatory practices under apartheid—acknowledged the existence of different groups within their borders and the right of each such group to their own respective cultural self-expression.

In this context, the term multiculturalism has largely come to be used in three distinct ways: a description of the nature of cultural diversity in a society; an ideology targeted towards intertwining cultural diversity within the socio-political structure of society; and as a public policy approach aimed at creating unity and harmony in an ethnically and culturally heterogenous society.[31] In essence, multicultural policies aim to create conditions for the peaceful co-existence of diverse groups of people by explicitly drawing attention to the differences between these groups while simultaneously calling for their treatment under the principles of equality, tolerance, democracy, and the recognition of the distinct needs of these groups.[32]

Conversely, cosmopolitanism emphasizes the crafting of a more homogenous, shared identity transcending cultural, religious, ethnic, and national elements of identity, in which factors such as global citizenship, globalization, or pan-regional associations hold greater significance than other features of identity. Cosmopolitanism can thus be viewed as another way to manage and ensure tolerance and harmony in societies with significant cultural and ethnic diversity, serving as a tool for reconciling diversity and unity.[33] Cosmopolitan approaches towards managing diversity within a polity generally tend to emphasize the overt adoption of what can be termed as symbolic cosmopolitan values. In this regard, education policy and school curricula, media, and popular culture all serve as crucial tools deployed to engineer association with these cosmopolitan values.[34] The shared understandings and experiences, as well as the homogeneity created by these values, serves to downplay other features of identity, such as ethnicity, religion, or culture.

Both multiculturalism and cosmopolitanism have been employed as significant approaches to managing diversity in non-Western, postcolonial states with socioculturally heterogenous polities; in these contexts, the colonial policy of divide and rule, pitting one ethno-cultural group against another, has led to the significance—or perceived significance—of ethnicity becoming even more magnified. In such postcolonial settings multiculturalism has been employed in a number of different policy frameworks; we see examples—including states like South Africa, India, Pakistan, and Malaysia—applying multicultural principles in different aspects of policymaking, including in their implementation of federalism, guarantees of constitutional protection to different ethnic groups and minorities, reserved legislative representation through quotas, etc.[35] Simultaneously, we also see cosmopolitanism playing a key role within certain postcolonial societies in states such as Nigeria and Ghana which, as a result of globalization, are experiencing increased immigration of labor and exchange of technology and ideas with the rest of the world.[36] Common elements observable across these various non-Western, postcolonial societies include, on one level, that these societies are highly ethnically diverse, particularly as a consequence of colonialism, and use the tools of multiculturalism and cosmopolitanism as mechanisms to engender cooperation, harmony, and tolerance amongst the different ethnic groups that would otherwise likely express a degree of hostility towards one another—if not be engaged in outright conflict. Moreover, in the attempt to engender greater cultural homogeneity, these societies emphasize going beyond the nation to focus instead on those aspects of identity not strictly tied to politics and the nation. However, what is also observed is that the implementation of and the eventual ways in which multiculturalism and cosmopolitanism play out across these different societies also vary greatly. Different states may implement the same principle in entirely different ways, and there are also instances where the principles of multiculturalism and cosmopolitanism overlap within these societies.

Certain key, easily identifiable, features exist that allow for and facilitate the successful implementation of multiculturalism within non-Western, postcolonial societies; of these elements, two in particular can be observed in certain contexts where multicultural policies have proven successful.[37] Firstly, these states have constitutional sovereignty[38]: i.e., that the rights guaranteed within the constitution are safeguarded with more ease, are less prone to being disregarded or violated by governments, and are much more likely to be enforced *vis-à-vis* state entities because the constitution does not place the national executive or legislature in a position of superiority over the state judiciary. Instead, in these contexts constitutional courts enjoy the legitimacy, mandate, and authority to enforce these constitutional norms upon the government and the people.[39] The second feature of such societies is the territorial dispersion of political power. This is often demonstrated as a division or delegation of power where the federating units have substantial devolved powers—for instance, the power to promulgate provincial constitutions, administer and raise taxes, and produce legislation on local government matters—while the central government has other wide-ranging overriding powers exercisable in the event of a conflict between provincial or between national and provincial legislatures.[40]

However, the fact that different states may implement the principle of multiculturalism in markedly different ways also needs to be given due recognition. In the case of Malaysia, the state has taken a widely disparate approach towards multiculturalism and the management of inter-ethnic strife. Malaysia started out with consociational policies that placed greater emphasis on ethnic/group recognition and representation within political bodies.[41] This appeared in the form of formal guarantees for minorities, such as the establishment of ethnically exclusive political parties, reserved seats for minorities, ethnically mandated voter registers, etc.[42] In context, therefore, Malaysia appears to be gradually moving towards a hybrid system, where centripetal policies are gradually being merged into the existing political system: for instance, pursuant to the policy of vote pooling, parties must now garner support across ethnic lines.[43] Thus, even parties ordered on ostensibly ethnic lines have to court voters from without their ethnic group to achieve political success.

Another means of promoting communal harmony, communitarianism, is a social and political philosophy emphasizing the significance of the community in the functioning of political life and society, providing meaning to the link between the individual and the community.[44] Will Kymlicka, a communitarian theorist, argues that a cultural community is required for the primary good of self-respect, and that without special group rights the cultural communities of aboriginal people would be vulnerable to destruction.[45] One distinction Kymlicka draws is between internal restrictions and external protection,[46] where he notes that external protections between groups might be justified for the promotion of equality (however, these interventions must not allow for exploitation or oppression by one group towards others). On the other hand, however, 'internal restrictions' which operate to unnecessarily restrict the autonomy of an individual within a minority group cannot be justified nor be acceptable within liberal ideology.[47] Referring to the tribal government of Pueblo Indians in the United States, Kymlicka illustrates how minorities may discriminate against certain subgroups such as girls and women by denying them education or the right to vote and hold office.[48] These illiberal tendencies would thus need to be addressed through the forms of intersectional internal protections Kymlicka discusses, where a distinct sociocultural group cannot be allowed to oppress members of the group—and remain inured from criticism through reliance upon external protections available to the group.[49]

Non-Western multi-ethnic states can significantly benefit from the realization of communitarianism to promote internal political stability; however, Western theories of communitarianism would need to be modified to be more efficacious in non-Western contexts such as Pakistan, as discussed in the proceeding sections of this chapter.

CONTEXTUALIZING THESE NORMS WITHIN PAKISTAN: INTERACTIONS WITH ETHNIC FEDERALISM, CIVIL-MILITARY IMBALANCE, AND CHINESE ECONOMIC INVOLVEMENT

This section will attempt to demonstrate certain specific ills inherent in Pakistan's federal and political architecture that have undermined the four democratic norms highlighted above, and how reforms predicated upon these four norms can work to remedy these sociopolitical ills, and eventually advance democracy within the country.

Since its independence, religious identity and theocratic forces have worked to transform the politico-legal system of Pakistan into a quasi-religious constitutional order.[50] While the country was ostensibly formed to provide a safe haven for India's large Muslim minority, Pakistan's founder, Mohammed Ali Jinnah, himself ascribed to Western liberal values, and avowedly envisioned a liberal state with a republican form of democracy. However, mere months after Pakistan's independence Jinnah passed away, leaving a political vacuum in the country. The 'founding father(s)' of a nation tend to speak with a non-trivial degree of authority on the nature of the country itself, and Jinnah's early demise deprived Pakistani liberalism of a powerful advocate, creating space for other, illiberal characteristics to gain traction.

Once the country was formed—ostensibly along 'religious' lines—however, ecclesiasts were quick to take advantage of the new political space, acting opportunistically not only to recognize the state, but by further attempting to change the narrative for its existence. This was done to gain political legitimacy and traction in a nascent political system that had yet to gain coherence. These ecclesiasts declared that Pakistan was solely formed to create an Islamic republican state—as opposed to a state formed to protect a religious minority which just so happened to be Muslim—effectively mobilizing with the end to 'Islamize' Pakistan. This 'Islamization' process began by exerting tremendous political and social pressure on the newly formed Constituent Assembly of Pakistan to adopt an Islamized constitutional order driven by their particular conceptions of Islamic norms of social justice.[51]

While Islamization processes continued throughout Pakistan's history, the most forceful form of Islamization, significantly eroding all forms of Western democratic norms in the country, took place under the auspices of military dictator Zia-ul Haq, who Islamized major parts of the criminal justice system of Pakistan and created a parallel Islamized federal court system. The Islamization of the Constitution in Pakistan has since been steadily proceeding for over seventy years, though there have been periods when secular dictators and progressive parliamentarians have resisted this process—with moderate successes in stalling or even reversing it in the short term. This Islamization, however, has left Pakistan particularly lacking in the application and assimilation of the basic values that would otherwise help multiethnic, postcolonial societies cohere; loosely defined and ineptly implemented local government models, with politically inept grassroots access, widened the distributive divide within society, perpetuated interethnic conflict, depressed minority protections, and led to the atomization of society. The extent of damage is acutely observed by Moeen Cheema in his article "Pakistan: State of Liberal Democracy," where he notes that democratic and liberal norms in Pakistan have been undermined by structural failings that no single institution or political actor can rectify in the short term.[52]

The outsized role played by Pakistan's military has also historically negatively impacted Pakistan's domestic and international affairs. For Levitsky and Ziblatt, independent checks and balances are a hindrance to most authoritarians, who work to neutralize them to stifle independent voices.[53] This is accomplished by, for example, either replacing a previously recalcitrant civil servant with a loyalist or by engaging in efforts to undermine and subvert, supplant, or influence them. Other methods include undermining influential and independent members of commercial or civil society who might presumably pose a threat to or who might instead be coopted into the illiberal project, blocking, and censoring free press and discourse, and suppressing votes, etc. All of these phenomena have been expressed in Pakistan from time to time and have contributed to the social and political harms plaguing the country.

The following subsections will illustrate the historical interplay of the four identified norms of distributive justice, grassroots democracy, the collective protection of minorities, and multiculturalism within Pakistan, and how these can be utilized to remedy three fundamental evils within the country's political and socioeconomic systems: interethnic conflict exacerbated by Pakistan's ethicized federal political framework, its civil-military asymmetry, and the challenges posed by Chinese economic investment in Pakistan.

Ethnic Federalism's Impact on Diluting Distributive Justice, Exacerbating the Vulnerability of Minorities, and Promoting Interethnic Conflict

While there exists a sizable corpus of literature on the normative theories of distributive justice, it is essential for the purposes of this chapter to evaluate the role of political power and engineering in attempting to achieve any form of parity or "justice" in the distribution of resources within society.

Pakistan is significantly socioculturally diverse, playing host to a large number of ethnic and religious groups extant throughout the country. Historically, however, only a handful of such groups have enjoyed any meaningful influence over the state—with an even smaller number still enjoying relative autonomy by way of the ethnic ordering of the country's federating units. This divergence between the country's diversity on one hand, and the inordinate control only certain select groups exercise over its power structures, must be addressed by a framework emphasizing the sociocultural value of such group identification while simultaneously divorcing it from political considerations. As will be discussed in this section, ethnic and religious sentiments inform Pakistani political and governmental considerations, which has contributed to the consolidation of power in the hands of members of elite or influential communities. By contrast, the goal is to 'tolerate'—if not celebrate—such sociocultural differences while stripping them of the political power they presently hold.

Presently, Pakistan's ethnic federalist framework lends an inordinate amount of influence to the larger ethnic groups in the country—the Punjabis for the most part; with this influence comes a great deal of control over the country's civilian and military bureaucracies and, consequently, over resource allocation in the country.[54] As a developing economy with limited resources to apportion across its federating units, it comes as little surprise that the interests of smaller ethnic groups and the provinces that house them are often left underserved. Pakistan's electoral processes ensure indirect representation of the polity in the country's legislative assemblies; these bodies, existing at the provincial and federal levels, wield a near-complete monopoly over the country's governance mechanisms—and governmental decision-making in particular.[55] This framework is replete with issues which erode democratic processes and work to engender authoritarian tendencies instead. Meaningful attempts at ensuring more direct forms of representation, or at least of ensuring accountability to the electorate, are often stymied by the institutional remove at which these governance mechanisms operate in relation to the polity. This distance creates an enabling environment for abusive and oppressive patterns of behavior which, in turn, serve to further factionalize a polity already scrambling for scarce resources allocated along ethnic—as opposed to equitable or socioeconomic—grounds.

While consociationalism—particularly as it has been expressed in Pakistan in the form of the country's ethnic federal organization—may ostensibly promote the interests of distinct sociocultural groups, it does so at the expense of all other, smaller such groups.[56] Organizing the state in this manner enables larger sociocultural groups—by virtue of sheer weight of numbers—to effectively dictate provincial and federal policy, leaving the political capacity of smaller such groups to either be subsumed within, coopted by, or ignored outright by their larger peers. By contrast, it is argued that uncoupling sociocultural identity from the way in which the state is ordered, and promoting local centripetalism by way of a form of collectivism predicated upon local and community empowerment would significantly curtail the instigation and perpetuation of the inter-communal tensions presently plaguing Pakistan. While sociocultural identity, including ethnicity, religious identification, or sexual identity, undoubtedly has political significance—i.e., the 'personal is political'—Pakistan's current federal architecture emphasizes ethnic membership to the near exclusion of all other identity markers, leaving persons not part of the dominant ethnicity on the political periphery.

The goal is thus to incorporate elements of distributive justice norms, which advocate for an equitable, 'socially just' distribution of these resources—much like affirmative action programs in the United States have sought to uplift historically disenfranchised elements of society. Doing so would entail decoupling resource allocation from ethnic considerations—presently a necessary corollary of the country's consociationalist and ethnic federalist structures—which not only affect inequitable resource distribution but also—as a result of such unfair allocations—serve to further exacerbate preexisting sociocultural tensions. The distributive divide, as it were, grows more stark when one examines it in light of the intersection between socioeconomics and faith; minority religious groups—particularly non-Islamic ones—are further excluded from the budgetary calculus of the country's provincial and federal governments; the lion's share of resources remains allocated to the country's significant Sunni Muslim community's interests, with disproportionately smaller amounts allocated to groups such as the indigenous Hindu, Sikh, animist, or Christian populations.

The roots of distributive injustice in Pakistan can be traced back to the colonial period. Classical liberal doctrine has attempted to provide moral and legal justifications to the subjecting of individuals to the political arrangements of a liberal system; more specifically, liberal doctrine has also been employed to justify forms of colonialism.[57] As Karuna Mantena writes: "(t)he liberal model of imperialism, which tied together a theory of imperial legitimacy with the project of improvement, represented the most fully developed moral justification of the Empire in nineteenth-century Britain. Liberal imperialism came to embody a coherent ideology, an intersecting set of justifications and governing strategies centered on the duty of liberal reform."[58] The central tenets of liberal imperialism began facing significant opposition from postcolonial societies in the realization of their own political, economic, and cultural rights.[59] In this vein, Duncan Ivison accurately highlights one of liberalism's primary defects in relation to postcolonial societies: "how could a philosophical and political creed of individual rights and human dignity not find favor with those suffering from racial or cultural discrimination and economic and political marginalization? There are a number of answers. The first is that liberalism is often equated with support for the unbridled supremacy of the market, and especially for what Gayatri Chakravorty Spivak has called the 'financialization of the planet'. Insofar as liberals support the expansion of free and unfettered markets and minimal governments on a global scale, they support the means through which the poorest and worst off are dominated and discriminated against."[60]

This association between liberalism and the British Empire, or with the expansion and legitimation of colonialism in general, has featured in the writings of numerous liberal political thinkers such as Edmund Burke, Adam Smith, John Stuart Mill, David Ricardo, and David Hume.[61] While liberalism asserts its values as 'politically inclusionary'[62] and universal,[63] a historical analysis of liberalism may suggest otherwise, as Uday Singh Mehta goes on to note:

"(a)nd yet, when viewed as a historical phenomenon, the period of liberal history is unmistakably marked by the systematic and sustained political exclusion of various groups and 'types' of people."[64]

While liberalism at home aligned itself with rights and citizens, the empire ruled over 'subjects.' The system of checks and balances developed in the form of the separation of powers in Britain, was not expressed in the Indian subcontinent,[65] where other expressions of liberalism—such as its take on property rights and the European 'civilizing project'—were imposed. Essentially, at its inception, Pakistan inherited a system that was fundamentally rigged against inclusive political participation, and the recognition of minorities and communal values.

In this context, notions of 'Multicultural citizenship' as advanced in Western societies may not be apposite to Pakistan unless first localized to address the issues undermining multiculturalism and communitarianism in the country; once these concepts are suitability aligned or even adapted to rid developing nations of social pathologies, many of which are as a result of colonialism, they can prove particularly useful in addressing the systemic aberrations that cause these ills.[66] In general, non-Western societies have criticized the 'universality' of human rights for being an overly simplistic notion of Western imperialism which fails to account for specific cultural and religious values.[67] If the narrative of rights can be framed in communal, cultural, religious, and social terms, the impact of these rights and their legitimacy between local populations is bound to be more significant. Most federating units in countries including Iran, Pakistan, Nepal, and India, for example, have been predicated upon ethnic parameters, with ethnic federalism being the fulcrum of the Pakistani Constitution in particular.[68] While this (ethnic) ordering of these states—particularly in the context of Pakistan—is largely a problematic relic of colonial practices, it nonetheless reflects the communal diversity present in these states, and simultaneously serves to highlight the importance these non-Western contexts place upon group identification, as opposed to individualism.

To counter the systemic exclusion of minorities, or indeed political parties representing smaller communities, a 'universally applicable' theory of justice—"the capabilities approach"—may also be well-suited to non-Western societies. This theoretical approach to deemphasizing sociocultural differences in heterogeneous polities, posited by theorists such as Amartya Sen and Martha Nussbaum, focuses on fostering and promoting central human capabilities, which include bodily integrity, sense, affiliations, and control over one's environment.[69] This approach focuses on the global citizen and is not premised upon an idealized theoretical political model of justice, but is instead driven by practical human realities. It espouses a more universalistic definition of citizenship and actively resists limitations associated with the central role and responsibilities of the state and state sovereignty.[70] To be effective, the theory needs to be adopted by non-Western societies and, for this purpose, must develop mechanisms that promote such adoption. It must develop means and methods of how local communities and groups, along with human rights actors, need to be mobilized, at times in resistance to the state for amassing human, political and social capital and realizing the "social minimum" that Nussbaum—in particular—outlines.[71] Amartya Sen challenges the traditional approach to development associated with economic growth, advancing two fundamental challenges. Firstly, the individual should be viewed as the 'unit of analysis'[72] and secondly 'the space in which progress is assessed is made of capabilities and freedoms instead of income';[73] Sen's approach therefore examines the opportunities available to each individual.[74] For instance, Sen's emphasis on basic education (and a rights-based approach to education) as a tool for enhancing and advancing human development can be adapted within education systems in non-Western societies.[75] Reframing policies intended to provide access to education for all and embracing cultural, ethnic, and religious differences could themselves be a means to embrace cultural, linguistic, and ethnic differences and as a result achieve social justice and empowerment for marginalized sections of society.[76] The capabilities approach also focuses on and prioritizes, perhaps in contrast to communitarianism, certain individual human rights focused on sentient living that will need to be reframed and indigenized to be impactful, in ways that are not presented or perceived as directly undermining preexisting social and gender roles that are central within non-Western collective societies.[77] In this vein, Muslim societies are, in any case, more comfortable with collective forms of justice in comparison to some Western forms focused on individual rights. For them, historically, the world is divided into the Muslim *Ummah* or 'community' and the other, with Muslim and minorities groups coexisting and enjoying similar cultural and social rights.[78]

Pakistan's postcolonial and Muslim-majority society, however, presents a case study to explore how certain federal structuring and power imbalances can further deepen intercommunal divisions and accentuate ethnic conflict, as opposed to preserving group rights and multiculturalism. The country's historic inclination towards consociationalism has meant that power has been concentrated amongst political—mostly Punjabi—elites and therefore that candidates and political parties have not been required to solicit votes from beyond their sociocultural blocs (see Chapter 2, this volume). These practices undermine the realization of grassroots democracy in the country; specifically, the Punjabi hegemony over the state apparatuses has been exercised at the expense and disenfranchisement of ethnic minorities within Pakistan. This centralized consolidation of power within a particular sociocultural group has resulted in adverse outcomes for smaller factions and cultural or religious minorities, thereby negatively impacting the application of norms of distributive justice and the realization of grassroots democracy.

The power struggle between the federal center (which happens to be the province of Punjab) and the smaller provinces, often entails a corresponding struggle between the federal and provincial governments, effectively discounting the third tier of government (i.e., local government).[79] This reluctance on the part of provincial governments to devolve financial and administrative authority to the local government tier further demonstrates how Pakistani politicians are "(not) interested in grassroots democracy because of their strong aversion to sharing power and resources with local public representatives."[80] Without an effective and meaningful devolution of competencies to the local tier of governance, as envisaged under the 18th Amendment to the Constitution of Pakistan, it is difficult to foresee participatory representation and grassroots democracy be realized within the country.

Even contemporaneously, self-governance in Pakistan is formally achieved through local government bodies, but more effectively by way of parallel extrajudicial systems such as the *panchayat* or *jirga*—i.e., a council of tribal elders—that dispenses justice expeditiously based on customary tribal norms.[81] Although these systems must be monitored and evaluated more stringently by the state to preclude internal restrictions and ensure their consistency with the constitutional rights-based framework—as such normative codes may often be discriminatory and repressive, sanctioning illegal and severe punishments predominantly on women and disenfranchised groups in direct violation of the Pakistani constitution's fundamental rights protections—they nonetheless still represent an important manifestation of a culture's right to self-govern, and can be a route to effective self-governance if reformed and employed correctly.

Group membership and identification fundamentally inform an individual's participation in the public sphere universally, and this partisanship—which is expressed globally—undoubtedly informs their political activity. Speaking to the specific context of Pakistan, the federating units have been ordered almost exclusively along ethnic lines, with the entire politico-legal framework privileging certain religious—i.e., sociocultural—groups over others, and where group membership—through quotas and special allowances—nets one tangible benefits. The idealistic touting of individual rights over collective ones thus comes across as particularly naïve when viewed from this context. The atomization of the polity—rendering the only legally enforceable rights exercisable by the individual alone—have the further consequence of making such rights more difficult for an individual—particularly one belonging to a marginalized community—to exercise them.

Much like union membership the world over empowers individual workers to leverage the collective bargaining power of the union as a whole, and so address the power imbalance inherent in the employer-employee relationship, so too does membership of a sociocultural group grant individual members capacities otherwise not exercisable as an individual. In the Pakistani context, however, these capacities have historically been leveraged by members of the larger, dominant social groups and to the detriment of other, marginalized, or disenfranchised groups, with the latter groups often unable to mobilize effectively enough to leverage their own—relatively smaller—group's influence. However, the proposed localized centripetalist federal framework (see Chapter 2) will seek to embed explicit protections not just for individuals as per traditional liberal thought, but also for groups themselves; just as certain historically marginalized groups of persons or 'classes' enjoy additional legal protections in the US context, so, too, is the proposed framework intended to ensure similar groups in Pakistan are protected at the community level.

Furthermore, on the topic of special group representation rights, Pakistan presently has a well-structured system of representation in the country's upper-bureaucracy in place via a quota system, and has reserved seats for women and minorities in its legislative assemblies; the country also has equal representation of its federating units—organized along ethnic lines—in the upper legislative house, regardless of the country's—and by extension each unit's—population demographics. A concern, however, is that many smaller ethnic groups are situated as enclaves within regions otherwise dominated by larger ones, with such smaller groups remaining unrepresented in the ordering of the provinces or in such quota systems, and hence deprived of meaningful political representation or engagement.

Despite these attempts to ensure representation for religious and ethnic minorities in Pakistan's federal structure (see Chapter 2), these weak federal mechanisms have not translated to the preservation of collective rights nor to ethnic minorities making meaningful contributions to national policy. Being the country's most populous province, Punjab dominates the National Assembly—the lower legislative house. Further, despite constitutionally mandated equal provincial representation in the upper legislative house, elected senators often align themselves with the federal government, thereby allowing the federally dominant Punjabi hegemony to seep into the Senate's workings as well (see Chapter 2). This effectively disenfranchises the other ethnicities and provinces, diluting the parity the ethnically balanced Senate is intended to achieve. Furthermore, smaller ethnic parties are often accorded cabinet positions to secure a majority in the National Assembly, as was the case with the Muttahida Qaumi Movement (MQM) in 2018. These positions, however, often do not translate into meaningful representation for such ethnic minorities—particularly in the upper echelons of government or the federal bureaucracy. The MQM, dissatisfied with Imran Khan's ruling party's lack of commitment to fulfilling electoral promises regarding additional development funds and ministries, quit the Cabinet to support the opposition in the latter's no-confidence vote against Imran Khan, ousting Khan's PTI government.[82] This is one instance of an ethnically oriented political party having to hedge its support with a majority party to garner any meaningful gains for itself or its community, and despite the fact that the MQM was able to successfully do so such often does not work in the smaller group's favor.

Immigrants and refugees are especially vulnerable in states lacking inbuilt collective minority protections, and where the movement of people—and boundaries—are more fluid and fungible constructs therein.[83] This is of particular concern in the Pakistani context, where—due to decades of violence in neighboring Afghanistan—the country plays host to over a million Afghan refugees. Voluntary immigration and what constitutes consent is also harder to assess in these political landscapes and the assimilation of minority groups in ethnically and religiously varied communities is, unlike in more homogenous Western contexts, often a direct corollary of active armed conflict in these and neighboring territories.[84] Under a communitarian model, immigrants and refugees should therefore also be accorded the same rights and privileges as indigenous ethno-cultural groups in such settings. However, it is important to refer to Kymlicka's categorization of immigrants and refugee populations within his theory, where he approaches the subject by way of the voluntary nature of migration as opposed to the influx of refugees in a particular territory. Given the 'voluntary' nature of immigration, Kymlicka classifies immigrants as an ethnic group that can only be accorded certain 'polyethnic rights';[85] further, he notes that such protections should not be limited to political and cultural recognition only but must also be substantiated and supported by concrete legal protections through legislation, with adequate implementation of these instruments through the executive. Similarly, communitarianism should also directly seek to challenge the nature and parameters of state citizenship, and in this process directly resist the absolutist international legal norm of state sovereignty.[86]

Of particular interest for this piece is a discussion of how sociocultural elements such as religiosity or ethnicity have been leveraged for political advantage, and how an emphasis on particular forms of cultural expression has served to disunite, rather than cohere, Pakistan's polity. This discussion will thus inform ways in which these sociocultural markers may be deemphasized to reduce points of distinction between the various groups extant within the country.

Developing states are unfortunately often rife with violations of political rights, with minorities, immigrants, and other marginalized groups principally the ones being deprived of these collective rights and individual freedoms.[87] In turn, many such groups resort to violence when repressed or subjugated, precipitating further state sanctions and thus perpetuating a cycle of violence. This cycle leaves the state in a constant state of emergency to maintain oppressive control over the populace and retaliate against these expressions of violence. As a result, both the internal and external self-determination of these minority groups are undermined.[88]

In Pakistan, the religious minority of the Ahmadiyya sect and the ethnic Baluchi group have been targeted for repression, both through state and nonstate violence.[89] Similarly, in Iran the minority Sunni, tribal population of the Baluchis continues to be deprived of their political rights of self-determination, and are instead placed directly under the authoritarian control of the Iranian Revolutionary Guard Corps, which targets Baluchi political actors and suppresses their political activities with impunity.[90] In India, the Hindu fascist government has, under the garb of secularism, stripped Muslim communities of their marital and divorce rights, previously secured under the framework of Muslim personal laws. The same Indian government responsible for demolishing a historical Muslim Mosque in Ayodhya—precipitating massive communal violence—has recently had the demolition legally sanctioned by the Indian Supreme Court and also managed to promulgate a law requiring Muslims, not Hindus nor those belonging to other Dharmic faiths, to provide their birth registry information for the purposes of determining their Indian citizenship. Independent India's first premier, Jawaharlal Nehru, often compared liberalism in the United States with that in India, describing the latter as more progressive and preferring it as the same valued and practiced multiculturalism and communalism in a way that legally provided space for religious minorities to practice their respective faiths such that—in the United States—would be seen as violating the public space or infringing upon equal protection clauses inherent in US law.[91] India's historically ecumenical approach to community rights has since, however, been significantly changed for the worse.[92]

From a theological perspective, sects within Islam broadly tend to view one another as equally valid; though tensions exist between various strands of Islamic thought, each of these have historically been viewed by the others, in the abstract at least, as equally legitimate, with this approach largely predicated upon theological notions regarding the fallibility of humans and as a counterpoint to absolutism which is largely perceived of as remaining within the realm of the divine. By contrast, in the past the Catholic Church in Europe has, through leveraging its inordinate temporal influence, been able to successfully categorize other, competing expressions of Christian thought as entirely invalid and heretical—ergo worthy of being eradicated outright. While this has since ceased to be the case, with contemporary Catholicism becoming less exclusionary and contemporary Islamic sects trending instead towards showing less tolerance for other ostensibly competing perspectives, it is opined that the historical degree of ecumenicism as expressed in both religions has led to different engagements with their respective governments.

Historically, Islamic societies did not experience the same violent history involving the church and state as seen in Christian Europe's history;[93] rather, Islamic jurists traditionally refused to be coopted by the state nor were used—or served—as tools of repression against political dissenters. Multiple jurists developed reputations for their insight and nonpartisanship, and, within any given region, disparate communities freely chose those legal traditions and sets of laws, including criminal laws, that would govern them—speaking of course about the minutiae of religious legal norms and praxis and not broader conceptions of legality or morality. This led to the classical Islamic tradition of tolerance, and freedom of expression and religion, as no one community at the time had or claimed to have the legal authority or legitimacy to question the authenticity of any particular Islamic legal system.[94] Simply put: when every community self-identified as a minority there was no majority to impose its own point of view upon others. Even today, Pakistan's Shia community continues to self-govern according to Shia Islamic law and the Sunni community by the Sunni legal traditions—largely Hanafi due to their more significant population—on matters of family law, property law, wills and estates, and certain criminal and financial matters.[95] Furthermore, the Ismaili Muslim community—predominantly situated in Hunza, Pakistan—has their own spiritual and political leader, the Agha Khan, with the Pakistani state refraining from interfering with the social and cultural norms of the community, even if at times such traditions appear to conflict with the Islamized provisions of the Constitution of Pakistan.

Civil-Military Imbalance and its Impact on Compounding Ethnic Conflict, Minority Repression, Perpetuating Distributive Injustice, and Ineffective Local Democracy

Pakistan's military has historically wielded inordinate influence over the country's governance mechanisms, particularly over areas such as the country's foreign relations or economy, areas traditionally not within the military's domain (see Chapter 3). This influence is compounded by—and in turn compounds—preexisting ethnic tensions prevalent in the country, with certain ethnic groups overrepresented among the officer corps. Historically, the highest-ranking office of the Chief of Army Staff, has predominantly been held either by a Punjabi or a Pashtun.[96]

This undue authority is further compounded by the Pakistani military's suppression of ethnic minorities in the smaller provinces. For instance, the Baloch population has always been disgruntled over the allocation of natural resources, so much so that such has precipitated secessionist movements backed by foreign powers in the region. Similarly, the Pashtuns have also been dealt with heavy-handedly by the army for contesting Punjabi hegemony over the center/federation (see Chapter 3). These trends have led the minority provinces to feel like the Pakistan Army is not a national institution, but instead a Punjabi force that wields its power against these provinces, rather than to protect their interests.[97] The fact that the composition of the Pakistani Armed forces is also—almost purposefully—ethnically skewed adds to the negative sentiment minorities have towards the military. Historically, close to 70 percent of the army has been populated by the Punjabi ethnicity, with Mohajir and Sindhi representation standing at a mere 3–5 percent, and the Baluchi ethnicity forming a dismal 0.3 percent of the military.[98] Even though the military has since made efforts to make the force more inclusive, credibly concerns about equitable ethnic representations within the institution's top brass still persist.[99] An oft-cited reason for this is that recruits from Sindh and Balochistan are simply not educationally at par with the military's standards, often requiring the expenditure of further resources to bring them up to the required standards.[100] If true, however, this claim further emphasizes the disparate treatment meted out to potential Sindhi or Balochi candidates who, by virtue of the inadequate educational opportunities afforded thereto, are excluded from the upper echelons of the military's power structures. The grassroots disadvantage these minorities experience, therefore, manifests in their ability to participate competitively on the national level. One way in which holistic inclusivity can be achieved, with military recruitment as just one example, is through collective minority protections—empowering minority ethnicities to negotiate more space within crucial national institutions, by allowing them to curate their own mechanisms and ideals for development.

As outlined in the preceding section, the successful implementation of democratic norms such as grassroots democracy is a crucial tool to ensuring representative participation in multiethnic societies such as Pakistan. While three separate attempts have been made to institutionalize local government by the Zia, Ayub Khan and Musharraf military regimes, these attempts have been weak as—due to certain loopholes—power remained centralized within certain ethnicities (see Chapter 2). Further, successive civilian governments have also failed to implement empowered, democratic local government systems; while the Eighteenth Amendment is a welcome move to empower provincial governments to institutionalize local government models, leading to greater representation and therefore accountability, it cannot be implemented in its truest sense without the political will to also institutionalize grassroots democracy.

The historical asymmetry between the military establishment and the civilian leadership and bureaucracy has also led to a growing corpus of 'military laws'—statutes that were promulgated for, and which serve to grant the Pakistani military and its personnel further protections and privileges within the state. In July 2023 Pakistan's lower legislative house the National Assembly passed the Pakistan Army (Amendment) Act 2023 in extreme haste; the bill was presented when attendance in the house was low and operates to effectively criminalize all domestic critique of the country's armed forces. The bill was similarly rushed through the upper cameral house, the Senate, even prompting members of the ruling coalition to walk out over the haste with which it was being pushed through the house and the inadequate time accorded for its review. The amendment effectively criminalizes the 'ridiculing, scandalizing, bringing into hatred, or lower the estimation of the Pakistani armed forces in the eyes of others,' yet it provides no clear boundaries or definitions of what these terms mean and how they are to be interpreted, and while proponents of the instrument have argued that its ambit is limited to 'personnel'—i.e., former or current members of the armed forces, itself alarmingly wide in scope—the language of the amendment is broad enough to raise serious concerns regarding its impact on domestic civil and political liberties.

The Official Secrets Act, 1923 was itself recently amended by way of the Official Secrets (Amendment) Bill, 2023, which grants sweeping powers to domestic intelligence agencies, allowing them to conduct raids, collect and confiscate what the agencies determine is 'evidence,' and detain citizens over suspected breaches of the legislation. The amendment, which faced fierce criticism over the 'draconian' nature of the powers accorded to these agencies, compelled the National Assembly to refer the bill to the Senate Standing Committee for review. Despite its opposition, and the patent civil liberties concerns it raises, the amendment nonetheless passed, ostensibly after clauses granting inordinately sweeping powers to Pakistan's intelligence agencies were removed. The bill's passage was not, however, uncontested, failing to placate legislators on either side of the legislative aisle, including members of the ruling coalition.

In context, it is crucial to recognize that corpus of laws—comprising the various military and intelligence agencies' statutes—has periodically been used by both the military as well as by civilian governments to bypass legal and constitutional protections in the name of 'emergencies,' with the superior judiciary often subsequently ratifying these excesses. This cycle of overreach and subsequent legitimization has led to the entrenchment of the already-powerful armed forces within a broad array of areas otherwise not within their purview and has rendered the country's military—and its personnel—largely immune from domestic critique. This impunity has only been formalized and reinforced through the passage of the 2023 amendments to the Pakistan Army and Official Secrets Acts.

Deemphasizing ethnicity among Pakistan's armed forces, and undoing decades of its judicial and legislative empowerment, will contribute significantly towards redressing these historical power imbalances, and reduce the scope such institutions otherwise have to distort federalism in Pakistan and the outlined positive values suitable for Pakistan. Specifically, diluting the role of ethnicity within the military's composition would enhance solidarity and promote realization of social justice—once ethnic grievances are displaced, the institution would be better equipped to effect cohesive national strategies and policies.

Furthermore, years of successive direct and indirect control by the military in Pakistan has also enabled it to become the largest commercial enterprise in the country.[101] The military's domestic primacy has meant that a significant proportion of the national budget is diverted towards defense spending, thereby negatively impacting the amounts left available to trickle down to social welfare programs in the fields of health care and education, and directly undermining norms of distributive justice for the polity. Additionally, it means that the military is able to strong-arm its way into getting disproportionately involved with various ministries of the government,[102] and even within crucial international economic projects such as the CPEC.[103] With the inordinate power to manipulate resources in its favor, the military, a non-democratic institution—problematically deepens the distributive divide. For one, the process of appointing retired senior military officials at the helm of critical national institutions such as the CPEC Authority is quite nontransparent and arguably not based on merit or value of service. There is, therefore, a constant, pernicious sentiment that the officer will act purely self-servingly—if not in the interests of their previous institution—and with relative impunity.[104] Secondly, the appointment of retired officers at such key posts is particularly alienating for the business community and other domestic stakeholders, which often do not share common practices or values with members of the military.

The military employed religion as a tool to keep political leaders in check, and to suppress certain religious minorities. For instance, following the declaration of Ahmadis as Non-Muslims under the Second Amendment passed by the then–Prime Minister Zulfiqar Ali Bhutto, Zia-ul-Haq further disenfranchised this minority by implementing separate electorates and requiring Ahmadis to register and vote as non-Muslims, effectively reducing Ahmadis to a non-Muslim minority, such as Hindus and Christians and diluting their electoral power (see Chapter 3).

In essence, if one were to borrow from Antonio Gramsci's "hegemony" thesis it appears that in Pakistan the military establishment is the major institution that holds power—economic, social, and political—to define "what is desirable, what is good, and, in a sense, what is the nature of their reality."[105] This leaves the majority of the polity with limited political power to change their circumstances, or the societies in which they live. If one hopes to revert the balance of power back in favor of the people—and not the military establishment—it is first essential to devolve political power to the grassroots level, where true democratic engagement and accountability takes place *vis-a-vis* giving the population the authority to decide the means and responsibilities of government.[106]

Effects of Economic Interactions with China (vis-a-vis the CPEC) on Distributive Justice, Local Self-Government, and Exacerbating Ethnic Conflict by Devaluing Communal Values

In addition to Pakistan's problematic federal structure and the imbalance between its citizenry and its powerful military, economic interactions, and transactions with neighboring China *vis-à-vis* the CPEC has also diluted distributive justice and grassroots democracy within the country, impeding the effective realization of multiculturalism.

As discussed above, the country's civil-military asymmetry, and successive tenures of military rule, all have played a significant role in the evolution of Pakistan's economic and fiscal policy. For instance, while policies adopted during General Ayub's regime led to economic growth, such was termed as "growth without development."[107] This economic growth formula, based on depressed wages and neglecting the norms of distributive justice, further empowered a particular class of social elite and contributed to mass poverty and increasing inequality.[108] Similarly, during the Zia regime, a significant flow of foreign aid trickled in as part of the 1970s' imposition of neoliberal agendas on the Global South through international governmental organizations such as the IMF and World Bank.[109]

As discussed in more detail in Chapter 4 of this volume, this neoliberal trajectory continued in successive civilian regimes, resulting in the elite capture of state-owned enterprises through privatization. Similarly, policies for the agricultural and industrial sectors have favored the elite operating within these sectors, thereby leaving very little in the way of resources that could be allocated towards the general social welfare. This situation, of favoring the political and bureaucratic Punjabi elites, directly undermines norms of distributive justice with regards to the other provinces and ethnicities, limiting their chances towards meaningful sociopolitical representation.[110]

For critics, the neoliberal state exacerbates existing inequalities within postcolonial, multiethnic polities; because its objectives are economic, the only class that stands to benefit is the capitalist sections of society. If economic expansion is prioritized over all else, only those who have preexisting capabilities to participate in the neoliberal agenda thrive, deepening the distributive divide and reinforcing preexisting class divisions and disparities (see Chapter 4 of this volume). State-led neoliberal agendas, such as China's economic expansion agenda prosecuted through the Belt and Road Initiative and the CPEC, necessarily require the centralization of decision-making within the state: the more state apparatuses are shaped to strengthen the central state's autonomy to enforce neoliberal policies, the more relentlessly neoliberal reforms are seemingly observed to disregard values such as social distributive justice and minority enfranchisement. Additionally, both traditional notions of neoliberalism and Chinese economic expansionism fail to consider the negative externalities of these policies and their effect on essential considerations, such as their impact on the environment or on sustainable forms of production, that do not damage the viability of ecosystems for future generations.[111]

Within the Pakistani context, the Chinese strain of economic development is particularly pernicious to preexisting—already-strained—interethnic and interprovincial relations. For example, the CPEC's focus on acquiring arable agricultural land has significantly impacted the rights of various ethnic groups, such as Balochis, agricultural communities around Peshawar, and fishing communities in Gwadar, leaving them disgruntled and disenfranchised.[112] The project has thus aggravated existing cries of neglect from the provinces of Sindh, Khyber-Pakhtunkhwa, and Balochistan against the Punjabi hegemony over resource allocation (discussed in more detail in Chapter 4).[113]

Another example of how Chinese expansionist projects can impact democratic norms and adversely impact minority populations is the implementation of Special Economic Zones ("SEZs") under the rubric of the CPEC (see Chapter 4). The governance of these SEZs under Special Economic Zone Authorities—which are provincial bodies—enables provincial governments to retain the right to acquire private land through the process of eminent domain under the Land Acquisition Act, 1894 (I of 1894).[114] This appropriation would be justified if the benefits accrued from the SEZs eventually trickled down to the locals—particularly those having to give up their land—thereby uplifting and empowering them. These SEZs, however, are instead like fortresses permitting access only to specialized persons who will further specific, state-determined objectives. The SEZs are therefore isolated from local sensibilities, and often heavily militarized, which only serves to further entrench negative local sentiment towards them. The implementation of SEZ mechanisms in areas such as Azad Jammu and Kashmir and Gilgit-Baltistan is even more problematic, as these territories are managed by the federal center which operates at a significant remove from local sentiments. What is thus effectuated is the very opposite of grassroots democracy—with power, decision-making, and accountability so far separated from local communities that they are ineffectual in asserting their rights and completely vulnerable to exploitation. In the context of grassroots democracy and the rights of local communities, for instance, while locals of Gilgit-Baltistan were initially promised 1.8 million jobs, in reality the federal government canceled the licenses of local miners to instead grant exclusive control of the mines to Chinese companies, also displacing thousands of locals without clear plans for their rehabilitation or resettlement.[115]

Additionally, as mentioned above, the fact that the CPEC Authority (created under an ordinance and not through ordinary legislative procedure) was headed by a retired military official not only deepens the country's civil-military asymmetry, but also the fact that this ordering of the CPEC—and the limited jurisdiction of courts[116] over it—leaves provincial governments with few legal options to challenge the federal government in relation to disputes arising under CPEC (see Chapter 4).

The public face of China's global economic policy is one of non-interference, valuing peaceful coexistence and harmony.[117] In practice, however, pressures from an economically superior country such as China to execute arrangements that are ostensibly for "mutual benefit" but instead have serious consequences and repercussions for locals, often strong-arm economically inferior countries such as Pakistan into implementing programs that harm its indigenous social and economic distributive justice systems (see Chapter 4). An example is the establishment of SEZs in Pakistan, where the continued appropriation of arable agricultural land for their construction is often touted a source of prosperity to the region, but the considerable costs of repurposing the land goes unaccounted for. For one, agriculture is the backbone of Pakistan's economy and employs almost a quarter of the nation's population; thus, there is a definite loss in local skilled livelihood if such arable land is reassigned from agricultural to industrial use. The timelines involved with re-skilling local labor are simply incompatible with the CPEC's developmental schedule—the Chinese CPEC-related presence in Pakistan is already notorious for their impatience with systemic time lags arising in Pakistan—and thus locals are being excluded from the eventual developmental benefits—if any—of these SEZs. Secondly, this repurposing may also have an effect in the form of its impact on land, food, or ecological objectives that would otherwise better cater to the needs of the Pakistani people. Another cost seldom accounted for is the loss of the ancestral and historical value inherent in the land acquired, compensated for—if at all—at bear market rates, which not only disenfranchises the indigenous agricultural economies and societies, pushing them either into abject poverty or towards militant resistance, but also alienates them from their cultural, historical, and ancestral heritage.

Drawing upon theories of international distributive justice, as referenced above, one could perhaps contend that independent states that set out to economically interact with one other have an international obligation to subscribe to certain minimum standards and rules of the trade regime, or to a system of internationally recognised property rights, which protect economically weaker states from being appropriated into debt traps and culturally damaging economic policies. Given that the impact of these economic interactions seep all the way down to the grassroots level of the distributive divide, independent nation-states must interact with one other in ways that are truly—and not merely rhetorically—non-interfering, inclusive, and harmonious.

CONCLUSION

Using Iran as a case study, Hussain Banai constructs the argument that classical Western liberal scholarship fails to adequately consider the nature of non-liberal societies—or indeed societies perceived as 'non-liberal' from a Western liberal perspective, particularly those which have recently experienced colonialism or which reside in postcolonial states—partly because these states lack the overtly 'liberal' institutions necessary for realizing the posited 'rights and justice' framework in line with the principles and norms of international law and practice, which traditional liberal theory prioritizes. While there is a fusion of various liberal theories as a 'universal philosophical creed,'[118] liberal doctrine as a whole often fails to identify parallels of liberal norms in non-liberal societies, and it is these 'hidden' values that may instead be synthesized for a cohesive response to counter autocratic power structures in these non-Western contexts, as opposed to traditional—'overt'—forms of liberalism, which would otherwise experience far more resistance.[119] These forms of hidden liberal expression find far greater traction within 'traditional' and 'non-liberal' non-Western societies, often because they are indigenously generated and not transplanted from a Western—often colonial—context, and because they can often be distinguished from more overt, 'traditional' expressions of liberalism which are usually associated in these contexts with hostile foreign states and cultures. Hidden liberalism thus seeks to preserve and provide similar or selected guarantees or 'liberties' by evolving, indigenizing, and revisiting 'traditionally' liberal concepts, more significantly, through institutional and state reform, as well as through the reinvention or re-expression of these liberal concepts through autochthonous norms and practices. Banai's arguments regarding 'hidden,' nontraditional expressions of liberal theory are thus far more consistent with the Pakistani experience, particularly with regards to communal democratic and liberal norms being incorporated into or by way of religious and indigenous normative frameworks.[120] While elements of Western scholarship often view Islamic ideologies as inherently illiberal, to refute this orientalist conception of Islam it is imperative to first understand the elaborate normative framework in Islamic thought which supports the implementation of political Islam in Muslim-majority societies, predicated upon Islamic theories of justice aimed at achieving and maintaining a free, equal society based on a just and fair system of government.

This thesis proposes that the four democratic values/norms discussed at length in this chapter can be indigenized and contextualized within the Pakistani context. Pakistan is presently overwhelmingly consociationalist in the way political participation is structured, resulting in a sharpening of ethnic, religious, and linguistic differences—and alienation—in the polity. This thesis, in the proceeding chapters, posits that a viable model of localized centripetalist federalism provides the means by which the political influence of these sociocultural differences can be minimized. This model incorporates the four norms described in this chapter, particularly by drawing upon strands of local communitarianism, so that the alienating influence of demographic interests in political expression can be minimized.

Historically, none of these norms are entirely alien to the Pakistani context; prior to the British colonial regime the region was a patchwork of small kingdoms and principalities, with periods of more consolidated rule under various Hindu and later Mughal Muslim dynasties. Ecumenicism in such a diverse context was the norm, and geopolitical boundaries were not maintained in the more contemporary post-Westphalian manner. The period of colonial rule, however, saw groups and communities being politically segregated on sociocultural grounds, culminating in the post-independence federal ordering of Pakistan. More recently, there have been efforts to inculcate forms of local governance and decentralize political and governmental decision-making; the Eighteenth Amendment to the Pakistani Constitution sought to devolve legislative and executive competencies that were historically solely exercised by the federal center, and while its implementation has been mixed, it nonetheless lays the groundwork for future, more ambitious reimaginings of Pakistan's federal structure. Giving effect to the Eighteenth Amendment in meaningful and universal ways, and possibly building upon earlier attempts at local governance made during the Musharraf regime, will decentralize legislative and executive activity, engendering greater transparency and accountability and rendering governmental processes more representative.

Through effective decentralization and devolution, the proposed localized centripetalist federative model will thus seek to shift decision-making processes and authority to the localized—'grassroots'—level to the fullest extent possible. While macro-level decisions must necessarily be deliberated upon by institutions with the broadest national purviews, shifting all other such processes to the local level will contribute significantly towards effecting transparency, representation, and accountability in the decision-making processes. The model will require constitutional and political reengineering, as well as modifications to present electoral systems and the arrangement of ethnic federalism and consociationalism currently in place. The proposed model will seek to ensure—and encourage—community identification and inter-communal tolerance, while simultaneously promoting the ability of minority communities to collectively articulate their rights.

Diluting the inordinate political impact of larger ethnic blocs and dissuading the polity from voting exclusively along sociocultural lines, will require modifications to the country's electoral processes; at present the Pakistani Senate is relatively more representative of the federating units, but its members are elected by members of the provincial legislative houses. Making senators directly elected would reduce the distance between the polity and its representatives in the upper house and would further deemphasize the influence of larger ethnic groups which are otherwise often overrepresented in these bodies. In the same vein, further empowering the Senate would shift the axis of legislative and governmental power away from Pakistan's lower house—the National Assembly—further decreasing the impact specific communities would otherwise have on national governmental processes and making space for minorities to exercise their political rights. At the national level, the centripetalist framework can be effected through electoral reforms, such as by introducing direct senate elections by way of alternative voting mechanisms such as alternative voting, single transferable or single non-transferable voting, or vote pooling etc.—moving from the first past the post system presently in place to alternative voting in the lower house—and by making changes in the parliamentary system of government, such as by creating more provinces and empowering the upper house.

Another way to deemphasize the influence ethnic identity has on Pakistani politics is to ensure multiparty registration at the national or federal representative levels, but to exclude the same from local elections and to gradually phase out ethnic representation in the legislative assemblies. While gender and religious minority quotas should be retained—and arguably expanded—to ensure groups historically marginalized or disenfranchised are able to effectively participate in the country's electoral processes, ethnic representation serves to perpetuate political tribalism and encourage political actors to cater only to the needs of the group they identify with. Similarly, breaking up the present provinces into smaller federating units—along ethnically agnostic lines—would serve to dilute the political impact larger provinces—and the ethnicities that dominate them—have over the country's governance mechanisms. While various such proposals have been considered in the past, the proposed provincial changes have always been drawn along distinctly ethnic lines and would likely only serve to prolong existing intercommunal political antagonism and factionalism.

Finally, by prioritizing cultural pluralism, multiculturalism appeals to non-Western societies—such as Pakistan—as a means of advancing communal rights by initiating the dialogue necessary to implement the politics of difference, and for identity formation as outlined by Charles Taylor. Taylor argues that Western philosophy disproportionality focuses on and favors individualism;[121] instead, multiculturalism can effectively be leveraged to protect cultures and groups on the precipice of extinction, such as the animist Kalash[122] people of Pakistan who are being forcefully converted to Islam due to sociocultural and economic pressures. So far, this theory has been applied in certain limited circumstances involving developed countries in peacetime, and in rarefied contexts such as the university setting; for it to be developed and applied to developing world and postcolonial countries—particularly those experiencing forms of overt conflict—and conflict zones marked by civil and religious strife (far removed from Quebec as studied by Taylor), more formalized and realistic engagements that account for human and group security will need to be devised to realize the process of dialogue central to identify formation. For instance, taking the approach adapted in South Africa, such groups could be protected through mandating a national commission for the protection of indigenous groups,[123] a commission given the necessary authority and legitimacy to effectively ensure the protection of such groups and the individuals comprising them.

After Pakistan instituted the Eighteenth Amendment to the Constitution, several areas previously within the legislative domain of the federal government were devolved to the provincial governments.[124] This devolution of power to the provinces was also perceived as a welcome move by proponents of a Seraiki province who view the decentralization and the creation of new provinces as a prerequisite to keeping a multicultural polity united.[125] Even earlier, a means of implementing local governance was instituted—surprisingly during the regime of the then military dictator Pervez Musharraf.[126] Initiatives such as these have worked to dilute the federal focus in the Pakistani political and legal contexts to a large degree, and while these are arguably still works in progress, initiatives such as these have served to shift the balance of power away from the center and towards the local. However, these actions have not always translated into the realization of social and political rights for ethnic and religious minorities and a far more targeted and nuanced approach to social emancipation via educational and developmental policies instead is also required to address certain continuing disparities. Furthermore, based on the South African experience (discussed above), devolution and the dispersion of territorial power will only succeed in addressing ethnic disparity where these provinces have significant powers and autonomy in terms of legislation, raising taxes, and perhaps also through establishing provincial constitutions and with the implementation of local government mechanisms.[127]

In the Pakistani context the localized forms of distributive justice; collective minority protections; localized self-governance; and autochthonous forms of communitarianism, multiculturalism, and cosmopolitanism, have historically seen significant traction and can provide the basis for the successful gradual and indigenized inculcation of progressive norms. In doing so, these will effectively address political distortions arising out of ethnic conflict and disparities, the asymmetry between the country's politically influential military and its civilian government, and neoliberalism, as will be discussed in later chapters.

These broad-ranging and systemic changes will serve to contribute towards fostering a more cooperative political environment at the federal level, which will effectively promote inter-communal harmony and communal values and foster a strong national civic identity distinct from ethnic identitarianism currently at play in the country. Military reforms effected through such political engineering will also help to promote civil-military parity in Pakistan and, in turn, better protect the rights of marginalized and disenfranchised groups within the country.

While the scope of these changes may seem ambitious, it is argued that these will be necessary to reverse the damage caused by divisive forms of consociationalism, which have contributed towards intercommunal tensions within the country.

NOTES

1. *See* Chapter 2 (this volume). ("In this context 'localized'—and particularly 'localized centripetalism'—refers to a model specific to Pakistan's postcolonial context, leveraging centripetal forces to counter interethnic discord, Punjabi hegemony, and the impact(s) of neoliberal policies that operate to exacerbate these issues. This proposed model differs from other hybrid models as it seeks to strengthen federal stability by way of splitting the existing, larger, provinces into smaller federating units—and thus dilute the overwhelming impact ethnic identity has on national politics—while simultaneously accommodating local and communal identity.").

2. Julian Lamont and Christi Favor, "Distributive Justice Stanford Encyclopedia of Philosophy," 2017 Available from: https://plato. stanford. edu/entries/justice-distributive. (2020).

3. John Rawls, *Justice as fairness: A restatement*. Harvard University Press, 2001.

4. *See supra* note 2. *See also* John Rawls, "A theory of justice." *Ethics*. Routledge, 2004. 229–34; Samuel Freeman. "Rawls on distributive justice and the difference principle." *The Oxford Handbook of Distributive Justice*. Oxford: Oxford University Press, 2018. 13.

5. *Ibid.*

6. *See supra* note 2.

7. *Ibid.*

8. *Ibid.*

9. Charles R. Beitz, "International liberalism and distributive justice: a survey of recent thought." *World politics* 51.2 (1999): 269–96.

10. *Ibid.*

11. *Ibid.*

12. Hugh Whalen, "Ideology, Democracy, and the Foundations of Local Self-Government." *Canadian Journal of Economics and Political Science/Revue canadienne de economiques et science politique* 26.3 (1960) : 377–95, 379.

13. *Ibid.* at 385–86.

14. *Ibid.*

15. John Stuart Mill, *Representative government*. Alex Catalogue; Net Library., 1924, 112.

16. *See supra* note 12 at 391.

17. *Ibid.*

18. Zsolt Körtvélyesi, "Transcending the Individual/Collective Minority Rights Divide: A Procedural Solution." *International & Comparative Law Quarterly* 71.1 (2022): 73–106.

19. *Ibid.*

20. Samuel Bagenstos, 'Litigation for the People,' (Fall 2020), accessed on November 22, 2022, <https://www.dissentmagazine.org/article/litigation-for-the-people>.

21. Will Kymlicka, "Defending diversity in an era of populism: Multiculturalism and interculturalism compared." *Multiculturalism and interculturalism: Debating the dividing lines* (2016): 158–77, 174.

22. *See supra* note 18.

23. Douglas Sanders, "Collective rights." *Human rights quarterly* 13.3 (1991): 368–86.

24. *Ibid.*

25. *Ibid.*

26. Bertrand G. Ramcharan, "Individual, collective and group rights: History, theory, practice and contemporary evolution." *International Journal on Minority and Group Rights* 1.1 (1993): 27–43.

27. *See supra* note 23. Essentially the "public face" of Quebec was legally French. Consequently, when the Quebec Government banned, by law, the use of any language other than French on commercial and public sign boards, the English-speaking population challenged it in court, saying that it compromised their freedom of expression—a right granted to them by the Canadian Constitution. The court ruled that freedom of expression is an individual right, which in this case is overruled by the collective right of the Quebecois French to assert their identity. However, the law was struck down because requiring a total ban on other languages was inordinate—although requiring a preponderance of the French language to be publicly visible was justified (the law was later re-instated through another legal lacuna). This is an example of where individual rights were allowed to be overridden by collective minority rights.

28. *See supra* note 23.

29. *Ibid.*

30. John Rex and Gurharpal Singh, "Pluralism and multiculturalism in colonial and post-colonial society—thematic introduction." *International Journal of Multicultural Societies* 5.2 (2003): 106–18.

31. Simon Bekker and Anne Leilde, "Is Multiculturalism a Workable Policy in South Africa?" *International Journal on Multicultural Societies (IJMS)* 5, no. 2 (2003): 119–34., 119.

32. Amaryll Chanady, "From difference to exclusion: Multiculturalism and postcolonialism." *International journal of politics, culture, and society* (1995): 419–37, 419.

33. David Ingram, "Between political liberalism and post national cosmopolitanism: Toward an alternative theory of human rights." *Political theory* 31.3 (2003): 359–91, 217.

34. *Ibid.* at 225.

35. *See supra* note 30.

36. Senayon Olaoluwa, "Crashed dreams in the Sahara: African cosmopolitanism in Across the Desert." *Alif: Journal of Comparative Poetics* 33 (2013): 114–35. Giles Mohan, "Embedded cosmopolitanism and the politics of obligation: the Ghanaian diaspora and development." *Environment and Planning A* 38.5 (2006): 867–83. *See also* Moses E. Ochonu, "Migration, Cosmopolitanism, and Africa in the Twenty-First Century" *African Collective* (22 Aug 2014), accessed on April 19, 2021,<https://theafricacollective.com/2014/08/22/migration-cosmopolitanism-and-africa-in-the-twenty-first-century-2/>. ("Perceptive scholars like Simon Gikandi and Stuart Hall have identified similar responses to cosmopolitanism, itself an outgrowth of various phases of globalization. In responding to cosmopolitan influences, communities in the global South and those with origins there adopt an ambivalent attitude. They reap the benefits of cosmopolitan openness while embracing and, at times, recreating

culturally parochial signs, symbols, and objects that can root them in specific locations, experiences, memories, and traditions. The celebration of cosmopolitanism proceeds in tandem with a retreat to parochially grounded identities that confer certitude in a world in flux—a world in which cosmopolitanism and globalization mask hegemonic Western cultural ascendancy.")

37. *See supra* note 31. As Simon Bekker and Anne Leilde highlight *viz* public policy in the South African context, the two broad features identified above stand out from within the 1996 Constitution: i.e., 'constitutional sovereignty' and the 'territorial dispersion of political power.' The authors note several other institutional changes and affirmative policies required to dilute intrasocietal ethnic and racial disparities. *See infra* note 40.

38. *See supra* note 31 at 121.

39. *Ibid.*

40. *Ibid.* Keeping in mind the features highlighted above, we can see that South Africa has been able to achieve a certain degree of success in implementing its multicultural policies. The country's 1996 Constitution is predicated upon the principles of non-racialism and non-sexism, guaranteeing the protection of cultural, linguistic, gender, and religious rights of individuals against discrimination. Moreover, the state also is obligated to take active, positive measures towards the protection of different ethnic communities, including elevating the status of indigenous languages, constituting a state commission for the protection of ethnic communities, recognizing the institution of traditional leadership, and ensuring that courts apply customary law where it is applicable. The implementation of affirmative action, the provision of local and national government roles and councils to traditional leaders, and recognition of the right to self-determination for any community that shares a distinct language and cultural heritage indicates what these steps look like as expressed and exercised within the political sphere. These policies have largely been successful and have resulted in a marked reduction in political violence within South Africa.

41. *See generally* Husin W.N.W., Rasyid W. I. W. and Mujani, W. K, Consociational Approach to Ethnic Resolution in Malaysia and Lebanon. *Journal of Social and Political Sciences*, Vol.3, No.2 (2020): 474–81.

42. Benjamin Reilly, "Ethnic Representation in Pacific Asia: A Report for the Southeast Asia Rules-Based Order Project."

43. Matthijs Bogaards, "Consociationalism and Centripetalism: Friends or Foes?" *Swiss Political Science Review* 25.4 (2019): 519–37.

44. Will Kymlicka, "Liberalism and Communitarianism." *Canadian Journal of Philosophy* 18.2 (1988): 181–203. *See also* Stephen Mulhall and Adam Swift, *Liberals and Communitarians*. Blackwell Publishers, 1992.

45. Will Kymlicka. *Multicultural citizenship: A liberal theory of minority rights*. Clarendon Press, 1995.

46. Will Kymlicka, *Contemporary Political Philosophy: An Introduction*. Oxford University Press, 2002, 340.

47. Chandran Kukathas, "Survey article: Multiculturalism as fairness: Will Kymlicka's multicultural citizenship." *Journal of Political Philosophy* 5.4 (2002): 406.

48. *See supra* note 45 at 153.

49. *Ibid.* at 362. Kymlicka highlights three group specific-rights: self-government, special group representation, and poly-ethnic rights, which include self-governance and affirmative action. ("National minorities require self-government rights which, in effect, devolve political power 'to a political unit substantially controlled by the members of the national minority, and substantially corresponding to their historical homeland or territory.' Immigrant groups, however, cannot claim self-government rights, but can enjoy 'polyethnic rights,' which are group-specific measures 'intended to help ethnic groups and religious minorities express their cultural particularity and pride without it hampering their success in the economic and political institutions of the dominant society.' Language rights would be one example of such a measure; exemption from some legal requirements (such as wearing motorcycle helmets for Sikhs) would be another. Both kinds of groups may also, in some circumstances, be entitled to special political representation as a temporary measure to deal with the systematic disadvantage or oppression they suffer in their societies."

50. *See* G. W. Choudhury, "Constitution-Making Dilemmas in Pakistan," *Western Political Quarterly* 8.4 (1955): 589–600; Fazlur Rahman, "Implementation of the Islamic Concept of State in the Pakistani Milieu." *Islamic Studies* 6.3 (1967): 205–23.; *See also* Fazlur Rahman, "Islam and the constitutional problem of Pakistan." *Studia Islamica* 32 (1970): 275–87.

51. *See* Mahboob Hussain, "ISLAMIZATION OF THE CONSTITUTION: THE ROLE OF RELIGIOUS PARTIES." *Journal of the Research Society of Pakistan* 51.2 (2014).

52. Moeen H. Cheema, "Pakistan: The state of liberal democracy." *International Journal of Constitutional Law* 16.2 (2018): 635–42.

53. *See supra* note 51 at pp. 78–84.

54. 'Punjab—the battleground for hegemony,' *News on Sunday* (Aug 24, 2014), accessed on 25 November 2022, <https://www.thenews.com.pk/tns/detail/556944-punjab-battleground-hegemony>.

55. *See* Chapter 2 (this volume).

56. Arend Lijphart, "Consociation Democracy," 2 *World Politics* 207 (1969); Arend Lijphart, "Cultural Diversity and Theories of Political Integration," 4 *Canadian Journal of Political Science* (1971); *see also* Arend Lijphart, *Democracy in plural societies: A comparative exploration*. Yale University Press, 1977; Arend Lijphart, "Consociationalism and Federation: Conceptual and Empirical Links," 12 *Canadian Journal of Political Science* (1979); Arend Lijphart, "Non-Majoritarian Democracy: A Comparison of Federal and Consociational Theories," 15 *Publius* (1985); *see also* Katharine Adeney, "The Limitations of Non-consociational Federalism: The Example of Pakistan," *Ethnopolitics: Formerly Global Review of Ethnopolitics*, 8:1, 87–106, 92–93.

57. Duncan Ivison, *Postcolonial liberalism.* Cambridge University Press, 2002, 14.

58. Karuna Mantena, "The crisis of liberal imperialism." *IDEAS IN CONTEXT* 86.1 (2007): 113–35.

59. *Ibid.*

60. *Ibid.* at 31.

61. Uday Singh Mehta, *Liberalism, and empire: A study in nineteenth-century British liberal thought*. University of Chicago Press, 2018. 4.

62. *Ibid.* at 46

63. *Ibid.*

64. *Ibid.*

65. *Ibid.* at 7 ("from the seventeenth century onward, the British, the Dutch and the French rightly conceived of themselves as having elaborated and integrated into their societies an understanding of political freedom, and yet during this very period they pursued and held vast empires where such freedoms were either absent or severely attenuated for the majority of the native inhabitants").

66. *See generally* Will Kymlicka, *Liberalism, community, and culture.* Oxford University Press, 1991.

67. Jonathan Russell, "Human Rights: The Universal Declaration vs the Cairo Declaration." *Middle East Blog* (2012).

68. *See generally* Sadaf Aziz, *The Constitution of Pakistan: A Contextual Analysis.* Bloomsbury Publishing, 2018. *See also* Caldarola, Carlo, ed., *Religion, and societies: Asia and the Middle East*. Vol. 22. Walter de Gruyter, 2011.

69. Martha C. Nussbaum, *The Cosmopolitan Tradition: A Noble but Flawed Ideal.* Harvard University Press, 2019, 240. Martha Nussbaum, Amartya Sen (eds.), *The Quality of Life*. Oxford University Press, 1993. *See also supra* note 4 '*A Theory of Justice.*' *See* "Global Ethics: Capabilities Approach." *International Encyclopedia of Philosophy*, accessed on April 19, 2021, <https://www.iep.utm.edu/ge-capab/> ("1. Life—Able to live to the end of a normal length human life, and to not have one's life reduced to not worth living. 2. Bodily Health—Able to have a good life which includes (but is not limited to) reproductive health, nourishment, and shelter. 3. Bodily Integrity—Able to change locations freely, in addition to, having sovereignty over one's body which includes being secure against assault (for example, sexual assault, child sexual abuse, domestic violence, and the opportunity for sexual satisfaction). 4. Senses, Imagination, and Thought—Able to use one's senses to imagine, think and reason in a 'truly human way'—informed by an adequate education. Furthermore, the ability to produce self-expressive works and engage in religious rituals without fear of political ramifications. The ability to have pleasurable experiences and avoid unnecessary pain. Finally, the ability to seek the meaning of life. 5. Emotions—Able to have attachments to things outside of ourselves; this includes being able to love others, grieve at the loss of loved ones and be angry when it is justified. 6. Practical Reason—Able to form a conception of the good and critically reflect on it. 7. Affiliation. 8. Other Species—Able to have concern for and live with other animals, plants, and the environment at large. 9. Play—Able to laugh, play and enjoy recreational activities. 10. Control over One's Environment").

70. *Ibid. The Cosmopolitan Tradition*, at 247–48.

71. Martha C. Nussbaum, *Frontiers of Justice: Disability, Nationality, Species Membership*. Harvard University Press, 2009, 70.

72. Adriana Conconi and Mariana Viollaz, "Poverty, Inequality and Development: a Discussion from the Capability Approach's Framework," in *The Age of Perplexity: Rethinking the World We Knew.* Penguin Random House, 2018, 354, accessed

on April 19, 2021, <https://www.bbvaopenmind.com/wp-content/uploads/2018/01/BBVA-OpenMind-The-age-of-perplexity-rethinking-the-world-we-knew.pdf>.

73. *Ibid.*

74. *Ibid.*

75. Amartya Sen and Sakiko Fukuda-Parr, "Development as capability expansion."*Readings in human development* (2003).

76. Abdullah Sahin, "Critical issues in Islamic education studies: Rethinking Islamic and Western liberal secular values of education." *Religions* 9.11 (2018): 335.

77. *See generally* Ingrid Robeyns, *Wellbeing, Freedom, and Social Justice: The Capability Approach Re-Examined.* Open Book Publishers, 2017.

78. *See generally* Derryl N. Maclean, *Cosmopolitanisms in Muslim Contexts: Perspectives from the Past: Perspectives from the Past.* Edinburgh University Press, 2012.

79. 'Grassroots power', *DAWN News* (Nov 17, 2021), accessed on November 22, 2021, <https://www.dawn.com/news/1658545>.

80. *Ibid.*

81. "Panchayat—Pakistan's Alternate Judicial System" *News International* (May 31, 2019), accessed on April 19, 2021, <https://www.thenews.com.pk/latest/478808-panchayat-pakistans-alternate-judicial-system>. The *jirga* system is prevalent in the west of Pakistan; similarly, the *panchayat* system is a similar alternative legal framework prevalent in the populous eastern province of Punjab, Pakistan and in neighbouring India.

82. 'MQM-P minsters call it quits,' *Express Tribune* (Mar 30, 2022), accessed on November 23, 2022 <https://tribune.com.pk/story/2350273/mqm-p-minsters-call-it-quits>.

83. *See generally* Navine Murshid, *The Politics of Refugees in South Asia: Identity, Resistance, Manipulation*. Routledge, 2013. De Wilde, Pieter et al., eds., *The Struggle Over Borders: Cosmopolitanism and Communitarianism*. Cambridge University Press, 2019.

84. For instance, the one-million-strong Hazara Shia community situated in the city of Quetta, (which is demographically Sunni majority Pathan and Baluchi) immigrated to this territory from Afghanistan and has still not been able to completely integrate itself, with its cultural and language not being granted any local or national recognition. *See* Iltaf, Maisam. "Hazaras Gripped by Religious Extremism in Balochistan," *Diplomat* (Apr 16, 2019), accessed on April 19, 2021, https://thediplomat.com/2019/04/hazaras-gripped-by-religious-extremism-in-balochistan/.

85. *Supra note* 45, ch.4.

86. Catherine Dauvergne, "Sovereignty, Migration and the Rule of Law in Global Times." *Modern Law Review* 67.4 (2004): 588–615.

87. Maria-Magdalena Fuchs and Simon Wolfgang Fuchs, "Religious Minorities in Pakistan: Identities, Citizenship and Social Belonging." *South Asia: Journal of South Asian Studies* (2019): 1–16.

88. Fozia Nazir Lone, *Restoration of the Historical Title and the Kashmir Question: An International Legal Appraisal*. BRILL, 2018.

89. Farahnaz Ispahani, *Purifying the Land of the Pure: A History of Pakistan's Religious Minorities*. Oxford University Press, 2017.

90. Peter Tatchell, "Iran's war on Sunni Muslims," *Guardian* (Oct 16, 2008), accessed on April 19, 2021 <https://www.theguardian.com/commentisfree/2008/oct/16/iran-humanrights>. *See also* "Iran's Beleaguered Sunnis," *Atlantic* (6 Jan 2016), accessed on April 19, 2021, <https://www.theatlantic.com/international/archive/2016/01/iran-sunnis-saudi/422877/>.

91. *See generally* Donald Eugene Smith, *Nehru and democracy: The political thought of an Asian Democrat*. Orient Longmans, 1958. In Nehru's secular India, Islamic practices, which actively interfered with public space, were considered consistent with the equal protection rights of other citizens. For instance, the Muslim call for prayer—'Azaan'—was not considered a public nuisance, and Muslims (as allowed under Islam) were allowed to have four wives at the same time, even though other male citizens belonging to other religions were not extended this right.

92. "Triple talaq: India criminalises Muslim 'instant divorce,'" *BBC NEWS* (Jul 20, 2019), accessed on April 19, 2021, <https://www.bbc.com/news/world-asia-india-49160818>; Sohini Chatterjee, "*Majoritarian State: How Hindu Nationalism is Changing India*: Angana P. Chatterji, Thomas Blom Hansen, and Christophe Jaffrelot (eds). Hurst and Company, 2019.

93. Karen Armstrong, "The Myth of Religious Violence," *Guardian* (Sep 25, 2014), accessed on April 19, 2021 <https://www.theguardian.com/world/2014/sep/25/-sp-karen-armstrong-religious-violence-myth-secular>.

94. *See generally* Reza Shah-Kazemi, *The Spirit of Tolerance in Islam*. Bloomsbury Publishing, 2012; Cook, Michael et al., eds. *Law and Tradition in Classical Islamic Thought: Studies in Honor of Professor Hossein Modarressi*. Springer, 2013.

95. The Muslim Family Laws Ordinance 1961. (VIII of 1961). [2 March 1961]; Zakat and Ushr Ordinance 1980. *See also* Andreas Rieck, *The Shias of Pakistan: An Assertive and Beleaguered Minority*. Oxford University Press, 2015.

96. Ayesha Siddiqa, "Pakistan military ethnic balance in the Armed Forces and problems of Federalism." *Manekshaw Paper No* 39 (2013): 149–62.

97. *Ibid.*

98. *Ibid.*

99. *Ibid.* at 18. ("[A] report published in 2007 and released by the Inter-Service Public Relations [ISPR], a public relations agency of the armed force, revealed a plan by the army to reduce the number of Punjabis. According to this report, the percentage of Punjabis in the army being 71 percent in 2001 was subsequently reduced and brought down to 57 percent. Furthermore, the report claimed that the number of Punjabis would be further reduced to around 54 percent by 2011. The reduction of Punjabis would be accompanied with an increase in human resource intake from other provinces. For example, from 2001–2011 the composition of Pushtoons in the army would increase by 1 percent to 14.5 percent. The recruitment from Sindh would increase from 15 percent to 17 percent. Recruitment of Baluchis, which stood at 0 percent in 2001 was increased to 3.2 percent with a further expansion by 2011 bringing the intake to 4 percent. Similarly, recruitment from Azad Kashmir and Northern Areas, which stood at 0 percent in 2001, would be brought to 9 percent by 2011. It is important to note that these numbers merely indicate domicile rather than the real

ethnicity of a recruit [domicile signifies the city of birth or residence of a citizen which may be different from his/her ethnicity].").

100. *See supra* note 96 at 20. ("Just like the army was suspicious of the quality of Bengali soldiers and officers, there appears to be a discomfort with the quality of manpower from Sindh and Baluchistan. However, the discomfort is also due to their unhappiness with the educational quality of a recruit from these areas. The army had relaxed its criterion to induct men from Baluchistan and Sindh. This means that it had to spend more resources to upgrade the capacity of the recruits before integrating them into the organization's system. . . . The military may continue to work towards integrating other ethnicities, but it is not likely to re-structure the organization or the recruitment pattern.")

101. *See generally* Ayesha Siddiqa. *Military Inc.: Inside Pakistan's military economy*. Penguin Random House India, 2017.

102. Examples of civilian institutions headed by ex-army officials include PIA, Pakistan Steel Mills, Suparco, WAPDA, PCSIR, etc. 'Pakistan's retired officers shouldn't head civilian organisations. Military is only for war,' *Print* (Oct 10, 2020), accessed on November 22, 2022,>https://theprint.in/opinion/pakistan-retd-officers-shouldnt-head-organisations-military-is-only-for-war/520900/>.

103. The CPEC Business Council, for example, has as a leading member of the steering committee a retired general of the Pakistan Army. *See also* 'With Military at the Helm, CPEC Fuels Centre-Province Tensions in Pakistan,' *Wire* (Oct 8, 2020), accessed on March 10, 2022, <https://thewire.in/south-asia/cpec-china-pakistan-military-belt-and-road-initiative>.

104. *Ibid.*

105. Michael Kaufman and Haroldo Dilla Alfonso, *Community power and grassroots democracy: the transformation of social life*. IDRC, Ottawa, ON, CA, 1997, 8.

106. *Ibid.*

107. Dr Aamer Taj, Dr Muhammad Nouman and Dr Saleem Gul, "The dynamics of international political economy relationships and its influence on the process of democratisation, institution building and national governance structure in Pakistan." *South Asian Studies* 30.1 (2020).

108. Hassan N. Gardezi and Soofia Mumtaz, "Globalisation and Pakistan's dilemma of development [with comments]." *Pakistan Development Review* (2004): 423–40.

109. Hussain H Zaidi, 'Neoliberal economics: the challenge within,' *News International* (Jul 21, 2018), accessed on March 10, 2022, <https://www.thenews.com.pk/print/344278-neoliberal-economics-the-challenge-within>.

110. 'What's wrong with our agricultural policies?' *Express Tribune* (Sep 5, 2013), accessed on November 25, 2022, <https://tribune.com.pk/story/600268/whats-wrong-with-our-agricultural-policies>. ("Unfortunately, successive governments in our country continue to rely on large landowners to achieve agricultural growth and boost its export earnings. The much-lauded 'Green Revolution' back in the 1960s had set the precedent of offering larger farmers access to state subsidies for them to engage in capital intensive farming rather than paying due attention to helping poorer subsistence farmers. This top-down model of agricultural development has continued to be endorsed due to the increasing emphasis on liberalisation of the agricultural

sector. Based on advice from development agencies like the World Bank, large landowners are either leasing their lands to commercial farmers or else engaging in capital-intensive farming themselves. Poor sharecroppers lacking the resources to pay upfront lease rents, in addition to purchasing the needed inputs required for cultivation, are instead finding it difficult to remain engaged in agricultural production to grow enough food for their own families.")

111. Kouser Shahzad and Abdul Subhan, "Uncovering pakistan's environmental risks and remedies under the China-Pakistan economic corridor." *Environmental Science and Pollution Research* 27.5 (2020): 4661–63, 4661. *See also* 'CPEC—challenges and solutions,' *Express Tribune* (Apr 18, 2018), accessed on March 10, 2022, <https://tribune.com.pk/story/1688108/6-cpec-challenges-solutions>.

112. 'Unmasking the China-Pakistan Economic Corridor,' *GRAIN* (May 12, 2021), accessed on March 10, 2022, <https://grain.org/en/article/6669-unmasking-the-china-pakistan-economic-corridor>. *See also* Roots for Equity and Pakistan Kissan Mazdoor Tehreek (PKMT) accessed on November 22, 2022, <https://rootsforequity.org/>, 'Peshawar Northern Bypass, pushing farmers to further destitution,' *PAN AP* (2020), accessed on March 10, 2022, <https://files.panap.net/resources/No-Land-No-Life-Land-Conflicts-and-Struggles-in-Asia.pdf>; Mariyam Suleman, 'How CPEC Left Behind the People of Gwadar,' *Diplomat* (Jun 2020), accessed on March 10, 2022, <https://thediplomat.com/2020/06/how-cpec-left-behind-the-people-of-gwadar/>; Ghulam Nabi et al., "China–Pakistan Economic Corridor (CPEC): an alarming threat to the biodiversity of Northern Pakistan." *Biodiversity and Conservation* 26.12 (2017): 3003–04.

113. *See generally* Filippo Boni and Katharine Adeney, "The Impact of the China-Pakistan Economic Corridor on Pakistan's Federal System: The Politics of the CPEC." *Asian Survey* 60.3 (2020): 441–65.

114. Land Acquisition Act (1 of 1894) art. 10 (4): Each SEZ Authority may acquire land in its respective Province in accordance with the Land Acquisition Act, 1894 (I of 1894).

115. Hamna Tariq, 'Gilgit-Baltistan: China's Golden Opportunity,' *Stimson* (Oct 8, 2020), accessed on March 10, 2022, <https://www.stimson.org/2020/gilgit-baltistan-chinas-golden-opportunity/>.

116. *See* CONST. of PAK. Art. 184(2). The Supreme Court of Pakistan (SCP) enjoys no executory authority in disputes between the provinces, or between the provinces and the federal government. Under Article 184 (2), the SCP can only exercise declaratory jurisdiction when adjudicating these kinds of disputes but lacks the authority to implement its judgments or entertain cases where the non-implementation of its orders thereof is alleged.

117. Muhammad Shakeel, "Chinese Co-Existence and Harmonious Policy and CPEC."

118. Hussein Banai, *Hidden Liberalism: Burdened Visions of Progress in Modern Iran*. Cambridge University Press, 2020.

119. *Ibid.*

120. These 'hidden' liberal norms however, being seriously under threat given the current political economy prevalent within Pakistan, particularly in the context of the

deep neoliberal engagement of neighbouring China into the Pakistani economy by way of the China-Pakistan Economic Corridor.

121. *See* Charles Taylor and Amy Gutmann, Multiculturalism*: examining the politics of recognition.* Princeton University Press, 1994. Multiculturalism imposes cultures on all individuals in society. This results in questions and considerations being taken into account. Secondly, the superiority of the hegemonic culture is assumed. Multiculturalism tries to free minorities from the imposition of the dominant image upon the subjugated. It is seen as a "culture for them" for minorities to learn about their heritage in a neutral setting. This way, their use for the hegemonic culture is extracted. This "us and them" undermines equality.

122. *Ibid.* at 50. The struggle for recognition can only be satisfactorily resolved through "a regime of reciprocal recognition among equals" and until that is achieved; multiculturalism will remain a challenge in Pakistan.

123. *See supra* note 31.

124. *See* Constitution (Eighteenth Amendment) Act, 2010. *See also* Adeney, Katharine, "A step towards inclusive federalism in Pakistan? The politics of the 18th amendment." *Publius: The Journal of Federalism* 42.4 (2012): 539–65.

125. '18th Amendment vital avenue to get Seraiki province,' *DAWN* (May 9, 2020), accessed on April 19, 2021, <https://www.dawn.com/news/1555645/18th-amendment-vital-avenue-to-get-seraiki-province>.

126. Sajjad Ali Khan, "Devolution Plan 2000: dictatorship, democracy, and the politics of institutional change in Pakistan." *Development in Practice* 25.4 (2015): 574–86. *See also supra* note 68, *The Constitution of Pakistan: A Contextual Analysis,* 180. ("Whereas the original 1973 Constitution had included the promise of local government amongst the principles of state policy, the introduction of Article 140A under the chapter titled 'provincial powers' provided a guarantee for its realisation. Previously, this third tier of government had been most ardently invigorated during periods of military rule. As with Ayub and Zia, Musharraf had also installed an apparatus for local government under the Devolution Act 2002. Replicating the form of previous systems, elections were held on a non-party basis under the devolution plan. Because these military leaders intended this level of government to provide a vent for local grievances and to legitimate central governance, the system was in all cases created by the federal and not the provincial government. Musharraf's plan went further than previous efforts in terms of devolving effective powers over service provisioning, including around education. Greater fiscal control was also accorded in this structure of local governments. With Musharraf's ouster from power and in the return to democratic rule, local government structures were also widely dismantled. Along with other reforms for devolution, the Eighteenth Amendment Act also provided a constitutional guarantee of local government in Article 140A: 'Each Province shall, by law, establish a local government system and devolve political, administrative and financial responsibility and authority to the elected representatives of the local governments.'").

127. *See supra* note 118.at 121.

BIBLIOGRAPHY

"18th Amendment vital avenue to get Seraiki province." *DAWN*, May 9, 2020. https://www.dawn.com/news/1555645/18th-amendment-vital-avenue-to-get-seraiki-province.

"CPEC—challenges and solutions." *Express Tribune*, April 18, 2018. https://tribune.com.pk/story/1688108/6-cpec-challenges-solutions.

"Grassroots power." *DAWN*, November 17, 2021. https://www.dawn.com/news/1658545.

"Iran's Beleaguered Sunnis." *Atlantic*, January 6, 2016. https://www.theatlantic.com/international/archive/2016/01/iran-sunnis-saudi/422877/.

"MQM-P minsters call it quits." *Express Tribune*, March 30, 2022. https://tribune.com.pk/story/2350273/mqm-p-minsters-call-it-quits.

"Pakistan's retired officers shouldn't head civilian organisations. Military is only for war." *Print*, October 10, 2020. https://theprint.in/opinion/pakistan-retd-officers-shouldnt-head-organisations-military-is-only-for-war/520900/.

"Panchayat—Pakistan's Alternate Judicial System." *News International*, May 31, 2019. https://www.thenews.com.pk/latest/478808-panchayat-pakistans-alternate-judicial-system.

"Peshawar Northern Bypass, pushing farmers to further destitution." *PAN AP*, 2020. https://files.panap.net/resources/No-Land-No-Life-Land-Conflicts-and-Struggles-in-Asia.pdf.

"Triple talaq: India criminalises Muslim 'instant divorce.'" *BBC NEWS*, July 20, 2019. https://www.bbc.com/news/world-asia-india-49160818.

"Unmasking the China-Pakistan Economic Corridor." *GRAIN*, May 12, 2021. https://grain.org/en/article/6669-unmasking-the-china-pakistan-economic-corridor.

"What's wrong with our agricultural policies?" *Express Tribune*, September 5, 2013. https://tribune.com.pk/story/600268/whats-wrong-with-our-agricultural-policies.

"With Military at the Helm, CPEC Fuels Centre-Province Tensions in Pakistan." *Wire*, October 8, 2020. https://thewire.in/south-asia/cpec-china-pakistan-military-belt-and-road-initiative.

Armstrong, Karen. "The Myth of Religious Violence." *Guardian,* September 25, 2014. https://www.theguardian.com/world/2014/sep/25/-sp-karen-armstrong-religious-violence-myth-secular.

Aziz, Sadaf. *The Constitution of Pakistan: A Contextual Analysis*. Bloomsbury Publishing, 2018.

Bagenstos, Samuel. "Litigation for the People." *Dissent Magazine*, Fall 2020. https://www.dissentmagazine.org/article/litigation-for-the-people.

Banai, Hussein. *Hidden Liberalism: Burdened Visions of Progress in Modern Iran*. Cambridge University Press, 2020.

Beitz, Charles R. "International liberalism and distributive justice: a survey of recent thought." *World politics* 51, no. 2 (1999): 269–96.

Bekker, Simon, and Anne Leildé. "Is multiculturalism a workable policy in South Africa." *International Journal on Multicultural Societies* 5, no. 2 (2003): 119–34.

Bogaards, Matthijs. "Consociationalism and centripetalism: Friends or foes?" *Swiss Political Science Review* 25, no. 4 (2019): 519–37.

Boni, Filippo, and Katharine Adeney. "The impact of the China-Pakistan economic corridor on Pakistan's federal system: the politics of the CPEC." *Asian Survey* 60, no. 3 (2020): 441–65.

Caldarola, Carlo, ed. *Religion and societies: Asia and the Middle East*. Flight. 22. Walter de Gruyter, 2011.

Chanady, Amaryll. "From difference to exclusion: multiculturalism and postcolonialism." *International journal of politics, culture, and society* (1995): 419–37.

Cheema, Moeen H. "Pakistan: The state of liberal democracy." *International Journal of Constitutional Law* 16.2 (2018): 635–42.

Choudhury, G. W. "Constitution-making dilemmas in Pakistan." *Western Political Quarterly* 8, no. 4 (1955): 589–600.

Conconi, A., and M. Viollaz. "Poverty, Inequality and Development: A Discussion from the Capability Approach's Framework." In N. Al-Rodhan, J. Andrews, M. Centeno et al., *The Age of Perplexity: Rethinking the World We Knew*. Penguin Random House Group Editorial (2018).

CONST. of PAK. (Eighteenth Amendment) Act, 2010.

CONST. of PAK. Art. 184 (2).

Dauvergne, Catherine. "Sovereignty, migration and the rule of law in global times." *Modern Law Review* 67, no. 4 (2004): 588–615.

De Wilde, Pieter, Ruud Koopmans, and Wolfgang Merkel, eds. *The struggle over borders: Cosmopolitanism and communitarianism*. Cambridge University Press, 2019.

Freeman, Samuel. "Rawls on distributive justice and the difference principle." In *The Oxford Handbook of Distributive Justice*, p. 13. Oxford: Oxford University Press, 2018.

Fuchs, Maria-Magdalena, and Simon Wolfgang Fuchs. "Religious minorities in Pakistan: Identities, citizenship and social belonging." *South Asia: Journal of South Asian Studies* 43, no. 1 (2020): 52–67.

Gardezi, Hassan N., and Soofia Mumtaz. "Globalisation and Pakistan's dilemma of development [with comments]." *The Pakistan Development Review* (2004): 423–40.

Gutmann, Amy. "Multiculturalism: Examining the politics of recognition." (1994).

Hussain, Mahboob. "ISLAMIZATION OF THE CONSTITUTION: THE ROLE OF RELIGIOUS PARTIES." *Journal of the Research Society of Pakistan* 51, no. 2 (2014).

Iltaf, Maisam. "Hazaras Gripped by Religious Extremism in Balochistan." *Diplomat*, April 16, 2019. https://thediplomat.com/2019/04/hazaras-gripped-by-religious-extremism-in-balochistan/.

Ingram, David. "Between political liberalism and post national cosmopolitanism: Toward an alternative theory of human rights." *Political theory* 31, no. 3 (2003): 359–91.

Ispahani, Farahnaz. *Purifying the land of the pure: A history of Pakistan's religious minorities*. Oxford University Press, 2017.

Ivison, Duncan. *Postcolonial liberalism*. Cambridge University Press, 2002.

Kaufman, Michael, and Haroldo Dilla Alfonso. *Community power and grassroots democracy: The transformation of social life*. IDRC, Ottawa, ON, CA, 1997.

Khan, Sajjad Ali. "Devolution Plan 2000: Dictatorship, democracy, and the politics of institutional change in Pakistan." *Development in Practice* 25, no. 4 (2015): 574–86.

Körtvélyesi, Zsolt. "Transcending the Individual/Collective Minority Rights Divide: A Procedural Solution." *International & Comparative Law Quarterly* 71, no. 1 (2022): 73–106.

Kouser, Shahzad, and Abdul Subhan. "Uncovering Pakistan's environmental risks and remedies under the China-Pakistan economic corridor." *Environmental Science and Pollution Research* 27, no. 5 (2020): 4661–63.

Kukathas, Chandran. "Survey article: Multiculturalism as fairness: Will Kymlicka's multicultural citizenship." *Journal of Political Philosophy* 5, no. 4 (2002): 406.

Kymlicka, Will. "Community and multiculturalism." *A companion to contemporary political philosophy* (2017): 463–77.

———. *Contemporary Political Philosophy*. 2nd ed. Oxford University Press, 2001.

———. "Defending diversity in an era of populism: Multiculturalism and interculturalism compared." *Multiculturalism and interculturalism: Debating the dividing lines* (2016): 158–77.

———. "Liberalism and communitarianism." *Canadian Journal of Philosophy* 18, no. 2 (1988): 181–203.

Kymlicka, Will, Okafor, Obiora Chinedu. "Multicultural Citizenship: A Liberal Theory of Minority Rights." *Canadian Journal of Law and Society* 11, Oxford: Clarendon Press, 1995," no. 2 (January 1, 1996): 267–70. https://doi.org/10.1017/s0829320100004981.

Lamont, J., and C. Favor. "Distributive Justice Stanford Encyclopedia of Philosophy, 2017" https://plato. stanford. edu/entries/justice-distributive. (2020).

Land Acquisition Act (1 of 1894) Art. 10 (4).

Lijphart, Arend. "Consociation and federation: Conceptual and empirical links." *Canadian Journal of Political Science/Revue canadienne de science politique* 12, no. 3 (1979): 499–516.

———. "Consociational democracy." *World politics* 21, no. 2 (1969): 207–25.

———. "Cultural diversity and theories of political integration." *Canadian Journal of Political Science/Revue canadienne de science politique* 4, no. 1 (1971): 1–14.

———. *Democracy in plural societies: A comparative exploration*. Yale University Press, 1977.

———. "Non-majoritarian democracy: A comparison of federal and consociational theories." *Publius: The journal of federalism* 15, no. 2 (1985): 3–15.

Lone, Fozia Nazir. *Historical Title, Self-Determination, and the Kashmir Question*. BRILL, 2018.

Maclean, Derryl N., ed. *Cosmopolitanisms in Muslim Contexts: Perspectives from the Past*. Edinburgh University Press, 2012.

Mantena, Karuna. "The crisis of liberal imperialism." *IDEAS IN CONTEXT* 86 (2007): 113.

Mehta, Uday Singh. *Liberalism and empire: A study in nineteenth-century British liberal thought*. University of Chicago Press, 2018.

Mill, John Stuart. *Representative government*. Alex Catalogue; NetLibrary, 1924.

Mohan, Giles. "Embedded cosmopolitanism and the politics of obligation: The Ghanaian diaspora and development." *Environment and Planning A* 38, no. 5 (2006): 867–83.

Mulhall, Stephen, Adam Swift, and Adam Swift. *Liberals and communitarians*. Oxford: Blackwell, 1992.

Murshid, Navine. *The politics of refugees in South Asia: Identity, resistance, manipulation*. Routledge, 2013.

Nabi, Ghulam, Suliman Khan, Shahid Ahmad, Ahsan Khan, and Rabeea Siddique. "China–Pakistan Economic Corridor (CPEC): an alarming threat to the biodiversity of Northern Pakistan." *Biodiversity and Conservation* 26, no. 12 (2017): 3003–04.

Nussbaum, Martha C. "The cosmopolitan tradition." In *The Cosmopolitan Tradition*. Harvard University Press, 2019.

———. *Frontiers of justice: Disability, nationality, species membership*. Cambridge, MA: Belknap Press, 2006.

Nussbaum, Martha, and Amartya Sen, eds. *The quality of life*. Clarendon Press, 1993.

Ochonu, Moses E. "Migration, Cosmopolitanism, and Africa in the Twenty-First Century." *African Collective*, August 22, 2014. https://theafricacollective.com/2014/08/22/migration-cosmopolitanism-and-africa-in-the-twenty-first-century-2/.

Olaoluwa, Senayon. "Crashed dreams in the Sahara: African cosmopolitanism in Across the Desert." *Alif: Journal of Comparative Poetics* 33 (2013): 114–35.

Rahman, Fazlur. "Implementation of the Islamic Concept of State in the Pakistani Milieu." *Islamic Studies* 6, no. 3 (1967): 205–23.

———. "Islam and the Constitutional Problem of Pakistan." *Studia Islamica*, no. 32 (1970): 275–87. https://doi.org/10.2307/1595225.

Ramcharan, Bertrand G. "Individual, collective and group rights: History, theory, practice and contemporary evolution." *International Journal on Minority and Group Rights* 1, no. 1 (1993): 27–43.

Rawls, John. "A theory of justice." In *Ethics*, pp. 229–34. Routledge, 2004.

———. *Justice as fairness: A restatement*. Harvard University Press, 2001.

Reilly, Benjamin. "Ethnic Representation in Pacific Asia: A Report for the Southeast Asia Rules-Based Order Project." https://researchimpact.uwa.edu.au/wp-content/uploads/2019/09/Ethnic-representation-Report.docx.pdf.

Rex, John, and Gurharpal Singh. "Pluralism and multiculturalism in colonial and post-colonial society—thematic introduction." *International Journal of Multicultural Societies* 5, no. 2 (2003): 106–18.

Robeyns, Ingrid. *Wellbeing, freedom, and social justice: The capability approach re-examined*. Open Book Publishers, 2017.

Roots for Equity and Pakistan Kissan Mazdoor Tehreek (PKMT) accessed on November 22, 2022 <https://rootsforequity.org/>

Russell, Jonathan. "Human Rights: The Universal Declaration Vs the Cairo Declaration." *Middle East Blog* (2012). https://blogs.lse.ac.uk/mec/2012/12/10/1569/.

Sahin, Abdullah. "Critical issues in Islamic education studies: Rethinking Islamic and Western liberal secular values of education." *Religions* 9, no. 11 (2018): 335.
Sanders, Douglas. "Collective rights." *Human rights quarterly* 13, no. 3 (1991): 368–86.
Sen, A. "Development as Capability Expansion. Readings in Human Development. S. Fakuda-Parr et al. New Delhi and New York." (2003).
Shah-Kazemi, Reza. *The spirit of tolerance in Islam*. Bloomsbury Publishing, 2012.
Shakeel, Muhammad. "Chinese Co-Existence and Harmonious Policy and CPEC."
Siddiqa, Ayesha. "Pakistan military ethnic balance in the Armed Forces and problems of Federalism." *Manekshaw Paper No* 39 (2013): 149–62.
Siddiqa, Ayesha. *Military Inc.: inside Pakistan's military economy*. Penguin Random House India, 2017.
Smith, Donald Eugene. *Nehru and democracy: The political thought of an Asian democrat*. Orient Longmans, 1958.
Suleman, Mariyam. "How CPEC Left Behind the People of Gwadar." *Diplomat*, Jun 2020. https://thediplomat.com/2020/06/how-cpec-left-behind-the-people-of-gwadar/.
Taj, Dr Aamer, Dr Muhammad Nouman, and Dr Saleem Gul. "The dynamics of international political economy relationships and its influence on the process of democratisation, institution building and national governance structure in Pakistan." *South Asian Studies* 30, no. 1 (2020).
Tariq, Hamna. "Gilgit-Baltistan: China's Golden Opportunity." *Stimson*, October 9, 2020. https://www.stimson.org/2020/gilgit-baltistan-chinas-golden-opportunity/.
Tatchell, Peter. "Iran's war on Sunni Muslims." *Guardian*, October 16, 2008. https://www.theguardian.com/commentisfree/2008/oct/16/iran-humanrights.
The Muslim Family Laws Ordinance 1961. (VIII of 1961).
W.N.W, Husin, Rasyid W. I. W., and Mujani, W. K. "Consociational Approach to Ethnic Resolution in Malaysia and Lebanon." *Journal of Social and Political Sciences*, Vol.3, No.2 (2020): 474–81.
Whalen, Hugh. "Ideology, Democracy, and the Foundations of Local Self-Government." *Canadian Journal of Economics and Political Science/Revue canadienne de economiques et science politique* 26.3 (1960) : 377–95.
Zaidi, Hussain. "Neoliberal economics: the challenge within." *News International*, July 21, 2018. https://www.thenews.com.pk/print/344278-neoliberal-economics-the-challenge-within.

Chapter 2

Ethnic Federalism and Pakistan

OVERVIEW

In the political sciences space, there exists a wealth of academic literature exploring the ways in which people societally organize themselves. John Locke laid down the foundations of liberalism as a political and moral philosophy, focusing on the individual and their expression of "consent"—explicit or tacit—in their participation in government.[1] Locke's positing of Natural—as opposed to Divine—law paved the way for peoples to organize themselves according to rules derived from logic and reasoning, divorced from conceptions of the divine derived from any particular religious framework.[2] This, coupled with the Hobbesian notion of the "social contract," emphasized the importance of individuals as members of a collective and their role in the collective's decision-making processes, culminating in the development and sophistication of contemporary governance mechanisms.[3] Similarly, Descartes and Kant each presented members of the polity as isolated individuals first, that then effect their agency in the formation of societies.[4]

Tangential to Western conceptions of individualism are theories focusing on other ways of political alignment, such as with a tribe, a clan, or a community. To this end, certain commentators have posited that people's identities are powerfully affected, if not determined outright, by the communities to which they belong, and that this sense of community or collective self is essential, even in individual-centric, "liberal" regimes.[5]

One of the ways in which a social contract can be expressed is through federalism, in which a political centre grants partial autonomy over subjects to geographically distinct sub-divisions of the polity. This mode of sociopolitical organization involves a compromise between the federal centre and its federating units, and between the units themselves, not least of which is the need to balancing minority groups' desires for recognition with the need to maintain federal stability and cohesion.

These federating units are often organized along sociocultural lines, where these regions are ordered based on the preponderance of ethnic groups. Organizing the federation along these lines, however, raises a key issue—particularly in diverse, ethnically pluralistic societies—which is, in turn, magnified by the federation's own ethnic ordering: i.e., the need to mitigate the divisive effects of such communal political ordering and to ensure that inter-communal tensions do not escalate into violence and conflict. These inter-communal frictions can often be managed and reduced by way of political engineering, political institutions, electoral systems, and by altering existing governmental arrangements, all to engender and foster stability between the federating units.[6] Federalism thus operates as a structure within which to mediate differences between these ethnic groups in a democracy,[7] granting socioculturally diverse polities—such as Pakistan's—the means to engage with the disparate communities comprising the society, and to potentially navigate a course that is mutually equitable.

Such is largely the case in Pakistan, where the four primary federating units—i.e., the provinces—are overtly ordered along ethnic lines. This organization has historically resulted in a non-trivial degree of intercommunal—and thus interprovincial—acrimony and has previously dissuaded political parties from reaching out to communities outside of their principal voter pool. In such an ethnically diverse context, therefore, the central question remains—as Timothy Sisk puts it:

> (i)n deeply divided societies, which kinds of institutions and practices create an incentive structure for ethnic groups to mediate their differences through the legitimate institutions of a common democratic state? Alternatively, how can the incentive system be structured to reward and reinforce political leaders who moderate on divisive ethnic themes and to persuade citizens to support moderation, bargaining, and reciprocity?[8]

In the Pakistani context, political activity has largely been predicated upon these communitarian lines, with little incentives for political actors to conduct outreach beyond their immediate sociocultural voter bloc.

This chapter will explore the ways in which forms of federalism can foster inter-communal harmony and federal stability within the Pakistani context. The chapter will begin with a brief discussion on the merits and demerits of communalism to organize power-sharing in an ethnically diverse polity such as Pakistan's, before transitioning to discuss the extant academic debate between the two classical and conflicting power-sharing models of Consociational and Centripetalist Federalism. Understanding these two distinct approaches to federal organization is essential when considering a context as ethnically, religiously, and culturally diverse as Pakistan, and the chapter will seek to assess whether one is better suited to the Pakistani context than the other. More specifically, the chapter will seek to present a localized form of centripetalist federalism as a means of achieving sociopolitical and inter-communal harmony in the country.

The chapter will also discuss federalism—and its interplay with communal democratic norms—more broadly and will explore the ways in which federalism may potentially offer the means to promote interethnic cohesion and stability, and thus foster healthy governance mechanisms which uphold values such as equality, justice, and liberty. The chapter will analyse these values specifically in the Pakistani context to identify the constitutional modifications required to realize a more equitable and stable form of federalism within the country. At present, a contextualized analysis of federalism in a densely populated and diverse postcolonial state such as Pakistan has not yet been undertaken in academic literature, with the corpus of South Asian legal-political literature merely touching upon the theoretical discourse of federalism and constitutional design. Similarly, Western discourse on the subject does not situate the theory in ways which would be relevant in South Asian countries far removed from the rarefied contexts within which such discourse is generated. This chapter seeks to fill this gap by prescriptively examining the ideal forms of federalist structures for Pakistan, and by analysing the ways in which attempts to achieve healthy forms of federalism may be—or, indeed, have been—undermined by other, competing, ideologies, such as neoliberalism as defined by some critical scholars, primarily in the form of the hugely significant China-Pakistan Economic Corridor (CPEC).

FEDERALISM: A WAY TO MEDIATE DIFFERENCES

Intercommunal frictions often arise in ethnically diverse countries since ethnic identity—and membership to any ethnic group—is a mutable, dynamic concept. Membership—whether perceived or otherwise—to a particular community varies based on proximity to or perspective from the group in question. At the same time, despite this apparent mutability, such communal markers nonetheless tend to be rigid for the purposes of communal—and intercommunal—organization. Twentieth-century United States, for example, expressed this apparent dichotomy in the form of "one drop" policies, where individuals who were otherwise 'white' or 'white passing' were—by virtue of a degree of black ancestry—nonetheless legally and socially categorized as black, with all the sociolegal outcomes associated with membership in the latter group. In the Pakistani context more specifically, we see how ethnic identity—and the distinctions between ethnic groups—is often expressed politicolegally through voting practices, with minority groups often choosing to vote for candidates belonging to their own ethnic groups.[9]

These voting patterns can result in factionalization and, particularly in new democracies, raises the risk of secessionism or internecine conflict. Simply banning the factions arising out of these intercommunal frictions often counterproductively results in an escalation of tensions, with some groups—feeling further disenfranchised by their exclusion from the political processes by such proscriptions—resorting to armed conflict to effect their and their community's rights.[10] Reynolds posits that "(i)n every successful case of peaceful and democratic conflict avoidance in the world, minority communities and their rights have been included and protected in the legislative process."[11] There do, however, also exist legitimate concerns that the entrenchment of such rights under the rubric of ethnic identity can, instead, further ingrain demands for recognition, resulting in the Balkanization of the polity.[12]

The compromise therefore, is a form of federalism which can balance a particular community's aspirations for ethnic autonomy with the competing need to ensure unity and stability at the federal or national level.[13] This is axiomatic as majorities necessarily desire majority rule, while minorities desire guarantees against it.[14] As such, federalism presents a form of governance in which pluralistic societies are able to allow for and accommodate ethnic diversity without fracturing or experiencing conflict along ethnic lines.[15] The federation thus needs to strike a balance between curbing sentiments of polarization, and achieving this depolarization in a way which reduces the likelihood of intercommunal conflict.[16] Minority groups in fledgling democracies may often be very self-conscious, possibly expressing a desire for greater autonomy and prominence within the nascent state, and as a result may politically organize themselves ethnically; this, in turn, can potentially position them at odds with other groups within the federation, precipitating interethnic conflict and violence.[17] The goal, therefore, is to construct a form of federal organization which protects the interests—and identities—of the different communities within the polity while, simultaneously, ensuring that these groups—and individuals ascribing to these groups—continue to coexist within the broader national purview.

MODELS OF FEDERALISM: COMMUNALIST, CONSOCIATIONAL, AND CENTRIPETALIST

Federalism's three classical, and ostensibly divergent, power-sharing models are Communalism,[18] Consociational Federalism, and Centripetalist Federalism.

Communalism

One proposed way to establish stable democratic forms of governance in countries with deep ethnic divides is communalism, which recognizes the various communal distinctions extant in society and employs these as the fundamental building blocks of the federal political system.[19] This system involves according institutional guarantees to these groups, such as separate electoral quotas for various ethnicities in the legislature and other significant state institutions which, in turn, often involves specifically reserving seats for representatives of specific communal groups. New Zealand, for example, reserves specific seats for representatives of its indigenous Maori population. Similarly, India reserves one-fifth of the seats in parliament for scheduled tribes and castes.[20]

The primary criticism levied at this approach is that, as communalism relies upon the official recognition and consequent determination of ethnic identity, with legal and constitutional outcomes associated with such recognition, it can often end up emphasizing and perpetuating ethnic differences. Under the model, it thus becomes harder to engender political integration, or develop political parties that are "national" in character—as opposed to purely serving the interests of a particular ethnic group—as the focus is on representing these communities.

Additionally, while ethnic identity is often flexible and mutable, and can change over time, communal or constitutional systems which rely on these forms of identification often fail to account for this fluidity, and therefore can be quite rigid and difficult to amend.[21] This can result in certain individuals—such as members of subgroups of a particular community—being excluded from the state's political calculus by virtue of their divergence from their 'parent' group. While an individual's membership in a particular sociocultural group carries a degree of political significance—i.e., 'the personal is political'—the rigidity of certain socio-legal systems, such as Pakistan's provincial ordering for instance, artificially coheres this sociocultural identity. Further, given that forms of communalism predate consociational forms of federalism the former neither requires nor relies upon the latter for its implementation; as this chapter will discuss at greater length, under a proposed local centripetalized framework sociocultural identity can be preserved at the local or communal level while, at the same time, be prevented from being politicized—and thus undermining localized, grassroots political activity.

Consociationalism

The consociational model of federalism requires the existence of robust federating units, with a correspondingly weaker federal centre. This association within the federal political framework centres upon leveraging existing internal divisions within a deeply divided and heterogeneous state, with the eventual goal of achieving a parity of rule within the federal government. Good governance is effected through a grand coalition comprising the political elites of all of the multiple—but segregated—social, political, and ethnic groups which otherwise exercise virtual independence in political decision-making within their own localities or over their own areas of influence.[22] Conceptually, the rationale for this model rests on inclusion, the recognition of group rights through representation, and the notion that one can best argue for one's rights through institutions designed to protect and reinforce group interests.[23] One of consociational federalism's proponents, Arend Lijphart, explains that the model is at its heart about recognizing ethnic distinctions, institutionalizing them by making multi-ethnic societies more plural, and employing these distinctions as constructive elements of a stable polity.[24]

By contrast, however, Donald Horowitz though claims that consociationalism is only possible when the majority is momentarily weak such as after violent upheaval.[25] This is in part because consociationalism maintains ethnic harmony by capitalizing on the independence and influence of ethnic groups through coalition governments, proportional representation, the division of government posts including in the army, and minority veto rights over issues that directly affect the welfare of their members.[26]

Stuart Kaufman argues that the most important group interests are linguistic, religious, and economic, the first two interests largely providing the reason for the group's aspirations for maintaining its distinct identity.[27] Economic interests, meanwhile, are significant when there exist natural resources in the area governed by that community. Consociationalism thus focuses on the balance of power brokered by ethnic leaders to encourage inter-ethnic power sharing through 'consensual' institutions.[28] Building on this, Lijphart offers a modified version of consociationalism and maintains that the most optimal system for societies with ethnic divisions is a list proportional representation system coupled with a decentralized political order, that he terms "consensus democracy," as this method produces multiparty parliaments within which all minorities can be represented.[29]

It has been argued, however, that consociationalism in fact deepens the preexisting ethnic divides it intends to address by treating ethnic groups as monoliths, thereby stifling internal diversity and institutionally entrenching them,[30] or that it may lead to a "tit-for-tat game of ethnic defection in which groups threaten violence or secession in return for concessions."[31] Arguments have also been presented that consociationalist forms of federal organization can produce or exacerbate communal differences—rather than ameliorate them—by allowing minorities to gain footholds of power and entrench the political dominance of small, nonrepresentative, extremist parties.[32]

Consociationalism operates to strengthen minority identities and politicizes ethnic identification;[33] in so doing it may, however, be even more conducive to factionalization and secessionism as it institutionalizes, and coheres these separate identities which may, in turn, act as a vehicle in increasing their individual capacities and their willingness to act unilaterally towards a bid for independence.[34] This 'codification' of ethnic identity might help concretize minority groups, according them greater unity and political leverage within a diverse, multipolar political context; however, it may also operate to exclude subgroups within each such community—such as smaller sects within a religious minority—from representation. Further, attempting to 'ossify' sociocultural identities in this way may prove problematic given the innate mutability and fluidity that comes with sociocultural identification. Attempting to categorize membership to such communities in such a rigid, systematic manner may invariably result in certain members of such communities being disenfranchised from participation or representation in the consociationalist federation's political processes simply due to their individual perceived cultural unorthodoxy.

Moreover, under a consociationalist federal framework, political elites are expected—if not required outright—to advance the interests of only the ethnic group they represent, as opposed to the electorate.[35] This insularity encourages these ethnic groups to jockey for position or resources with one another within the overarching weak federal framework, discouraging attempts at achieving consensus and eroding any sense of national identity. Reynolds summarizes the issue by stating that "consociationalism allows antagonism to become the default position of political engagement, rather than creating space in which a new, more transcendent logic might begin to emerge."[36]

A consociationalist ordering of the federation can also arguably contribute to or exacerbate oppression by placing primary significance on political elites.[37] While the expectation under consociationalism remains that these elites will effectively represent their communities' interests, this expectation does not preclude these elites from abusing their positions and authority, nor does it place sufficient political checks and balances on any bad actors within these elites. Further, the strict delineation of these groups in order for them to participate politically in the federation places pressures on members of these groups to either conform to the legal or constitutional boundaries of their parent-group or be excluded from participation entirely; this, in turn, serves to discourage dissent within the group for fear of being 'other-ized' and excluded therefrom, effectively disenfranchising dissenters from the state's political apparatus.

Consociationists prefer the model of ethnic federalism as it allows for the concentration of ethnic groups in certain areas;[38] when federal power is devolved to these territories, this allows for the rule of the minority over the minority in an area which is its exclusive domain.[39] This therefore necessitates that these territories be as ethnically homogenous as possible to capitalize on each group's control over the territory, its resources, and its people.[40] This ethnic homogenization, however, serves to constrain the polity's rights of freedom of movement, discouraging individuals' mobility in favour of maintaining a particular group's majority in its 'native' region, while further entrenching the influence ethnic elites exert over the region.

As already touched upon, the consociational federal model is consistent with the recognition of group rights, including those of minority groups extant within the state. The model, however, may not prove ideal for countries such as Pakistan where a particular ethnic group (Punjabis in the case of Pakistan) dominate national power structures and the federal political arena, putting other minority ethnicities at a disadvantage. In *Multicultural Citizenship* Kymlicka suggests the need to advance group-specific rights, stating that ethnic conflict is often part and parcel of the processes of nation building, aimed at producing a common national identity across the state's territory to be shared by all its citizens.[41] However, as Sujit Choudhry notes in *Bridging comparative politics and comparative constitutional law: Constitutional design in divided societies*:

> Kymlicka has played a major role in encouraging the adoption of multinational federalism as a constitutional device to accommodate the claims of national minorities for over a decade. Moreover, although in recent work he has become more sceptical regarding the possible transplantation of this model outside North America and Western Europe, he is still arguing that it has been successful in those regions.[42]

This is a significant critique, signalling that while multicultural citizenship may have worked in Western contexts, it may not be as successful—particularly in its unmodified form—in postcolonial, heterogenous, and deeply divided societies such as Pakistan's.[43]

For instance, Pakistan's failure to successfully implement the forms of multiculturalism posited by Kymlicka are evinced in its actions towards minority groups, particularly its Ahmadi minority. To this end, an amendment was made to Pakistan's Constitution in 1974 declaring Ahmadis to be non-Muslims in 1974, effectively excluding them from mainstream Islam as practiced in the country, even though this contravenes the fundamental freedom to practice religion guaranteed under Article 20 of the Constitution. Further, owing to the state's inability or unwillingness to protect them, many members of Pakistan's religious minorities have emigrated to protect themselves from differential—often hostile—treatment meted out to them by the Sunni Muslim majority. Furthermore, when the state has employed emergency powers, such as during times of armed conflict or terrorism, the target has largely been men from the smaller provinces of Khyber Pakhtunkhwa and Baluchistan, who are often subject to ethnic profiling and incarceration under special penal laws.

Consociationalism's tendency to accentuate ethnic differences between minority communities, and its failure in postcolonial contexts, can also be observed through studying the models adapted in Iraq and Lebanon.[44] In the case of Lebanon, consociational federalism "exactly cemented what it was supposed to overcome, namely vertical and horizontal inequality."[45] This, in turn fuelled, ethnic conflict in Lebanon's deeply divided multi-ethnic and multi-sectarian polity. Severely impacted by French colonial influences and internecine conflict, Lebanon's consociational arrangement was repeatedly revised over the course of its history.[46] In 1943, "corporate consociationalism" was advanced to implement power-sharing between the various factions;[47] this 'confessional' concentration of power left the state inordinately concerned with the individual needs of each discrete sociocultural group, rendering it ill equipped to address broader issues facing the entire polity and resulting in a deeply divided state.[48] As such, the Lebanese case study clearly demonstrates the inability of classical Western forms of federalism to be feasibly applied to postcolonial, diverse societies far removed from the—relatively homogenous—Western contexts within which these forms were first developed.[49] More recently, Lebanon's consociational system has been undergoing reform, with proposals made to further decentralize its federal framework in favour of smaller provinces. Problematically, however, Lebanon's confessional electoral system has been retained, which has undermined power-sharing efforts in the country.[50]

Similarly, Iraq's reformed consociational framework has also failed to achieve a unified national identity. Iraq's federal constitutional setup allows for representation of various religious sects;[51] despite this federal arrangement, however, Iraq has still experienced an amplification of identity politics, as well as overt attempts at secession by the Kurdistan Regional Government.[52]

More recent constitutional reforms in Iraq have made further revisions to the country's consociational federal ordering, requiring a supermajority for election to the posts of President, Prime Minister, and the Council of Ministers under the 2005 Constitution.[53] Although the current framework requires the eighteen governorates across the country (electing their own regional governments) to collaborate with the federal government, these demarcations have exacerbated sectarian differences, rather than reduced them.[54]

As outlined in this section, consociationalism has been implemented in deeply divided societies to aid peace building processes in several countries such as Bosnia and Herzegovina, Burundi, Iraq, Kenya, Lebanon, and South Sudan.[55] However, the model has been facilitated and sometimes been artificially maintained by external actors, bringing into question the model's ability to sustain itself.[56] Although the format has advanced various forms of power-sharing in these countries, its failure to maintain peace and advance democratic values has resulted in calls for reforming these arrangements.[57]

For instance, judicial interventions have often sought to "tackle the terms of power-sharing agreements, especially in favour of the rights of individuals over consociationalism's emphasis on group rights."[58] Similarly, there has been a move away from consociationalism in Burundi, where the consociational arrangement "promoted autocratization and undermined power-sharing, with the three post conflict elections fundamentally altering Burundi's political landscape compared to the political context at the time of the Arusha Agreement."[59]

Another example is that of Northern Ireland where, despite several politically initiated reforms instituted, power-sharing has been suspended in "2017 for three years as a result of a renewable heating energy scandal, marriage equality, an Irish language act, and Brexit."[60] More recent frictions between the UK and the EU over the implementation of the Northern Ireland Protocol to the Brexit Withdrawal Agreement have, in turn, served to undermine meaningful political participation of the region's inhabitants and complicate the post-Troubles armistice brokered under the 1998 Good Friday Agreement.

Both Lebanon and Iraq present cases of consociational frameworks that have been unable to alleviate ethnic conflict and disparities within their territories, hindering the progression and realization of liberal and democratic norms.[61] It can be argued that a move towards a hybrid model of power-sharing with centripetal features would instead assist in minimizing sectarian differences, and consequently reduce the potential for intranational conflict.[62] Horowitz and Reilly both argue that centripetalism better achieves the desired outcome of a peaceful and self-sustaining democracy, and thus the proceeding section will examine the centripetalist federal model, as well as its localized formats, and how these forms of federalism have been more successful.

Centripetalist Federalism: Theory and Practice

Centripetalism[63] strives to achieve political stability through centralization, endeavouring to establish and maintain a strong federal government that engages with comparatively weak federating units with the goal of militating against sociocultural distinctions—such as ethnicity, religion, or linguistic diversity—in political life. Ultimately, internal unity and consensus are achieved at all levels of government, which itself works towards the realization of political egalitarianism without prioritizing or promoting the interests of one federating unit—or community—over another. Essentially, the model aims to dilute the ethnic character of politics by promoting multi-ethnic outcomes and inter-group accommodation instead.[64] This form of political ordering is focused on promoting inclusive, moderate, accommodating, and compromising policies at the centre of a divided, heterogenous sociopolitical spectrum to create an integrative institutional framework.[65]

The emphasis under a centripetalist federal framework is on moderation, with the core aim being to depoliticize ethnicity and undermine its importance—rather than to reflect ethnic divisions in the state's power dynamic—and thereby to reduce intranational tensions by essentially 'defanging' ethnic considerations in politics.[66] The model therefore encourages the establishment of political systems which encourage parties to court votes from all ethnicities, and to moderate their own rhetoric on divisive issues, such as through the alternative vote (AV) system.[67] This encourages policies which are less extremist and which hold greater universal appeal, and promotes a more diverse range of policies presented by political actors in an effort to engender votes from multiple communities.[68]

As a result, centripetalist approaches to federalism prefer a unitary state or federation segregated on non-ethnic lines to deemphasize and reduce communal frictions.[69] Under the centripetalist framework, ethnic factionalization and polarization is avoided through competitive, broad-based elections; political electioneering cutting across ethnic lines; and the establishment and maintenance of more fluid senses of selfhood not intrinsically linked to community membership.[70] Through these—and other processes—the goal under a centripetalist federal ordering is to dilute and deemphasize the political significance of the ethnic group—particularly in diverse, heterogenous polities.

Under this system the federal government can govern effectively, avoiding meting out any preferential treatment to any ethnic groups; arguably it is also robust enough to keep other central institutions of government not directly subjected to democratic controls—such as the military or the judiciary—in check.[71]

Centripetalism does, however, raise certain concerns that political power under its framework may be monopolized by majorities and particular minorities willing to cooperate in co-opting some of the state's power, leaving other groups relatively unprotected and precluded from access to power.[72] In *Ethnic Groups in Conflict*, Donald Horowitz[73] argues for the promotion of multi-ethnic political parties, which would in turn ensure a moderate approach to inter-group accommodations,[74] and thus work to ameliorate some of the concerns regarding the co-option of the federal architecture by groups working in concert. Following up in *Ethnic Power Sharing: Three Big Problems*,[75] Horowitz further identifies certain underlying issues for consociationalist or centripetalist models of federal power-sharing which need to be addressed to ensure equitable political outcomes for the entire polity: firstly, the adaptability of the model[76] particularly to settings far removed from that where the model was conceived; secondly, the 'degradation' of the electoral system through manipulation by a particular majority or a coalition of minorities in a given power-sharing setting;[77] and lastly the 'immobilism' or rigidity within a model to evolve (especially consociationalism),[78] and how capable it is of adapting to the changing sociocultural and politicolegal context of the state it is applied to.

Horowitz comments on the failure of consociationalist models of federalism, stating that:

"As the immobilism of consociational institutions sets in, in nearly every case some proposals for change are geared toward centripetal institutions, especially vote-pooling electoral systems"[79]

before going on to specifically advocate for the "alternative vote" (AV) electoral system which would, in turn, allow for electoral candidates to make appeals across ethnic lines.[80] In a similar vein, Brian Shoup notes: "the main point of AV systems is to force ethnic communities to pool votes around more moderate political parties",[81] discouraging political—and power—organization along ethnic lines and diminishing the impact of such sociocultural considerations on the organization and functioning of the state.

Reilly argues that strong centripetalism requires multi-ethnic political parties, incentives for ensuring vote-pooling across ethnic groups, and the need to avoid formal criteria for determining ethnic selfhood.[82] Moderate centripetalism, on the other hand, requires the inclusion of all ethnic groups on electoral party lists, with voters basing their decisions on politics and policies, and not on ethnic identity(ies).[83] Finally, weak centripetalism focuses on providing guaranteed representation for ethnic groups in institutions otherwise dominated by the ethnic majority.[84] Horowitz argues against this latter form of centripetalism, stating that

> proportionate minority office-holding does not guarantee that minority interests will receive attention in the legislative process. Indeed, minority office-holding may come at the expense of minority representation in the larger sense, for the creation of ethnically concentrated constituencies means not only more minority-dominated constituencies, but also more constituencies in which majority-group voters dominate and in which majority-group candidates do not need to worry about minority support or minority interests.[85]

In the Pakistani context, attempts at effecting weak centripetalist elements—specifically by guaranteeing representation of certain communities in federal institutions—have done little to address historical interethnic disparities. Despite ensuring the representation of otherwise marginalized groups—such as religious minorities and individuals from the smaller provinces—in the federal bureaucracy, these weak expressions of centripetalism have not ensured that such groups are adequately represented in the manner and at positions where they can meaningfully inform regional or national policy.

It becomes increasingly apparent, the more these competing models of federalism are analysed, that a localized model of centripetalism may prove to be most apposite for many fledgling postcolonial democracies.

Contrasting centripetalism against consociational and hybrid consociational models, it becomes clear that a locally adapted centripetal framework emphasizing an AV electoral system, cross-ethnic political parties, and the depoliticization of ethnicity, is better positioned to provide fora for more reciprocal arrangements on issues that affect the polity. Such systems contribute towards a stable federal architecture in postcolonial, multi-ethnic societies, engendering stability and decreasing the incidence of intercommunal frictions in these otherwise often turbulent and fractious postcolonial contexts. Such a shift towards localized centripetal tendencies and away from federal frameworks with embedded consociational elements—such as grand coalitions and ethnic parties—"encourage(s) cross-ethnic behaviour, such as electoral and party systems which encourage the pooling of votes across ethnic lines,"[86] with variations of this model successfully applied across South Asia in countries such as Indonesia, the Philippines, Malaysia, and Singapore,[87] as well as in Nigeria: all postcolonial states with tremendous sociocultural diversity, and each having historically experienced degrees of intercommunal antipathy which have since been curbed. Centripetal organizational processes thus attempt to dilute and deemphasize these ethnic divisions—particularly the political impact these distinctions may hold—by instead promoting intergroup political accommodation moderation at the institutional level.[88]

Discussing Indonesia specifically, the country's shift to centripetalism demonstrates key elements of the model, such as "cross-regional party registration and presidential election requirements; a necessity for broad cross-party coalitions to both nominate presidential candidates and form executive government; and a highly ambitious and (mostly) non-ethnic model of administrative decentralisation."[89]

In this context, significant emphasis is placed on multi-regional parties and party coalitions, with the law requiring political parties to establish electoral support and presence across the country's seventeen thousand island-strong archipelago,[90] with similar coalition requirements applied to the presidential nomination process.[91] Benjamin Reilly describes this 'distributive requirement' of requiring broad-base, multi-ethnic support for political activity as an example of the restructuring of electoral processes to "require successful candidates to gain support across different regions of a country, thus helping to break down the appeal of narrow parochialism or regionalism."[92] These centripetal incentives have thus far served to "manage and limit ethnic mobilization, particularly of a secessionist form."[93] Furthermore, even though religion has played a part in the political landscape of the country, centripetal reforms have also served to minimize the polarizing effect faith may have.[94] Overall, as Reilley notes:

> (t)his proliferation of administrative regions has multiplied points of power, shifting the locus of political contestation across a greater range and to a lower level within the political system, fragmenting Indonesia's political map and broadening the possibilities for ethnic coalition building. This has also led to a propensity to split potentially separatist provinces such as Papua into new units to undercut potential ethnic identification and mobilization.[95]

Singapore's "Group Representation Constituencies,"[96] and the AV system, recently adopted in the Asia-Pacific regions of Papua New Guinea and Fiji,[97] all provide persuasive examples of the efficacy centripetalist processes enjoy in diminishing inter-communal friction and effecting greater minority representation in hugely diverse, postcolonial Southeast Asia.

As touched upon earlier, similarly, positive outcomes have also been achieved in Nigeria, with its federal arrangement described as a strong example of localized centripetalism at play.[98] This was achieved primarily through repeated geographic divisions during and after the "the Biafran war into 12 and then 19, and eventually 36 regions."[99] As Alison McCulloch writes:

> (t)his territorial engineering apparently made it much more difficult for the large Hausa-Fulani community to dominate and opened "considerable intra-ethnic tension" within the three large communities, particularly in the Muslim North, where the existence of just one region had muted latent intra-Muslim diversity.[100]

To further increase parity, the 'federal character principle' was promulgated as part of the Nigerian Constitution in 1979.[101] Although the principle does have some consociational tendencies, it nonetheless operates to achieve "a balance between large segments and, in this manner, constitutes some form of revision of centripetal institutions."[102] Nigeria's model therefore presents a classic case of employing a centripetal framework, combined with certain 'informal consociational' arrangements, to prevent majorities from otherwise dominating the polity.[103]

CONSOCIATIONALISM OR CENTRIPETALISM FOR PAKISTAN

The interactive dialectic between Arendt Lijphart and Donald L. Horowitz significantly informed the existing academic discourse on the nature of an ideal political order for the realization of a stable constitutional system. The discussion began when Lijphart, a strong proponent of consociationalism,[104] conducted a detailed study of the Netherlands' political system in his 1976 work *Politics of Accommodation*[105] (though Lijphart had also previously described the consociational model in *Consociational Democracy*.)[106] Lijphart reiterated his support for the consociational model in 1977's *Democracy in Plural Societies*,[107] presenting the model as a panacea for the political distortions arising in deeply divided societies. His solution relied on the co-option of political elites by enticing them to collaborate to defeat centrifugal forces, resulting in increased political stability in otherwise divided societies. Lijphart's analysis was however limited to smaller and relatively developed and homogenous communities,[108] and as such had its limitations.

The debate over the nature of consociational forms of government has continued to evolve over time; Lijphart, or proponents of his theories, have, however, failed to explore how the model would operate in complex, post-colonial states such as Pakistan. More recent advocates of consociational federalism, such as Brendan O'Leary, reiterate the argument that consociationalism effects the realization of a national society where all "peacefully co-exist, with none being institutionally superior to the others, and in which the relevant communities co-operate politically through self-government and shared government";[109] however, the gap in the discourse regarding consociationalism's place in the global south persists unaddressed.

While Lijphart has attempted to examine the roles played by consociationalism and democratic institutions at a global level,[110] his analyses remain somewhat broad and policy oriented, and do not provide strong evidentiary support to substantiate his assessment. This has opened his political model to critique from his detractors for being undemocratic and for unnecessarily empowering political elites through his support for "grand coalitions" and "cartel(s) of elites."[111]

Additionally, the favourable factors identified by Lijphart[112] that help determine the success of the consociational model in each polity, when viewed from Pakistan's perspective, leads one inevitably to the conclusion that this model would be inapposite to the Pakistani context. Specifically, Lijphart proposes consociational models for small populations, with each ethnic segment of the population being geographically distinct, with 'overarching loyalties' to the state and an absence of significant socioeconomic differences between them.[113] Lijphart's favourable factors, however, are lacking in the context of Pakistan; the country's exclusionary policies towards minority groups not considered a disparate ethnic group—such as the Ahmadi community—renders it difficult for such groups to entertain any sort of overarching loyalty towards the state in the manner Lijphart envisions. In fact, because such groups are not visible as nor are treated like an ethnic group, they often cannot avail the kinds of protections and rights that Lijphart envisages for such groups. In short, a variety of circumstances, including the political elite's refusal to share power with other minority ethnic groups such as the Ahmadi or Hazara communities; conflicts over disproportionate resource allocation by the centre; and the excessive influence and control of particular ethnic groups—such as the majority Punjabis—over the centre, all contribute significantly towards nonconsociationalism in Pakistan.[114] Additionally, infusing consociationalist elements in Pakistan, particularly the kind that have to be facilitated and sometimes propped up by external actors,[115] is inherently nonviable, as it not only questions the model's ability to sustain itself but also challenges the state's sovereignty; with problems such as a concentration of power in the Punjab, and intensifying sectarian and ethnic strife in Balochistan, it is untenable to seek support and influence from across the border.[116]

Centripetalism is posited in direct contrast to consociationalism, with the theories advancing it gaining prominence through the works of scholars such as Donald L. Horowitz, who was studying ethnic conflict in diverse societies and its correlation to democratic models of power-sharing. Horowitz developed his theory of ethnic divides through his seminal 1985 work: *Ethnic groups in conflict*,[117] in which he examines a diverse array of societies, tracing the roots and characteristics of interethnic conflict—as well as intranational political arrangements—and considering the interplay between these tensions and expressions of democracy in these contexts.

Horowitz further refined his analyses in his more recent piece: *Ethnic Power Sharing: Three Big Problems*,[118] advocating for deeper forms of collaboration between minorities and moderates as a solution to resolve or minimize interethnic conflict. However, in his review of the various adaptations of consociational models, Horowitz primarily focus was placed on Cyprus, Northern Ireland, Bosnia, Burundi, and Belgium—all small nations with ethnic patterns and electoral frameworks far removed from Pakistan's.

Horowitz's customized, hybrid model—as adapted in Cyprus—has recently been reviewed by McGarry in *Centripetalism, Consociationalism and Cyprus: The "Adoptability" Question.*[119] In carrying the discussion forward, McGarry does not review the feasibility of a particular political model—centripetalism or consociationalism—but rather addresses the prior question of whether a certain system may be better "adapted" in or to a particular society. McGarry studies are, however, focused on Cyprus, a "partitioned polity, which currently lacks any common power-sharing institutions. Indeed, no functioning common institutions have existed in Cyprus since its consociational arrangements collapsed in December 1963."[120] Thus, McGarry provides a degree of insight into the applicability of centripetalism over consociationalism, or *vice versa*, in a deeply divided context like Cyprus', where the polity is split along largely ethnic lines. Cyprus' size and relative homogeneity might not make it an ideal point of comparison to Pakistan, a large and socioculturally heterogenous polity of over two hundred and twenty million, playing host to a diverse array of ethnic, religious, and cultural groups, but given the former's federal and constitutional ordering along explicitly ethnic lines—something mirrored in Pakistan's ethnically ordered provinces—McGarry's work provides certain understandings which can be transposed to the Pakistani context.[121]

The comparison between the models of consociationalism and centripetalism is particularly relevant for the populous, deeply divided, and geographically distinct—arguably segregated—communities extant in Pakistan, as power-sharing accommodations have proven to be difficult to establish and maintain from the country's inception. Identifying a suitable political model to address such intercommunal and political discord in Pakistan would contribute significantly to the corpus of literature on constitutional design and, given Pakistan's long familiarity with consociational constitutional frameworks—and the problems these have caused—an examination of the applicability of centripetalist constitutional frameworks would not only be unprecedented in the body of academia on Pakistan, but would also—it is theorized—provide useful and viable solutions to Pakistan's sociocultural frictions. A localized model would, it is argued, offer tailored and indigenously viable prescriptions to modify centripetal federalism (and other similar constitutional models) to effect electoral reform, institutional change, and the devolution of federal or constitutional powers, as well as develop mechanisms to counter the adverse impacts associated with neoliberal policies, with the goal being the safeguarding of individual rights—particularly those of minority group members. As a result, it is argued that localized forms of centripetalism, ones informed by and predicated upon pre-existing sociocultural arrangements, will work to engender and maintain social and political harmony in conflict-ridden and ethnically diverse countries such as Pakistan.

In this context 'localized'—and particularly 'localized centripetalism'—refers to a model specific to Pakistan's postcolonial context, leveraging centripetal forces to counter interethnic discord, Punjabi hegemony, and the impact(s) of neoliberal policies which operate to exacerbate these issues. This proposed model differs from other hybrid models as it seeks to strengthen federal stability by way of splitting the existing, larger, provinces into smaller federating units—and thus dilute the overwhelming impact ethnic identity has on national politics—while simultaneously accommodating local and communal identity. The model also advances reforms to the National Finance Commission NFC award[122] to alleviate the negative effects of neoliberal policies pushed forward by the federal centre to the detriment of the provinces and proposes electoral and Senate reforms aimed at alleviating distortions caused by Punjabi hegemony—or by the preponderance of the Punjabi population—at achieving parity among the country's federating units. Further, another point of divergence from models in other countries such as Nigeria, is localized centripetalism's focus on leveraging and protecting certain specific democratic values—as previously discussed in Chapter 1; collective—as opposed to individual—minority protections and an emphasis on communitarianism or multiculturalism.

With the increasing democratization of states worldwide it is evident that theories on centripetalism, and its relation to federalism, are becoming increasingly practically significant. In this regard, Horowitz's observations in *Constitutional Design: An Oxymoron?*[123] are highly revealing of the role centripetalism will play in the coming years around the globe. In his work, Horowitz expounds upon how, in the absence of centripetal institutions and structures, societies with deep ethnic divides are instead more likely to exclude minorities or individuals otherwise deviating from the society's conception of what membership in the majority would be. This would operate to exclude not only members of minority groups, but also erstwhile members of the majority which, for political or personal reasons, have been excluded therefrom. Among other objectives, Horowitz promotes political moderation by—among other proposals—structuring voting policies in a manner that accommodates ethnic minorities to drive majority decision-making.[124]

The two models of federal organization—i.e., consociationalism and centripetalism—while presented and often examined as a means of inculcating and fostering democratic norms within a diverse polity can, instead, present challenges to or undermine democratic political structures; this is since the aims and objectives of these federal models are specific and limited in scope, and do not necessarily prioritize democratic governance. In fact, these models relate entirely to the organization of a state—and the role sociocultural identity plays therein; thus, there is little that is inherently democratic, or which lends itself to democracy, within them.

Critics of centripetalism's misfires in Pakistan cite the bloody secession of East Pakistan (now Bangladesh) from the federation, and the prevailing unrest in Baluchistan as evidence in support of their position that the model is inapposite to the Pakistani context. According to such consociationalists, a Punjabi-dominated federal government has historically disenfranchised all other provinces and their populations under the garb of centripetalism. This ability of one province—and the ethnic majority therein—to dominate the country's politics has proven to be a perennial source of instability and insecurity.[125] Despite the political entrenchment of the Punjabi ethnic group in Pakistan, according to Breen the country nonetheless has strong multi-ethnic parties, in addition to those organized along predominantly ethnic lines, with two of them, the Pakistan People's Party (PPP) and Pakistan Muslim League-Nawaz (PML-N), both promoting ethnically pluralistic policies despite otherwise comprising a preponderance of a particular ethnic group. These policies include establishing new provinces along ethno-linguistic lines, such as a Seraiki province (also supported by the incumbent Pakistan Tehreek-e-Insaaf), as well as declaring the four provincial languages as national ones.[126]

The forms of power-sharing arrangements that consociationalism posits would instead further empower undemocratic forces in Pakistan, which are directly responsible for challenging and upsetting the country's constitutional stability and, in turn, for promoting civil conflict in the country. The concentration of power and positions in a 'cartel of elites' drawn predominantly from particular ethnic groups further deepens discord between ethnicities by depriving disenfranchised groups of their rights and autonomy (as seen in the consociational experiments in Iraq and Lebanon).[127] Therefore, consociationalism is ill-suited for Pakistan, while its opposite—centripetalism—in a modified form instead presents a viable means of effecting social, political, and even cultural reconciliation in Pakistan.[128]

Given the less than ideal outcomes the more 'pure' forms of consociationalism have had for Pakistan's constitutional ordering, there is thus a pressing need for a federal model drawing upon the best, most apposite elements of communalism/communitarianism,[129] consociationalism, and centripetalism to meet the needs and interests of Pakistan's diverse polity—including its minority and local communities—to reduce intercommunal frictions and enhance political stability.[130] Merely applying a singular political framework in its entirety, without adapting it for the Pakistani context, has only served to consolidate power in the hands of political elites, and exacerbate inter-communal differences.

FEDERALISM VERSUS NEOLIBERALISM IN PAKISTAN

To fully understand the interplay between the political models in Pakistan, there is a need to first consider the relationship between federalism and neoliberalism, and the ways both are expressed, paradoxically, in Pakistan's democratic system. Superficially, neoliberalism and federalism are predicated upon similar norms—competition between individuals and subunits with a minimal, non-intrusive role for the state. In practice, however, the two views are inimical to one another, in large part because neoliberalism for many concerns itself exclusively with an individual's economic identity to the exclusion of all else. Federalism, on the other hand, values multiple identities in a political rights and capabilities-based approach.

As a political and economic theory, for Noam Chomsky, neoliberalism is realized through economic policies[131] that focus on strong property rights, grassroots competition between economic actors, free markets, and free trade to enhance individual and—by extension—collective well-being.[132] As per David Harvey, neoliberalism is characterized by its trust in the market's ability to aggregate information, allocate resources, and govern production and consumption decisions at both the individual and collective levels. These market-based ideals have, over time, permeated cultural norms and redefined personal and sociocultural relations.[133] The role of the state in neoliberal theory is minimal: it exists to create a framework within which neoliberalism can thrive, but then must remove itself from the context to reduce the influence it may exert on the market. Consequently, a key prescription of neoliberalism is the privatization of most state functions and deregulation of the—increasingly privatized—market.[134] Neoliberal philosophy accepts social and economic disparities between individuals as a necessary incentive for competition and innovation, incentivizing the economically disadvantaged to increase their financial well-being by participating in the market.[135] In such a society, everyone is "free," and eventually, better off.[136] Neoliberal deregulation can thus be distinguished from a *laissez faire* system as the former does not entail a complete absence of government intervention.[137] It requires state regulation to protect the banking and monetarist systems, and thus prioritizes centralization over devolution.[138]

In other words, neoliberal states have enacted extensive regulations to protect their financial institutions, demonstrating the inconsistency at the heart of neoliberalism: it is highly protective of certain private actors, while remaining unconcerned with others.[139] As some critiques of neoliberalism point out, this is the inherent paradox within neoliberalism, in which it touts the rollback of the state on one hand, while actually promoting state intrusion on the other—particularly by insisting upon the necessity of state control to maintain the supremacy of competition, and to ensure and promote the protection of certain property and contractual rights over others.[140] A stark example of neoliberalism's need for a degree of governmental intervention is the outcome of the global 2008 Financial Crash, during which an extended period of financial adventurism in the US precipitated neoliberal state intervention in the form of bailouts and the renationalization of banks.[141]

As touched upon earlier, federalism is often a compromise aimed at resolving conflicts between disaffected communities and the political centre. Like neoliberalism, federalism also promotes competition, but among political subunits instead of economic actors. A federalist structure grants partial autonomy to geographically defined subunits within the state,[142] distinguished by ethnicity, culture, linguistics, political identity, or even geography.[143] Federalism is thus a compromise rather than a solution, as disconnected communities often regard subunit status as suboptimal to complete independence and secession.[144] Although federalism is intended to protect politically distinct peoples from the tyranny of the centre, it is often an unstable arrangement that can prompt disillusioned communities against centralized governments within the federation towards secession. This inherent instability in federalism is thus termed the 'tragedy of federalism,' and this disbalance often provokes or propagates friction between the various groups within the federation. This is particularly problematic in a consociationalist federation such as Pakistan, where certain ethnic groups enjoy dominance within each federating unit, while others remain on the federal periphery.

Additionally, federalism as a system is arguably unconcerned with democracy, simply assigning definitive authority to government subunits, and informing the power dynamic between these units and between the units and the centre, regardless of the democratic—or undemocratic—character of these relationships.[145] Constitutional federalism in Pakistan has also been observed to remain largely unaffected by extended periods of autocratic rule—seemingly even when large-scale decentralization was undertaken,[146] belying the presumption that the model is somehow intrinsically tied to democratic norms. It thus becomes clear that to foster and preserve liberal norms—not least of which is some form of democratic, representative governance—federalism is insufficient.

In this discussion, federalism and decentralization must also be distinguished as, at times, the achievements or failures of decentralization are wrongly attributed to federalism.[147] Constitutional federalism does not imply a policy of decentralization—and vice versa,[148] and while federalism refers to the constitutional structure of the state, decentralization—instead—is a policy decision. While a centralized state government can decentralize by establishing independent regulators or by instituting deregulating policies;

federated states, instead, can centralize certain state functions—such as national defence and international trade—by agreement.

Decentralization achieved, for example, through a devolution of powers from the centre to the subunits, is often necessary in heterogeneous societies and can, in diverse polities such as Pakistan's, engender inclusivity in political activity and self-determination for communities. As a policy tool, therefore, decentralization can be of significant value in ameliorating pre-existing ethnic discontent and alienation. Being, in essence, a managerial strategy by which the centre can ensure effective operations in the subunits, decentralization fosters diversity in how common state goals can be realized. For example, in the Pakistani context the decentralization of administrative authority to the provinces, i.e., the federating subunits, would, theoretically empower them to monitor processes more effectively in the provision of administrative services to the public.[149] This would also—in theory—empower communities to manage themselves in ways particular to them, ensuring greater efficiency in the allocation and utilization of resources, a more effective addressal of the community's needs, and decreasing ethnic frictions arising from divisive policies deployed at the central level, far removed from the contexts to which they are applied.[150]

As previously discussed, federalism is not a panacea for the issues prevalent in a diverse, postcolonial state, nor is it a guarantee of applying and effecting liberal norms such as democratic governance. As evinced by the extended periods of military rule in Pakistan, authoritarian regimes may, for instance, allow for the election of local authorities, only to compel strict compliance with the centre's dictatorial policies.[151] As Feely and Rubin (2008) note,

> "Federalism reserves particular issues to sub-national governmental units, regardless of the political process that exists within these units, whereas local democracy establishes a particular political process in the subnational units without granting these units any particular area of authority."[152]

This is not to say that local democracy is without its merits—to name a salient few, it can increase public participation and allow elected representatives to be more closely answerable to the public that elected them. The problem arises when local democracy systems obfuscate a democratic deficit elsewhere in the constitutional framework or frustrate the ends for which they were implemented.

What remains to be examined is the extent to which these various policies work to help empower the federating units, and the ways in which "decentralization" has been effective in addressing the causes and concerns that originally brought into focus the need for such large-scale exercises. In the Pakistani context, it has been effectively argued that the aftermath of the

Local Government Ordinance resulted in an unfortunate increase in centralization, in fact reinforcing the same problems it was intended to solve.[153]

Federalism also encounters many issues in practice which require the involvement of the state; the establishment of a federalist structure itself, with its costly need for duplicating facilities, functions, and personnel, necessitates state involvement. Moreover, to ensure a stable form of federalism there must be parity of powers across federating units which are equal in size and reasonable in number,[154] and the initial establishment and demarcation of the federal structure requires the involvement of the state. State intervention is also necessary where devolutionary federalism may result in a tyranny of the majority group within the subunit, or the differential treatment of minorities within subunits may conflict with the state's constitutional architecture. Such discrimination could trigger judicial intervention to protect and effect minority rights, such as was witnessed during the US' Civil Rights movement.[155]

In short, aside from the degree of centralized decision making that both frameworks require, neoliberalism's inherent focus on the individual puts it at odds with federalism, which is focused instead on a shared, communal identity. This tension can be seen to play out in Pakistan, between the neoliberal economic order imported into the country and the ethnic federalism upon which it was based.[156]

Neoliberalism's genesis in Western academia, and its translation to and application in other non-Western contexts—such as China—also need to be considered considering its more recent 'importation' to Pakistan, most notably by way of the CPEC megaproject. To this end, contrasting the experiences of developed and developing states with neoliberalism is vital to evaluating the interaction of the economic model with other, more fragmented models of federalism in postcolonial societies such as Pakistan, where the implementation of neoliberal policies has served to deepen class divides and economic inequality.[157] This widening socioeconomic gap, in turn, exacerbates pre-existing intranational conflict, consequently undermining the application and perpetuation of liberal values.[158] As Danish Khan notes:

"The central proposition of neoliberal policies which divorces the state from the economy cannot be treated as a serious developmental strategy."[159] This is where the application of a local centripetalist federal model can play a crucial role in countering the adverse impacts of neoliberal policies,[160] potentially disrupting or dampening the impact of the kinds of predatory economic relationships that find fertile ground under neoliberal regimes.[161]

While the interplay between a local centripetal federal model and neoliberal policies will be discussed at greater length in Chapter 4, it is pertinent here to point out that the proposed localized model places significant emphasis on communalism and multiculturalism as a means of strengthening federalism—while simultaneously pushing back against neoliberal policies—in

Pakistan. The model seeks to encompass a stronger federal architecture, an empowered Senate, and more representative and transparent electoral processes to ultimately limit the inordinate power presently wielded by domestic elites—the country's influential military particularly, a primary beneficiary of the neoliberal nexus in Pakistan.

CENTRAL DYSFUNCTIONALITIES WITHIN ETHNIC FEDERALISM IN PAKISTAN

This section will explore the fundamental processes and legislative provisions associated with federalism in Pakistan that have operated to destabilize intranational democratic processes, infringed upon the rights of various ethnicities, and stymied the realization of core liberal norms in the country. To uncover these dysfunctions, this section will examine Pakistan's historical problems associated with postcoloniality, defects in the functioning of its senate, voting mechanisms, discrepancies in devolutionary federalism, the use of religion to influence and effect political disenfranchisement, and the adverse impact of neoliberal policies and the CPEC on Pakistani ethnic federalism.

Historical Overview

In Pakistan, as with other countries in South Asia such as India and Malaysia, majoritarianism combines with ethnofederalism to create a strong centre and ethnic autonomy.[162] Pakistan has an ethnofederalist system under which the provinces are based on ethnic identity, with certain special rights extended by the state to certain ethnic groups or provinces.[163] Federalism in Pakistan is beset by grievances between the central government and the provinces as well as by interprovincial tensions, directed primarily towards Punjab which is the most populous province and which dominates recruitment to all governmental and military posts.

Post-independence, most Pakistani governments have showed a preference for adopting centripetalist versions of federalism,[164] a propensity further aided through the Islamization of the constitution; an undertaking that has attempted to diminish all forms of social, political, or cultural distinctions except those based on religion. This assessment is clearly demonstrated through a survey of the jurisprudence of the highest courts in the country.[165] Nine years after its independence Pakistan altered its federal architecture, merging all provinces in West Pakistan to create parity with the more populous East Pakistan.[166] This restructuring, however, failed to ease tensions and instead, following a violent civil conflict, East Pakistan seceded to form the state of Bangladesh. Subsequently, Pakistan restored the original ethnically based provinces in its western territories, subsequently adding the Federally and Provincially Administered Tribal Areas and the semi-autonomous Gilgit-Baltistan region.[167]

At the time of its independence from the British regime, Pakistan was conceived as a liberal state with a binary federal system in the form of East and West Pakistan. This liberal and federal system, however, immediately came under pressure, firstly from Bengali demands for secession, and secondly from traditionalist Islamist elements in the polity, which came to bear when the first Constituent Assembly began its work on the first constitution.[168] Subsequently, Pakistan adopted a quasi-religious constitutional order which has persisted to this day, as well as a conventional federalist model in which an association of four provinces retain their respective autonomy in many respects whilst simultaneously sharing power with the central government. The 1973 Constitution introduced a bicameral legislature, creating an upper house comprising equal representation of all provinces, and introduced an ethnic federation which organized political power along ethno-linguistic lines.[169] This federalist model has, in the proceeding period, come under considerable strain due in no small part to a concentration of power in the Punjab province, civil-military asymmetry, and varying neoliberal economic policies.[170]

Main Dysfunctionalities in Pakistan's Federalism

Senate Processes and Defects

The Senate—the upper legislative house—has equal representation from all four provinces;[171] additionally, the President also appoints four senators from the Federal Capital.[172] Provinces also nominate women, technocrats, and minorities on reserved seats allocated to each province, to serve in the Senate. Once appointed, most of these senators also tend to align themselves with the powerful federal government in the hopes of netting better rewards as the federating units are unable to recall them.[173] Thus, the federal government enjoys immense influence over the Senate and, because the Punjabi ethnic group enjoys a position of dominance over the federal government, it consequently exerts similar influence over the Senate as well.

Punjab's dominance is at its most overt when the Senate is confronted with legislation, both generally and relation to CPEC. Under the Constitution, the Senate cannot table a "money bill" under the Constitution[174] and thus lacks fiscal legislative power, being virtually excluded from the financial planning of and decision-making over federal expenditure. The National Assembly—the 'lower' house of parliament—on the other hand, exercises effective control over Pakistan's national exchequer. However, this control vests in the Punjab province, which enjoys an absolute majority in the National Assembly. This consolidation of power in a particular ethnic group—and by extension their province of primary domicile—severely imbalances the power dynamic between the centre and the provinces (despite formal equal representation of each province within the Senate) and highlights the need to implement localized centripetalist reforms such as the creation of smaller provinces to break Punjabi hegemony, an overhaul of the Senate's polling process to prevent the practice of buying and selling of votes that are a result of the indirect election through secret ballot,[175] and the empowering of the Senate with regards to finance bills.

The Pakistani Senate's relative weakness is compounded by the fact that, unlike the US Senate, the Senate in Pakistan lacks treaty-making power, or indeed any constitutional role over the country's foreign relations.[176] Further, under Article 70(3) of the Constitution, if a disagreement develops between the Senate and the National Assembly over proposed legislation, both houses vote in a joint sitting and the bill becomes law when approved by a simple majority; because the National Assembly enjoys a numerical advantage over the Senate, and because the Punjabi ethnic group enjoys an absolute majority in a joint sitting of both houses, Punjab can thus pass or reject any law it desires.[177]

In summary, the existing constitutional framework allows the province of Punjab to pass any federal legislation or veto any bill tabled by other provinces in relation to CPEC or any associated fiscal measures or policies. The fact that the Senate has equal representation from all the provinces is rendered inconsequential due to its constitutional exclusion from the country's foreign relations and fiscal policy, as well as its hamstrung role in domestic legislation. As a result, Punjab has been able to set the terms for the country's relationship with neighbouring China, and the arrangements under CPEC, with little oversight or involvement of the remaining provinces.

Electoral Processes

In addition to the existing power imbalance between its two legislative houses, according to members of a particular ethnic group disproportionate say in the country's governance mechanisms, Pakistan's voting processes have also contributed to a largely non-representative system which has, in turn, exacerbated ethnic discord within the country. Following elections in the First-Past-The-Post (FPTP) system—a relic from the country's colonial period—(plus reserved seats for minorities), parties are able to form a government without holding fifty percent of the seats in the National Assembly, resulting in a government that "may not be the true representative of the majority of the electorate".[178] While proponents of the FPTP system praise it for its simplicity, as opposed to more complex voting systems which—they argue—may not be feasible given literacy levels in the country.[179] However, given the prior discussion (and consociationialism's failure to subdue ethnic conflict in the country), along with Pakistan's heterogenous ethnic makeup, a move to a more centripetalist voting system is required.[180] Outlining this alternative "preferential option" Rielley notes: "(a)ll preferential electoral systems share a common, distinguishing feature: They enable electors to indicate how they would vote if their favoured candidate was defeated and they had to choose among those remaining. Such systems include the "alternative vote" (AV) and the "single transferable vote" (STV)."[181]

Fiji's experiment with the AV system has achieved certain favourable results, such as the application of vote pooling and formation of pre-election alliances, which ensured that "(s)ince cross ethnic preference exchanges underpinned both coalitions, the new rules also prompted the development of new bargaining arenas that brought together former adversaries from across the ethnic divide, encouraging a degree of cross cultural communication that had been conspicuously absent at previous elections".[182]

Similarly, Papua New Guinea presents another compelling case for the use of AV systems to encourage cooperation between diverse societies. Due to the sociocultural diversity prevalent in the Papua New Guinean polity, candidates were required to go beyond their own communities to garner support as a 'second-best' candidate for other groups.[183] Subsequently, the electoral system was changed to a plurality system in 1975 which led to disastrous outcomes for the electoral process and election. The dissolution of incentive for tribes to cooperate across ethnic lines was replaced with electoral violence to secure votes,[184] prompting a return to "preferential voting," "with voters required to list at least three preferences . . . (a)long with moves to strengthen executive government, weed out corruption in politics, and promote the development of political parties . . . "[185]

Pakistan requires the implementation of a similar 'preferential voting' system that will require candidates to gain support across ethnic lines; such systems would work to foster a stronger sense of accountability towards the electorate and require the distribution of resources amongst various groups—including to members of other groups—thereby incentivizing intercommunal political outreach and deemphasizing the political impact of sociocultural considerations.

Pakistan's FPTP electoral system—itself a holdover from the country's colonial rule—politically entrenches larger ethnic groups, the Punjabis in particular, in the country's politicolegal architecture; and the country's turbulent constitutional history, marred by extended periods of military rule, ethnic conflict and an unstable economy, have all contributed significantly towards weakening and diluting national and intranational democratic processes and electoral institution such as the Election Commission of Pakistan (ECP).[186] Elections have also been manipulated through the disenfranchisement of large sections of society, and the imposition of problematic qualification criteria for candidates.[187]

Pakistan's politically influential military—in which the Punjabi ethnic group is also disproportionately represented—has also exploited and distorted the electoral system to promote a legislative assembly that tilts legislative and constitutional amendments in its favour to further consolidate power in the military's realm and that of its 'civilian allies.'[188]

Devolutionary Federalism

The 18th Amendment to the Pakistani constitution repealed some of the more overt distortions in the electoral system effected by the Musharraf military regime, by introducing amendments to enhance the ECP's role,[189] and instituted a form of devolutionary federalism. This amendment devolved several competencies which were previously within the legislative domain of the federal government to the provincial governments,[190] and restructured the National Finance Commission (NFC) Award which was previously responsible for determining the formula for the distribution of financial resources from the centre to the provinces and between the provinces themselves.[191] Consequently, the federating units could now receive financial support from the centre, which only intervened to ensure the stability of the monetarist policies being implemented.

At the time of its independence, Pakistan was divided into provinces along ethno-linguistic lines. This federal ordering, however, excluded several distinct ethnic groups such as the Saraiki-speaking people in southern Punjab; the Hindko-speaking people of Hazara; and the Muhajir, Urdu-speakers in Sindh. These minorities have since, with varying degrees of force, argued for a province of their own, in which they would constitute the majority population.[192] There have also been demands by Baluchi Pashtuns pushing for the division of Balochistan into two provinces, one for the Baluchistan's Pathan community and the other for the province's other ethnic groups.[193] These calls for new provinces gained further traction following the promulgation of the 18th Amendment as the instrument served to devolve several powers and redistributed many resources from the centre to the provinces.[194]

These calls for a reordering of the country's federal architecture are further highlighted by the fact that the NFC Award assigns a disproportionate weightage to each province's population, leading to the award favouring the most densely populated province, Punjab, over others.[195] This is further complicated by Punjab's dominance in the federal legislature, bureaucracy, and military, fomenting resentment among the other provinces—and ethnic groups—and even within the province, with South Punjab expressing discontent at resources being focused in the province's north.[196] This imbalance in favour of Punjab, and its political parties dominating the legislative houses essentially frustrates the objects of devolutionary federalism.[197]

One of the primary purposes of devolution of power in a federation is to ensure that local tiers of government are less marginalized by centralist and patronage-based governance mechanisms. This is significant as, in Pakistan, decentralization was attempted by way of the devolution of power from the centre to the provinces in three disparate stages of enforced local government systems, each imposed by a different military regime: firstly through Ayub Khan's "Basic Democracy" plan;[198] secondly, through Zia's "Local Government" plan;[199] and, most recently, through Musharraf's "Devolution Plan"[200] in 2000, adopted by the provincial governments as the Local Government Ordinance (LGO) in 2001.[201] This latter plan was "based on five fundamentals: devolution of political power, decentralization of administrative authority, deconcentration of management functions, diffusion of the power-authority nexus, and distribution of resources to the district level (LGP 2000)".[202] A critical observation at this stage is that, as all three decentralization plans were undertaken during periods of autocratic military rule, this lent a certain degree of ambiguity to the motivations driving their implementation.[203] Additionally, each phase of devolution has been proceeded by a civilian government's failure to implement or revive local government, with unelected administrators often being appointed instead of holding elections.[204]

Therefore, even though political parties are ostensibly on board with local government, and legislation has been moved to give effect to this system, the "institutionalisation of empowered, democratic local government in Pakistan remains a doubt";[205] with civilian governments repeatedly failing to hold local government elections, instead running these local governments through unelected administrators.[206] Thus, "the democratic parties' disconnection from local government has created local political vacuums that have been repeatedly exploited by nondemocratic forces to undermine the national system of civilian governance".[207] This disconnect, it is argued, exists because political representatives at the national and provincial level see local government officials as competitors for patronage and power, and thus a real transfer of power through the conduct of holding elections at the local bodies' level does not sit well with the power retention motives held at the central and provincial levels.[208] While the 18th Amendment represents a welcome shift in the power dynamic between the provinces and the centre, to capitalize upon the advances made under the amendment it is crucial to effectively leverage local government models, to ensure better representation and accountability; care must be taken, however, to ensure that these models deemphasize—rather than magnify—interethnic differences.

The current local government acts were not imposed on the provinces by the federal government—instead, each province drafted and promulgated their own individual acts, the result being that the scale and scope of devolution varies significantly across the provinces. KPK has the largest scope of devolution, giving specific powers beyond the district, tehsil and union council levels of local government, extending even to the lower tiers of village and neighbourhood councils.[209] By contrast, Punjab and Sindh have developed their devolution plans in a more centrist way; both have done away with the tehsil-level tier of local government,[210] leaving no local government structures beyond the union council levels, and resulting in a heavily asymmetric relationship between the local and provincial governments.[211] In Balochistan, though the province was one of the first to formulate legislation to enact the devolution process, and among the first to conduct local government elections, the provincial government has been unable to transfer the essential administrative, financial and political powers necessary to enable the local governments to function effectively. This is a consistent issue across all the provinces, which all lack sufficient funding to ensure the effective implementation of their respective devolutionary plans. Further complicating the situation are allegations of widespread corruption, the underutilization of funds, and a lack of resources, all of which have led to the establishment of ineffectual local bodies which are failing to fulfil the roles they were created for.[212]

The provinces each developing and implementing their own devolutionary processes has also caused serious inconsistencies between them regarding the timelines for their execution, the tenures of local governments, electoral processes, and even the extent to which provincial powers are to devolve to local governments.[213] Compounding these problems is the fact there exists no effective means of moderating or coordinating these core devolution processes between the provinces as the 18th amendment, which delegated these devolutionary powers to the provinces, also dissolved the federal ministry for local government and rural development, which would otherwise have served a pivotal role in effecting a degree of uniformity between each province's devolutionary processes.[214] However, despite these inconsistencies, all provincial local governments nonetheless exhibit a common thread of centralization; by giving the provincial chief minister—elected through the provincial assemblies—the prerogative to remove or suspend the heads of the elected local government, the centre has retained effective control over the local governments despite having ostensibly given all provincial governments control authority over policies and operations relating to various core subjects.

Finally, in an ethnic federation like Pakistan, one that is fundamentally socioculturally heterogeneous, the primary goal of the state is often to reorient ethnically based collective action into non-violent politics.[215] The FATA's merger into KPK is *prima facie* aimed at easing inter-ethnic conflict and addressing the underlying issues fomenting secessionist sentiment. However, unless electoral and parliamentary reforms are introduced to bolster the outcomes of this merger and ensure the subsequent devolution of powers to the local bodies, and existing administrative and procedural issues ironed out, the principal goal of easing inter-communal frictions will continue to elude national policymakers.[216]

The Role of Neoliberal Policies in Perpetuating Civil-Military Imbalance, and Weakening Devolutionary Federalism

Pakistan was first exposed to neoliberal forces in the 1980s, during the regime of military dictator Zia-ul-Haq who aligned the country politically and economically with the US; at the time the latter was competing with the USSR through various proxy-states across the globe. Succeeding the more socialist Bhutto regime, Zia's introduction of neoliberal policies further compounded the imbalance of power between provinces and the institutional apparatus,[217] aligning the country's powerful military apparatus along neoliberal lines. These reforms were forcefully imposed on the country throughout the 1980s, largely through western diktat,[218] with the military regime disregarding all domestic political input. At the time, Pakistan had—at the prompting of the US and its allies—received numerous loans from international lending agencies including the IMF and World Bank—during the reign of a military dictator—and when the country was on the verge of defaulting, these institutions mandated strict privatization schemes and austerity as prerequisites for debt restructuring.[219] These conditions included the privatization of virtually all state-owned enterprises, the deregulation of its financial markets, and the de-unionization of the workplace.[220] As discussed above, the implementation of these neoliberal policies had severe deleterious effects on the institutions of devolutionary federalism in Pakistan.[221]

The policies imposed by the Zia regime significantly retarded attempts at addressing systemic, intercommunal conflict. Punjabi elites enjoyed a bolstering of their economic and political dominance, while the other provinces—Baluchistan in particular—suffered as de facto colonies of the federal centre. Under the neoliberal economic policies instituted by the military dictatorship, the country was burdened with tremendous international debt, with much of the elements of the intranational welfare framework either severely compromised, if not abolished outright; this further exacerbated economic disparities between the centre and the provinces, and between the provinces themselves. While previous military regimes have—to varying degrees—tinkered with the country's socioeconomic frameworks, the imposition of neoliberal policies under the Zia regime, at the behest of its Western allies, represented the most significant departure from the welfare state envisioned at the time of the country's formation, and laid the groundwork for the widening of socioeconomic and intercommunal divisions in the Pakistani polity.

As discussed in chapter three, the Pakistani military has repeatedly accumulated power beyond its traditional sphere, engaging in political and economic activities traditionally within the realm of civilian governance, and Zia's imposition of a neoliberal order further contributed to this civil-military asymmetry.[222] The colonial policies of military landholding rapidly gained pace under neoliberalism, with the military transforming itself into the largest, most successful corporate entity in the nation, and recent reports suggesting that the country's military is also its largest landholding entity. The perpetuation of these policies in Pakistan has, in turn, given rise to massive food insecurity, poor levels of human development, water scarcity, and immense oppression of the rural poor. The political and economic disenfranchisement of broad swathes of Pakistani society under the neoliberalism's rubric have served to foster discontent, contributing to the rise of extremism and terrorism in Pakistan and the Muslim world in general, with the vacuum left behind by the state ceding its obligations to unelected oligarchies—including the military's—linked with the rise of fundamentalism in Islam.[223]

While the country has struggled with the imposition of neoliberalism for decades, the CPEC represents a more recent flashpoint in the frictions caused by the doctrine, with the project serving to exacerbate existing inter-communal and socioeconomic disparities. The implementation of federalism in Pakistan has brought with it several challenges due in no small part to a constitutional order which consists of parliament seats being allocated by population, thus paving the way for Punjabi dominance over the centre, with any political party wishing to come into power therefore obliged to appeal to this ethnic group almost exclusively.[224] Despite the promulgation of the 18th Amendment, due in no small part to the centralization of its implementation and administration, coupled with the continued neglect of KP and Baluchistan under the project, the CPEC has given new life to pre-existing grievances between the provinces and the centre—and between the provinces and Punjab in particular—which the amendment sought to address. It is to these issues that we now turn.

The CPEC exemplifies the tensions between neoliberal forces and federalism in Pakistan, involving the siphoning of resources and investments from disenfranchised Pashtuns and Balochs to Punjabi elites, which foments resentment between the federating subunits.[225] Concerns that the larger Punjab intends to appropriate the project at the expense of the smaller provinces persist, particularly as all major development projects associated with CPEC are being planned and executed by the federal government along the Eastern route, which will pass through Punjab,[226] with one senator from Balochistan lampooning the project as the "China-Punjab Economic

Corridor".[227] Moreover, the way neoliberal practices has been employed by the Chinese under the CPEC regime potentially transforms Pakistan's political economy by deploying the state and its machinery to ensure that this direct foreign investment goes unhindered. These neoliberal economic policies, implemented for CPEC, risk destabilizing Pakistan's fragile federalism even further, exacerbating pre-existing intercommunal tensions and fuelling secessionist sentiments in the country's smaller provinces.

The Pakistani Constitution allows the federal legislature to amend the constitution with relative ease, requiring only a two-thirds supermajority in Parliament, requiring no prior provincial consultation nor according a constitutional role to the provinces enabling them to effectively challenge such a legal reordering.[228] This leaves open the possibility that the federal legislature might exercise this prerogative—particularly in light of the tensions between the devolutionary processes instituted under the 18th amendment and the centre's desire to unilaterally implement the CPEC and its associated projects—to accommodate the project in ways that further antagonizes the smaller provinces. The mismanaged or exploitative implementation of CPEC will militate against an efficient and equitable form of federalism, as envisioned under the 18th amendment and the 7th NFC award, and it thus becomes imperative to effect reforms which serve to accord the provinces a degree of meaningful input and oversight over the project to counter this imbalance.

Significantly, many of the projects being implemented under the CPEC rubric are located and function within the SEZs governed and monitored by provincial SEZ Authorities,[229] which exclude the application of Pakistani law in favour of other legal regimes.[230] This raises the risk of imposition of neoliberal and investor focused legal arrangements which facilitate continued Chinese investment, possibly at the expense of compromising the fundamental rights accorded by the Pakistani constitution.[231] Moreover, given the relative ease with which the Pakistani constitution can be amended, it would not be improbable for the federal legislature—dominated as it is by the Punjabi ethnic group—to amend the constitution to facilitate Chinese investment and their own resource extraction from these investment projects. With these specific enclaves carved out of the broader legal landscape, it would be increasingly difficult for marginalized and disenfranchised groups either living within or affected by these SEZs to peacefully agitate for their rights with any degree of success.

Several reasons have been cited in defence of the centralized control over CPEC, including the Pakistani military's view that the project would be a chance to further deepen relations with China and expand the latter's role within Pakistan.[232] To this end, China has already stated it would prefer that the Pakistani armed forces play a greater role in CPEC's implementation, which will only serve to enhance perceptions of Punjabi control over the project given the overrepresentation of that group in the country's armed forces. Further, the military's role in CPEC has continued to grow over time, with a National Development Council established in June 2019 to include key members from the army such as the Chief of Army Staff.[233] This promises to further the power imbalance within the problematic civil-military relations in Pakistan, already skewed in favour of the military.

The extant political rhetoric, acrimony, and inter-provincial friction will only continue as CPEC transitions into its implementation phase, bringing with it a re-introduction of and emphasis on neoliberal policies; in this milieu Punjab can—and likely will—expropriate many CPEC projects and their dividends to derive the highest amounts of economic rent for itself, further distorting Pakistan's ethnic federalist architecture. Additionally, due to the ambiguous territorial status of Gilgit-Baltistan, uncertainty also persists regarding the sharing of revenues or rents with these administrative units which otherwise do not fall within the provincial mold prescribed by the constitution. These issues greatly imperil the devolutionary federalist processes begun under the 18th amendment by asymmetrically equipping certain federating units with greater power and relevance over others.[234]

The Use of Religion to Weaken Federalism

Islam remains a key factor in Pakistan's constitutional design. While the faith presents an opportunity to deemphasize other sociocultural concerns such as ethnicity, the inordinate emphasis placed on the religion—particularly on its Sunni sect—by the state's architecture often serves instead to exclude other religious groups, or members of other Islamic denominations. The 1973 constitution declares Pakistan an Islamic Republic,[235] with Islam as the state religion.[236] It also empowers a Council of Islamic Ideology[237] to ensure the conformity of all legislation promulgated with the injunctions of the faith, and while the Council operates at the federal level, it is nonetheless empowered to recommend amendments to provincial legislation as well to effect national legislative consistency with Islamic religious norms. Though not binding in nature, the Council and its pronouncements nonetheless represent another expression of the centre's involvement in provincial decision-making and legislative capacity, curtailing their autonomy while simultaneously applying the normative framework of a particular faith on an otherwise religiously diverse polity.

Pakistan's military has leaned into the use of Islamic rhetoric, presenting itself as the sole guardians of the Islamic faith—and by extension the Islamic Republic itself—in the face of opposition from Hindu-majority India to its East. Given the historic tensions between the two states, this use of rhetoric serves to justify military adventurism into civilian affairs—including economic concerns—and inures the country's already-influential military from domestic critique. This self-designation of the Pakistani military as Islam's bastion in the face of non-Islamic opposition allows the country's armed forces to deploy religion as a rhetorical and policy tool to further undermine Pakistan's ersatz provincial parity, with dissidents characterized either as 'agents' of hostile non-Muslim states—India and Israel being popular choices—or 'terrorists' who 'subvert or distort' the articles of the faith.[238]

FEDERALISM IN SOUTH ASIA AND LESSONS FOR PAKISTAN

Given the significant impact the British colonial imposition has had on South Asia—and the collective colonial and postcolonial experiences arising out of that shared history—South Asian countries often borrow elements of federal or constitutional organization from one another, learning from each other's experiences. Federal processes adapted by Nepal, India, and Sri Lanka offer key examples to explore "post-peace-agreement efforts to sustain peace, address the root causes of the conflict [these countries] face, and promote reconciliation and social justice"[239] in the region.[240] These developments can provide insight into elements, models, and frameworks that might prove applicable in conflict-ridden, postcolonial societies, and it is arguable that these learning experiences may prove to be more apposite to the Pakistani context than the 'imported', alien ideologies—such as neoliberalism—imposed by the colonial regime or by their neo-colonial antecedents.

Important Experiences of India, Nepal, Bangladesh, and Sri Lanka with Federalism

Defects in Federal frameworks and electoral processes

Given the indelible historical ties between south Asian polities, examining federalism, and its evolving status, in this context is crucial to understanding federalism and its characteristics in Pakistan.[241]

Postcolonial India, and its federal evolution, represents an ideal case study owing to the sociocultural and historical elements it shares with Pakistan. Following the 1857 mutiny it became clear to the East India Company that it was losing its power to effectively rule India's colonized population.[242] Thus, India began its progression towards a decentralized federal framework.[243] Legislative councils established in 1861 were extended further by the Government of India Act 1909,[244] which further strengthened the federal framework through—among other initiatives—the creation of separate electorates for Muslims.

The commitment to federalism was further strengthened through the Government of India Act 1935,[245] which allowed Congress leaders to govern "under an act that ' . . . committed India to a federal form of government. . . . The provinces are for the first time recognized in law as separate entities, exercising executive and legislative powers in their own field . . . '".[246]

Nehru's opposition to federalism notwithstanding, India's constitutional processes continued to evolve in line with federal values, with Gandhi laying

> the foundations for a post-independence federal state by replacing Provincial Congress Committees (PCCs), based on British provinces, with 20 language based PCCs. By using a federal structure to democratize communication within the Congress, Gandhi not only arranged for shared sovereignty among India's linguistic regions but also was able to create a truly national organization that could speak to and mobilize village India.[247]

Despite this initial progress towards a framework accommodating multiculturalism, India was nonetheless unable to avoid the 1947 partition, failing to implement a system of shared sovereignty with the subcontinent's significant Muslim minority.[248] Post-partition, India and Pakistan inherited similar governance structures, predicated on a strong centre with weaker federating units—the provinces in Pakistan and states in India.

India also implemented party reforms which shifted its political topography from "a dominant party to a multi-party system and from majority governments to coalition governments. The change had a profound effect on the federal system. State-based parties played an increasingly decisive role in the formation of coalition governments. The equilibrium change wrought by a federal market economy was compounded by the change in the party system."[249]

Currently, India' employs the First-Past-The-Post electoral voting system, a product of its colonial heritage, which has resulted in disproportional representation.[250] Despite India's pluralistic society "the electoral system has retained a considerable degree of support, due in part to the practice of reserving seats for socially underprivileged groups".[251] More recently, however, the FPTP system implemented to forestall fragmented legislatures and stabilize the political arena has instead resulted in "an era of political instability and uncertainty".[252]

Like the Pakistani Senate, the voting processes in India's Rajya Sabha (the upper legislative house) is also plagued with elements which detract from federal cohesion, such as indirect elections and the conduct of secret ballots.

While recent reforms have attempted to curb vote buying by partially lifting the secrecy of the ballot, they have yet to achieve the desired results.[253]

In the Nepalese context, decades of exclusion and disempowerment of the country's minority ethnic groups have resulted in endemic poverty and intercommunal conflict, prompting repeated calls to implement decentralized federal structures and democratic norms within the country.[254] Nepal can be viewed as a country in transition to federalism, with the federal structure clearly defined in the 2015 Constitution including the three tiers of government.[255] However, although this can be viewed an attempt at strengthening federalism, the devolution of power to states has instead resulted in further strained relations with the federal government.[256] Nepal's attempts to address these issues are discussed at greater length under 'devolutionary federalism' below.

Devolutionary Federalism

India's federal architecture has historically demonstrated more stabilized progress toward the inculcation and application of democratic norms. For instance, during a national financial crisis in 1991, economic liberalization reforms were instituted to "move India from a planned to a market economy".[257] This, in turn, shifted the balance of power from the centre to India's federating units—its states.[258]

Another keystone of India's federal framework has been the judiciary.[259] The Supreme Court of India, through its proactive and activist approach towards human rights issues and—more importantly—its jurisprudence on the role of the President, has furthered federalism and entrenched it within the country's fundamental constitutional framework.[260] With the weakening of the dominant multi-party system, however, as Saxena and Swenden note:

> (t)he re-emergence of a majority government headed by the Hindu nationalist Bharatiya Janata Party may put (the Indian Supreme Court) under pressure to read some state rights more restrictively, especially where they could be interpreted as strengthening India as a pluralized and multiculturally diverse country and not just as a 'federal' state. This will require closer scrutiny of where the Court is headed in years to come, particularly in cases relating to federal asymmetry, national identity, and citizenship.[261]

As previously discussed, federalism itself requires a degree of intervention by federal institutions—such as the judiciary—to function effectively. In the Pakistani context, the Supreme Court of Pakistan (SCP)—as the guardian of the Constitution—could play a key role in safeguarding minority rights and balancing the allocation of power and resources between the centre and the subunits. So far, the SCP has been unable to assume its role as a final arbitrator between the centre and the provinces[262] and historically, has predominantly favoured the former when the issue has presented itself before the apex court.[263]

In Nepal's recent reforms of its federal structure—despite clearly defined powers for the federal, state, and local governments –significant tensions have arisen between the federal government and the state. To address these issues,

> infrastructure that may have once suited a traditional unitary structure must be upgraded to serve a purpose in the context of federal governance. To do this, the government has taken actions to dissolve several ministries and departments at the federal level. States, in turn, have started establishing new organisations to carry out their responsibilities as envisioned in the constitution. Local governments have also followed suit.[264]

Further, for devolution to be effective, it is important for reforms in the bureaucracy to retrain and reintegrate officials formally trained to work for a historically centralized government, as has been the case in postcolonial societies such as Nepal and Pakistan.

In Sri Lanka, the first real attempt to tackle the country's ethnic divide, by breaking its Unitary system through federalism, came in 1995.[265] Historically, the country has adopted a piecemeal approach to devolution, and has encountered several challenges to the effectivity of this process due in no small part to the fact that it has been implemented through the 13th amendment.[266] The introduction of provincial councils has largely been viewed by the Sri Lankan polity as "another layer of bureaucratic and political malpractices and corruptions".[267] Therefore, it is imperative to devolve power to the local government tiers to ensure greater engagement with the polity and to serve local issues of the populations. Further, there is a pressing need to ensure that these reforms are enacted in a manner which bolsters the polity's confidence in them, to further ensure their effective application.

Bangladesh has also experimented with decentralization through its local government (LG) bodies; this process has, however, encountered difficulties in achieving local development and improving public services.[268] For instance, less.

"Then one per cent of Bangladesh's GDP funds 85 per cent of LG development expenditures. Undeniably, LG bodies are heavily dependent on direct grants from the central government and on sharing tax revenue with the land department."[269]

Additional problems have arisen through a lack of accountability and participation from locals, with the process suffering from veiled centralization where MPs are allowed to 'advise' local government bodies.[270]

There are important lessons to be drawn for Pakistan from the experiences of its neighbouring South Asian states, and their approaches towards federal organization. Given the constitutional role the 18th amendment was envisioned to play in Pakistan's federal architecture, a constitutional mandate for local governments needs to be guaranteed, along with simultaneous reforms to the bureaucracy, to better implement the devolution envisioned through the enactment of the amendment. Further, economic liberalization and the management of the state's financial burden through reforms to the NFC award system and revenue collection and generation needs to be ensured at the provincial level. The deleterious effects of neoliberalism on the Pakistani polity's economic and sociocultural well-being must also be countered, to deescalate ethnic strife in the country. Lastly, as the judiciary can play an important role in balancing the powers between the provinces and the centre, as envisioned under the 18th amendment,[271] it needs to lean into its role as a counter majoritarian guardian of the country's marginalized groups.

Neoliberal Policies and their Impact on Federalism

As discussed above, although India's early economic liberalization programs and policies facilitated a balance of power between the federation and states, more recent neo liberalization is accelerating cultural majoritarianism and therefore weakening the idea of citizenship, thereby adversely affecting the rights of weaker populations.[272] As Ajay Guhavarthy notes:

> At the same time, even as cultural majoritarian politics is eroding trust and dividing one group from another, it built on rhetoric that emphasizes forging a united, stronger India. Majoritarianism creates a complex web of both inclusion and exclusion. As it excludes religious minorities from basic citizenship rights, it provides an immediate sense of inclusion for the most deprived of Hindu caste groups. So even though Dalits are today experiencing a frontal assault on their rights and dignity, many feel more included in national life than Muslims do.[273]

It becomes clear that neoliberal economic policy will also negatively impact a country's domestic and foreign policy, and further accentuate inequality between various ethnicities, adversely impacting minorities. Sri Lanka is no stranger to the neoliberal project, with " . . . [p]ost-war Sri Lanka was to be connected through a vast array of highways and road networks, ostensibly uniting warring communities through the common endeavour of national development and economic growth."[274] Sri Lanka is also a party to China's Belt and Road Initiative, and in addition to debt trap concerns around the initiative, the project may also have serious impacts on the country's environment and labour relations if left unchecked.[275]

With Pakistan's already fragmented polity and with increasing discontent between provinces over the CPEC project and impacts on local populations, it is crucial to institute provincial powers and additional checks to ensure that the growth and development promised under the CPEC rubric proves beneficial for elements of Pakistani society, across its various provinces and ethnicities, to prevent the further fragmentation of the polity.

The Use of Nationalism to Undermine Federalism

India's transition towards coalition governments demonstrates inherent consociational tendencies in the Indian political apparatus;[276] however, as highlighted by Katherine Adeney, "the electoral success of Hindu nationalism and the increasing acceptance of ethnic majoritarianism has reduced the degree of power-sharing in India."[277] The 'coalition government' model has, however, not enjoyed as much traction in Pakistan due to the disenfranchisement of the smaller provinces and the concentration of power in the Punjabi elite, which obviates the need for the dominant politico-cultural group to court political outsiders. In contrast to India, Pakistan has historically had its electoral landscape dominated by a two-party system, interrupted by—or arguably interrupting—extended periods of military rule, with the country's ethnic factions largely remaining concentrated in specific territorial pockets in their respective four provinces.

While India has historically been perceived as a pluralistic state with robust federal structures, this has been in large part due to the sharing of sovereignty and autonomy between its multinational, multicultural, and multilingual states. Recent political changes in the country and the rise of 'national federalism,' however, present serious challenges to India's federal architecture,[278] with attempts now being made to redefine what constitutes a shared or collective Indian identity—and by extension to identify which groups do and do not share in it. Similarly, electoral reforms to ensure a level playing field for all ethnicities and parties are needed in societies such as India and Pakistan; as Ambar Kumar Ghosh writes: "unless the third level of Indian federalism, i.e., the local self-governments, are not further politically empowered, efforts to strengthen the federal discourse will fail."[279]

Case studies from other South Asian states such as India, Bangladesh, Nepal, and Sri Lanka provide valuable lessons for the Pakistani context, highlighting the need to have a strong federal model based on centripetal elements to counter ethnic discord, financial, and political disenfranchisement, and to peacefully discourage secessionist sentiments. Ethnic identity cannot be ignored entirely when implementing federal policies towards constitutional reforms, and a localized centripetal model must consequently accord a degree of space to such sociocultural considerations: for instance, in demarcating new provinces predicated upon the ethnolinguistic lines of smaller cultural groups, such as the Seraiki community in southern Punjab. Such initiatives can ensure the realization of cultural and linguistic rights, while simultaneously encouraging cooperation between populations—particularly in southern Punjab and Sindh, where the provinces are dominated by one ethnic group but house nontrivial minority groups within them. Similarly, as the 18th amendment fails to provide an adequate framework for the provinces' financial empowerment and self-reliance, this needs to be addressed with changes to the NFC award and to neoliberal policies imposed by the centre.

While India has enjoyed a degree of federal stability and ecumenicist harmony, recent political developments highlight the need to ensure effective political representation of all communities—particularly minority groups—at the grassroots level, to ensure the continued stability and cohesion of the Indian state. To preclude secessionist attempts in states such as India and Pakistan, and to ensure the continued survival of federalism, it is thus imperative to strengthen the capacities of the federating units to establish and maintain trust between the centre and the provinces.[280] To this end, strong and effective devolution mechanisms can counter calls for self-determination from ethnicities as that form of autonomy dilutes the 'self'.[281]

ETHNIC FEDERALISM AND COMMUNAL DEMOCRATIC NORMS

Pakistan's ethnic federal structuring - with a strong Punjabi hegemony within the various levels of government and state apparatuses - has been at the root of intercommunal and interprovincial acrimony in the country. This hegemony is expressed at every level of socio-economic transactions undermining distributive justice within the polity: specifically, for example, as the National Finance Commission (NFC) Award's calculus is still overwhelmingly based on the strength of a province's population, Punjab continues to draw inequitably larger portions of the Award.

Additionally, the current consociational political framework in Pakistan serves to alienate minorities and subverts multiculturalism. Pakistan's political parties are currently ordered along ethnic lines, with minority parties having to align themselves with the mainstream parties to enjoy any political representation. This is sub-optimal, not only because they often make large compromises to their political ideals, but also because it leads to an eventual political assimilation within the larger party. This also leads to minorities creating smaller, non-representative and extremist parties, which can often work to damage national identities and cohesiveness.

Not only have group-specific rights, aimed at protecting minorities, not been granted—in fact, discrimination against certain minorities, for example the Ahmadis, has been entrenched by the State, thereby alienating them further. Sociocultural identity, as Horowitz proposes, can be depoliticized through the promotion of multi-ethnic parties and ensuring inter-group accommodations, thereby producing meaningful regional and national policies, without compromising on a common national identity. Pakistan's current framework based on politicized ethnicity does not provide incentives for political actors to conduct outreach beyond their sociocultural bloc.

The current ordering of local government mechanisms in Pakistan are still quite heavily centrist and patronage based, which makes the current system ineffectual in diluting Punjabi hegemony, and providing a system that is representative and accountable to the public. The federal government has repeatedly been unable—and arguably unwilling - to hold effective local government elections, resorting instead to filling the representative positions with unelected administrators. This is because political representatives at both the federal centre and the provincial governments see local government officials as competitors for patronage and power and are therefore resistant to initiating any meaningful electoral processes that would shift the power dynamic away from them.

PRESCRIPTIONS

The prevalent tensions between neoliberal economic policies and devolutionary federalism, electoral processes and senate defects can be ameliorated through the implementation of certain prescriptions. The inter-provincial power imbalance can be addressed through an increase in the number of federating units, with greater interprovincial diversity to allow for a system of federalism that fosters cooperation between a diverse array of political actors, as opposed to one divided along predominantly ethnic lines.[282] Coupled with the introduction of more languages at the national level, the splitting up of larger, more influential federating units—such as Punjab—would help prevent the mobilization of political power along ethno-linguistic lines, allowing for greater and practically equal representation in the Senate and fostering a healthier parity between the units.[283]

Judicial activism and constitutional restraint may also be applied to effect a transition towards a lasting civil-military balance, and to extend the judiciary's protection to marginalized elements of Pakistani society most in need of the same; in a similar vein, the socio-economic rights enshrined in the Constitution must be made operative in nature—as opposed to the aspirational nature they presently enjoy—to fully realize their protective potential.[284]

The units' autonomy to directly transact with foreign entities must also be strengthened, perhaps by reducing the involvement of the centre in such endeavours,[285] and the federation must enable the provinces to strengthen their public health and education institutions—especially in light of the detrimental, exclusionary impact of economic policies during the COVID-19 pandemic—and must look to re-nationalize the service-provision of critical utilities—such as health care—to protect its public structures from neoliberal pressures.

The realization of a localized form of centripetalist federalism in Pakistan would require major constitutional modifications that would deeply impact the country's current political landscape, such as by altering the current number, status, and powers of existing federating units, reforming the legislative electoral system, formally institutionalizing traditional alternative dispute resolution mechanisms such as *jirgas* and *panchayats*, revising the powers of constitutional bodies tasked with resolving contestations between the provinces and/or the centre, and revisiting the gender quota system with the aim to work towards guaranteeing meaningful representation for women in the country's legislative bodies.

Firstly, to effect electoral and structural reforms of the state apparatus, it is crucial to blunt the political influence wielded by the Punjabi majority and its *de facto* control over the federal legislature.[286] Doing so would ensure that no one province or ethnic group would be able to exercise effective hegemony over the parliament.[287] The division of the province of Punjab into several smaller provinces would work to break its inordinate collective power and numerical superiority, consequently diminishing the antagonism from other provinces. This territorial re-demarcation can employ local centripetalist approaches, such as those employed in Nigeria, to dilute the concentration of political power in the Punjabi community.[288] Furthermore, specific constitutional provisions should be implemented to ensure the unrestricted movement and relocation of ethnic groups throughout the country, resulting in a provincial identity not principally centred on ethnic identities.[289] This, in turn, would serve to discourage ethnically motivated political decision-making at both the federal and provincial levels. While ethnic identities must continue to be valued for their social and cultural significance, the aim of this project should only be to strip ethnicity of the primarily alienating political construction it holds in Pakistan today.[290]

Secondly, electoral reforms (at both the institutional and party levels) are also desperately needed to decrease ethnic discord within the country. As already outlined earlier in this chapter, the FPTP system (with the addition of reserved seats) has led to unrepresentative governments and a disgruntled electorate, and Pakistan's propensity for the system has only served to further entrench Punjab's inordinate influence over the country. In this context, the further sub-division of the existing provinces (Punjab in particular) into more federating units would serve to dilute the hegemony exercised by the province in national politics and, given the necessity for an equitable inter-provincial allocation of resources by way of the NFC award, also serve to guarantee greater financial autonomy for the other provinces—and the ethnic groups they consist of—to effect their social development through the consensus-based NFC award.[291]

The success of 'preferential' voting formats, such as Alternative Voting, is prescribed for Pakistan to encourage political moderation and require electoral candidates to accommodate minority populations as they become reliant on their votes.[292] A limited preferential system can be adapted like that employed in Papua New Guinea, requiring citizens to vote for three candidates in order of their preferences. This system will encourage citizens to vote across ethnic lines, thereby defeating the disproportionality that comes with FPTP systems and "raising the bar to representation — in order to get elected parties [sic] need to garner widespread support — and because it is preferential and allows voters to have a say on all candidates, it is able to address the FPTP weakness of wasted votes".[293] Furthermore, at the party level, political parties might also be required by law to have a cross-regional presence, similar to the 'national party' scheme in Indonesia.[294]

Thirdly, reforms are also required through constitutional amendments to the Senate's electoral processes, the conduct of its elections, and the powers constitutionally allocated to it.[295] Like most bicameral parliamentary systems, elections to the upper house are presently held indirectly by sitting legislators. This system, however, dilutes the accountability senators may otherwise have to the electorate, preventing unaligned groups from fielding senatorial candidates and forcing them instead to have to 'sell their votes.' Blocs not part of nor otherwise aligned with a larger ethnicity—particularly the dominant one in the province—are denied representation in the Senate and must instead negotiate with the dominant group to achieve any sort of tangential impact on the Senate. In the Pakistani context this often results in the smaller group forced to acquiesce to the larger's senatorial candidate or remain entirely unrepresented in the body, negotiating from a position of relative weakness given their relative lack of political influence for whatever concessions the dominant group may deign to extend in exchange for the smaller bloc's electoral power. To overcome these issues, a constitutional amendment requiring direct elections to the Senate is imperative, with senators representing geographical constituencies, resulting in a more representative upper house, and thereby contributing to a stronger federal structure.[296]

Fourthly, the Senate's powers need to be enhanced to accord it greater oversight over finance bills and the use of emergency provisions as enshrined in the Constitution.[297] In addition to these recommendations, it is also imperative that article 73 of the constitution be amended to ensure that finance/money bills introduced in the lower house be passed by both houses prior to their submission for presidential assent. Furthermore, the Senate should also have a stronger constitutionally mandated role in oversight over the proclamation of a state of emergency within a province, with the mechanism allowing for provincial veto powers in virtually all circumstances on the centre's proclamation of emergency.

Fifthly, civilian democratic regimes in Pakistan must adopt and develop a functional and coherent system of elected local governments, with the aim of strengthening the foundations of federal democracy in Pakistan.[298] Democratically representative local governments promote communitarianism by valuing and prioritizing local choices, and by allowing communities to elect representatives that are more relatable, reachable, and responsive to their needs and concerns. Incentivizing the development of cross-communal or -ethnic electoral bases and rewarding popularity across communities will promote a localized form of centripetalism, further deemphasizing the exclusionary political role ethnicity has come to play in the country. Another tool to help political representatives garner cross-ethnic support is the "Alternative Vote" (AV) and "Single Transferable Vote" (STV) already discussed above.

Within this context, devolution would ensure the grant of significant powers to the local government, which would then reduce the inordinate lobby Punjab enjoys within the centre and empower local governments to develop policies and undertake administrative actions responsive to the needs of the people.

Sixthly, as most of the Pakistan's population resides in rural settings, the use of local governance frameworks such as the '*panchayat*' and '*jirga*' can advance socio-economic development at the local level in these nonurban settings. In India, the 'Panchayati Raj Institutions' enjoy constitutional cover, and have been a strong feature in terms of rural self-governance and community development under the country's federal architecture.[299] The system has made considerable headway towards facilitating participatory decision-making at the grassroots level, and has also ensured the meaningful participation of women in the political process.[300] The use of these systems can also indirectly aid in the realization of multiculturalism and ethnic rights, though it remains crucial to ensure that fundamental constitutional rights and democratic norms are assimilated in *jirga/panchayat* procedures.[301]

Seventhly, the current political party framework and gender quota system in Pakistan yields ineffective participation from women as they are more often than not obliged to align their political preferences with filial or party positions, thereby defeating democratic values and hindering their effective representation.[302] It therefore becomes necessary to implement reforms to the electoral process to ensure the larger, more representative, and more impactful participation of women in Parliament.[303] This can be achieved through implementing a "special nationwide tier for female candidates only" as implemented in Uganda,[304] which will require amendments to the relevant legislation—such as the Elections Act of 2017 and the Constitution—to revise the existing reserved quotas. Furthermore, for representation to truly be substantive, and not merely descriptive, additional measures to empower women and remove historical patriarchal hurdles is necessary, possibly through legally mandating women's participation in party decision-making.

Eighthly, to further the effect of the 18th amendment and prevent the progress garnered thereunder from being rolled back, it is necessary to ensure greater financial independence for the provinces. Pakistan's historic, centralized approach to federalism has led to the collection and accumulation of resources and capacity at the centre, leaving provinces financially exhausted and dependent thereon. Although the provincial share has been raised to 57.5 percent post 2010 (to be distributed horizontally), this has not been sufficient to equip the provinces to perform better. The NFC award thus needs to be revisited to develop a resource allocation mechanism based on population needs, resource generation (by the centre and the provinces), and incentives and rewards for provinces creating additional revenue resources through—for example—tax reforms. These policy measures can ensure better cooperation between the centre and provinces and diffuse consociational competitiveness which would otherwise lead to a weaker federal system in the country's post-colonial, ethnically divided context. Territorial divisions and strengthened mechanisms of local self-governance can also aid in averting discord over revenue allocation, as has been attempted in Nigeria.[305]

Localized centripetalist federalism also faces a grave threat from recent neoliberal policies, most visibly through the CPEC and its associated projects. Presently, the smaller provinces—with no small degree of justification—fear a complete appropriation of the CPEC and its benefits by the Punjabi-dominated centre and demonstrate significant mistrust towards Punjab and the federal government. As a compromise to resolve conflicts between disaffected communities and the political centre, a localized form of centripetalist federalism may thus operate to circumvent the destabilizing effects of neoliberalism and ensure that the dividends of foreign investment—including the CPEC—are not monopolized by any one ethnic group.

The Pakistani military predominantly comprises Punjabis and Pashtuns which—given the inordinate political, social, and economic influence Punjab wields—further aggravates existing inter-ethnic frictions in the country. Similarly, the reins of the country's second most powerful institution, the bureaucracy, has also historically remained in the hands of Punjabis.[306] To effectively implement and maintain a localized, centripetalist form of federalism in Pakistan, central institutions of the government—such as the military, the bureaucracy, and the judiciary—must be kept in check, as these may otherwise end up challenging or undermining the intended federal structure as their aims and objectives, of national security and rule of law respectively, do not prioritize democratic governance.

As discussed in more detail in Chapter 4, the military must be reordered at every level;[307] specifically, all stakeholders—the military, the political elites, and the citizenry—must agree on the composition of the officer corps, the recruitment and style of the military, and the political decision-making process, so that the current inter-institutional frictions are converted instead into a collaborative framework with clearly spelled out civilian supremacy. To this end a binding and authoritative legal instrument, establishing a national oversight council and clearly delineating the individual areas of competence and roles of stakeholders, with mechanisms to address potential issues which may arise in each area of national significance, can be prepared outlining the bases for constructive consultative dialogue to take place.

Moreover, is imperative that the state's judicial arm upholds its responsibility to protect and preserve the Constitution and maintain parity between the centre and the provinces considering the 18th amendment.[308] In this context, the Supreme Court can employ its judicial oversight function to safeguard the fundamental rights enshrined in the Constitution. The historical legitimization of military coups, the application of laws discriminatory towards minorities, and rendering of verdicts that themselves work to undermine judicial independence have all been contributing factors to the promotion of an unhealthy form of federalism in the country, whereas an independent and powerful judiciary is *a sine qua non* for the existence of a robust federation.[309]

An independent and reformed judiciary would serve not only to help underpin the rule of law and constitutionalism but would also greatly minimize the possibility of further authoritarian interventions. The Constitution of Pakistan outlines rules and safeguards for the independence of the Judiciary—the problem arises in the suspension of these rules, or their circumvention outright by acting "extra-constitutionally".[310] The judiciary must thus be willing and able to push back when this is attempted, to ensure that the institution is never co-opted by authoritarian elements seeking to destabilize or distort the country's constitutional architecture, and to minimize the space within which such interventions can occur. To bolster its own effectiveness, the criterion for the appointment of judges must also be improved and made transparent, to ensure those called to the bench are capable and impartial, and to minimize the effect extraneous factors—such as religious or ethnic identity—do not inform judicial appointments. Doing so will ensure that the Pakistani judiciary is empowered and capable enough to protect its constitutional role—and thus better protect individuals' rights—and will also contribute towards ensuring the judges so appointed are able to conduct their duties in an environment free from any extrinsic pressures or influence.

CONCLUSION

In essence, federalism serves as a bulwark against tyranny in ethnically diverse democratic societies and is necessary to ensure stability within the state. It is a compromise negotiated between unity and dissociation, which allows people's identities to be expressed and recognized without allowing this expression to lead to secession and atomization. Furthermore, federalism operates at odds with neoliberalism, which for critics focuses solely on an individual's economic identity; by contrast, federalism values multiple identities, including ethnicity and religious affiliation. Pakistan's political system has historically been centred on ethnic, religious, and linguistic diversity, providing for a state that is majoritarian and ethnofederalist in that there is ethnic autonomy and a strong centre. Progress has been made towards deemphasizing the ethnicized nature of the Pakistani federation under the 18th amendment to the Pakistani constitution; however, the country remains beset by pre-existing grievances between the central government and the provinces and by interprovincial tensions, largely due to Punjab's dominance over the federation—and its institutions—as a whole.

This, as well as the inimical interplay between neoliberalism and federalism, has been exacerbated by CPEC, which has already proven to be a serious flashpoint in inter-provincial politics, and which may prove to further escalate ethnic tensions in the country. The project encapsulates the key issues with both these forms of political engineering, bringing to the fore the inherent incompatibility of neoliberal arrangements with any meaningful, stable form of federalism. The realization of a localized form of centripetalist federalism is thus the core solution posited in this chapter; this would, as previously discussed necessitate fundamental, structural constitutional modifications to the country's existing politico-legal framework and its political economy, that would deeply impact Pakistan's current political topography.

NOTES

1. Crawford Brough Macpherson, "The theory of possessive individualism: Hobbes to Locke." *Oxford: Clarendon Press* 8 (1962): 121.
2. *Ibid.*
3. *Ibid.*

4. Rene Descartes, "Discourse on Method and the Meditations. 1637." *Trans. FE Sutcliffe. Harmondsworth: Penguin* (1968). *See also* Immanuel Kant, *The Cambridge Edition of the Works of Immanuel Kant: Critique of Pure Reason*/Transl. and Ed. by Paul Guyer; Allen W. Wood. Cambridge University Press, 1998.

5. *See generally* Arnold Leonard Epstein and Athena S. Leoussi, *Ethos and identity: three studies in ethnicity*. Routledge, 2017; Cohen P. Anthony, "Self–consciousness: an alternative anthropology of identity." (1994); Benedict Anderson, "Census, map, museum." *Imagined communities: Reflections on the origin and spread of nationalism* (1991): 163–85; and David Miller. *On nationality*. Clarendon Press, 1995.

6. Benjamin Reilly, "Institutional designs for diverse democracies: Consociationalism, centripetalism and communalism compared." *European Political Science* 11.2 (2012): 259–70.

7. *Ibid.*

8. Timothy Sisk, *Power sharing and international mediation in ethnic conflicts*. US Institute of Peace Press, 1996, 33.

9. Michael G. Breen, "Federal and Political Party Reforms in Asia: Is There a New Model of Federal Democracy Emerging in Ethnically Diverse Countries in Asia?" *Government and Opposition* (2020): 1–22. *See* Laurent Gayer, Christophe Jaffrelot, 'Do Pakistanis vote on an ethnic basis?,' *Herald* (Mar 7, 2018), accessed on October 17, 2021 <https://herald.dawn.com/news/1153691>. ("By requesting political candidates to refrain from seeking votes 'on the basis of religion, sect, caste or ethnicity' and threatening violators with a three-year jail term, the Electoral Commission of Pakistan recently confirmed the persisting relevance of ethnic bonds in shaping electoral choices.").

10. *Ibid.* 'Federal and Political Party Reforms in Asia: Is There a New Model of Federal Democracy Emerging in Ethnically Diverse Countries in Asia?' at 14.

11. Andrew Reynolds, *Electoral systems and the protection and participation of minorities*. London: Minority Rights Group International, 2006, 1.

12. *Ibid.* at 210.

13. *See supra* note 9 'Federal and Political Party Reforms in Asia: Is There a New Model of Federal Democracy Emerging in Ethnically Diverse Countries in Asia?' at 14.

14. Donald L. Horowitz, "Ethnic power sharing: Three big problems." *Journal of democracy* 25.2 (2014): 5–20, 8.

15. *See supra* note 6.

16. *Ibid.*

17. *Ibid.*

18. Communalism here is used synonymously with Communitarianism. Communitarianism is a political structure which stresses the importance of kinship and community, along with a sense of common purpose and tradition. In this context, Reilly uses the term communalism to reflect the same ethos as Communitarianism, and so for the purposes of this piece, the commonalities between the two are sufficient to use them synonymously.

19. *See supra* note 6.

20. *Ibid.*

21. *Ibid.*

22. Arend Lijphart, "Consociation Democracy," 2 *World Politics* 207 (1969); Arend Lijphart. "Cultural Diversity and Theories of Political Integration," 4 *Canadian Journal of Political Science* (1971); *see also* Arend Lijphart, *Democracy in plural societies: A comparative exploration.* Yale University Press, 1977; Arend Lijphart, "Consociationalism and Federation: Conceptual and Empirical Links," 12 *Canadian Journal of Political Science* (1979); Arend Lijphart, "Non-Majoritarian Democracy: A Comparison of Federal and Consociational Theories," 15 *Publius* (1985); *see also* Katharine Adeney, "The Limitations of Non-consociational Federalism: The Example of Pakistan," *Ethnopolitics: Formerly Global Review of Ethnopolitics*, 8:1, 87–106, 92–93.

23. Krzysztof Trzciński, "Hybrid power sharing: On how to stabilize the political situation in multi-segmental societies." *Politeja-Pismo Wydziału Studiów Międzynarodowych i Politycznych Uniwersytetu Jagiellońskiego* 15.56 (2018): 85–105, 88.

24. *See supra* note 22 '*Democracy in Plural Societies: A Comparative Exploration,*' 42.

25. *See supra* note 14 at 8.

26. *See supra* note 6.

27. *See Supra* note 23. *See also* S.J Kaufman, "Ethnicity as a Generator of Conflict", in K. Cordell, S. Wolff (eds.), *Routledge Handbook of Ethnic Conflict,* London 2011.

28. *See supra* note 6 at 261.

29. Arend Lijphart, *Patterns of Democracy. Government Forms and Performance in Thirty-Six Countries*. New Haven: Yale University Press 1999, 1.

30. Donald Horowitz, D. Russel, and I. O'flynn (eds)., *Power Sharing: New Challenges for Divided Societies* Pluto Press, 2005, 4.

31. John Gerring and Strom C. Thacker, *A centripetal theory of democratic governance*. Cambridge University Press, 2008, 43.

32. *See supra* note 6.

33. *See supra* note 23 at 91.

34. *See supra* note 31.

35. *See supra* note 11 at 45.

36. *Ibid.* at 51.

37. *Ibid.* at210.

38. *See supra* note 6 at 261.

39. *Ibid.*

40. *Ibid.*

41. Will Kymlicka, *Multicultural citizenship: A liberal theory of minority rights.* Clarendon Press, 1995.

42. Sujit Choudhry, 'Bridging Comparative Politics and Comparative Constitutional Law: Constitutional Design in Divided Societies,' in Sujit Choudhry eds. *Constitutional Design for Divided Societies: Integration or Accommodation*, New York: Oxford University Press, 2008, 39.

43. For instance, the one-million-strong Hazara Shia community situated in the city of Quetta (which is demographically Sunni majority Pathan and Baluchi) immigrated to this territory from Afghanistan and has still not been able to completely integrate itself, with its cultural and language not being granted any local or national recognition. *See* Maisam Iltaf, 'Hazaras Gripped by Religious Extremism in Balochistan,' *Diplomat* (Apr 16, 2019), accessed October 19, 2021, <https://thediplomat.com/2019/04/hazaras-gripped-by-religious-extremism-in-balochistan/>. *See also* Navine Murshid, *The Politics of Refugees in South Asia: Identity, Resistance, Manipulation.* Routledge, 2013; De Wilde, Pieter et al., eds. *The Struggle Over Borders: Cosmopolitanism and Communitarianism.* Cambridge University Press, 2019.

44. Ibrahim Halawi, "Consociational Power-Sharing in the Arab World as Counter-Revolution." *Studies in Ethnicity and Nationalism* 20.2 (2020): 128–36. Toby Dodge, "Iraq's Informal Consociationalism and Its Problems." *Studies in Ethnicity and Nationalism* 20.2 (2020): 145–52. Eduardo Wassim Aboultaif, "Revisiting the semi-consociational model: Democratic failure in prewar Lebanon and post-invasion Iraq." *International Political Science Review* 41.1 (2020): 108–23.

45. Samir Makdisi and Marcus Marktanner, "Trapped by consociationalism: The case of Lebanon." *Topics in Middle Eastern and North African Economies* 11 (2009), 1. Lebanon's consociational system was unable to reduce vertical inequality, and it must be borne in mind that any economic development in post-colonial contexts must include a horizontal dimension. *See* Adib Nehmeh, 'Horizontal and Vertical Expansion of Poverty in Lebanon,' *Alternative Policy Solutions* (Sep 21, 2020), accessed on October 12, 2021 <https://aps.aucegypt.edu/en/articles/511/horizontal-and-vertical-expansion-of-poverty-in-lebanon>.

46. Petros Petrikkos, "Building Bridges in Divided Societies: Sustaining Democratic Transition Through Complex Power-Sharing in Lebanon and Iraq." *Federal Governance* 15.2 (2019): 18–32, 24.

47. Imad Salamey, "Failing consociationalism in Lebanon and integrative options." *International Journal of Peace Studies* (2009): 83–105, 83. ("The consociational system allocated the presidency to a Christian Maronite, the premiership to a Muslim Sunni, and the Speakership to a Muslim Shi'ite. All public offices were corporate according to confessional and sectarian affiliations. They were assigned confessions on the proportional principle of 5 Muslims to every 6 appointed Christians. Along the same confessional office-allocation principle, all elected seats of the National Assembly were divided.") However, this model of consociationalism resulted in the capture of governmental power by the sectarian elite which lacked accountability, undermining a fair electoral process by preventing the participation of independent opponents. The built-in majority for Christians was removed following the 1992 elections, with the 128 seats now equally divided between Muslims and Christians. *See* 'International Religious Freedom Report for 2021,' *United States Department of State—Office of International Religious Freedom*, accessed on November 8, 2022, <https://www.state.gov/wp-content/uploads/2022/04/LEBANON-2021-INTERNATIONAL-RELIGIOUS-FREEDOM-REPORT.pdf>. ("Parliament is elected on equal representation between Christians and Muslims, and cabinet positions must be allocated

on the same basis. Druze and Alawites are included in this allocation within Muslim communities.").

48. *Ibid.* at 84. ("The immediate result was a spread of social and political insecurity among its citizens, forcing sectarian groups to rely on their own social and security networks, and to look for support beyond Lebanon's borders."). *See also infra* note 50.

49. *See supra* note 47.

50. 'Lebanon's confessional system keeps change just out of reach,' *Electoral Reform Society* (Sep 2, 2020), accessed on October 17, 2021, <https://www.electoral-reform.org.uk/lebanons-confessional-system-keeps-change-just-out-of-reach/> ("Lebanon's political system is based around confessionalism, wherein its various religious groups are guaranteed representation relative to their presence across the country's electoral districts, with Parliament's 128 seats split equally between Christians and Muslims and the branches within each of the religions. This differs significantly to other democracies in which seats are specifically reserved for minorities to ensure representation is the face of the majority ethnic group.") *See also supra* note 46 at 24–25. ("Nonetheless, minorities that are often side-lined, like the Lebanese Druze, have become increasingly concerned with the existing consociational framework not giving them a strong voice, as they have become increasingly marginalised.")

51. *Ibid. See also* Renad Mansour, "Iraq's 2018 government formation: unpacking the friction between reform and the status quo." (2019).

52. 'The Kurds' Quest for Independence,' *Council on Foreign Relations*, accessed on October 17, 2021, <https://www.cfr.org/timeline/kurds-quest-independence>.

53. *See supra* note 46 at 26. *See* CONST. of Iraq. Art.70(1): ("The Council of Representatives shall elect a President of the Republic from among the candidates by a two-thirds majority of the number of its members"). *See also* CONST. of Iraq: Art. 76 and 77.

54. *See supra* note 46 at 26. ("The system further increased sectarian tensions. . . .This is evident in the example of 2006, where no federal government was able to be conceived in the period of 3 months, due to a disproportional allocation of seats in the legislative chamber, which prevented the selection of cabinet ministers.")

55. Brigitte Rohwerder, "Reform of consociationalism arrangements in deeply divided societies." *Institute of Development Studies*, 2020.

56. Allison McCulloch and Joanne McEvoy, "'Bumps in the Road Ahead': How External Actors Defuse Power-Sharing Crises." *Journal of Intervention and Statebuilding* 13.2 (2019): 216–35, 217.

57. *See supra* note 55.

58. *See Supra* note 55 at 2. ("Bosnia and Herzegovina is an example of consociationalism arrangement where attempts have been made to reform it through judicial interventions. . . . In 2000, Bosnia's Constitutional Court made the controversial ruling that the constitutions of both Entities had to extend 'constituent peoples' status to all three recognised groups. . . . This introduced reforms that would constitute the upper chambers of the two entities on the basis of parity (regardless of population)

and mandated that government be formed on the basis of proportional representation, moving away from ethnic homogeneity in the Entities.")

59. *Ibid.* at 14. ("The 2000 Arusha agreement marked the end of ethnic civil war in Burundi with a consociational power-sharing arrangement. A major achievement of the agreement was felt to be the 'de-ethnicization of political competition.' However, Vandeginste (2017, 6) details how Burundi's consociational power-sharing arrangement came under increasing threat, against a wider background of democratic backsliding towards a de facto one party state.")

60. *Ibid.* at 10 ("Power-sharing has restarted this week (13th January 2020) with the support of the British and Irish governments, who drafted a New Decade New Approach deal to restart power-sharing and provided substantial sums to sweeten the deal. . . . The governments have provided a compromise 'whereby the rights of Irish speakers are balanced with rights for the Ulster Scots/loyalist tradition.' . . . Unhappiness with the main parties had led to the loss of thousands of votes in the recent general election, which added to the pressure on the parties to return to devolution and power-sharing.")

61. These elements include the concentration of fiscal power in the elite (Lebanon), retention of the confessional system (Lebanon), side-lining minorities in the legislative decisions-making processes and the amplification of sectarian differences by limiting ethnicities to territories (Iraq).

62. For instance, a localized form of centripetalism can target ethnic tensions and divisiveness by guaranteeing greater fiscal autonomy. Additionally, electoral reform can increase chances of political participation by ethnic and religious minorities. Tailored territorial divisions can help in dispersing ethnic concentrations, thereby reducing chances of secessionist movements.

63. Donald L. Horowitz, "The many uses of federalism." *Drake L. Rev.* 55 (2006): 953. John McGarry, Brendan O'Leary, and Richard Simeon, 'Integration or Accommodation? The Enduring Debate in Conflict Regulation', in Sujit Choudhry (ed.), *Constitutional Design For Divided Societies: Integration or Accommodation*, New York: Oxford University Press, 2008.

64. *See supra* note 6 at 261.

65. *Ibid.* at 263.

66. *Ibid.*

67. *Ibid. See infra* note 81.

68. *Ibid.*

69. *Ibid.*

70. Benjamin Reilly, "Cross-ethnic voting: An index of centripetal electoral systems."*Government and Opposition* 56.3 (2021): 465–84, 465.

71. *See infra* note 307.

72. *See supra* note 23 at 91.

73. *See supra* note 63.

74. Donald L. Horowitz, "Ethnic groups in conflict." *University of California* (1985); Horowitz, Donald L. *Ethnic groups in conflict, updated edition with a new preface*. Univ of California Press, 2000.

75. *See supra* note 14.

76. *Ibid.* at 8–9. The adoption of a particular model in conflict-ridden societies is the first core problem according to Horowitz. He cites issues with prescribing inter-ethnic accommodation for divided societies, namely asymmetric preferences, general risk-aversion, negotiators' biases, visibility of interest, and the availability of alternatives.

77. *Ibid.* at 11–12. Horowitz argues that centripetal electoral institutions are degraded by manipulations on behalf of the majority which ensure that they exclusively benefit. These manipulations also cannot be checked by a judiciary which enforces political negotiations.

78. *Ibid.* at 12. He makes the point that consociational arrangements can be difficult to modify and modification is often desired. It is difficult because each participating group is often able to block the claims and demands of other groups, thereby immobilizing the system, a stalemate which may lead to a majority desire to modify the arrangement. This is particularly so once peace has been achieved.

79. *See supra* note 14 at. 15.

80. For Horowitz's discussion with a focus on post-apartheid South Africa, *see* Donald L. Horowitz. *A democratic South Africa?: Constitutional engineering in a divided society*. Vol. 46. University of California Press, 1992.

81. Brian Shoup, *Conflict and cooperation in multi-ethnic states: institutional incentives, myths and counter-balancing*. Routledge, 2007, 27. ("AV systems require voters to rank candidates in order of their preferences. If, after the first round of counting, a candidate has an absolute majority of first-place votes he or she is declared the winner. If no candidate receives a majority of first-place votes, then the candidate with the fewest first-place votes is eliminated and his or her ballots are redistributed according to second preferences. . . . Horowitz argues that the imperatives of reaching across ethnic boundaries to receive enough second- and third-place votes are such that the system will promote moderation by ethnic parties.")

82. *See supra* note 70.

83. *Ibid.*

84. *Ibid.*

85. Donald L. Horowitz, "Electoral Systems a Primer for Decision Makers' *Journal of Democracy* Volume 14 Number 4." (2003), 119–20.

86. *See supra* note 6, n42. ("Horowitz identifies four other mechanisms which characterize his approach to moderating the potentially harmful effects of inter-ethnic competition: arrangements which proliferate the points of power "so as to take the heat off a single focal point", such as a constitutional separation of powers or federalism; devolution or ethnically-reserved offices to foster intra-ethnic conflict at the local level; public policies which encourage the growth of less damaging 'cross-cutting cleavages', such as class identification, to act as counterweights to ethnic identification; and measures which serve to reduce inter-ethnic inequalities and disparities "so that dissatisfaction declines").

87. *Ibid.*

88. *See supra* note 6 at 260.

89. Benjamin Reilly, "Ethnic Representation in Pacific Asia: A Report for the Southeast Asia Rules-Based Order Project." 20.

90. *Ibid.* at 21. ("This "national party" scheme requires parties to have branches and permanent offices in all 34 provinces, in at least 75 percent of the municipalities in each province, and in at least 50 percent of the sub-districts within each municipality. Parties which fail to do so cannot run in national or even local elections. National parties with a cross-regional organizational basis are thus privileged, winnowing the party system over time.")

91. *Ibid.* ("Indonesia's two-stage, double-majority model of presidential elections follows a similar logic, encouraging aspiring presidents to form cross-regional coalitions by requiring the support of a quorum of the legislature in the nomination process. Once past this nomination threshold, presidents are then required to gain not just a majority of the vote, but a spread of votes across different parts of the country in their actual election. Only parties or coalitions controlling 20 percent of lower-house parliamentary seats or winning 25 percent of the popular vote in the preceding parliamentary elections are eligible to nominate a presidential candidate.")

92. *Ibid.* However, this approach can lead to the exclusion of tribal, indigenous and smaller local communities from the political process as they will not have the resources and outreach to compete at the regional level.

93. *Ibid.* at 21. *See also* Marcus Mietzner, 'Comparing Indonesia's Party Systems of the 1950s and the Post-Suharto Era: From Centrifugal to Centripetal Inter-Party Competition'. *Journal of Southeast Asian Studies*, 39(3), 2008 431–53, 431.

94. *Ibid.* For instance to minimize the potential impact of religion towards secession, the region of Aceh ("was exempted from two key national laws as part of a 2005 peace agreement to resolve the long-running separatist conflict. The special autonomy provisions for Aceh permit the application of Sharia Law and also allow local parties to compete in national elections."). *See also* Benjamin Reilly, "Political reform and the demise of consociationalism in Southeast Asia." Palgrave Macmillan, 2011. 114–30. 124. ("Indonesian policymakers have explicitly rejected the orthodoxy that regional governments should be representative of their own constituents. Rather, they have taken the national bias in the electoral system to an extraordinary level: instead of allowing regional governments to be representative of their own constituent populations, the law forces them to be comprised of the same parties which compete at the national level. Indonesia's current party rules are thus the exact opposite of what consociationalists would recommend, and are one of the most extreme versions of centripetal incentives to be found anywhere in the world.").

95. *Supra* note 89 at 24. *See also* Krzysztof Trzciński, 'The Consociational Addition to Indonesia's Centripetalism as a Tactic of the Central Authorities: The Case of Papua,' *Hemispheres: Studies on Cultures and Societies*, 4:31 (2016), 5–20.

96. *See supra note* 94 'Political reform and the demise of consociationalism in Southeast Asia,' 123. ("There, parties and alliances contesting any of the 14 multi-member GRCs must include candidates from designated ethnic minorities on their ticket, and voters must choose between competing party slates rather than individual candidates—arrangements which effectively require a degree of cross-ethnic voting, while guaranteeing that parliamentarians of Chinese ethnicity will retain 3/4 of the parliament's 93 seats, but that at least nine will be occupied by Malays, and five by Indian or other minorities.").

97. *Ibid.* ("Because they make politicians from different parties reciprocally dependent on preference transfers from their rivals, such systems present candidates who wish to maximize their electoral prospects with an incentive to try to attract secondary preference votes from other groups, so as to ensure the broadest possible range of support for their candidacy.").

98. *See* Matthijs Bogaards, "Electoral systems, party systems, and ethnicity in Africa." *Votes, Money and Violence* (2007): 168–93.

99. Allison McCulloch and John McGarry, eds. *Power-sharing: Empirical and normative challenges*. Taylor & Francis, 2017, 27.

100. *Ibid.*

101. Krzysztof Trzciński, "Centripetal Federalism." (2020). 5. ("This rule allows members and representatives of different ethnic groups and religious communities to participate in these bodies. In keeping with the 1999 Constitution of Nigeria (art. 318 [1]), the federal character principle is to promote national unity, support national loyalty, and to give each Nigerian citizen a sense of belonging to the nation, irrespective of ethnic or religious affiliation. Its wider aim is to strengthen the integration of a multi segmental society, to achieve political stability and to facilitate civilizational development.").

102. *Ibid.*

103. *Ibid.* ("the formal federal character principle is supplemented by some informal institutions of consociational type. In Nigeria, the rotation of the presidency between the North and the South (in fact between Muslims and Christians), similarly to that of the presidency and vice-presidency for different religious communities and ethnic groups, increases the balance of power between Muslims and Christians and, at the same time, between the main ethnic groups.").

104. Lijphart describes his theory as an evaluation and reiteration of the model already employed in the Netherlands since 1917. Lijphart explores the two basic causes of divide in Dutch society: class and religion. He then pins his consociational theory based on the "grand coalition" of the four divides/elites under the Dutch system (namely: Calvinist, Socialists, General and Catholics). Lijphart bases his theory on pluralism and how sets of elites came together to attain a workable model in the interest of society. His model promotes national consensus through a mutual veto and proportionality in politics which creates a sense of autonomy allowing the instantiation of individual identity for different segments of society. Lijphart terms Dutch politics as a good example of the politics of accommodation.

105. Arend Lijphart, *The politics of accommodation: Pluralism and democracy in the Netherlands*. Vol. 142. Univ of California Press, 1975.

106. Arend Lijphart, "Consociational democracy." *World politics* 21.02 (1969): 207–25.

107. *See supra* note 22 '*Democracy in plural societies: A comparative exploration.*'

108. *See supra* note 29. Lijphart outlines consensus democracy by using the EU, Belgium and Switzerland as case studies.

109. Brendan O'Leary, "Consociation: What We Know or Think We Know and What We Need to Know." *Conference on National and Ethnic Conflict Regulation at the University of Western Ontario*. 2002. However, these conditions do not reflect the

scenario in Pakistan, where a particular ethnicity commands control over the legislature, army, and the economic infrastructure, causing serious discontent and opposition from other ethnicities.

110. *See supra* note 29.

111. *See supra* notes 22 and 29.

112. *See* Mohammad Mushtar, Ayaz Muhammad and Syed Khawlja Alqama, "Examining the Favorable Factors for Consociational Democracy in Pakistan." *European Journal of Social Sciences*, Volume 20, No. 2 (2011), 277.

113. *See supra* note 22 "Democracy in Plural Societies. A Comparative Exploration." at 82. ("Overarching loyalties are even more important if they provide cohesion for the society as a whole and thus moderate the intensities of all cleavages simultaneously. Nationalism is potentially such a cohesive force. Not only its strength is important, but also the question of whether it truly unites the society or instead acts as an additional cleavage by providing a loyalty to a 'nation' that is not coterminous with the states.").

114. Veena Kukreja, "Ethnic Diversity, Political Aspirations and State Responses: A case Study of Pakistan". *Indian Journal of Public Administration* (2020).

115. *See supra* note 56 at 218. ("External actors—states, international organizations or nongovernmental organizations—often support power-sharing institutions in their efforts to resolve intra-state conflicts. Power-sharing has been facilitated and even imposed by external actors in deeply divided societies ranging from Bosnia and Herzegovina, Burundi, Iraq, Kenya, Lebanon, South Sudan to Macedonia and it has been recommended by external actors for Cyprus, the Democratic Republic of Congo, Liberia, Nepal, and Syria. In many cases, external actors have gone beyond supporting the adoption of power-sharing to playing an integral role in its maintenance.").

116. *See generally* Yunus Samad, "Understanding the insurgency in Balochistan." *Commonwealth & Comparative Politics* 52.2 (2014): 293–320. Mir Sherbaz Khetran, "Indian Interference in Balochistan." *Strategic Studies* 37.3 (2017): 112–25.

117. *See supra* note 74.

118. *See supra* note 14.

119. John McGarry, "Centripetalism, Consociationalism and Cyprus: The "Adoptability" Question." *Political Studies* (2016).

120. *Ibid.* at 2.

121. *Ibid.* at 14 onwards. Specifically, he mentions the importance of "the equality of veto power"—or where a strong minority still holds an equal veto power on policies when confronted by a majority—in maintaining a balance in policies. He also points out that, based on the Cyprus experience, "centripetal electoral systems like the AV or distributive systems are unlikely to be the first preference of political minorities. This is because both electoral systems are biased in favor of majorities. It is also unclear why majority elites would opt for such electoral systems instead of straightforward majoritarian electoral systems such as the two-round run-off system that is commonly used in presidential elections." An additional observation is that "centripetal federalism, with its emphasis on fragmentation, looks infeasible where minorities are nationally mobilized or already enjoy collective self-government and are capable of resisting what they will code as "partition. In contrast, it looks more

feasible where the communities in question are not nationally (collectively) mobilized, where collectively self-governing minorities are too weak to resist, or where fragmented self-government represents the most attainable advance on a centralized status quo."

122. *See infra* note 191.

123. Donald L. Horowitz, "*Constitutional Design: An Oxymoron?*" (2000), 253. ("debates have begun about institutions appropriate to the consolidation of new democracies. Lively controversies have raged about the respective merits of presidential and parliamentary systems, proportional and plurality electoral systems, unitary and federal governments. No sooner have these debates captured the imagination of academicians and policymakers than it has become clear that a peculiar set of problems surrounds the maintenance of democracy in societies severely divided along ethnic lines.")

124. Horowitz describes his model as the "incentives approach" which can adapt to different electoral frameworks by offering electoral incentives and constitutional reforms to tackle group (ethnic) polarization. Horowitz notes: "If the goal is to produce a moderate, interethnic center, it is necessary to provide ethnically based parties with electoral incentives to take moderate positions on issues of interethnic relations and to form electoral alliances and governing coalitions with moderate parties of other ethnic groups."). *Ibid.* at 260.

125. *See supra* note 9 'Federal and Political Party Reforms in Asia: Is There a New Model of Federal Democracy Emerging in Ethnically Diverse Countries in Asia?'at 14.

126. *Ibid.* at 1.

127. *See supra* note 47.

128. *See supra* note 123, at 260. ("Because this approach is designed to reward political leaders for interethnic moderation, sustaining the system, once it is adopted, will be much easier than sustaining consociational arrangements that are based merely on exhortations and constitutional constraints, devoid of political incentives."). For proposed recommendations on a localized model, see the 'Prescriptions' section of this paper.

129. Preserving gender quotas at a local level and continuing the provision of localized justice through jirgas are both communalist strategies, which can be retained in a proposed localized centripetal model, to indigenize it, lend it greater legitimacy, and better embed it within the Pakistani sociocultural context.

130. *See supra* note 23 at 104.

131. Noam Chomsky, *Profit over people: Neoliberalism and global order*. Seven Stories Press, 1999, 22–56. For Chomsky, the corporate giants are nothing but culprits—those that feed off the larger masses. He views them as profit aggrandisement machines which carry out all transactions in impersonal and inhumane ways. He argues that with the advent of neoliberal economic policies, while global profit has certainly maximised, disparity has also astronomically increased as more and more people are now subject to a system of exploitation. This new system, as he suggests, can be fully blamed for reducing the identity of all humans to mere consumers—something that needs to be immediately overturned through the use of social activism.

132. David Harvey, *A brief history of neoliberalism*. Oxford University Press, USA, 2007.

133. Wendy Brown, *Undoing the demos: Neoliberalism's stealth revolution*. Mit Press, 2015.

134. Wendy Brown, *In the ruins of neoliberalism: The rise of antidemocratic politics in the west*. Columbia University Press, 2019.

135. *See Supra* note 132.

136. *See generally* Friedrich A. Von Hayek and Milton Friedman, *The road to serfdom*. Chicago: University of Chicago Press, 1944. For Friedrich Hayek, who is credited with inventing neoliberalism, this state of freedom is not a naturally occurring political state; it has to be created and maintained through a social contract at the local and communal levels. This, according to him, was achieved in early utopic Greek society.

137. Richard L. Harris and Melinda J. Seid, "Critical perspectives on globalization and neoliberalism in the developing countries." *Journal of Developing Societies* 16, no. 1 (2000): 1–26.

138. *See supra* note 132, at 97–167. For critics, neoliberal policies undermine local and communal social systems, while it strengthens elite economic actors through undemocratic venues. Additionally, while neoliberalism ostensibly espouses deregulation and competition at the national levels, at the global and local levels it does not. It has also promoted an imperialist and exploitative ideology. Its hegemonic champions, the United States and China, still both internally operate under the auspices of Keynesian economics, which is illustrated from their present debt burden and the extensive domestic labor regulations they have put in place.

139. *See supra* note 132, at 73.

140. The realization of individual economic rights also requires a strong banking and monetarist system. *See* Denise Mifsud, "'Decentralised' neoliberalism and/or 'masked' re-centralisation? The policy to practice trajectory of Maltese school reform through the lens of neoliberalism and Foucault." *Journal of Education Policy* 31, no. 4 (2016): 443–65. Gillian MacNaughton and Diane F. Frey, eds., Economic and social rights in a neoliberal world. Cambridge University Press, 2018; Audrey Chapman, "Being Bold about Rights in a Neoliberal World." *Health and human rights* 21, no. 1 (2019): 287.

141. 'Bush outlines radical plan to part-nationalise banks,' *Guardian* (Oct 14, 2008), accessed on November 1, 2021 <https://www.theguardian.com/business/2008/oct/14/us-banks-bailout-bush>.

142. Malcolm M. Feeley and Edward L. Rubin, *Federalism: Political identity and tragic compromise*. University of Michigan Press, 2009.

143. *Ibid.*

144. *Ibid.*

145. *See supra* note 142.

146. Refer to discussion ahead on decentralization in Pakistan.

147. Lorenz Blume and Stefan Voigt, "Federalism and decentralization—a critical survey of frequently used indicators." *Constitutional Political Economy* 22, no. 3 (2011): 238–64.

148. *See supra* note 9 'Federal and Political Party Reforms in Asia: Is There a New Model of Federal Democracy Emerging in Ethnically Diverse Countries in Asia?' at 32; Furthermore, constitutional federalism does not imply devolution: there exist numerous alternatives to devolutionary federalism, such as consociational systems and local democracy. *See supra* note 106.

149. A. Cheema, I. Khwaja, and A. Qadir, (2005) Decentralization in Pakistan: Context, Content and Causes. Kennedy School Working Paper Number: RWP05–034. *See also* A Cheema and A. U. Sayeed (2004), 29. ("These reforms have all involved decentralizing from the Province to local levels but often a recentralization at the Federal levels. Our interpretation is that these reforms have been used as a means for a non-representative centre to gain legitimacy by by-passing the political agents at the provincial and national levels.") *See also* "Bureaucracy and Pro-Poor Change," Paper written for the "Pakistan Drivers of Pro-Poor Change Study conducted by Institute of Development Studies UK, Collective for Social Science Research, Karachi. DFID, UK.

150. *Ibid.* at 32. ("While these local governments' future is still uncertain given the lack of constitutional support and conflict with the provincial governments, what is clear is that if they remain, we are likely to see an impact on the delivery of these public services. Whether this will be for the better, as local governments may become more accountable to the general public, or for the worse, if local governments fall into patronage and 'biraderi' politics, remains to be seen.") *See also* Syed Mohammad Ali, Devolution of Power in Pakistan, Special Report 422 for USIP, (2018).

151. *See supra* note 142.

152. *Ibid.* at 41.

153. *See supra* note 149.

154. *See* Mikhail Filippov and Olga Shvetsova, "Federalism, democracy, and democratization." *Federal Dynamics* (2013): 167–84, 167. *See also* Asma-ul-husna [VNV] Faiz. *Making federation work: federalism in Pakistan after the 18th amendment*. 2015.

155. *See generally* Michael J. Klarman, *Brown V. Board of Education and the civil rights movement: Abridged edition of From Jim Crow to civil rights: the Supreme Court and the struggle for racial equality*. Oxford University Press, 2007; Brown v. Board of Education of Topeka, 347 US 483 (1954). The Supreme Court ruled in favor of desegregation in *Brown v. Board of Education*, even though the South had its own distinctively racial policies. Similarly, in Pakistan, the institution most likely to intervene for minority rights within provinces is the Supreme Court; *see* Maryam S Khan, "Ethnic Federalism in Pakistan: Federal Design, Construction of Ethno-Linguistic Identity & Group Conflict." *Harv. J. Racial & Ethnic Just.* 30 (2014): 77.

156. Hamza Rifaat and Tridivesh Singh Maini, 'China-Pakistan Economic Corridor.' *Stimson*, accessed on October 19, 2021, 15 <https://www.stimson.org/wp-content/files/file-attachments/The percent20China-Pakistan percent20Economic percent20Corridor percent20- percent20Final.pdf>. ("Alongside security related challenges to the corridor, Pakistan has witnessed considerable provincial discord regarding CPEC's proposed route. Given that each of Pakistan's four provinces is

ruled by distinct political parties with diverse views on economic prosperity, provincial disagreements are common.").

157. Danish Khan, 'DON'T BELIEVE THE HYPE: NEOLIBERALISM HAS FAILED PAKISTAN', *Center for Popular Economics* (Sep 3, 2015), accessed on October 19, 2021 <www.populareconomics.org/dont-believe-the-hype-neoliberalism-has-failed-pakistan/>. ("What the neoliberal theoretical framework ignores is the fact that a society like Pakistan is highly unequal in terms of wealth/income distribution, gender relations and caste differentiations. As a consequence, when the state does not steer the direction of development, then market forces simply reproduce and reinforce existing realities of Pakistani society, i.e., intensified socio-economic inequalities.").

158. *See* Chapters 1 and 4 (this volume).

159. *See Supra* note 157.

160. Manzoor Ali Khan, 'Stabilisation or overkill,' *SZABIST* accessed on October 19, 2021 <www.szabist.edu.pk/pdf/Stabilisation percent20or percent20overkill.pdf>. ("the PTI government decided to approach the IMF for a bailout package. Some of the IMF conditionalities are fixed and there are a few situational factors, such as the IMF suggesting it wants 'absolute transparency' of Pakistan's debts from China to determine Islamabad's debt sustainability. The Fund has also proposed cuts in the share of the provinces in the NFC award. This means that the IMF wants cuts from funds required for the development of the social sector.")

161. *See* infra—discussion on CPEC's Neoliberal policies and devolutionary federalism in Pakistan.

162. *See supra* note 9 'Federal and Political Party Reforms in Asia: Is There a New Model of Federal Democracy Emerging in Ethnically Diverse Countries in Asia?' at 1.

163. *See supra* notes 41 and 9 'Federal and Political Party Reforms in Asia: Is There a New Model of Federal Democracy Emerging in Ethnically Diverse Countries in Asia?' at 1.

164. *See generally* Ramon Maiz and Safran William, *Identity and Territorial Autonomy in Plural Societies*, Routledge, 2015, 204 ("In 1955, the 'one unit' system was introduced. By this system, a false parity was introduced between East and West Pakistan, by consolidating them into the two federating units in the state. The four constitutive provinces of West Pakistan were merged to create that unit. The idea was that this would help the west balance the numerical dominance of the east. That is, the population of East Bengal was so much larger than that of the provinces in the west that the east would have dominated any federal legislature. By creating two units of equal importance, the potential dominance of the east was diminished. From the perspective of the East, it would now be underrepresented in the federal legislature. On the other hand, regional parties and leaders were unhappy over their displacement as their spheres of influence disappeared overnight. More importantly, 'one unit' meant greater centralization and the result saved no one save the centre.")

165. *See Islamic Republic v. Abdul Wali Khan* PLD 1976 S.C. 57.

166. *See supra* note 9 'Federal and Political Party Reforms in Asia: Is There a New Model of Federal Democracy Emerging in Ethnically Diverse Countries in Asia?' at 1.

167. *Ibid.*

168. Sadaf Aziz, *The Constitution of Pakistan: A Contextual Analysis*. Bloomsbury Publishing, 2018.

169. *Ibid.*

170. I.A. Rehman, 'Provinces vs centre,' *DAWN* (June 11, 2020), accessed October 19, 2021, <https://www.dawn.com/news/1562775>. ("within a few years of independence, the ideal of a federation was smothered by a strong alliance of the upholders of the viceregal system, a power-hungry central bureaucracy, a conservative religious lobby, and a succession of men on horseback. The way Article 92-A was inserted into the provisional constitution, and its use to demolish provincial governments, constitute a regrettable chapter in the history of Pakistan. Although Section 92-A was replaced with Section 93 in 1955, which considerably reduced the arbitrary nature of actions against the provincial governments, federal inroads into provincial autonomy continued till the 1980s. A federation in name, the country was run as a unitary state and its dismemberment was the price paid for this folly.").

171. Following the Twenty-Fifth Amendment to the Constitution of Pakistan 1973, and FATA's merger with KPK, the 4 seats for FATA were removed. 'National Assembly green-lights Fata-KP merger by passing "historic" bill,' *DAWN* (24 May, 2018) https://www.dawn.com/news/1409710 ("Once the bill is passed, the strength of the Senate will reduce from 104 to 96 members as Fata will no longer have separate representation. Likewise, the number of seats in the National Assembly will be cut to 336 from 342. Meanwhile, the KP assembly will have 145 seats, including 115 general, 26 reserved for women and four for minorities. Fata will have 21 seats in the KP Assembly, including 16 general, four for women and one reserved for non-Muslim.").

172. *See* CONST. of PAK. Art59(c): ("two on general seats, and one woman and one technocrat including aalim shall be elected from the Federal Capital in such manner as the President may, by Order, prescribe.").

173. Asid Ezdi, 'Power, People and the Senate,' *News International* (January 26, 2015), accessed on October 19, 2021, <http://www.thenews.com.pk/print/20504-power-people-and-the-senate>.

174. CONST. of PAK. Art. 73(2) (2): ("For the purpose of this Chapter, a Bill or amendment shall be deemed to be a Money Bill if it contains provisions dealing with all or any of the following matters, namely:—(a) the imposition, abolition, remission, alteration or regulation of any tax; (b) the borrowing of money, or the giving of any guarantee, by the Federal government, or the amendment of the law relating to the financial obligations of that Government; (c) the custody of the Federal Consolidated Fund, the payment of moneys into, or the issue of moneys from, that Fund; (d) the imposition of a charge upon the Federal Consolidated Fund, or the abolition or alteration of any such charge; (e) the receipt of moneys on account of the Public Account of the Federation, the custody or issue of such moneys; (f) the audit of the accounts of the Federal Government or a Provincial Government; and (g) any matter incidental to any of the matters specified in the preceding paragraphs.").

175. Hassan Niazi, 'Senate reform,' *Express Tribune* (Feb 01, 2021), accessed on October 19, 2021, <https://tribune.com.pk/story/2282260/senate-reform>.

176. *See generally* Tahid Mahmood, 'A Comparative Analysis of the Functioning of the Senate in USA and Pakistan,' *South Asian Studies—A Research Journal of South Asian Studies* 30:2 (2015), 265–62.

177. CONST. of PAK. Art. 70(3): ("If a Bill transmitted to a House under clause (1) is rejected or is not passed within ninety days of its laying in the House or a Bill sent to a House under clause (2) with amendments is not passed by that House with such amendments, the Bill, at the request of the House in which it originated, shall be considered in a joint sitting and if passed by the votes of the majority of the members present and voting in the joint sitting it shall be presented to the President for assent.").

178. Raja Rafi and Nadeem Ul Haque, 'Electoral Systems,' *News International* (Apr 20, 2021), accessed on October 19, 2021, <https://www.thenews.com.pk/print/822809-electoral-systems>. ("For example, in the last two general elections for the National Assembly (NA), the PML-N (2013) and the PTI (2018) won 33 percent and 32 percent of votes respectively and yet were able to form majority governments by bringing in independent winning candidates and MNAs from various regional parties. In simpler terms, it means that every two out of three of those people who cast their votes did not vote for the party that eventually formed the government in both 2013 and 2018.").

179. *Ibid.*

180. Benjamin Reilly, "Electoral systems for divided societies." *Journal of Democracy* 13.2 (2002): 156–70.

181. *Ibid.* at 157–58. ("AV is a majoritarian system used in single-member electoral districts that requires the winning candidate to gain not just a plurality but an absolute majority of votes. If no candidate has an absolute majority of first preferences, the candidate with the lowest number of first-preference votes is eliminated and his or her ballots are redistributed to the remaining candidates according to the lower preferences marked. . . STV, by contrast, is a proportional system based around multimember districts that. . . . Voters rank candidates in order of preference on the ballot in the same manner as AV. The count begins by determining the "quota" of votes required to elect a single candidate. Any candidate who has more first preferences than the quota is immediately elected. If no one has achieved the quota, the candidate with the lowest number of first preferences is eliminated, and his or her second and later preferences are redistributed to the candidates left in the race. At the same time, the "surplus" votes of elected candidates (that is, their votes above the quota) are redistributed at a reduced value according to the lower preferences on the ballots, until all seats for the constituency are filled.").

182. *Ibid.* at 163. However, the 2001 election following military rule, produced varied results. Although it broke the imbalance in favor of the labour party (compared to the 1999 election), but it also reduced cross ethnic voting.

183. Benjamin Reilly, "Papua New Guinea: Electoral Incentives for Inter-Ethnic Accommodation." *The International IDEA Handbook of Electoral System Design* (1997): 40–42.

184. The Electoral Knowledge Network, accessed on October 19, 2021 <https://aceproject.org/ace-en/topics/es/annex/esy/esy_pg/mobile_browsing/onePag>. ("The

different incentives provided by the new FPTP system led to quite different results from those expected. . . . There was no incentive to cooperate with anyone else. Electoral violence increased because it was in some candidates' interests to stop opponents' supporters from voting rather than to campaign for their second preferences as they had done under AV. Also, because there were so many clans all trying to win the seat, candidates learned that they could be successful with very limited support.") *See also supra* note 180 at 166 ("With no incentives for cooperation, elections almost immediately became zero-sum contests between rival tribal groups. Most seats were contested by scores of clan-backed candidates, resulting in winners being elected on the basis of increasingly minuscule vote shares. At the most recent national election in 1997, over half of all seats were won with less than 20 percent of the vote, and 15 with less than 10 percent.").

185. *Ibid.*

186. *See* CONST. of PAK. Art. 213–26.

187. 'Reforming Pakistan's Electoral System,' *International Crisis Group* (30 March, 2011), accessed on October 19, 2021 <https://www.crisisgroup.org/asia/south-asia/pakistan/reforming-pakistan-s-electoral-system>. ("Highly inaccurate voters lists are responsible for disenfranchising millions. Polling procedures are often manipulated; accountability mechanisms for candidates and political parties seldom employed; and the electoral code of conduct routinely flouted. Dysfunctional election tribunals, characterised by corruption and prolonged delays, prove incapable of resolving post-election disputes. . . . Many discriminatory laws remain in place, including easily manipulated qualification criteria requiring electoral candidates to be of good Islamic character.").

188. *Ibid.* ("General Pervez Musharraf's eight-year rule gravely eroded the ECP's already limited independence, impartiality and competence, reducing the institution to providing a façade of legitimacy to military rule. Handpicked chief election commissioners (CECs) oversaw widespread rigging of two local government elections, a presidential referendum, and a general election. Musharraf's Legal Framework Order, enshrined in the constitution though the seventeenth amendment, massively distorted the political system, tilting the electoral playing field towards the military's civilian allies, including the Islamist parties.").

189. *Ibid.* ("The amendment package enhanced the ECP's independence by making the appointment of its key officials more transparent and subject to parliamentary oversight. The CEC and other ECP members, previously appointed by the president, will now be selected through consultations between the prime minister and the leader of the opposition in the National Assembly, and subsequently vetted and approved by a joint parliamentary committee comprising, equally, government and opposition members.").

190. *See supra* note 168 at 152–76. The Eighteenth Amendment abolished the previously controlling Concurrent Legislative List (CLL), which enumerated the concurrent powers and jurisdiction of both the federation and the provinces over various subject matters, and has now replaced it with a list enumerating federal powers, while vesting all residual powers in the provinces.

191. Ijaz Nabi and Hina Shaikh, "Fiscal Federalism in Pakistan: A radical departure and some new challenges." *Development Policy Research Center Working Paper, LUMS, Lahore* (2010), 9. ("Under the seventh NFC award, provinces could raise domestic and foreign loans with the approval of the National Economic Council. Additionally, the share of each province was determined by considering four key indicators namely HDI, backwardness and poverty, revenue collection and generation, inverse population density (IPD), and revenue generation–was weighted 82 percent, 10.3 percent, 5 percent, and 2.7 percent respectively. The provinces remain dependent on the NFC award to overcome the deficit in their expenditure and revenue potential, with the provinces accounting for a 57.5 percent share of the total resources distributed. The award was well-received by provinces because it froze each province's share for the duration of its five-year tenure and allocated greater funding to previously neglected provinces such as Balochistan.").

192. Katharine Adeney, *Federalism and ethnic conflict regulation in India and Pakistan*. Springer, 2016.

193. Farhan Hanif Siddiqi. *The politics of ethnicity in Pakistan: the Baloch, Sindhi and Mohajir ethnic movements*. Routledge, 2012.

194. Katherine Adeney, "A step towards inclusive federalism in Pakistan? The politics of the 18th amendment." *Publius: The Journal of Federalism* 42, no. 4 (2012): 539–65. "18th Amendment vital avenue to get Seraiki province," *DAWN* (May 9, 2020), accessed on October 17, 2021, <https://www.dawn.com/news/1555645/18th-amendment-vital-avenue-to-get-seraiki-province>.

195. Nighat Bilgrami Jaffery and Mahpara Sadaqat, "NFC awards: commentary and agenda." *Pakistan Economic and Social Review* (2006): 209–34.

196. *See supra* note114. Pakistan's attempts at the devolution process have also favored the Punjabis: the dominant ethno-national group has consistently maintained its primacy in the federal government, the country's armed forces and the civil bureaucracy. 'The origin and politics of the Seraiki movement' *DAWN* (24 May, 2009), accessed on October 17, 2021. https://www.dawn.com/news/881086/the-origin-and-politics-of-the-seraiki-movement.

197. '8th NFC Award: Provinces demand more tax revenue from Centre,' *Express Tribune* (29 Apr, 2015), accessed on October 19, 2021, <https://tribune.com.pk/story/877678/8th-nfc-award-provinces-demand-more-tax-revenue-from-centre/>.

198. *See* Aneela Salman, *Decentralization in Pakistan: Lessons and Challenges*, University of Albany, SUNY, 2012.

199. *See infra* note 201.

200. *Ibid.*

201. M. Malik and Ahsan Rana, "The History of Local Governance in Pakistan: What Lessons to Learn?" (2019), 34. ("The major distinction of the Local Government Ordinance (LGO) 2001 compared to previous ordinances was that it overcame the urban-rural divide and established the local government at three levels: Union Council, Tehsil Council, and District Council. . . . The LGO removed the previously existing hierarchical relationship between the local and provincial governments. Local governments were instead directly linked to the President's office through several institutions, such as the National Reconstruction Bureau and

the Devolution Trust for Community Empowerment. . . . Despite several distinctions, however, the LGO 2001 had some similarities with previous local government systems. For example, Musharraf also followed the legacy of previous military regimes and conducted local government elections on the non-party basis that further entrenched the politics of personalised patronage based on clan and caste loyalties. Moreover, though Musharraf gave a short-term constitutional status to the local government up till 2009 through a Presidential Order . . . the local governments were still not given a constitutional status permanently.").

202. *Ibid.*

203. *Ibid.*

204. Ali Cheema, Adnan Q. Khan, and Roger, B. Myerson, *Breaking the Counter Cyclical Pattern of Democracy in Pakistan* (2014), accessed on October 19, 2021, <http://home.uchicago.edu/~rmyerson/research/pakdemoc.pdf>.

205. *Ibid.*

206. 'Devolution matters,' *News International* (Aug 27, 2021), accessed on October 19, 2021, <https://www.thenews.com.pk/print/883591-devolution-matters>.

207. *See supra* note 204.

208. *Ibid.*

209. *Ibid.*

210. A *tehsil* is a local unit of administrative division in some South Asian countries, including Pakistan.

211. *See supra* note 198.

212. *Ibid.*

213. *Ibid*

214. *Ibid.* Specifically: Punjab, for example, provides for direct elections for the posts of chairmen and vice chairmen of its union councils, whereas Sindh envisages indirect election of these officials via its councilors. KP provides for direct elections for all seats—including those reserved for women and minorities—in the village and neighborhood councils, whereas in other provinces reserved seat members are selected indirectly.

215. *See supra* note 155 'Ethnic Federalism in Pakistan: Federal Design, Construction of Ethno-Linguistic Identity & Group Conflict.'

216. *See* Syed Mohammad Ali, "Devolution of power in Pakistan," *United States Institute of Peace* (2018) Special Report 422, accessed on October 19, 2021, <https://www.usip.org/publications/2018/03/devolution-power-pakistan>.

217. *See* chapter 3 (discussion on the military's involvement and control over CPEC).

218. Geoff Brown, "Pakistan: failing state or neoliberalism in crisis?" *International Socialism: A Quarterly Review of Socialist Theory* 150 (2016).

219. Muhammad Shoaib Butt and Jayatilleke S. Bandara, *Trade liberalisation and regional disparity in Pakistan*. Routledge, 2008, 24–30.

220. *Ibid.*

221. *See generally supra* note 149.

222. *See* Ayesha Siddiqua, *Military Inc.: Inside Pakistan's military economy*. Penguin Random House India, 2017.The Military's role is to aid the federal government

in the protection of its citizens, instead it engages in its own neoliberal exploits weakening civilian institutions through their military prerogative, Ayesha Siddiqa refers to this as 'Milbus.' *See also* Christophe Jaffrelot, *Pakistan at the Crossroads: Domestic Dynamics and External Pressures*. Random House India, 2016, 24–49.

223. *See* Chapter 3 (this volume).

224. Marking a watershed moment in the country's constitutional history, the Eighteenth Amendment allowed for factors other than population to be taken into account by the center when allocating resources to the federating units. Further, in abolishing the Concurrent List, the Eighteenth Amendment created the Federal Legislative List which devolved legislative competencies to the provinces. Part 1 of the list identifies subjects controlled by the center, while Part 2 lists those that fall under the competency of the Council of Common Interests and also includes subjects of relevance to the CPEC, including electricity, railways, ports, and national planning.

225. *See* Andrew Small, *The China Pakistan axis: Asia's new geopolitics*. Random House India, 2015.

226. *See* Siegfried O Wolf, *The China-Pakistan Economic Corridor of the Belt and Road Initiative*. Springer International Publishing, 2020. These comprise projects dealing with investment and energy, including fiber optic links, railway tracks, gas and oil pipelines, and so forth.

227. Syed Irfan Raza, "Senators Say CPEC Turned into 'China-Punjab' Corridor," *DAWN* (Nov 24, 2015), accessed on October 19, 2021, <https://www.dawn.com/news/1221849>.

228. There is no provincial role for Constitutional Amendments unless an amendment is altering the boundaries of a province. CONST of. PAK. Art. 238: Amendment of Constitution. Subject to this Part, the Constitution may be amended by Act of [Majlis-e-Shoora (Parliament); CONST. of PAK. Art. 239: ("Constitution Amendment Bill. (1) A Bill to amend the Constitution may originate in either House and, when the Bill has been passed by the votes of not less than two-thirds of the total membership of the House, it shall be transmitted to the other House. (2) If the Bill is passed without amendment by the votes of not less than two-thirds of the total membership of the House to which it is transmitted under clause (1), it shall, subject to the provisions of clause (4), be presented to the President for assent. (3) If the Bill is passed with amendment by the votes of not less than two-thirds of the total membership of the House to which it is transmitted under clause (1), it shall be reconsidered by the House in which it had originated, and if the Bill as amended by the former House is passed by the latter by the votes of not less than two-thirds of its total membership it shall, subject to the provisions of clause (4), be presented to the President for assent. (4) A Bill to amend the Constitution which would have the effect of altering the limits of a Province shall not be presented to the President for assent unless it has been passed by the Provincial Assembly of that Province by the votes of not less than two-thirds of its total membership. (5) No amendment of the Constitution shall be called in question in any court on any ground whatsoever. (6) For the removal of doubt, it is hereby declared that there is no limitation whatever on the power of the Majlis-e-Shoora (Parliament) to amend any of the provisions of the Constitution.").

229. Karim Khan and Saba Anwar, "Special economic zones (SEZs) and CPEC: Background, challenges and strategies." *Pakistan Development Review* (2016): 203–16. These SEZs operate with different regulatory and fiscal regimes than the rest of the country which are typically more liberal and administratively efficient.

230. Asifa Jahangir, Omair Haroon, and Arif Masud Mirza, "Special Economic Zones under the CPEC and the Belt and Road Initiative: Parameters, Challenges and Prospects," in *China's Belt and Road Initiative in a Global Context*, Palgrave Macmillan, 2020, 289–328.

231. The Pakistani constitutional framework already allows for the selective application of its fundamental rights; while article 8 of the constitution nullifies any laws "inconsistent with or in derogation" of the fundamental rights guaranteed by Chapter 1 of the constitution, the article goes on to explicitly exempt a number of legislative instruments—listed in the First Schedule to the constitution—from this proscription. Further, Pakistan's constitutional history is replete with instances where the superior judiciary has either interpreted these constitutional liberties in a highly restrictive manner, or has outright justified 'exceptions' to their application.

232. Filippo Boni and Katharine Adeney, "The Impact of the China-Pakistan Economic Corridor on Pakistan's Federal System: The Politics of the CPEC." *Asian Survey* 60.3 (2020): 441–65, 449.

233. *Ibid.*

234. *See supra* notes 190 and 191.

235. CONST. of. PAK. Art. 1.

236. CONST. of PAK. Art 2.

237. CONST. of PAK. Art. 228. *See generally* Ahmed Mahmood Zahid, 'Institutional Analysis of Council of Common Interests' (Dec 2013), accessed on October 19, 2021. <http://www.pk.undp.org/content/dam/pakistan/docs/Democratic percent-20Governance/Federalism/CCI percent20Manual percent20(1).pdf>.

238. 'RELIGION, NATIONALISM AND INSURGENCY IN BALOCHISTAN,' *DAWN* (14 Jul, 2019), accessed on October 19, 2021, <https://www.dawn.com/news/1493929>. ("But religion is reshaping the socio-political ethos of the province and the state is also using religion as a tool to glue disparate groups together. The establishment feels easy using religious actors and it feels it has mastered this art," says Zulfiqar explaining "why the establishment does not instead engage with other aggrieved segments of society.") *See generally* Sheikh Md Ziaul Haque and Zahid Shahab Ahmed. "Military, authoritarianism and Islam: A comparative analysis of Bangladesh and Pakistan." *Politics and Religion* 13.2 (2020): 333–60.

239. Mark Tushnet and Madhav Khosla, eds., *Unstable constitutionalism: Law and politics in South Asia*. Cambridge University Press, 2015, 291.

240. *Ibid.* at 75. (It is interesting to note the parallel with the construction of Pakistan's new Islamic capital of Islamabad in Punjab between 1959 and 1963 under General Ayub Khan's regime (1958–1969) and the promulgation in the same period of a new constitution in 1962. It is significant that in Ayub's Islamabad—as in Panchayat-era Kathmandu—the fulcrum of the capitol and of political authority was the seat of the Head of State.").

241. Llyod I. Rudolph and Susanne Hoeber Rudolph, "Federalism as state formation in India: A theory of shared and negotiated sovereignty." *International Political Science Review* 31.5 (2010): 553–72.

242. *Ibid.* at 560.

243. *Ibid.* ("Lord Ripon, Viceroy from 1880 to 1884, introduced elected municipal councils and rural district boards. As Ripon saw it, India lacked indigenous local government institutions. These British-style arrangements would introduce 'a measure of political and popular education.").

244. *Ibid.* at 561. ("by enlarging their non-official membership and allowing them to discuss financial matters. Although those seeking movement toward 'responsible government' found their expectations disappointed, the Morley–Minto reforms kept alive and marginally strengthened federal state formation in India.").

245. *See* Government of India Act 1935.

246. *See supra* note 241 at 563.

247. *Ibid.*

248. *Ibid.* at 564. *See also* Ayesha Jalal, *The sole spokesman: Jinnah, the Muslim League and the demand for Pakistan.* No. 31. Cambridge University Press, 1994, 38. ("there seemed little point in paying much heed to the League—an assessment which seemed reasonable enough in the first flush of victory in 1937, but one which was to prove to be one of the gravest miscalculations by the Congress leadership in its long history.").

249. *Ibid.*

250. The Electoral Knowledge Network, accessed on October 19, 2021, <https://aceproject.org/main/english/es/esy_in.htm> ("the FPTP electoral system resulted in the ruling Congress party securing stable majorities in the Lok Sabha, usually against a fragmented opposition. But since 1977, when the opposition parties combined to form coalitions and started putting up common candidates against the Congress candidates [as was the case in the 1977 and 1989 general elections], the Congress majorities have vanished. . . . The overall results of elections to the Lok Sabha have never been proportional. Because the candidate who obtains the most votes, but not necessarily a majority of votes polled, is declared elected, support can often be divided by setting candidates of the same caste, religion, or region against each other.").

251. *Ibid.* ("Minority Provisions. The Indian Constitution reserves 22 percent of all seats for historically disadvantaged groups known as Scheduled Castes [79 reserved seats] and Scheduled Tribes [41 reserved seats]. In these constituencies, only a member of the Scheduled Castes or Tribes may contest the polls, although all electors have voting rights. This has ensured that their parliamentary representation is in line with their proportion of the population.").

252. *Ibid. See also* 'Why India Needs to Change its Electoral Voting System,' *Caravan* (13 Sept, 2017), accessed on October 19, 2021, <https://caravanmagazine.in/vantage/why-india-needs-to-change-its-electoral-voting-system>. ("It is increasingly becoming clear that the first-past-the-post system of voting is fraught with serious problems. In the 2014 Lok Sabha elections, despite the 'Modi wave,' only 37 percent of the elected candidates, or 201 MPs, obtained a majority of the votes in the elections. In the 2009 elections, only 22 percent, or 120 MLAs, had secured a majority.

. . . These instances reflect the main shortcoming of the FPTP system—the lack of legitimacy of political parties who are voted to a majority of seats by a minority of voters. . . . Another consequence of the winner-takes-all nature of the FPTP system is that it rewards parties who target and treat preferentially specific segments of the electorate, or 'vote banks,' rather than the majority of electors.").

253. 'Case for direct Senate elections' *DAWN* (13 March, 2018), accessed on October 19, 2021 <https://www.dawn.com/news/1394959>. ("Rule 39AA of the elections to the Rajya Sabha requires the electors to show their marked ballots to their party's polling agent. Even if we ignore the debate on the political freedom of elected members that this rule restricts, it has had a limited impact on corruption. The rule does not obviously apply to independents, or members of the smaller parties that lack numbers to propel their own candidate consider themselves free to sell their vote to the highest bidder.").

254. *See supra* note 239 at 296.

255. Damodar Adhikari. "Nepal's Road to Federalism: From the Perspective of Grassroots Democracy." RTI International, NC (2020), 7, accessed on October 19, 2021, <https://www.rti.org/publication/nepal percentE2 percent80 percent99s-road-federalism/fulltext.pdf>. ("The Constitution established a federal structure with multi-level governance consisting of three spheres of government—Federal (sangh), State/Province (pradesh) and Local Level (palika). Each sphere of government has exclusive power in some areas and concurrent powers in others. All levels are expected to work in harmony as per the constitutional principles of cooperation, coordination and coexistence.").

256. 'Nepal's fight for federalism, Asia and the Pacific Policy Society,' *Policy Forum* (26 March 2019), accessed on October 19, 2021, <https://www.policyforum.net/nepals-fight-for-federalism/>.

257. *See supra* note 241 at 565. *See also* Douglas A. Irwin, "India's trade reforms 30 years later: Great start but stalling," *Peterson Institute of International Economics* (July 22, 2021), accessed on October 19, 2021, <https://www.piie.com/blogs/trade-and-investment-policy-watch/indias-trade-reforms-30-years-later-great-start-stalling> ("India devalued the rupee and moved toward a flexible exchange rate and current account convertibility. It extensively dismantled the license raj that had blocked imports and made exports uncompetitive, while unshackling constraints on domestic investment that limited competition. It also took steps to open the economy to foreign investment.").

258. *Ibid.*

259. *See* Rekha Saxena and Wilfried Swenden, "The Indian Supreme Court and federalism." *Federalism Regionalism* (2017). ("One may assume that the political climate which had become more favorable to state rights since the 1990s enabled the Supreme Court to adopt more state-favorable positions in those recent rulings. In contrast, the Court has upheld a restrictive reading of the powers of the states in treaty-making powers, state reorganization and [of increasing relevance but beyond the purview of this paper] in matters of national security.").

260. *Ibid.* ("In State of West Bengal vs. Union of India [1963], the state challenged the constitutionality of the Coal Bearing Areas [Acquisition and Development] Act

[1957] enacted by the Parliament because the ownership of the land was vested in the state government. The Supreme Court ruled that the state right in the matter was subject to the Union right and national interest under the Constitution. . . . In a more recent case, *State of West Bengal vs. Keshoram Industries Ltd.* [plus a group of similar cases 2004], the Supreme Court examined the constitutional allocation of legislative and taxation powers between the Union and the States at great length. . . . (2) The Union's power to regulate and control does not result in depriving the States of their power to levy tax or a fee within their legislative competence without trenching upon the field of regulation and control (3) Every effort should be made as far as possible to reconcile the seeming conflict between the provisions of the state legislation and the union legislation.'").

261. *Ibid.*

262. Under Art. 184, the Supreme Court of Pakistan has original jurisdiction in case of a dispute between the Federal and Provincial governments. However, the jurisdiction is limited to pronouncing declaratory judgments only and therefore cannot provide a remedy to the provincial party. (*See* CONST. of PAK. Art 184[2]); for the Supreme Court of Pakistan's inclination towards a historically centralized model, *see also* Hassan Niazi, 'The 18th Amendment and the Supreme Court,' *Express Tribune* (19 May 2020), accessed on October 19, 2021, <https://tribune.com.pk/story/2224292/18th-amendment-supreme-court>.

263. *Ibid.* 'The 18th Amendment and the Supreme Court.'

264. *See supra* note 256.

265. *See supra* note 239 at 302.

266. Ranjanee De Alwis. "Federalism or devolution of power? Sri Lanka's perspectives." *Asia & the Pacific Policy Studies* 7.1 (2020): 124–30. ("The 13th Amendment to 1978 Constitution of Sri Lanka indicates the 'devolved subjects' to the provincial councils under List I, while categorizing the 'reserved subjects' for the central government under List II. This specifies the reserved subjects as 'national policy on all subjects and functions.' The List III specifies the 'concurrent subjects' those concurrently managed by the centre and the provinces. According to Gunawardena (n.d.), 'national policy on all subjects and functions' in the List II has been always interpreted by the centre to control the actions of provincial councils. Duplication of work and lack of clarity in devolved functions hinder effective service delivery. Further, lack of effective authority over finances and human resources and lack of skills in enactment of statutes by provincial staff have contributed to weakened provincial administration. According to the World Bank [The World Bank, 2003], Sri Lanka's provincial councils depend on the centre for more than 80 percent of its financing.").

267. *Ibid. See also* De Alwis, R. K, "The history of and prospects for public sector reforms in Sri Lanka." (2009).

268. 'Bangladesh: In Quest of a Decentralised Local Representative Bodies', *Urbanet* (4 Aug, 2020), accessed on October 19, 2021 <https://www.urbanet.info/bangladesh-in-quest-of-a-decentralised-local-representative-bodies/>.

269. *Ibid. See also* 'Are Bangladesh's local government bodies democratic?' *LSE Blogs* (24 Nov, 2017), accessed on October 19, 2021 <https://blogs.lse.ac.uk/southasia/2017/11/24/are-bangladeshs-local-government-bodies-democratic/>.

270. *Ibid.* ("As stipulated in the Upazila Parishad Act 2009, it is acceptable that Members of Parliament (MPs) act as advisers to the local government bodies if they are watchful of the wellbeing of the people in his/her constituency. However, the reality suggests that the 'advice' of MPs often turns into an 'executive order,' letting them override and control the development planning and actions by the elected representatives at the UP.").

271. *See supra* notes 262 and 263.

272. 'Please Mind The Gap: Winners and Losers of Neoliberalism in India,' *E-International Relations* (11 Mar, 2017), accessed on October 19, 2021, <https://www.e-ir.info/2017/03/11/please-mind-the-gap-winners-and-losers-of-neoliberalism-in-india/>. ("Neoliberalism in India, far from alleviating poverty and encouraging sustainable development, has only widened the inequality gap, created a staggering number of losers, roughly the entire agrarian population and majority of the country. In return, the winning minority, the business elites who promoted the country's economic liberalisation in the first place, knew that it would increase their wealth and social and political influence.").

273. 'Neoliberalism is killing the very idea of citizenship in India,' *Quartz India* (2 Sept 2019), accessed on October 19, 2021, <https://qz.com/india/1700542/neoliberalism-is-killing-the-very-idea-of-citizenship-in-india/>.

274. 'Poverty of Vision: Neglecting growing class inequality in post-war Sri Lanka?' *LSE Blogs* (30 Oct, 2019), accessed on October 19, 2021, <https://blogs.lse.ac.uk/southasia/2019/10/30/poverty-of-vision-neglecting-growing-class-inequality-in-post-war-sri-lanka/>.

275. 'The Belt and Road in Sri Lanka: Beyond the Debt Trap Discussion,' *Diplomat* (7 May, 2020), accessed on October 19, 2021, <https://thediplomat.com/2020/05/the-belt-and-road-in-sri-lanka-beyond-the-debt-trap-discussion/.>

276. Arend Lijphart, "The puzzle of Indian democracy: A consociational interpretation." *American political science review* 90.2 (1996): 258–68. ("India has been the one major deviant case for consociational (power-sharing) theory, and its sheer size makes the exception especially damaging. A deeply divided society with, supposedly, a mainly majoritarian type of democracy, India nevertheless has been able to maintain its democratic system. Careful examination reveals, however, that Indian democracy has displayed all four crucial elements of power-sharing theory. In fact, it was a perfectly and thoroughly consociational system during its first two decades. From the late 1960s on, although India has remained basically consociational, some of its power-sharing elements have weakened under the pressure of greater mass mobilization.").

277. Katharine Adeney and Wilfried Swenden, "Power-sharing in the world's largest democracy: Informal consociationalism in India (and its decline?)." *Swiss Political Science Review* 25.4 (2019): 450–75.

278. Ambar Kumar Ghosh, "The Paradox of 'Centralised Federalism': An Analysis of the Challenges to India's Federal Design." (2020).

279. *Ibid.*

280. As outlined earlier, the NFC award has often been contested by the smaller provinces in Pakistan due to favourable shares routed towards Punjab. *See generally*

'It Is High Time We Revisited the NFC Awards in Pakistan,' *PIDE BLOG* (19 May, 2021), accessed on October 19, 2021 <https://pide.org.pk/blog/it-is-high-time-we-revisited-the-nfc-awards-in-pakistan/>.

281. Katharine Adeney, "Centrifugal and centripetal elements of Indian federalism." *Indien heute: Bennpunkte seiner Innenpolitik* (India today: domestic priorities), Hanns Seidel Stiftung, Munich (2003): 47–54. Local government reforms in Pakistan can also offer a forum for accommodating rights of minority and vulnerable groups in a cooperative setting without fanning ethnic competition.

282. *See supra* note 155 'Ethnic Federalism in Pakistan: Federal Design, Construction of Ethno-Linguistic Identity & Group Conflict.'

283. *Ibid.*

284. CONST. of PAK. Part 2, Chapter II.

285. *See* Ikram Ullah, "Reko Diq Case: Another Intervention from Supreme Court of Pakistan." *International Arbitration Law Review* 17, no. 6 (2014): N61–N64; Maulana Abdul Haque Baloch v Government of Balochistan PLD 2013 SC 641 (Reko Diq case). Reko Diq; the Government of Balochistan entered into an agreement with the Tethyan Copper Company which was later struck down by the Supreme Court.

286. *See supra* note 9 'Federal and Political Party Reforms in Asia: Is There a New Model of Federal Democracy Emerging in Ethnically Diverse Countries in Asia?' at 6. In comparison to other South Asian countries Michael G. Breen notes: ("Pakistan has an ethnofederal system, but it is not ethnoterritorial because the largest group [Punjabi and before that Bengali] has been consolidated in one province.")

287. Based on the discussion above, it is apparent that Punjabi hegemony is due to the concentration of population in one province. Namwar Yusuf Rahman, *Punjabi Domination and the Biopolitics of the Census and Statistics in Pakistan*. Diss. Central European University, 2018.

288. *See* Allison McCulloch and John McGarry, "Seeking stability amid deep division: consociationalism and centripetalism in comparative perspective." (2009), 105. ("The federal arrangement... did work to "break up the hegemony of Nigeria's largest ethnic groups" that had been so pronounced under the First Republic. Under the new system, the three main groups were spread out across dozens of new states; this did constrain their ability to dominate the centre").

289. *See* CONST. of PAK Art. 15: ("Freedom of movement, etc.—Every citizen shall have the right to remain in, and, subject, to any reasonable restriction imposed by law in the public interest, enter and move freely throughout Pakistan and to reside and settle in any part thereof.")

290. *See* Moonis Ahmar, "The Dynamics of Pakistan's Intra-National Security: The Role of the New Provinces." *India Quarterly*, Volume 72. No.1. (2016). The demand for disparate provinces extends beyond dividing Punjab to create Janoobi (southern) Punjab, comprising Bahawalpur, and the Saraiki regions around it. There is a simultaneous call for a disparate Hazara Province in KPK, and for the creation of Southern Sindh, covering the regions of Karachi and Hyderabad. There are also talks of the division of Balochistan along Baluch and Pashtun Lines. The creation of these provinces will not only have the significantly positive outcome of discouraging power disparities by empowering local governments, and ethnically-motivated

decision-making at federal and state levels, but also will increase decentralization and improve and ease administration of public services.

291. Manzoor Ahmed, "Fiscal decentralisation and political economy of poverty reduction: Theory and evidence from Pakistan." Diss. Durham University, 2013, 152. ("the biggest objection of other provinces has been that the population should not be the sole criterion for horizontal resource distribution. And retreating to the current Award inherently implies the perpetuation of population-based distribution that obviously advantages the Punjab. Thus, in a game theoretic framework the Punjab being an influential stakeholder frustrates any move driving to diversify the distributional criteria.").

292. *See supra* note 183.

293. *See supra* note 288 at 50. ("Because AV is both majoritarian and preferential, political leaders in heterogeneous polities will have to campaign outside their own ethnic group to receive enough votes to get elected. To capture the lower-ranked votes of members of other groups, they will have to make explicit cross-ethnic appeals and in so doing will have to moderate their own claims and broaden their platforms. AV is further desirable, its advocates argue, because it empowers supporters of candidates unlikely to get elected as they can still influence the election of a majority candidate with their preference votes. This creates a scenario in which minorities help to get moderates from the majority elected. The majority is thus dependent on minority support and must accordingly take their demands seriously to enhance its own electoral success.").

294. *See supra* note 86 at 20–21. ("Indonesian parties are today required by law to establish an organizational network across the nation's vast archipelago, no easy task in a nation of 17,000 islands. . . . This 'national party' scheme requires parties to have branches and permanent offices in all 34 provinces, in at least 75 percent of the municipalities in each province, and in at least 50 percent of the sub-districts within each municipality. Parties which fail to do so cannot run in national or even local elections.").

295. *See* CONST. of Pak. Art 59: ("The Senate (1)The Senate shall consist of [ninety-six], of whom- (a)fourteen shall be elected by the members of each Provincial Assembly; (c)two on general seats, and one woman and one technocrat including aalim shall be elected from the Federal Capital in such manner as the President may, by Order, prescribe; (d) four women shall be elected by the members of each Provincial Assembly; (e)four technocrats including ulema shall be elected by the members of each Provincial Assembly; and (f) four non-Muslims, one from each Province, shall be elected by the members of each Provincial Assembly: Provided that paragraph (f) shall be effective from the next Senate election after the commencement of the Constitution (Eighteenth Amendment) Act, 2010. (2) Election to fill seats in the Senate allocated to each Province shall be held in accordance with the system of proportional representation by means of the single transferable vote.").

296. 'Pakistan parties allege votes "bought" in Senate elections,' *Al Jazeera* (6 March, 2018), accessed on November 7, 2022, <https://www.aljazeera.com/news/2018/3/6/pakistan-parties-allege-votes-bought-in-senate-elections>. ("Pakistan's Senate election is held through an indirect ballot, with members of the four provincial

assemblies and the national assembly voting in nominees. As such, the outcome of the polls tends to be predictable, based on the proportional representation of each party in the assemblies. Cricketer-turned-politician Khan, however, alleged that some legislators, whose votes are kept secret, sold their votes to rival parties to help them secure greater representation in the Senate. Legislators voted for 52 vacant Senate seats on Saturday, with the PML-N emerging as the largest party in the 104-member house, with 33 seats.") The indirect election to the senate seats should be replaced by direct elections and be held through one of the following formats: 1) Each province be broken up into the same designated number of single-member districts [across provinces] according to population size within a province and senators are elected in each single member- district through alternative vote (AV); or 2) Each province comprises one multi-member district where the designated number of senators are elected through the Single transferable vote (STV)system, where voters' rank their candidates in order of preference, and candidates are elected when they pass a specified quota, with surplus votes apportioned to remaining candidates in order of voters' preference, until all seats are filled; or 3) Each province is considered one multi-member district and the designated number of senators are elected through the Single Non-Transferable Vote (SNTV) system.

297. *See* CONST. of PAK Art 73. *See also* 'Finance Bill 2021: Senate adopts nearly 300 recommendations,' *Business Recorder* (25 June, 2021), accessed on October 19, 2021, <https://www.brecorder.com/news/40102876>. ("Constitutionally, the Upper House of the Parliament can hold extensive debate on the Finance Bill and devise recommendations accordingly but it has practically no role in budgetary legislation since it is completely up to the National Assembly to either completely or partially accept those recommendations or hand them an outright rejection.").

298. *See supra* note 204.

299. 'Panchayats as instruments of social and economic progress,' *Hindu Business Line* (Apr 24, 2020), accessed on October 19, 2021, <https://www.thehindubusinessline.com/opinion/panchayats-as-instruments-of-social-and-economic-progress/article31421460.ece>. ("The 73rd Constitutional Amendment passed by the Parliament in the year 1993 was a pioneering step in decentralising political power in India. It required Indian States to enact laws for creation of the Panchayat Raj institutions.").

300. Nupur Tiwari, 'Panchayati Raj in India: Are They Really Successful in Participatory Decision-Making?' *Forum of Federations* (2008), accessed on October 19, 2021, <www.forumfed.org/library/panchayati-raj-in-india-are-they-really-successful-in-participatory-decision-making/>. ("Panchayati raj in India, in terms of the size of the electorate, the number of grass roots institutions (about 240,000), the number of persons elected [3.6 million in the panchayats and nagarpalikas], and in terms of the empowerment at the grass roots of women, is the greatest experiment in democracy ever undertaken anywhere in the world or at any time in history. No less than one million women have been elected to the panchayati raj institutions, constituting some 37 per cent of all those elected and rising to as high as 54 per cent in Bihar, which has 50 per cent reservations for women. . . . One of the key objectives of panchayati raj is to ensure that the process of planning for development in the country follows a

bottom-up approach and commences at the grass roots level. The core approach is that the village panchayat plans, prepared with peoples' participation, are joined by plans prepared by the intermediate and district panchayats and then these are consolidated by the district planning committee [DPC] along with Municipal Plans into the Draft District Development Plan, in accordance with Article 243 ZD of the Constitution.").

301. 'Basit Mahmood, Pakistan's Jirgas and Women's Rights,' *Diplomat* (Jan 4, 2018), accessed on October 19, 2021,<https://thediplomat.com/2018/01/pakistans-jirgas-and-womens-rights/>. ("When the government decided to pass the Alternate Dispute Resolution (ADR) Bill in 2017, it did so knowing fully well that the system of jirgas would gain added legitimacy. The bill makes some minor changes, allowing the government for example to appoint 'neutrals' to each jirga, who must approve their verdicts. Yet these 'neutrals,' consisting of retired judges and religious scholars, are more likely than not to be men with conservative principles. . . . The bill itself, which will undoubtedly have a major impact on the lives of women across the country, was voted on by only 23 out of the 342 members of the lower house.").

302. *See generally* Ayesha Khan and Sana Naqvi, "Dilemmas of Representation: Women in Pakistan's Assemblies." *Asian Affairs* 51.2 (2020): 286–306.

303. 'General elections: Women quota law fails to yield results,' *Express Tribune* (23 Sept, 2018), accessed on October 19, 2021, <https://tribune.com.pk/story/1809319/general-elections-women-quota-law-fails-yield-results>. ("The Elections Act of 2017 made it mandatory for all political parties to set aside at least five per cent of tickets to women on general seats. Women participation in the July 25 general election witnessed a slight improvement. A total of 183 women contested polls on 272 general seats of the National Assembly. Of the total, only eight were successful in entering the National Assembly. This number is the lowest since 2002.").

304. The Electoral Knowledge Network, accessed on October 19, 2021, <https://aceproject.org/ace-en/topics/ge/ge2/ge22/gender-quotas-in-elections/legislated-reserved-seats>. ("This method takes a number of different forms, for example: (1) the election of a set number of women from districts designed for electing female parliamentarians only (in Rwanda, where women are elected in 24 provinces through a specially designated electoral college); (2) a separate tier of female MPs directly elected in single-member districts [in Uganda]; and (3) a separate tier reserved for women to be elected from a special all-women national lists [such as the 60 reserved seats for women in Morocco elected through a women-only list PR system/closed list and in Mauritania, which elects 20 women through a women-only nationwide list].").

305. Antigha Okon Bassey, "The making of Nigeria as a sovereign state—A theoretical prognosis and analysis of a balanced federalism." *Geografia-Malaysian Journal of Society and Space* 10.2 (2017), 41–42. ("Fiscal federalism [Revenue Allocation] in Nigeria is a major area of federal imbalance as the federal government controls the fundamental sources of revenue, causing states and local governments to depend solely on federal government for revenue allocation. . . . The purpose of state creation was to solve the primary problem of ethno-structural imbalance engendered by the disproportional size of the North. State creation was also to create federal structure [in terms of sub-national units] in which the interest of minority ethnic groups were protected. States and local government areas were also created to reduce

the obviously insatiable distributive pressure in revenue allocation, as well as, bring government and development closer to the people.").

306. S. Mahmud Ali, *The fearful state: power, people, and internal war in South Asia*. Zed Books, 1993; H.A Rizvi, *Military, State and Society in Pakistan*. London: Macmillan, 2000.

307. Morris Janowitz, *The professional soldier: A social and political portrait*. Simon and Schuster, 2017. Morris Janowitz, "The social demography of the all-volunteer armed force." *Annals of the American Academy of Political and Social Science* 406.1 (1973): 86–93.

308. *See supra* notes 259–63.

309. Mohammad Akram Sheikh, Revival of the Constitution and Judiciary in Pakistan, *Policy Perspectives*, Vol. 5. No. 3. (2008).

310. *Ibid.* ("Zulfiqar Ali Bhutto himself, in whom the credit for the passage of our unanimous constitution vests, was responsible for the 4th Constitutional Amendment, which struck the powers of the Judiciary, as well as the 5th Constitutional Amendment, which took away the tenure of the judges. . . . Again, in November, 2007, courtesy Pervaiz Musharraf: "the structure of the Judiciary was disintegrated and the Constitution tossed aside to send 60 judges home.").

BIBLIOGRAPHY

'The Belt and Road in Sri Lanka: Beyond the Debt Trap Discussion,' *The Diplomat* (7 May, 2020), accessed on October 19, 2021 <https://thediplomat.com/2020/05/the-belt-and-road-in-sri-lanka-beyond-the-debt-trap-discussion/.>

"18th Amendment vital avenue to get Seraiki province." *DAWN*, May 9, 2020. https://www.dawn.com/news/1555645/18th-amendment-vital-avenue-to-get-seraiki-province.

"8th NFC Award: Provinces demand more tax revenue from Centre." *The Express Tribune*, April 29, 2015. https://tribune.com.pk/story/877678/8th-nfc-award-provinces-demand-more-tax-revenue-from-centre/.

"Are Bangladesh's local government bodies democratic?" *LSE Blogs* November 24, 2017. https://blogs.lse.ac.uk/southasia/2017/11/24/are-bangladeshs-local-government-bodies-democratic/.

"Bangladesh: In Quest of a Decentralised Local Representative Bodies." *Urbanet* August 4, 2020. https://www.urbanet.info/bangladesh-in-quest-of-a-decentralised-local-representative-bodies/.

"Bush outlines radical plan to part-nationalise banks." *The Guardian*, October 14, 2008. https://www.theguardian.com/business/2008/oct/14/us-banks-bailout-bush.

"Case for direct Senate elections." *DAWN*, March 13, 2018. https://www.dawn.com/news/1394959.

"Devolution matters." *The News International*, August 27, 2021. https://www.thenews.com.pk/print/883591-devolution-matters.

"Finance Bill 2021: Senate adopts nearly 300 recommendations." *Business Recorder*, June 25, 2021. https://www.brecorder.com/news/40102876.

"General elections: Women quota law fails to yield results." *The Express Tribune*, September 23, 2018. https://tribune.com.pk/story/1809319/general-elections-women-quota-law-fails-yield-results.

"International Religious Freedom Report for 2021." *United States Department of State—Office of International Religious Freedom*. https://www.state.gov/wp-content/uploads/2022/04/LEBANON-2021-INTERNATIONAL-RELIGIOUS-FREEDOM-REPORT.pdf.

"It Is High Time We Revisited the NFC Awards in Pakistan." *PIDE BLOG*, 19 May 2021. https://pide.org.pk/blog/it-is-high-time-we-revisited-the-nfc-awards-in-pakistan/.

"National Assembly green-lights Fata-KP merger by passing 'historic' bill." *DAWN*, May 24, 2018. https://www.dawn.com/news/1409710.

"Neoliberalism is killing the very idea of citizenship in India." *Quartz India,* September 2, 2019. https://qz.com/india/1700542/neoliberalism-is-killing-the-very-idea-of-citizenship-in-india/.

"Nepal's fight for federalism' Asia and the Pacific Policy Society." *Policy Forum*, March 26, 2019. https://www.policyforum.net/nepals-fight-for-federalism/.

"Pakistan parties allege votes 'bought' in Senate elections." *Al Jazeera*, March 6, 2018. https://www.aljazeera.com/news/2018/3/6/pakistan-parties-allege-votes-bought-in-senate-elections.

"Panchayats as instruments of social and economic progress." *The Hindu Business Line*, April 24, 2020. https://www.thehindubusinessline.com/opinion/panchayats-as-instruments-of-social-and-economic-progress/article31421460.ece.

"Please Mind the Gap: Winners and Losers of Neoliberalism in India." *E-International Relations*, March 11, 2017. https://www.e-ir.info/2017/03/11/please-mind-the-gap-winners-and-losers-of-neoliberalism-in-india/.

"Poverty of Vision: Neglecting growing class inequality in post-war Sri Lanka?" *LSE Blogs*, October 30, 2019. https://blogs.lse.ac.uk/southasia/2019/10/30/poverty-of-vision-neglecting-growing-class-inequality-in-post-war-sri-lanka/.

"Reforming Pakistan's Electoral System." *International Crisis Group*, March 30, 2011. https://www.crisisgroup.org/asia/south-asia/pakistan/reforming-pakistan-s-electoral-system.

"RELIGION, NATIONALISM AND INSURGENCY IN BALOCHISTAN." *DAWN*, July 14, 2019. https://www.dawn.com/news/1493929.

"The Kurds' Quest for Independence." *Council on Foreign Relations*. https://www.cfr.org/timeline/kurds-quest-independence.

"The origin and politics of the Seraiki movement." *DAWN*, May 24, 2009. https://www.dawn.com/news/881086/the-origin-and-politics-of-the-seraiki-movement.

"Why India Needs to Change its Electoral Voting System." *The Caravan*, September 13, 2017. https://caravanmagazine.in/vantage/why-india-needs-to-change-its-electoral-voting-system>.

Aboultaif, Eduardo Wassim. "Revisiting the semi-consociational model: Democratic failure in pre-war Lebanon and post-invasion Iraq." *International Political Science Review* 41, no. 1 (2020): 108–123.

Adeney, Katharine, and Wilfried Swenden. "Power-sharing in the world's largest democracy: Informal consociationalism in India (and its decline?)." *Swiss Political Science Review* 25, no. 4 (2019): 450–475.

Adeney, Katharine. *Federalism and ethnic conflict regulation in India and Pakistan.* Springer, 2016.

———. "A step towards inclusive federalism in Pakistan? The politics of the 18th amendment." *Publius: The Journal of Federalism* 42, no. 4 (2012): 539–565.

———. "The limitations of non-consociational federalism: The example of Pakistan." *Ethnopolitics* 8, no. 1 (2009): 87–106.

———. "Centrifugal and centripetal elements of Indian federalism." *Indien heute: Bennpunkte seiner Innenpolitik (India today: domestic priorities), Hanns Seidel Stiftung, Munich* (2003): 47–54.

Adhikari, Damodar. "Nepal's Road to Federalism: From the Perspective of Grassroots Democracy." *RTI International*, NC (2020). https://www.rti.org/publication/nepal percentE2 percent80 percent99s-road-federalism/fulltext.pdf.

Ahmar, Moonis. "The Dynamics of Pakistan's Intra-national Security: The Role of the New Provinces." *India Quarterly* 72, no. 1 (2016): 16–29.

Ahmed, Manzoor. "Fiscal decentralisation and political economy of poverty reduction: Theory and evidence from Pakistan." PhD diss., Durham University, 2013. http://etheses.dur.ac.uk/7288/1/Manzoor_final_thesis percent5B percent5D.pdf?DDD2+.

Ali, S. Mahmud. *The fearful state: Power, people, and internal war in South Asia.* Zed Books, 1993.

Ali, Syed Mohammad. "Devolution of power in Pakistan," *United States Institute of Peace* (2018) Special Report 422. https://www.usip.org/publications/2018/03/devolution-power-pakistan.

Ali, Syed Mohammad. "Devolution of power in Pakistan," *United States Institute of Peace* (2018) Special Report 422. https://www.usip.org/publications/2018/03/devolution-power-pakistan.

Anderson, Benedict. "Census, Map, Museum." In *Imagined Communities: Reflections on the Origin and Spread of Nationalism,* 163–185. 1991.

Aziz, Sadaf. *The Constitution of Pakistan: A Contextual Analysis.* Bloomsbury Publishing, 2018.

Bandara, Jayatilleke S. *Trade Liberalisation and Regional Disparity in Pakistan. Routledge Studies in the Growth Economies of Asia.* Taylor & Francis, 2008.

Bassey, Antigha Okon. "The making of Nigeria as a sovereign state-A theoretical prognosis and analysis of a balanced federalism." *Geografia-Malaysian Journal of Society and Space* 10, no. 2 (2014).

Blume, Lorenz, and Stefan Voigt. "Federalism and decentralization—a critical survey of frequently used indicators." *Constitutional Political Economy* 22, no. 3 (2011): 238–264.

Blume, Lorenz, and Stefan Voigt. "Federalism and decentralization—a critical survey of frequently used indicators." *Constitutional Political Economy* 22, no. 3 (2011): 238–264.

Bogaards, Matthijs. "Electoral systems, party systems, and ethnicity in Africa." *Votes, money, and violence. Political parties and elections in Africa, Uppsala: Nordic Africa Institute* (2007): 168–193.

Boni, Filippo, and Katharine Adeney. "The impact of the China-Pakistan economic corridor on Pakistan's federal system: the politics of the CPEC." *Asian Survey* 60, no. 3 (2020): 441–465.

Breen, Michael G. "Federal and Political Party Reforms in Asia: Is There a New Model of Federal Democracy Emerging in Ethnically Diverse Countries in Asia?" *Government and Opposition* 57, no. 2 (2022): 296–317.

Brown v. Board of Education of Topeka, 347 US 483 (1954).

Brown, Geoff. "Pakistan: Failing state or neoliberalism in crisis?" *International Socialism: A Quarterly Review of Socialist Theory* 150 (2016).

Brown, Wendy. *Undoing the demos: Neoliberalism's stealth revolution*. Mit Press, 2015.

———. *In the ruins of neoliberalism: The rise of antidemocratic politics in the west*. Columbia University Press, 2019.

Chapman, Audrey. "Being Bold about Rights in a Neoliberal World." *Health and human rights* 21, no. 1 (2019): 287.

Cheema, Ali, Adnan Q. Khan, and Roger Myerson. "Breaking the countercyclical pattern of local democracy in Pakistan." *Is decentralization good for development* (2015): 68–79.

Cheema, Ali, and Asad Sayeed. "Bureaucracy and Pro-poor Change." *Working Papers & Research Reports* 2006 (1961): 2006–03.

Cheema, Ali, Asim Ijaz Khwaja, and Adnan Khan. "Decentralization in Pakistan: Context, content and causes." *Content and Causes (April 2005)* (2005).

Chomsky, Noam. *Profit over people: Neoliberalism and global order*. Seven Stories Press, 1998.

Choudhry, Sujit. "Bridging Comparative Politics and Comparative Constitutional Law: Constitutional Design in Divided Societies." In Sujit Choudhry eds. *Constitutional Design for Divided Societies: Integration or Accommodation*. New York: Oxford University Press, 2008.

Cohen, Anthony. *Self-consciousness: An alternative anthropology of identity*. Routledge, 2002.

CONST. of PAK. Art. 1.

CONST. of PAK. Art. 15

CONST. of PAK. Art. 184 (2).

CONST. of PAK. Art. 2.

CONST. of PAK. Art. 213–226.

CONST. of PAK. Art. 228.

CONST. of PAK. Art. 238.

CONST. of PAK. Art. 239

CONST. of PAK. Art. 59.

CONST. of PAK. Art. 70 (3).

CONST. of PAK. Art. 73 (2)(2).

CONST. of PAK. Art. 73.

CONST. of PAK. Part 2, Chapter II.

De Alwis, Ranjanee Kusumsiri. "The History of and Prospects for Public Sector Reforms in Sri Lanka." (2009). https://researcharchive.vuw.ac.nz/xmlui/handle/10063/1444.

De Alwis, Ranjanee. "Federalism or devolution of power? Sri Lanka's perspectives." *Asia & the Pacific Policy Studies* 7, no. 1 (2020): 124–130.

De Wilde, Pieter, Ruud Koopmans, and Wolfgang Merkel, eds. *The struggle over borders: Cosmopolitanism and communitarianism*. Cambridge University Press, 2019.

Descartes, René. *Discourse on Method and the Meditations*. Penguin UK, 1968.

Dodge, Toby. "Iraq's informal consociationalism and its problems." *Studies in Ethnicity and Nationalism* 20, no. 2 (2020): 145–152.

Epstein, Arnold Leonard, and Athena S. Leoussi. *Ethos and identity: Three studies in ethnicity*. Routledge, 2017.

Ezdi, Asid. "Power, People and the Senate." *The News International*, January 26, 2015. http://www.thenews.com.pk/print/20504-power-people-and-the-senate.

Feeley, Malcolm, and Edward Rubin. *Federalism: Political identity and tragic compromise*. University of Michigan Press, 2009.

Filippov, Mikhail, and Olga Shvetsova. "Federalism, democracy, and democratization." *Federal dynamics* (2013): 167–184.

Gayer, Laurent, and Christophe Jaffrelot. "Do Pakistanis Vote on an Ethnic Basis?" *Herald Magazine*, March 7, 2018. https://herald.dawn.com/news/1153691.

Gerring, John, and Strom C. Thacker. *A centripetal theory of democratic governance*. Cambridge University Press, 2008.

Ghosh, Ambar Kumar. "The paradox of 'Centralized Federalism': an analysis of the challenges to India's federal design." *ORF Occasional Paper No* 272 (2020). https://www.orfonline.org/research/the-paradox-of-centralised-federalism/.

Government of India Act, 1935.

Halawi, Ibrahim. "Consociational Power-Sharing in the Arab World as Counter□Revolution." *Studies in Ethnicity and Nationalism* 20, no. 2 (2020): 128–136.

Harris, Richard L., and Melinda J. Seid. "Critical perspectives on globalization and neoliberalism in the developing countries." In *Critical perspectives on globalization and neoliberalism in the developing countries*, pp. 1–26. Brill, 2000.

Harvey, David. *A brief history of neoliberalism*. Oxford University Press, USA, 2007.

Hayek, Friedrich August. *The Road to Serfdom*. University of Chicago Press 1944.

Horowitz, Donald L. "Constitutional design: An oxymoron?" *NOMOS: Am. Soc'y Pol. Legal Phil.* 42 (2000): 253.

———. *A democratic South Africa? Constitutional engineering in a divided society*. Vol. 46. Univ of California Press, 2022.

———. "The many uses of federalism." *Drake L. Rev.* 55 (2006): 953.

———. "Ethnic power sharing: Three big problems." *Journal of democracy* 25, no. 2 (2014): 5–20.

———. *Ethnic groups in conflict, updated edition with a new preface*. Univ of California Press, 2000.

———. "Electoral systems: A primer for decision makers." *Journal of Democracy* 14, no. 4 (2003): 115–127.

Horowitz, Donald, D. Russel, and I. O'Flynn (eds). *Power Sharing: New Challenges for Divided Societies.* Pluto Press, 2005.

Iltaf, Maisam. "Hazaras Gripped by Religious Extremism in Balochistan." *The Diplomat*, April 16, 2019. https://thediplomat.com/2019/04/hazaras-gripped-by-religious-extremism-in-balochistan/

Irwin, Douglas A. "India's trade reforms 30 years later: Great start but stalling" *Peterson Institute of International Economics*, July 22, 2021. https://www.piie.com/blogs/trade-and-investment-policy-watch/indias-trade-reforms-30-years-later-great-start-stalling.

Islamic Republic v. Abdul Wali Khan PLD 1976 S.C. 57.

Jaffery, Nighat Bilgrami, and Mahpara Sadaqat. "NFC awards: commentary and agenda." *Pakistan Economic and Social Review* (2006): 209–234.

Jaffrelot, Christophe. *Pakistan at the Crossroads: Domestic Dynamics and External Pressures*. Random House India, 2016.

Jahangir Asifa, Omair Haroon and Arif Masud Mirza. "Special Economic Zones under the CPEC and the Belt and Road Initiative: Parameters, Challenges and Prospects." In *China's Belt and Road Initiative in a Global Context*, pp. 289–328. Palgrave Macmillan, 2020.

Jalal, Ayesha. *The sole spokesman: Jinnah, the Muslim League, and the demand for Pakistan*. Vol. 31. Cambridge University Press, 1994.

Janowitz, Morris. "The social demography of the all-volunteer armed force." *The ANNALS of the American Academy of Political and Social Science* 406, no. 1 (1973): 86–93.

Kant, Immanuel. "Critique of pure reason, trans. Paul Guyer and Allen W. Wood." *Cambridge: Cambridge University Press* 177 (1998): A27.

Kaufman, Stuart J. "Ethnicity as a generator of conflict." In *The Routledge handbook of ethnic conflict*, pp. 109–119. Routledge, 2016.

Khan, Ayesha, and Sana Naqvi. "Dilemmas of Representation: Women in Pakistan's Assemblies." *Asian Affairs* 51, no. 2 (2020): 286–306.

Khan, Danish. "DON'T BELIEVE THE HYPE: NEOLIBERALISM HAS FAILED PAKISTAN." *Centre for Popular Economics*, September 3, 2015. www.populareconomics.org/dont-believe-the-hype-neoliberalism-has-failed-pakistan/.

Khan, Karim, and Saba Anwar. "Special economic zones (SEZs) and CPEC: Background, challenges and strategies." *The Pakistan Development Review* (2016): 203–216.

Khan, Manzoor Ali. "Stabilisation or overkill." *SZABIST* www.szabist.edu.pk/pdf/Stabilisation percent20or percent20overkill.pdf.

Khan, Maryam S. "Ethnic federalism in Pakistan: federal design, construction of ethno-linguistic identity & group conflict." *Harv. J. Racial & Ethnic Just.* 30 (2014): 77.

Klarman, Michael J. *From Jim Crow to civil rights: The Supreme Court and the struggle for racial equality*. Oxford University Press, 2004.

Kukreja, Veena. "Ethnic diversity, political aspirations and state response: A case study of Pakistan." *Indian Journal of Public Administration* 66, no. 1 (2020): 28–42.

Kymlicka, Will. *Multicultural citizenship: A liberal theory of minority rights*. clarendon Press, 1995.

Lijphart, Arend. "Consociation and federation: Conceptual and empirical links." *Canadian Journal of Political Science/Revue canadienne de science politique* 12, no. 3 (1979) : 499–516.

———. "Consociational democracy." *World politics* 21, no. 2 (1969): 207–225.

———. "Cultural diversity and theories of political integration." *Canadian Journal of Political Science/Revue canadienne de science politique* 4, no. 1 (1971) : 1–14.

———. *Democracy in plural societies: A comparative exploration*. Yale University Press, 1977.

———. "Non-majoritarian democracy: a comparison of federal and consociational theories." *Publius: the journal of federalism* 15, no. 2 (1985): 3–15.

———. *Patterns of democracy: Government forms and performance in thirty-six countries*. Yale university press, 1999.

———. *The politics of accommodation: Pluralism and democracy in the Netherlands*. Univ of California Press, 2022.

———. "The puzzle of Indian democracy: A consociational interpretation." *American political science review* 90, no. 2 (1996): 258–268.

MacNaughton, Gillian. "Equality rights beyond neoliberal constraints." *Economic and social rights in a neoliberal world* (2018): 103–23.

Macpherson, Crawford Brough. "The political theory of possessive individualism: Hobbes to Locke." (2010).

Mahmood, Basit. "Pakistan's Jirgas and Women's Rights." *The Diplomat*, January 4, 2018. https://thediplomat.com/2018/01/pakistans-jirgas-and-womens-rights/.

Mahmood, Tahir. "A Comparative Analysis of the Functioning of the Senate in USA and Pakistan." *South Asian Studies* 30, no. 2 (2020).

Máiz, Ramón, and Safran William. *Identity and territorial autonomy in plural societies*. Routledge, 2014.

Makdisi, Samir, and Marcus Marktanner. "Trapped by consociationalism: The case of Lebanon." *Topics in Middle Eastern and North African Economies* 11 (2009).

Mansour, Renad. "Iraq's 2018 government formation: unpacking the friction between reform and the status quo." *LSE Middle East Centre*, February 2019. https://eprints.lse.ac.uk/100099/1/Mansour_Iraq_s_2018_government_formation_2019.pdf.

Maulana Abdul Haque Baloch v Government of Balochistan PLD 2013 SC 641 (Reko Diq case).

McCulloch, Allison. "SEEKING STABILITY AMID DEEP DIVISION: CONSOCIATIONALISM AND CENTRIPETALISM IN COMPARATIVE PERSPECTIVE," 2009. https://qspace.library.queensu.ca/bitstream/1974/1708/1/McCulloch_Allison_200902_PhD.pdf.

McCulloch Allison and Joanne McEvoy. "'Bumps in the Road Ahead': How External Actors Defuse Power-Sharing Crises." *Journal of Intervention and Statebuilding* 13.2 (2019): 216–235

McCulloch, Allison and John McGarry, eds. *Power-sharing: Empirical and normative challenges*. Taylor & Francis, 2017.

McGarry, John. "Centripetalism, consociationalism and Cyprus: The 'adoptability' question." *Political Studies* 65, no. 2 (2017): 512–529.

Mietzner, Marcus. "Comparing Indonesia's party systems of the 1950s and the post-Suharto era: From centrifugal to centripetal inter-party competition." *Journal of Southeast Asian Studies* 39, no. 3 (2008): 431–453.

Mifsud, Denise. "'Decentralised' neoliberalism and/or 'masked' re-centralisation? The policy to practice trajectory of Maltese school reform through the lens of neoliberalism and Foucault." *Journal of Education Policy* 31, no. 4 (2016): 443–465.

Miller, David. *On nationality*. Clarendon Press, 1995.

Murshid, Navine. *The politics of refugees in South Asia: Identity, resistance, manipulation*. Routledge, 2013.

Mushtaq, Muhammad, Muhammad Ayaz, and Syed Khawja. "Examining the Favourable Factors for Consociational Democracy in Pakistan." *European Journal of Social Sciences* 20 (2011): 275–287.

Nabi, Ijaz, and Hina Shaikh. "Fiscal Federalism in Pakistan: A radical departure and some new challenges." *Development Policy Research Centre Working Paper, LUMS, Lahore* (2010).

Nehmeh, Adib. "Horizontal and Vertical Expansion of Poverty in Lebanon." *Alternative Policy Solutions*, September 21, 2020. https://aps.aucegypt.edu/en/articles/511/horizontal-and-vertical-expansion-of-poverty-in-lebanon.

Niazi, Hassan. "Senate reform." *The Express Tribune*, February 01, 2021. https://tribune.com.pk/story/2282260/senate-reform.

———. "The 18th Amendment and the Supreme Court." *The Express Tribune,* May 19, 2020. https://tribune.com.pk/story/2224292/18th-amendment-supreme-court.

O'Leary, Brendan. "Consociation: What We Know or Think We Know and What We Need to Know." In *Conference on National and Ethnic Conflict Regulation at the University of Western Ontario*. 2002.

Petrikkos, Petros. "Building Bridges in Divided Societies: Sustaining Democratic Transition Through Complex Power-Sharing in Lebanon and Iraq." *Federal Governance* 15, no. 2 (2019): 18–32.

Rafi, Raja, and Nadeem Ul Haque. "Electoral Systems." *The News International*, April 20, 2021. https://www.thenews.com.pk/print/822809-electoral-systems.

Rahman, Namwar Yusuf. "Punjabi Domination and the Biopolitics of the Census and Statistics in Pakistan." PhD diss., Central European University, 2018. http://www.etd.ceu.edu/2018/rahman_namwar.pdf.

Raza, Syed Irfan. "Senators Say CPEC Turned into 'China-Punjab' Corridor." *DAWN*, November 24, 2015. https://www.dawn.com/news/1221849.

Rehman, I.A. "Provinces vs Centre." DAWN.COM, June 11, 2020. https://www.dawn.com/news/1562775.

Reilly, Ben. "Institutional designs for diverse democracies: Consociationalism, centripetalism and communalism compared." *European Political Science* 11, no. 2 (2012): 259–270.

———. "Papua New Guinea: Electoral Incentives for Inter-Ethnic Accommodation." *The International IDEA Handbook of Electoral System Design* (1997): 40–42.

———. "Ethnic Representation in Pacific Asia: A Report for the Southeast Asia Rules-Based Order Project." https://researchimpact.uwa.edu.au/wp-content/uploads/2019/09/Ethnic-representation-Report.docx.pdf.

———. "Cross-ethnic voting: An index of centripetal electoral systems." *Government and Opposition* 56, no. 3 (2021): 465–484.

———. *Political Reform and the Demise of Consociationalism in Southeast Asia*. Palgrave Macmillan, 2011, pp. 114–130. p. 124.Murdoch University, n.d.

Reynolds, Andrew. *Electoral systems and the protection and participation of minorities*. London: Minority Rights Group International, 2006.

Rifaat, Hamza and Tridivesh Singh Maini. "China-Pakistan Economic Corridor." *Stimson.* https://www.stimson.org/wp-content/files/file-attachments/The percent20China-Pakistan percent20Economic percent20Corridor percent20- percent20Final.pdf.

Rohwerder, Brigitte. "Reform of consociationalism arrangements in deeply divided societies." (2020). https://opendocs.ids.ac.uk/opendocs/bitstream/handle/20.500.12413/15000/730_Reform percent20of percent20consociationalism percent20arrangements.asd.pdf?sequence=1.

Rudolph, Lloyd I., and Susanne Hoeber Rudolph. "Federalism as state formation in India: A theory of shared and negotiated sovereignty." *International Political Science Review* 31, no. 5 (2010): 553–572.

Salamey, Imad. "Failing consociationalism in Lebanon and integrative options." *International Journal of Peace Studies* (2009): 83–105.

Salman, Aneela. *Decentralization in Pakistan: Lessons and Challenges*, University of Albany, SUNY, 2012.

Samad, Yunas. "Understanding the insurgency in Balochistan." In *State and Nation-Building in Pakistan*, pp. 136–163. Routledge, 2015.

Saxena, Rekha, and Wilfried Swenden. "The Indian Supreme Court and federalism." *Federalism Regionalism* (2017).

Sheikh, Md Ziaul Haque, and Zahid Shahab Ahmed. "Military, authoritarianism and Islam: A comparative analysis of Bangladesh and Pakistan." *Politics and Religion* 13, no. 2 (2020): 333–360.

Sheikh, Muhammad Akram. "Revival of the Constitution and Judiciary in Pakistan." *Policy Perspectives* (2008): 73–84.

Shoup, Brian. *Conflict and cooperation in multi-ethnic states: Institutional incentives, myths and counterbalancing*. Routledge, 2007.

Siddiqa, Ayesha. *Military Inc.: Inside Pakistan's military economy*. Penguin Random House India, 2017.

Siddiqi, Farhan Hanif. *The politics of ethnicity in Pakistan: The Baloch, Sindhi and Mohajir ethnic movements*. Routledge, 2012.

Sisk, Timothy D. *Power sharing and international mediation in ethnic conflicts*. US Institute of Peace Press, 1996.

Small, Andrew. *The China Pakistan axis: Asia's new geopolitics*. Random House India, 2015.

The Electoral Knowledge Network. https://aceproject.org/ace-en/topics/es/annex/esy/esy_pg/mobile_browsing/onePag.

———. 2021. https://aceproject.org/ace-en/topics/ge/ge2/ge22/gender-quotas-in-elections/legislated-reserved-seats.

Tiwari, Nupur. "Panchayati Raj in India: Are They Really Successful in Participatory Decision-Making?" *Forum of Federations*, 2008. www.forumfed.org/library/panchayati-raj-in-india-are-they-really-successful-in-participatory-decision-making/.

Trzcinski, Krzysztok. "Centripetal Federalism." *PhilPapers*, 2020.p.5. https://philpapers.org/rec/TRZCF.

———. "The Consociational Addition to Indonesia's Centripetalism as a Tactic of the Central Authorities: The Case of Papua." *Hemispheres* 31, no. 4 (2016).

———."Hybrid Power Sharing: On How to Stabilize the Political Situation in Multi-segmental Societies." Politeja 15 (2018): 85–107. doi:10.12797/Politeja.15.2018.56.06.

Tushnet, Mark, and Madhav Khosla, eds. *Unstable constitutionalism: Law and politics in South Asia*. Cambridge University Press, 2015.

Ullah, Ikram. "Reko Diq Case: Another Intervention from Supreme Court of Pakistan." (2015).

Wolf, Siegfried O. *The China-Pakistan Economic Corridor of the Belt and Road Initiative*. Springer International Publishing, 2020.

Zahid, Ahmed Mahmood. "Institutional Analysis of Council of Common Interests." December 2013. http://www.pk.undp.org/content/dam/pakistan/docs/Democratic percent20Governance/Federalism/CCI percent20Manual percent20(1).pdf.

Chapter 3

Civil-Military Relations

INTRODUCTION

Civil-military relations are often fraught by the paradox: "(t)he very institution created to protect the polity is given sufficient power to become a threat to the polity."[1] While true for states—and the professional armies that defend them—worldwide, this inherent contradiction in the national constitutional framework has been uniquely expressed in the Pakistani context.

This chapter will begin with a discussion of this apparent incongruence in civil-military relations, exploring the extent to which institutions tasked with protecting and advancing the polity's interests should simultaneously be constrained to ensure they themselves do not pose a threat to the polity. An imbalance favouring the military has serious implications on the dynamics of a democratic federation, and consequently often on internecine struggles for power and autonomy playing out within the state as well. In this regard, this chapter will examine the theoretical debates on the presence of a military within a state's institutional context, its ordering, and its optimal engagement with the civilian government. The chapter will then move on to an exploration of the state of civil military relations in a non-Western context, with a view towards analysing contexts analogous to Pakistan's.

Managing this dichotomy requires balancing powers between two indispensable and potentially conflicting authoritative institutions: the civilian government and the military. The military needs to be strong enough to effectively repel external thrcats; however, inordinately concentrating power in the institution engenders the threat of it misusing its coercive authority against the polity to further its own vested interests, such as consuming or reallocating the state's resources or enforcing its will on the people.

The objective control of the civilian government over the military is essential in a democracy. Bearing the costs of policy adventurism, as well as the brunt of the fallout for potential failures, the civilian electorate is ideally positioned to assess and ascribe value to the potential risks associated with these endeavours, and in a representative form of government is the institution that must necessarily be able to wield maximum influence over political decision-making and resource allocation—including in relation to the military.

While the military may have the technical expertise and capability to both assess and address risks to national security, only a civilian government can be charged with the authority to assess what constitutes an "acceptable amount of risk", and consequently to embody the polity's willingness for, or tolerance to accepting such a risk.[2] These normative values are often reflected and preserved in constitutions, and academia has long debated increasing the separation of powers between the civilian organs of the state. This separation of powers grants each branch of the state some degree of control over the military, blunting its domestic political clout, enhancing military accountability to the civilian electorate, and prescribing checks and balances,[3] while simultaneously preserving the military's capacity to protect the parent state.

This crucial interplay between the need to ensure a degree of participation by the armed forces in the decision-making process, particularly in relation to national defence, and the equally significant need to ensure that the military does not opportunistically co-opt such participation to its own ends, has been explored by David Easton in his book, *A Systems Analysis of Political Life*. Easton writes: "(i)f politics is concerned with the authoritative allocation of values and power within a society, the military as a vital institution in the polity can hardly be wished out of participatory bounds . . . "[4], going on to acknowledge that this degree of participation can range from "minimal legitimate influence through recognized channels by virtue of their position and responsibilities within the political system" to the "total displacement of the civilian government in the form of illegitimate overt military intervention in politics".[5]

The possibility of the latter necessitates the institution of balancing mechanisms which—on the one hand—ensure that the military's meaningful participation on issues of national defence remains uncompromised, while—on the other—guarantee that its level of engagement with strategic issues does not lend itself to intruding in areas of policymaking, which must remain within the purview of the civilian government.

Historically, this precarious balancing act has rarely been maintained in Pakistan. Instead, the country has been under military rule, in varying forms, for much of its postcolonial history, with the military continuing to exert nontrivial influence over domestic politicking and policy formation even during periods of civilian rule. With this in view, this chapter will explore why an imbalance in civil-military relations in Pakistan exists in favour of the military, what the historical and sociocultural antecedents of this imbalance are, and how this imbalance has adversely impacted the presence of essential democratic values and the state of federalism in the country.

Ultimately, this chapter will highlight how the historical concentration of inordinate amount of power within the Pakistani military establishment enabled and exacerbated internal ethnic conflict which, in turn, has perpetuated the consolidation of power within the military establishment. The democratic norms of distributive justice, localized self-government, collective minorities rights and multiculturalism, which must be realized effectively to progress political stability in Pakistan, have been deeply impacted by the civil-military imbalance in the country. By outlining the asymmetrical dynamic of increased military power, both on paper and in practice, this chapter will discuss more specifically how Pakistan's armed forces have consistently exploited historical inter-communal frictions, consolidated the federation's organization upon ethnic lines, and promoted exploitative forms of neoliberal policies, to further their interests. It will explore the reasons and incentives for the Pakistani armed forces, both from a historical and strategic perspective, to influence and undermine the civilian government, at times by forcing the invocation of emergency powers vested in the executive by the Constitution of Pakistan.

It is a given that all states would have some form of military apparatus, coupled with a balanced civil-military relationship, where the state's armed forces protect the state's espoused political values from internal and external threats. In democratically weak states, however, this balance may be askew, with the military often exerting undue influence over otherwise civilian matters. While what constitutes an 'appropriate' relationship between a state's civilian and military apparatuses is derived, in some way, from Western political ideology, and in third world states this relationship is often informed—and thus distorted—by historical factors; in Pakistan, for instance, much of this dysfunction can be attributed to the country's postcolonial status, as well as its status as a developing country that has often been employed as a means of—or as the context for—external political and economic intrusions. The country's civilian and military bureaucracies have historically been overdeveloped in relation to its civilian political arrangements, necessarily tipping the scales in favour of the former two institutions. In the case of Pakistan's military in particular, the perennial threat of violent extremism within the country, and the presence of an unfriendly and a volatile state on its eastern and western borders—in the form of India and Afghanistan respectively—have served to further entrench the Pakistani armed forces' disproportionate boot print on the country's governance structures.

This chapter will conclude with a brief exploration of how the Pakistani military has controlled and affected the CPEC project to strengthen its grip over the political economy of Pakistan. While a more detailed discussion of this topic is undertaken in Chapter 4, this chapter will outline how the Pakistani military is transforming and undermining existing political relationships and is exacerbating pre-existing ethnic and provincial grievances brought into sharper distinction by the CPEC project. The chapter will also put forward the proposition that measures taken to adopt local centripetalism, an indigenously viable form of federal organization discussed in the preceding chapter, may transform the ordering of Pakistan's military, and prevent it from continuing to undermine both federalism and democratic values within the country, curbing the influence it exerts over the bureaucratic and political workings of the civilian government.

THEORIZING CIVIL-MILITARY RELATIONS

This section will outline the evolution of civil-military relations (CMR) theories and their impact on government. It will review the works of leading experts such as Huntington[6], Feaver[7], Schiff[8], and Janowitz[9] among others and critique how classical CMR theory has fared in predicting military power in postcolonial, non-Western contexts, such as in Pakistan. While CMR theory regularly examines civil-military relations in a variety of geo-political settings, it's exploration of such imbalances in postcolonial, non-Western contexts are lacking. A comparative review of some of the major contributions to CMR theory in postcolonial settings will help elucidate the optimal ways of promoting civil-military symmetry, political stability, national security, and democracy in postcolonial, non-Western societies. Contextualizing these theories to Pakistan will contribute significantly towards determining how local centripetalism restructure—and potentially stabilize—civil-military relations in Pakistan.

In *The Soldier and the State* Huntington postulates that the fundamental distinction between the civilian government and the military is in their respective attitudes and values—the military trending towards conservatism and the civilians towards liberalism. Recognising the paradoxical relationship between empowering the military to achieve its designated role of protecting the polity, but at the same time its ability to use this power to threaten the polity, Huntington sought to propose a secure solution to ensuring effective civilian control over the armed forces.[10] A key conceptual part of Huntington's solution was "military professionalism." According to Huntington, the "professionalization" of the military accentuates areas of comparative advantage of the institution, such as its structure and order, and relegates the military to a separate sphere where the officers, and collectively the officer corps, are recognized as professional experts in their respective fields. Recognition of their expertise would then, Huntington argued, reduce the need for interference in, or direct control of the military realm by civil authority, eventually leading to what he referred to as "objective civilian control."[11]

Huntington's idea of "professionalism" within the military corps encapsulates an "autonomous military ethic of expertise, political neutrality and professional competence";[12] in essence, a recognition by the military that it is a tool of the state to achieve, in the most effective and competent ways, the goals and objectives defined by the state. This recognition within the military is what Huntington proposes creates "objective civilian control," contradistinguished from "subjective control"[13] in which civilian direction of the military is more intrusive, objective civilian control seeks to maximize military professionalism by separating political and military decision-making. This separation ensures that neither group can interfere with the workings of the other: political leaders formulate and set end goals and broad conditions for the conduct of military operations, and military commanders enact these ordered operations autonomously and "professionally."[14]

Peter Feaver instead uses a principal-agent framework to explain how actors in superior positions influence those in subordinate roles. A defining feature of all agency relations is that once principals delegate authority to agents, they "often have problems controlling them because '(1) agents' interests often differ from theirs, and (2) agents often have better information about their actions than do principals".[15] The principal-agent model can explain both the legislature-bureaucracy relationship and the legislature-military relationship. In a sense, Feaver's model is a straightforward extension of Huntington's.[16] Huntington concedes that the military has expertise the civilian government does not, and the military has a sphere of competence where the civilian government does not—or cannot—interfere; the latter's lack of expertise in and control over the former's area of expertise renders it unable to monitor the military's work. Feaver, on the other hand, poses the question that necessarily follows: what does the military do when it knows that the civilian government cannot observe it perfectly?

Feaver's work compares the incentives of the civilian government and the military. One of the key determinants of his theory is the extent to which civilian and military expectations coincide; as expectations diverge, the challenges of control grow.[17] According to Feaver, the principal is the civilian leadership, entrusted with the responsibility of deciding policy, with the military as the agent which may either work—i.e., perform the task—or shirk—subverting the principal's desires to further its own interests.[18] The issue for the principal is ensuring that the agent does as instructed: theoretically, if the costs of monitoring the latter are low, the former will use "intrusive" methods of control to ensure that the agent is complying with its directions.[19] The incidence of shirking, then, is inversely proportional to the perceived costs and likelihood of punishment. By extension, the result of a regime of intrusive monitoring by the civilian leadership, combined with a shirking military would lead to the highest levels of civil-military conflict.[20] Feaver's working-shirking paradigm may be extended to any number of principals, for example, to construct a model with the legislature as the principal and the judiciary, the bureaucracy or executive, and the military as its three agents.[21]

Rebecca Schiff, by way of her concordance theory, argues that the military, the political elite and the citizenry must seek agreement on four indicators: (i) the social composition of the officer corps; (ii) the political decision-making process; (iii) the method of recruiting military personnel; and (iv) the style of the military.[22] Applying her theory to a variety of historical case studies worldwide, she claims that agreement among these three partners, with reference to these four indicators, indicates that military intervention is less likely to occur. Just as Feaver's theory can be read as an extension of Huntington's, Schiff's can be seen as corollary of Feaver's. Where Feaver suggests that agency problems will be reduced if the agent shares the principal's incentives or goals, Schiff attempts to address the question: what specific issues must the principal and agent agree on?

Morris Janowitz postulates in his book *The Professional Soldier*[23] that military and civilian institutions tend to converge within the host state; the result of this convergence is either the civilization of the military or militarization of the society. Despite this confluence, Janowitz posits that the military would remain discernibly military in nature and distinct from the civilian sphere, viewing the convergence as a solution to inter-institutional frictions. For Janowitz, this convergence nonetheless provides the state with an opportunity to imbue the military with the norms and expectations of the society that formed it. This necessitates a new self-conception of the military: "(t)he military establishment becomes a constabulary force when it is continuously prepared to act, committed to the minimum use of force, and seeks viable international relations, rather than victory."[24]

Janowitz proposed a professional military education which acquaints servicemen with the ideals and norms of civilian society, ensuring the "civilization of the military."[25] Janowitz, then, can be read as a corollary to Schiff: where Schiff notes the issues on which the military and the civilian government must agree to avoid military takeovers, Janowitz provides a method to promote such agreement.[26]

Under Acemoglu and Robinson's model a distinction is drawn between *de facto* and *de jure* power to make the claim that even in the absence of one, the other remains.[27] In a sense, Acemoglu's and Robinson's writings extend from where Feaver left off: what happens when a traditional principal-agent relationship breaks down, or is reversed? An ostensible agent such as the military may in fact be the principal: in Acemoglu and Robinson's terms, the *de jure* agent may instead be the *de facto* principal.

> There can be equilibrium changes in political institutions and thus *de jure* political power; but these induce offsetting changes in the distribution of *de facto* political power. Put differently, when elites who monopolize *de jure* political power lose this privilege, they may still exert disproportionate influence in politics by increasing the intensity of their collective action (e.g., in the form of greater lobbying, bribery, or downright intimidation and brute force), and thus ensure the continuation of the previous set of economic institutions.[28]

From the military's perspective then, any loss in *de jure* power (for example, the support of the legislature or the judiciary) triggers increased military investment in *de facto* political power; this investment can take several forms, such as the precipitation of armed conflict or other security crises to justify any adventurism, greater lobbying of and intrusion in political parties, greater influence over the country's economy, and increased expenditure on public relations and cultivating grassroots support.

Insights from Huntington's work have also informed studies of post–Cold War civil-military relations. Michael Desch revived Huntington's strain of thought, using international systemic structural theory to examine the behaviour of states in achieving civil-military balance,[29] positing that "the best indicator of the state of civilian control is who prevails when civil and military preferences diverge. If the military does, there is a problem; if the civilians do, there is not".[30] He goes on to present a matrix within which to determine the civil-military balance of power using the level of "internal or external threat" to the nation.[31] He outlines four possible situations of threat: high internal and external threat, low internal and external threat, high external and low internal threat, and low external and high internal threat. He then posits that, historically, civilian control seems to be most effective when there is a high external but low internal threat to a state, as in this situation the interests of the civilian government and military align, and both institutions act most cohesively—where the civilian leadership can count on the military defending the state and realizing the end goals set out by the civilian government.[32]

While Huntington's work remains one of the most influential starting points in the corpus of civil-military relation academia, informing political science scholarship throughout the world, the work is not without its limitations. The critique of Huntington's approach to CMR can be framed in terms of three broad ideas: the tautological nature of his argument, overemphasis on the aspect of civilian control, and an inability to define his concept of "professionalism." Before engaging further into a critique of Huntington's model however, it is crucial to first note that his work is a normative theory of civil-military relations as opposed to an empirical work based on the testing of variables to establish causal links.[33] The theory revolves arounds prescribing what civil-military relations "should" look like instead of how they might—and have—actually shaped out in actuality as informed by varying, real-world circumstances. Taken out of this context, however, Huntington's theory is often misapplied to contexts it was never meant to explain.

For some critiques, Huntington's approach is based on a tautology—premised on the argument that a military that obeys civilian authority is 'professional,' and a military that defies it is not. Huntington's establishment of objective civilian control depending on the voluntary subordination of the military seems both circular and inapplicable in practical terms. For Huntington, military professionalism is the tool that keeps the officer corps separated from the civilian branches of the state; Feaver contests this characterization, arguing instead that Huntington presents a definition of professionalism more so than an actual description of a causal relationship.

Florina Matei contests Huntington's emphasis on democratic control by highlighting how, in the current global context, militaries have far more diverse roles than armed combat, requiring them to be effective not only in terms of managing violence on the battlefield, but also in engaging in non-combat activities and decision-making. Militaries today are engaged in nation-building both within and outside the borders of their host country, including humanitarian efforts following natural disasters, maintaining everyday law and order in cases of civil unrest, and combating crimes that are typically situated in remoter parts of the country or borders, such as smuggling or the international drug trade.[34] This diversity of roles also highlights the need for fluidity and cooperation between the roles of civilian and military institutions in the realization of these goals, which require the combination of expertise and logistical support of the armed forces; civilian law enforcement; intelligence agencies; civilian democratically elected policymakers and legislators, and technocrats.[35]

Huntington's normative separation of the civilian and military spheres may also exacerbate problems of accountability. As his theory proposes that civilians authorize the use of force and subsequently let the military manage the actual prosecution of hostilities, the consequences of battleground outcomes come to be associated with the civilian political leadership rather than the military which, self-evidently, nonetheless plays a primary role in shaping these outcomes. Cohen rejected Huntington's theory on this basis, using this reasoning to urge then-US President George W. Bush to hold his military leadership accountable for the US military's strategic failures in Iraq in 2006.[36]

Huntington also fails to define what his conception of "professionalism" exactly entails, particularly considering the constantly evolving nature of military professionalization considering changing policies, sociopolitical mores, and operational realities. Instead, Thomas Bruneau contends that "professionalism," like "culture," is not a static concept but is instead dynamic and mutable by virtue of educational programs,[37] shifts in the sociocultural context the military is embedded in, and variances in the operational conditions the military finds itself in. Professional norms are also institutionalized through legally approved, transparent policies for recruitment, training, education, promotion, usually consistent with the goals of the democratically elected civilian leadership.[38] This demonstrates that Huntington's professionalism, as a concept, cannot be taken as an absolute and should neither be generalized nor applied to contexts alien to that which the concept originated from; the differing definitions it may take, depending upon the peculiarities of its context, will determine how military professionalism will practically pan out.

Given these points of critique, Matei responds with a tripartite framework defining civil-military relations that attempts to fill in the gaps within Huntington's model. Matei's trinity involves, firstly, democratic civilian control of the armed forces predicated upon institutional control mechanisms, democratic oversight of the military, and the inculcation of professional norms within the military.[39] The second element of Matei's trinity is ensuring the effectiveness of security forces, which involves the development of a clear plan, strategy, or doctrine for security forces; structures to implement those doctrines such as defence ministries, national security councils, coordinating agencies, and so on; and the commitment of resources towards realization of the former two.[40] The final element is the efficiency of military action, i.e., the maximization of goal fulfilment using the least possible amount of resources.[41] Within Matei's framework all three components are essential and mutually reinforce each other, and the absence or diminishment of one hinders the optimal functioning of the other two, thus distorting civil-military relations and the efficient attainment of national goals.

Given the wealth of discourse on the subject, it nonetheless remains important to recognize that theories of civil-military relations may not enjoy universal relevance and are likely to vary considerably in their application—if possible—to non-Western contexts. Given that these locales may often have low levels of institutionalization, it is thus important that theories of civil-military relations be adapted to suit these contexts.

CIVIL MILITARY RELATIONS IN NON-WESTERN CONTEXTS AND THEIR RELEVANCE FOR PAKISTAN

While the theoretical frameworks within which to analyse civil-military relations are both varied and comprehensive, their practical applicability across a diversity of contexts remains to be seen. To this end, it is useful to first examine other developing or postcolonial states through the lens of these various theoretical frameworks, and to compare Pakistan's civil-military relations to those in these other developing countries. This comparison will aid in identifying issues within the domestic civil-military dynamic unique to the Pakistani context, while simultaneously serving a prescriptive purpose in aiding Pakistani and international policy makers in policymaking *vis-à-vis* domestic civil-military relations. Citing and drawing upon experiences from other developing or postcolonial states may also provide insights into analogous situations or issues arising in the Pakistani context. This section thus discusses two distinct types of developing states: global south countries and non-Western, Islamic states.

Studies on Latin American and Soviet/Post-Soviet states have highlighted several incompatibilities with applying Western-standardized approaches to these non-Western contexts. Three primary issues arise with generalizing Western approaches to these states: (i) the assumption of statehood, (ii) divisions between the civilian and military spheres, and (iii) the presumed norm of civilian control.[42] One example of this sort of incompatibility, for example, is Iraq's Kurdistan regional government: in this context there is no gap between the civilian and military spheres, nor a cogent understanding of professionalism or institutionalism—as applied to civil-military interactions.

David Pion-Berlin introduces the concept of formal and informal spheres of civil-military relations, an attribute crucial in laying the groundwork for an understanding of civil-military relations in disparate contexts. 'Formal relations'[43] refer to the contact between civilian and military leaders through formal avenues, such as defence organizations, tied through a formalized and official chain of command. This organizational ladder, using official lines of communication and abiding by official procedures, characterizes formal civil-military relations. Informal relations, on the other hand, relate to such interactions not ordained by law or an official source, but instead take place outside of such official avenues or hierarchies and depart from formalized rules and procedures.[44] This distinction will contribute towards our understanding of civil-military relations in areas where these two spheres are not clearly divided—as classical theories presume, particularly where levels of institutionalization are low. Specifically, Pakistan seems to lie in Pion-Berlin's "informal" category of civil-military interaction; in Pakistan's case, the National Security Council (NSC), which was founded with the intention of being the foremost institution coordinating relations between civilian and military leaders, has remained in the background in interactions between the civilian and military leadership. While it has convened a handful of formal meetings between civil and military leaders, the dominant culture is still largely ad hoc, private contact between members of the leadership, which suggests that the institutional role the Council was designed to fulfil remains lacking or underutilized.[45]

Frederick M. Nunn draws an important distinction between "military professionalism" and "professional militarism"[46] in his discourse on the South American Military. According to him, military professionalism, like Huntingtonian professionalism, is a condition based on education and expertise, involving autonomous institutional governance.[47] Professional militarism, on the other hand, "is the willingness and propensity to provide solutions to a country's problems—economic, political or social—based on a military ethos".[48] This professional militarism can be "latent", when the military thinks and behaves in a way that displays its conflict with the civilian leadership in politicking, or "manifest", when it also forces its solutions onto the civilian leadership.[49]

Nunn formulated his theory in the context of the South American states of Argentina, Chile and Paraguay, which gained independence from their Spanish colonizers in the early 19th Century, and have since hosted—to differing degrees—a growing and increasingly-professionalized military.[50] Since their independence, several of these states have undergone periods of authoritarian rule; Pakistan has shared a similar fate, both in terms of the increasing professionalization of the military as well its extended periods of authoritarian rule. At a minimum, many such states "retain the civilian form of government but to circumscribe its democratic content, rather than to opt for military rule as an alternative."[51] Increased "professional militarism" may thus become an informal, non-institutionalized, and non-regulated form of otherwise usurping power and control from the civilian government, without drawing overt negative attention towards the military.

An important distinguishing factor for some South American states, such as Chile, is that the professionalization of their military began after their independence, while upon its independence Pakistan inherited a professional, strong, standing military trained by the British colonial presence.[52] When the South American states did gain sovereignty, it was natural for them to follow and adopt the political changes taking place in Europe.[53] At the time Europe was in the throes of modernization, a process which gave rise to the professionalization of many institutions, including the military. The professionalization of South America's military was thus a social process running parallel to similar developments in Europe, as best illustrated in the continental models of France and Prussia (soon to be known as Germany in 1871).[54]

During this period, professionalized militaries were made to believe that, in addition to their traditional role of prosecuting wars and providing security from external foes, they were also expected to play an integral role in the preservation of domestic or internal state apparatuses—beyond what was historically envisioned of them. From this shared perspective European and South American military development diverged; the European experience involved building up states internally while—at the same time—embarking on external colonial projects aimed at 'civilizing' natives they came into contact with and ensuring resource extraction from these newly-colonized regions. By contrast, South America's military was almost entirely internally focused, and since there was no 'civilizing mission' directed abroad, it was often the underdeveloped civil society institutions that bore the brunt of the military's European inspired mission to govern in a 'civilized' manner.[55] The fact that these institutions were underdeveloped was itself used to justify significant military intervention into the civilian political and bureaucratic spheres. This ethic was so prominent in Cold War politics that most Third World countries also found themselves also embroiled in similar processes. As Nunn notes: "Both the Cold War—in many respects an era whose significance in Latin America may still be misunderstood—and the US military presence—the impact of which has certainly been exaggerated—reinforced internal role assignments dating from early in this century".[56] Furthermore, the US turning a blind eye towards strong domestic military intervention within these states, intervention which fostered favourable domestic economic conditions, was also considered tolerable. When the Cold War came to an abrupt close, however, the South American militaries found themselves on shakier ground in light of the US's ostensibly more critical view of authoritarian regimes overseas.[57] The fact of the matter remains, however, that in the South American context, more than for any geopolitical reasons, the military regimes failed to achieve any significant economic development while—at the same time—committing many human rights abuses, despite being given the chance to fully and directly participate in the political realm.[58]

The Pakistani experience has been both similar and dissimilar to the South American nations' civil-military relationship. Pakistan gained independence half a century after South America when global geopolitical realities were markedly different. Also, while in postcolonial South American states political dictators and autocratic parties were removed and subsequently displaced by the military on the premise of protecting democracy, in Pakistan, as will be discussed further on, the military was authoritarian from the very beginning. This difference has had an impact on the political system and the psyche of the civilian populations who might view the permanent role of the military in politics differently because of these varied historical contingencies. Additionally, Pakistan's "social process" has also been dissimilar to South America's; not only was it born with a "professional" army trained in the colonial British military ethos and hierarchy of service, but the transition to "professional militarism" took place relatively seamlessly as well due to weaknesses in the country's early civilian leadership and the natural lead role the military played in internal and external conflicts which plagued the country in its early years.

Not only was Pakistan's military internally focused (as South America's was), but it also contended with external existential threats from India, and a brewing separatist movement from the Bengalis. While the latter was—at the time—constitutionally and federally a part of the state—for geographical and sociocultural reasons it was often treated as disparate—almost 'foreign'—territory. Finally, much like in South America, American intervention in Pakistan had and continues to have a nontrivial impact on Pakistan's internal, domestic policies and the organization of its civil-military relations.

There are perhaps some peculiar, arguably unique factors in postcolonial states with an Islamic character, which have contributed to civil military imbalance, and which can also be observed in the Pakistani context. Egypt is one such example where, in addition to its involvement in Egyptian politics, the country's military also operates several institutions within civilian society including commercial interests. To protect these interests, the Egyptian military places retired officers from the army at senior positions within the state's bureaucracy to subvert civilian oversight over these industries.[59] In addition to the Egyptian military's own commercial interests, the US—seeking to retain Egypt's support as a regional ally—has also provided significant aid, consequently strengthening the Egyptian military's influence over civil society institutions. As per Robert Springborg "(t)he United States has inadvertently helped to strengthen the military's control over the polity, society, and economy, rather than to create a more effective and efficient military subject to civilian control. This is reflected in the US Agency for International Development's multi-year, cross-national empirical study of the effects of democracy promotion, which finds that US military assistance has actually worked at cross-purposes to assistance from the United States intended to improve Egypt's governance and promote democracy".[60] This is a form of post- or neo-colonial economic imperialism, a strategic tool employed by first-world powers to exert influence and control over third-world institutions—and by extension the global southern states that host them.

In a similar vein is Turkey which, like Egypt, became a sovereign state with the assistance of its army, including General Mustafa Kemal Attaturk who was instrumental in the prosecution of Turkey's war of independence. Unlike Egypt however, Turkey's preferred governmental mode was ostensibly democratic, and protecting the Turkish state—and its governance mechanisms—from external and anti-democratic forces became a priority termed Kemalism.[61] Turkish Kemalism has historically had far more traction than Nasserism has had in Egypt, with the Turkish military going as far as to periodically intervene in Turkey's civilian politicking on the pretext of protecting the norm of Kemalism from what it—i.e the Turkish armed forces—deemed to be 'undemocratic' or inconsistent with the norm.

Iran has had a unique experience with its own military: while there is an official Iranian army tasked with protecting Iran's borders, there is also the Islamic Revolutionary Guard Corps (IRGC), a parallel strategic military presence mandated by the Iranian Constitution to execute "an ideological mission of jihad in God's way; that is extending sovereignty of God's law throughout the world".[62] Examining the IRGC's evolution over time illustrates the novel way in which Islamic sectarianism was used by the militant IRGC to further Iran's geopolitical and strategic foreign policy. Iran, already an Islamic Republic, leveraged the Shi'a Islamist Ideology to gain support and recruitment from within and beyond Iran, with a specific view towards defending against threats—real or perceived—to the Shi'a Muslim identity, and to further a revolutionary Shi'a Islamist ideology.[63] Iran's military, specifically the IRGC, is unique in the sense of not only using sectarian differences to effect its political will domestically, but also to further its ideology beyond its national borders, garnering support and traction from Shi'a political pockets across the region.[64] The IRGC, despite having fewer troops than the Iranian Army, is nonetheless considered to be the dominant military force in Iran, and once established as a counterweight to the traditionalist regime's military strength, has now evolved into a force to be reckoned with, both locally and internationally.[65]

Islam has historically held significant sociocultural significance in Muslim-majority Pakistan, even being touted as the basis for the Two-Nation Theory leading to the nation's partition from British India. Invariably, since the country's independence sectarian political parties, such as the Jamaat-e-Islami (JI) and more recently the Tehrek-e-Labbaik Pakistan, have come to organize themselves along religious—i.e., Islamist—lines; these parties have, however, been allowed by the military to freely participate in national politics without facing the kinds of resistance their counterparts in Muslim-majority Turkey or Egypt experienced at the hands of their own respective militaries.[66] Conversely, their participation, and the extent to which Islamization could occur, in politics was, in fact, closely regulated by the Pakistani military.[67]

Examining these non-Western, Muslim-majority states allows one to position Pakistan on a spectrum of civil-military interactions and provides a clearer understanding of the potential courses of action (if any) that should be pursued to address imbalances in Pakistani civil-military relations. Three primary observations stand out considering this comparison: firstly, Pakistan's geostrategic security concerns arising out of its tense border with India and the ongoing Kashmir issue are far more formidable than Egypt's regional rivalry with Israel. Not only was Nasser able to instigate a war against Israel in 1967 but, when the need arose, Sadat was also able to put Egypt's differences with Israel aside to sign the Camp David accords to retain continued

United States aid and support. Conversely, India poses a much more credible existential threat to Pakistan, and the Kashmir issue has sparked armed conflict thrice in Pakistan's history. The fact that both countries possess nuclear weapons further escalates this regional rivalry and lends it international significance beyond South-Asia, and despite repeated attempts by the US and other global powers, relations between India and Pakistan have never normalized. This automatically places Pakistan's military in a position of strength *vis-à-vis* civilian institutions, as their perceived role as protectors of national borders and effectors of geostrategic security goes unchallenged.

Secondly, the Pakistani military, unlike Egypt's and Turkey's but like Iran's, presents itself as the guardian of Islamic values and justice. As Kukreja highlights: "The Pakistan Army, according to Dixit, 'claims to be the shadow of God responsible for exercising state sovereignty for the welfare of the Pakistani people of which they claim to be the most competent judge'".[68] In the Pakistani context the military lacks the basic democratic orientation by which it would otherwise consider itself an apolitical instrumentality of a democratic state;[69] unlike the development of the Deep State in Egypt,[70] the Pakistan's armed forces did not directly involve themselves in the execution of arrests and clamping down on domestic enemies: "(f)or the army, it was a situation of having your cake and eating it too. They determined policy in areas most important to them without getting into the mess of day-to-day governance. They formulated the Kashmir policy, the Afghan policy, and where they failed, the blame was put on the civilian government."[71]

Putting the non-trivial weight of Sunni Islam—the dominant Islamic sect in the region—behind an institution like the military, which presents itself as the primary—if not sole—guardian of the faith, further empowers the Pakistani military and inures it from civilian oversight, accountability, and checks and balances. Additionally, given the inherently undemocratic nature of an institution like the military, this enabling of the Pakistani armed forces further entrenches non-democratic norms in society—norms which previously would have been confined to the internal military hierarchy.

Thirdly, active US involvement cannot be discounted when comparing Pakistan's civil-military asymmetry to similar relations in other Muslim-majority states. The US proxy war fought against the Soviet invasion of Afghanistan, with the active support of the Pakistani armed forces, saw a massive influx of military and financial aid to Pakistan, resources which were used to bolster the Islamized regime of then-military dictator General Zia who actively served as a conduit to arm religious extremists including the precursors to the Afghan Taliban, eventually leading to the militarization of political Islam in the region.[72] Much like in the Egyptian context, US involvement in Pakistan's military presence and strength has been significant; in 1954, Pakistan signed the Mutual Defence Assistance Agreement, pursuant to which it became associated with the US in four distinct mutual security arrangements—becoming America's "most allied ally".[73] Aside from its strategic defence interests in increasing Pakistan's military prowess to better serve as a proxy in the region, the US has historically remained relatively unconcerned with the disproportionate political power the Pakistani military wields and the consequences this has for Pakistani democracy; in fact it can credibly be argued that Washington has historically tacitly supported the Pakistani armed forces' intrusions into the civilian-political realm, all while publicly espousing the ideals of democracy and political pluralism.[74]

Lastly, much like in Egypt and Iran, Pakistan's military also has significant interests embedded deeply within the country's economy. Various commercial powerhouses such as the Fauji Foundation, Shaheen Foundation, Bahria Foundation—controlled by the Pakistani army, air force, and navy respectively—as well as the Defence Housing Authority, along with their many subsidiaries, occupy a huge commercial space within the country, with operations as diverse and lucrative as food and beverage, construction materials, and housing and development.[75] Estimates place the Pakistani military as the largest urban real estate developer and manager, with the Army Welfare Trust—a foundation established in 1971 with the express purpose of identifying and capitalizing on potentially profitable ventures for the military—operating a commercial airline and one of the country's largest financial institutions—the Askari Commercial Bank. According to the United Nations Development Programme's Pakistan National Human Development Report, 2020—published in early 2021—"the military establishment owns the largest conglomerate of business entities in Pakistan, besides being the country's biggest urban real estate developer and manager, with wide-ranging involvement in the construction of public projects".[76]

Given its inextricable ties to the country's commercial framework, its nontrivial stake in the national economy, and its position as an economically stable and self-sufficient—arguably self-serving—institution, it has become increasingly difficult for the civilian government to control or curb the influence the Pakistani military wields domestically.

THEORIZING PAKISTAN'S CIVIL-MILITARY RELATIONS

The balance-of-power paradox between civilian and military institutions discussed above are theoretical frameworks developed from a uniquely Western perspective,[77] particularly from that of the United States and European states in the post–World War II and Cold War periods.[78] It must be therefore understood right at the outset, that these theoretical models—as expressed in the bulk of existing literature on the subject—cannot be applied in their entirety, or in the same ways, to postcolonial and non-Western societies such as Pakistan. In addition to the shortcomings of directly applying these Western perspectives on civil-military relations in Pakistan, a further pertinent point to consider is Pakistan's unique political and sociocultural dynamics, specifically demonstrated in the overlap between the military, Islamization and militancy in Pakistan, and how that impacts civil-military relations.[79] Much like it has within the broader politico-legal framework in Pakistan, Islam has played also a key role within the military's structure and practices. The religion has often been used as a unifying tool, cutting across cultural, ethnic, and political divides. Furthermore, the military has often been portrayed as the defender of Islam, especially in contradistinction to Hindu-majority India.[80] In his book *Pakistan: Between Mosque and Military*, Hussain Haqqani provides a comprehensive overview of the role of religion and the military in influencing and driving the country's domestic and foreign policies,[81] identifying that the source of the military's strength lies in the country's national insecurity plaguing the state since its inception.[82] Today, however, Pakistan's military might also be evolving in its role, pivoting away from its historical associations with Islamist groups and towards collaborating with the civil branch.[83] Following the 2018 general elections in particular, which marked the second consecutive democratic transfer of power in Pakistan's history, the military's role and involvement in civilian politics, and even its alleged inclination towards particular political parties, came into sharp focus,[84] with the current political opposition's chief contention regarding the outcome of the 2018 elections that the election was inappropriately supported and influenced by the military establishment. Despite ostensible civilian supremacy, as asserted in formal constitutional documents, the military is nonetheless widely considered to be Pakistan's major arbiter of external defence, foreign policy, and internal security and stability.[85]

Given this context of misplaced and inordinate military influence on civilian politicking, it becomes essential to examine certain theoretical models relating to political economy which help to better understand the reasons for, and provide potential remedies to, Pakistan's civil-military imbalance of power.[86]

Applying Huntington's model to Pakistan, the Pakistani military is autonomous and professional, and civilians generally recognize the military's expertise in its domain. The professionalization of the military has not, however, prevented it from interfering in the civilian sphere; instead, it may be argued that this professionalism—and the perceived competency associated with it—engenders greater confidence in the military's capabilities, even in areas traditionally falling within the domain of the civilian government.[87] In this context therefore, the professionalization of the military may instead enhance domestic perceptions of the military as the primary bearer of expertise and decision-making capabilities, beyond the perceived capacity of civilian governments, furthering its political aspirations and empowering it to overstep its role as an assessor and mitigator of risk by portraying itself as the sole capable arbiter of risks.

Whereas Huntington's idea of indoctrinating the ethos of civilian control at every level of the military, starting at the recruiting level, to achieve objective civilian control over the military is theoretically a tempting mode to adopt, it remains to be seen how this theory would effectively translate to a postcolonial context such as Pakistan's, where—at its inception—the military was already far more empowered than its nascent civilian leadership.[88] Huntington's model assumes a willingness on the part of the military to be educated in a way that entrenches the objective control of the civilian leadership—and necessarily at the expense of any political power the military may already wield. The first fundamental resistance to this model's application to Pakistan would thus be the patent lack of appetite for such a shift in the national power equilibrium. Not only has the balance of power between the civilian leadership and the military always been tipped in favour of the latter, but also there has been a conscious effort on the part of the military to maintain that imbalance, and even in certain instances to increase that ambit of influence. Considering the military's concerted effort to consolidate its own power, it is unlikely that it would be willing to yield the space so gained to the civilian leadership.

Another way this theory may not find fertile soil in the Pakistani context is in the very idea of "professionalism" that Huntington postulates: whereas Huntington's professionalism includes a recognition by the military that it is a tool of the state, and that the state is the dictator of policy, for Pakistan the military has often found itself in the position of either filling a political vacuum, or outrightly assuming control where it independently finds the civilian leadership lacking in some way. From the state's inception the military's role in Pakistan has been to "guide democracy to best represent its interests"; it can even be credibly argued that the military has "allowed democratic governments to rule intermittently, so long as they protected the interests of the military".[89] This significant—if not primary—role the Pakistani military has assumed exhibits the military's transcendence of its "professional" domain, assuming instead the role of dictating state policy and directing civilian actions as opposed to the converse. Put differently, Pakistan demonstrates that the military's professionalization, while significant, is not sufficient for ensuring the military's detachment from civilian affairs and can, in fact, arguably be seen to exacerbate military adventurism into civilian matters.

In a democratic state the civilian leadership must be able to oversee and direct military behaviour through established norms and institutions; in

Pakistan, however, the opposite holds true, with the military's autonomous power to influence and direct civilian entities woven deeply into these various institutions.

A strong army inarguably generates benefits for the host state; however, the stronger this military is, the easier it is for it to influence the state directly or obliquely. Members of the military are self-interested and so have an incentive to do so, since this allows them to redirect state resources to themselves. Civilian leadership may respond to this in two ways: build a strong army but accord it sufficient monetary and economic incentives to ensure a potential coup would be less attractive; or by 'downsizing' the army, thereby emaciating it and making it incapable of mounting coups. A "tin pot" army like this may not be large enough to exercise the state's monopoly of violence, but civilian politicians may view this as a more desirable outcome than having to economically maintain a large army—one which could potentially challenge the civilian government.

While the civilian government can remain in power with a cheap but ineffectual army, this presents the danger of potential internal or external threats to the nation's sovereignty[90] which, in Pakistan's case, are significant. India is perceived and presented as a perennial existential threat—a fear empowering the military to set goals and policies that would normally be within the civilian government's purview. Just as anti-Semitic rhetoric and propaganda in Nazi-era Germany portrayed the Jewish community as "parasites" on the German "body", whose destruction was a "last-ditch defensive survival strategy", and emboldened the German military to attempt to exterminate the community, so too does India present an ever-present 'threat' to the polity, justifying the continued empowerment of Pakistan's military.[91] This perception of India as an existential threat is magnified by the fact that the two states have gone to war four times, and have engaged in perennial smaller skirmishes and conflicts since their independence from the British colonial regime.

Another way in which application of Huntington's work may be inapposite to Pakistan's context is in his contention that the military and civilian regimes work under fundamentally different values and ethos; according to Huntington, the military expresses conservative values while the civilian sphere is inclined to articulate more progressive values.[92] While this conservatism may be ascribed to the Pakistani military, the domestic civilian sphere has not always been concurrently liberal. Pakistan, ostensibly created as a homeland for Muslims, has instead seen a strong inclination throughout its history towards the reform of legal and political structures to incorporate and overtly reflect Islamic principles and practices,[93] thereby resulting in the inculcation of a strong streak of social conservatism in the populace.

Samuel Finer identifies five preconditions for military intervention: the professionalization of the officer corps; the rise of nationalism and the nation state; substitution of divine authority of kings with the sovereignty of the people; insurrectionary armies; and the emergence of new, independent states.[94] This framework, applied to Pakistan's postcolonial context, further helps understand why the military dominates the domestic power dynamic within the country. Historical peculiarities in Pakistan have led to a highly-professionalized—as per Finer—and coherent officer corps, uneasily coexisting with a historically less disciplined or organized civilian government.

Moreover, the opportunity costs of professionalization are even greater for a newly partitioned postcolonial state such as Pakistan; the limited assets gained as a result of the country's independence processes were inordinately invested into the military, leaving civil institutions relatively too weak and underdeveloped to be able to exert sufficient control over the military, thereby further intensifying the pre-existing disparity in civil-military relations. The military inherited by Pakistan upon its independence was already well-trained and equipped, and deeply entrenched in the colonial power structure, as a tool of domination and power-projection for the British colonial regime. Given the regime's relationship with the colonized sub-continent, where the British Raj's primary interests were resource extraction and maintaining regional influence, the military that would later devolve to Pakistan was often deployed to subjugate the indigenous population, a population that subsequently—through civilian democratic processes—would presumably be superior. Due to these—and other—historical exigencies, the demarcation between Pakistan's military's internal and external goals has remained unclear, resulting in a weak and divided civil authority and an inordinately-internally focused military.[95]

Huntington's conception of the professionalization of the military may thus not always suffice to prevent the military from impinging upon the civilian sphere. Feaver, noting that the Huntingtonian professionalization of the military does not guarantee unfettered civilian control,[96] instead advances his principal-agent theory, which accords superior and subordinate roles to the civilians and military, respectively. Feaver's theory also falls short in its application to Pakistan, however, where the military has in fact directly wielded power several times and has therefore held a role superior to that of the civilian government.[97] Even though civilian governance structures may exist, and the military and civil society outwardly present themselves as two distinct entities, the military continues to exert *de facto* authority, reversing the principal-agent relationship as envisioned under Acemoglu and Robinson's model, with the military—in a position of dominance—inordinately influencing the subordinate civilian establishment,[98] rendering the *de jure* agent the *de facto* principal.[99] Further, the military continues to exert a nontrivial degree of influence over areas of governance which would ordinarily fall within the civilian government's scope. This is most explicitly exemplified by the military's key role in the development and projection of Pakistan's foreign policy, which is perceived in the west to ordinarily lie within the civilian sphere.

Therefore, in the case of Pakistan, the roles of principal and agent seem to have been—if only partially—reversed. The military is the principal that both supervises and incentivizes—financially and politically—the civilian establishment, which also includes corporate and commercial actors, to further its—i.e., the military's—interests. Military, corporate, and commercial enterprises thus become civilian agents, rewarded if profits are forthcoming and the military's interests are served; similarly, political actors willing to further the military's interests during periods of ostensible democratic rule are also politically and financially rewarded. Feaver's model can thus be seen to be working perfectly, with the exception that—in Pakistan's case—the roles between civilian and military leadership as principal and agent respectively are inverted. The Pakistani military—growing unfettered in stability, internal organization, and resources since its inception—demonstrates superior ability and political strength to assert itself as the principal, with the civilian architecture—repeatedly challenged and struggling towards stability—assuming a corollary role as agent.

In her book *The Military and Domestic Politics: A Concordance Theory of Civil-Military Relations,* Rebecca L. Schiff, has sought to go beyond traditional theories on civil-military relations by applying the concordance theory to India, Pakistan, Israel, Argentina, and Post-Revolutionary America.[100] While it acknowledges Huntington's separation theory as over-simplistic, Schiff's theory, however, also fails to acknowledge broader issues that cannot be solved—as she posits—via 'concordance'.

With reference to Pakistan, Schiff attempts to explain why the country—unlike its Eastern neighbour India, despite their shared colonial and pre-colonial history—has historically suffered from military intervention. Schiff argues that Pakistan embraced the Western separation model in its nascent stages: a political and military tradition inherited from the British colonial regime;[101] this tradition was, however, incompatible with Pakistan's indigenous cultural and political realities.[102] As a result, a political vacuum gradually began to develop, accentuated by the alienation of the Bengali community which the Pakistani political elite failed to address until it was too late.[103] The subsequent lack of concord among the military, political elites, and citizenry instead led to several military coups; greater agreement, Schiff argues, would have enabled Pakistan to avoid the repeated domestic military intervention it experienced.

Using concordance theory, Schiff attempts to explain the occurrence of military coups in Pakistan, arguing that these were the result of divergence and disagreement among the three primary, concordance actors (i.e., the military, political elites, and citizenry) over the four indicators (the officer corps composition, military recruitment method, political decision making, and military style), further exacerbated by extant ethnic strife among groups in Pakistan's diverse, multi-ethnic population and—most particularly—the attempted severe political disenfranchisement of the Bengali community.[104] Schiff's concordance theory as applied to Pakistan has both its detractors[105] and supporters[106], and arguably the theory fails to acknowledge that a 'discord' may not be the only prerequisite for a military intervention.[107] In this vein, as Zulfiqar Ali responds in his critique to the Schiff's hypothesis, the theory inevitably and unknowingly overlooks the many political and security issues extant in Pakistan, which could have contributed or precipitated military intervention, and seeks instead to impose a Western model of governance on a context vastly disparate from that from which such models originated.[108] Most significantly, Schiff's theory fails to take into account the renewed role of the military as a key stakeholder in development, investment, and related security, particularly relating to infrastructural projects such as the CPEC.[109] Fundamentally, Schiff's four "indicators" do not include concordance by the three "actors" in the fields of economic development and investment, perhaps because this is typically considered by Western theorists to be an exclusively civilian-political subject.

In '*The Professional Soldier*'[110] Morris Janowitz emphasizes the 'civilization of the military' through professional military education; this 'civilization' would, presumably, prevent discord between the military and civilian governments, reducing the risk of military interventions. While this theory may, in a sense, operate to keep the military within its domain, it overlooks situations where the militarization of the state apparatus may instead happen via soft coups; in point of fact, this consolidation of non-military power by the military has more recently been on the rise in Pakistan.[111] Moreover, it can be argued that the military's influence over civilian governance and decision making has developed to the point where it need not overtly assume the reins of power—and the concomitant diplomatic and public relations concerns that come with such a *coup d'état*—and can nonetheless continue to achieve its own internally-set goals.

Following the death of Pakistani military dictator Zia-ul-Haq in 1988, a new pattern of 'soft' or 'non-takeover' intervention developed, in which the emphasis shifted from assuming power directly, to playing a more subtle, but still ubiquitous, role from the side-lines. The military exerted—and continues to exert—nontrivial influence over key national issues, including the country's foreign security and policy, and has continued to moderate between feuding politicians or state institutions.[112] This 'velvet glove' approach persisted throughout the post-Zia period until the October 1999 coup conducted by Pervez Musharraf and, following Musharraf's resignation as self-appointed president in August 2008, has since been reinstated. Pakistan thus represents a counterexample to Janowitz's position; arguably, instead of a civilization of the military, we see a convergence towards the militarization of other—non-military—institutions, evinced in war-like political campaigns; the exile and incarceration of prominent politicians; and a strict, militaristic, hierarchy instituted in political parties and non-military institutions.

Lastly, under the Acemoglu and Robinson model, on the pretext of the threat of global terrorism and rising inter-ethnic conflict, the military recently conducted full scale military operations, including *Zarb-e-Azb* and *Radd-ul-Fasad,*[113] in the country's restive north-western regions. These—and other—campaigns eventually led to the *de jure* empowerment of the armed forces through legislative instruments, such as the 2014 Protection of Pakistan Ordinance and other, newly proposed, and promulgated amendments to the extant criminal law, further inuring the military from critique. As overt conflict can prove particularly costly and risky, the military also increases its *de facto* power through large-scale commercial enterprises such as the Defence Housing Authority or the Fauji Foundation, and through grassroots campaigning and public relations efforts through the Inter-Services Public Relations (ISPR) wing of the Pakistani armed forces.[114] The success and economic stability of these military-controlled enterprises, along with the narrative of the military as custodians of stability, progress, and strength—communicated through the ISPR and other platforms—inculcates within the polity the impression that the military—as opposed to civilian institutions—are the preferred institution within which to place one's trust, investment, approval, and expectations of progress and development. This combination of 'hard' power—through legislative instruments and military might—and 'soft' power—through public relations campaigns and commercial enterprises—all come together to further tilt the balance of power in Pakistan in its armed forces' favour.

From the above it thus becomes clear that Pakistan's military has historically been—and remains—overwhelmingly influential within the national context, enjoying political and financial capital while maintaining and promoting a heroic ideal to garner popular support. This has transformed the military into one of the most—arguably the most—powerful institutions in the country; the professionalization of the military and its concordance, as well as the alignment of broader civil society perceptions and engagements with the military along lines conducive to the military's own interests, have all served to entrenched its position as the principal, as Feaver would put it, with the civilian government relegated to the role of the agent in this inverted principal-agent model.[115] With this consolidation of a broad array of power; the support, co-option, and collaboration of major ethnic groups like the Punjabis; and atrophied systems of transparency and accountability, the intrusion of the military in civilian politics distorts entirely the federalist structure otherwise ostensibly aimed at empowering ethnic minorities and according them greater autonomy and security within the national context. This confluence of power within this one institution has resultantly served to exacerbate—rather than ameliorate—pre-existing sociocultural and ethnic frictions; the military's self-description as the guardian and proponent of Sunni Islam and it's drawing heavily from the Punjabi ethnic population for recruitment of the officer corps has served to marginalize non-Sunni, non-Muslim, and non-Punjabi communities within the state.

DEMOCRATIC VALUES V. ETHNIC CONFLICT AND NEOLIBERAL POLICIES IN PAKISTAN: THE ROLE OF THE MILITARY AND HOW LOCAL CENTRIPETALISM CAN PROMOTE HEALTHY CIVIL-MILITARY BALANCE AND POLITICAL STABILITY

This section begins with a brief overview of the Pakistani military's postcolonial history; exploring the influence it continues to wield over Pakistan's economy, foreign policy and—most importantly—national federal structures and politics; and illustrating how the military's continued intrusion into civilian politicking has given rise to the civil-military imbalance in Pakistan. Building upon this historical understanding, this section will then discuss the ways in which this imbalance stunts the realization of the positive democratic norms of distributive justice, collective minority rights, multiculturalism and local self-government in Pakistan, the absence of which have fomented political instability, and fostered ethnic conflicts and predatory neoliberal practices in the country. The section will conclude by positing prescriptions, framed through "local centripetalism," for how best to achieve civil-military symmetry and promote inter- and intra-communal harmony.

As will be elaborated upon further on, Pakistan has historically relied on unelected institutions, such as the military it inherited from the British colonial regime, to maintain its political systems and secure national solidarity. This has not always resulted in successes: the alienation of the Bengali population led to the secession of Bangladesh from the country, and—more recently—the Punjabi-dominated military's adventurism in and neo-colonial approach toward the provinces of Baluchistan and Khyber-Pakhtunkhwa have stoked the flames of separatism and discord in those regions. This historical inclination towards power being wielded by unelected institutions has also been intensified during the nontrivial periods of direct military rule in the country, where federal structures and institutions have inevitably declined, with the federal parliament and judiciary often acting subserviently *vis-à-vis* the—often unelected—executive.[116]

Historical Overview of Civil-Military Relations in Pakistan

Military coups and interventions seem to be a perennial feature of the postcolonial state; viewed as an instrument to keep the newly-autonomous state in a cycle of dependency and prevent it from leaving the former colonizer's sphere of influence, these military interventions are a means to essentially maintain the postcolonial state in a state of permanent infancy, constantly needing the support of a paternalistic military—itself a holdover of the colonial regime—to oversee and guide it.

The colonial heritage of the armed forces in Pakistan is a clear precursor to the country's continuing civil-military asymmetry. Following the 1857 mutiny in pre-partition India,[117] the British colonial regime realized "the strategic importance of the Punjab as well as the Punjabis who had earlier supported the 'military-fiscal state' of the [East India Company's] rule",[118] and moved to capitalize on this newfound understanding. This cultivation of the military to achieve the East India Company's capitalist interests proved to be the basis for the establishment of what Ejaz Hussain describes as the "praetorian oligarchy".[119] Pakistan's military has since inherited this colonial understanding of the organization of the state and the military and the interplay between the two, as well as the colonial-era policy of the 'Punjabicisation' of the armed forces, which have continued to express itself in the dominance by the Punjabi ethnic group of the Pakistani military's hierarchy, thereby contributing to inter-ethnic tensions.[120] This is most evident in the Pakistani military's approach to the province of Baluchistan, treated as a colony itself within the country, and subjected to forceful resource appropriation and disenfranchisement by the Punjabi-dominated armed forces.

Following the country's independence, Pakistan's military has continued to exercise its control by suppressing ethnic minority voices across the various 'smaller' provinces.[121] The disenfranchised Balochi population, for instance, has always contested the exploitation of its natural resources by the centre, specifically Punjab.[122] Unsurprisingly, the army has been a key player in suppressing Balochi secessionist movements, which have been alleged to receive support from an array of foreign actors including India, Iran and Afghanistan.[123] The CPEC project has only magnified this historical suppression of minority rights.[124] Other ethnic minorities have been dealt with in the same strong-armed manner by the armed forces, and while the Pashtun population—perceived of as a 'martial race' by the British colonial regime—has enjoyed significant representation in the armed forces, this has not prevent Pashtun nationalists from contesting suppression by the Punjabi-Muhajir nexus at the centre.[125] The United States' "global war on terror" and the rise in terrorism within the country have since led the Pakistani military to conduct extensive military operations, such as the *Zarb-e-Azb* and *Radd-ul-Fasad*, in the former—Pashtun-majority—tribal areas, with the Pakistani military employing a number of tactics previously relied upon by the colonial regime, including collective punishments and "forced disappearances"—i.e., state-sanctioned abductions, and a complete lack of any form of due process applied to the use of force. This sparking a response in the form of the Pashtun Tahafuz Movement (PTM)—literally the 'Pashtun protection movement', which demanded "an end to extra-judicial killings and arbitrary detentions of Pashtuns in the name of the war on terror.[126] The PTM is not novel in its ethnically-organized resistance to military oppression; similar movements have also arisen among the Sindhi and Muhajir populations (discussed in greater detail in chapter 2),[127] which have—in turn—provided the military apparatus with an easily-available justification for further uses of force.

The colonial legacy of Pakistan's armed forces has manifested itself in several other ways as well, the most significant of which is in the military's historic and repeated efforts to interfere with the state's civilian politics, often assuming direct control on the pretext of a political breakdown, or state of "emergency." These repeated interventions—direct or otherwise—have contributed to political instability in the country, co-opting the judiciary and over-emphasizing the role of the executive over that of the legislature, stymieing the country's political development and democratic progression and, in a self-fulfilling manner, laying the groundwork for justifying the next such intervention. This colonial heritage is also evinced by the military's operational practices,[128] attributable to the British colonial regime which viewed the then-British Indian Army as another instrument of its "divide and rule" policy.[129] The Pakistani military continued this legacy post-Partition—demonstrated, for example, through the military's disproportionate recruitment from Punjab, already politically and economically significant, to the detriment of representation from other provinces or ethnic groups. This policy of ethnically informed recruitment has since proved to be increasingly detrimental towards inter-provincial and inter-ethnic harmony, exacerbating historical, pre-existing ethnic, regional, and religious antagonisms.[130]

Domestic ruling elites—predominantly Punjabi—have refused to allocate space and accept Pakistan's vastly multicultural society,[131] and with the pre-Partition Punjabisation process firmly in place, all subsequent nation-building has since been viewed through this unitary lens. Any ethno-linguistic movement was thus viewed by "centrists, who have held power uninterruptedly since the partition . . . their opponents' demands as 'autarchic,' and anti-Pakistan. They have rapidly stressed on a doctrinaire uniformity whose basis is the conformity to the principle of 'one nation (Pakistan), one language (Urdu), and one people (Muslim)'".[132]

The first military coup in Pakistan, occurring in 1958, arose out of widespread conditions of social and political unrest: at the time there were agitations in Sindh,[133] secessionist movements in Baluchistan and the then-NWFP (now the province of Khyber-Pakhtunkhwa) against the "political and economic authority given to Punjab, while fear and mistrust was growing vis-a-vis politicians in the Awami League within East Pakistan".[134] Pakistan faced considerable headwinds in its early years and the emerging sentiment was that the civilian political leadership had failed to effectively address these challenges. The assassination of Liaquat Ali Khan—Pakistan's first Prime Minister—further exacerbated this perception of civilian incompetence, creating a political vacuum which allowed Pakistan's military the space to assert itself politically. This sentiment of civilian incapacity was shared by General Ayub Khan, the first Commander-in-Chief of Pakistan's Army who was—at the time—hugely influential and deeply engaged in the formulation of Pakistan's internal and foreign policy.[135] Capitalizing on the widespread civil unrest in the country, he advanced the argument that Pakistan's survival was "vitally linked with the establishment of a well-trained, well-equipped and well-led army"[136], a view substantiated by the Pakistani Supreme Court, which legitimized Khan's 1958 coup under the rubric of "doctrine of necessity"[137], a principle which has since seen several different iterations—each effectively creating a corpus of judicial precedent legitimizing military intervention into civilian affairs.

Major structural changes were enacted to the country's economic policies under the Ayub Khan regime, implemented through the civilian bureaucracy;[138] these were not only economically ineffective but were also discriminatory, disenfranchising the Bengali population in particular,[139] and the policies—and military intrusion into civilian affairs—precipitated massive public outcry and opposition, further aggravating inter- and intra-provincial dissonance. Ayub Khan stepped down in 1969, following a decade of direct military rule in Pakistan, succeeded by yet another member of the military, the then-Army Chief of Staff General Yahya Khan, to "ease the transition to democracy"[140].

It is with no small degree of irony to note that, at a time when Huntington was proposing that postcolonial states first need a stable political order to affect their successful social and economic development—one that necessarily must be an "authoritarian, modernizing dictatorship"[141]—Pakistan's political outcomes were the stark opposite. Ayub Khan's dictatorship seriously damaged Pakistan's political framework, and directly contributing to inter-ethnic strife within the country, culminating in the 1971 war with India and the successful secession of East Pakistan to form Bangladesh.[142]

The transition from Ayub Khan to Yahya Khan saw the consolidation of Pakistan's military's metamorphosis from a colonial to a postcolonial—and arguably neo-colonial—entity, deeply involved in the running of its state's government and entrenched in its sociocultural power centres, all while retaining the trappings of its colonial heritage.[143] Ensuing anti-military sentiment extended beyond the civilian populace and into the junior officer corps as well, with the collective pressure forcing Yahya Khan to step down in December 1971 and hand the reins of government over to civilian premier Zulfikar Ali Bhutto, the hugely popular founder of the Pakistan People's Party[144] (the "PPP"). The bulk of Bhutto's support nonetheless came from Punjab—the army's principal recruitment centre—and the military remained contented in the belief that Bhutto consequently would not act to hurt its interests.[145]

Over time however, as Bhutto made serious gains towards rectifying Pakistan's civil-military imbalance, promulgating the 1973 Constitution of Pakistan which persists—albeit heavily amended—to this day, and strengthening state institutions like the bureaucracy and judiciary, all of which sparked conflict with the military's top brass.[146] At the same time Bhutto, still struggling to subdue the various continuing insurgencies in the provinces—Baluchistan in particular—resorted to calling upon the army to help restore order and provide assistance in the wake of natural disasters.[147] These events not only allowed the army to whitewash its reputation and garner public support but also helped instil and reinforce in the Pakistani polity the notion that the civilian political leadership was using the army to further its own political goals, and that consequently the military was the only reliable and effective state institution.

During the 1977 general elections the Pakistan National Alliance (PNA), a right-wing, hardline Islamist bloc of political parties allied under their distaste for the left-of-centre PPP sought to contest the PPP's control of the government. Despite performing poorly in the elections, the PNA—with its not-inconsiderable street power, however, engaged in violent political activism, sparking widespread violence and civil unrest. While the PPP attempted to quell the violence through the deployment of civil paramilitary organizations, simultaneously negotiating with the PNA for a peaceful resolution to the ongoing political crisis, elements from the PNA approached the military leadership and—citing the lack of agreement between the PPP and PNA—sought to have the armed forces stage a coup to oust Bhutto's government. Once again, the military felt compelled to step in before the country fell to anarchy;[148] headed by General Zia-ul-Haq, the Chief of Army Staff under Bhutto, the military enacted a bloodless coup, ushering in the longest period of military rule in Pakistan's history.[149] Once again, the Pakistani Supreme Court legitimized the coup under the "doctrine of necessity", further inhering in the Pakistani legal framework and public consciousness the notion that the armed forces were the sole authority competent to oversee the state.

Zia's period of military rule was principally occupied with the promotion of an arch-conservative perspective on Islam; the 'Islamization' of state institutions, the legislative framework, and Pakistani society; and mass crackdowns on progressive political and civil groups.[150] Decades after the end of his regime, 'Islamists' persist in rallying for control over the civilian government, and jealously guard the Islamicized elements of the legal system—instruments that often operate to effect preferential legal outcomes for Muslims over non-Muslims.[151] Following Zia's death in 1988 general elections were conducted, ushering in a decade of civilian governance, with the two largest political parties alternating in power: the PPP lead by Bhutto's daughter Benazir Bhutto and the Pakistan Muslim League N (the "PML(N)") lead by Nawaz Sharif. This eleven-year span of democratically elected leadership ended abruptly when the Chairman of the Joint Chiefs and the Chief of the Army Staff General Pervez Musharraf instituted another bloodless coup, ousting Sharif's PML(N) government.[152]

This coup was yet another overt assertion of military authority over civilian decision-making; prior to the intervention Sharif found Musharraf rankling at instructions issued by the civilian government, fomenting tensions between the civilian and military leadership.[153]

Once again, the Supreme Court of Pakistan was called upon to adjudicate upon the legitimacy of the coup, and once again the "doctrine of necessity" was used to provide this legal fig leaf. Thus began a lengthy legal battle between Sharif and Musharraf.[154] It was evident that the judiciary's vacillation was guided by oppositional pressures—the military's on one hand and civilian on the other.

Musharraf consolidated his regime by amending the Constitution to further empower the executive—and the presidency within it—and by legislating through executive pronouncements—'ordinances,' reducing the role of the legislature to essentially a decree-stamping institution[155] and running the state from between 2002 and 2007 with little to no democratic input. The 17th amendment[156] to the Constitution—enacted by Musharraf's regime itself—however, required that by 2007, Musharraf had to choose between remaining the president or retaining his position as Chief of Army Staff, with the only institution standing between him and the abrogation of this choice being the judiciary. Iftikhar Chaudhry, the then-Chief Justice of the Pakistani Supreme Court, was unwilling to indulge the Musharraf regime on the matter, however, and so was summarily dismissed on the pretext of misconduct.[157] This sparked massive, nationwide demonstrations, bringing pro-democracy elements within Pakistan, including lawyers, students, and members of civil society, out on to the streets to protest this blatant abuse of power.[158]

Faced with mounting domestic and global opposition Musharraf had little choice but to step down as both President and Army Chief and announce elections in January 2008. Musharraf's ouster ushered in the longest unbroken period of democratic rule in Pakistan, but despite the outward trappings of democratic civilian-led governance, however, the country's powerful military continued to retain much of its economic and political clout.[159] Frederick Grare has argued that the then-Chief of Army Staff Ashfaq Parvez Kayani held the judiciary as a 'sword of Damocles' over the PPP government headed by Benazir Bhutto's widower Asif Ali Zardari at the time, to render it more pliant to the military's influence.[160]

From this historical context, the Pakistani military—already a formidable institution under the previous colonial regime—has since emerged to be the dominant institution within the national milieu. Manoeuvring emergency powers—those directly granted to it and those it has come to employ; state institutions; and domestic understandings of ethnicity, religion, and neoliberalism it has not only created a favourable environment for itself, but has also indirectly distorted patent and 'hidden' democratic values—such as localized governance, minority rights, multiculturalism, and distributive justice—to further stymie civil resistance that may be mobilized against it.

The military's ability to consolidate power has not been unilateral; over the years it has enjoyed the support of several institutions, including foreign governments,[161] but more significantly the national judiciary,[162] which has frequently provided strength and legitimacy to military coups by applying the 'doctrine of necessity'.[163] These legal artifacts, as well as other direct and indirect attempts at constitutional engineering in the form of emergency powers have further destabilized Pakistan's federal framework, leaving the military as an overt power at the cost of the polity's elected representatives and the state's civilian bureaucracy.[164]

Following the events of 9/11, and the subsequent inception of the United States' 'global war on terror,' Pakistan became a frontline state in the fight against religious extremism, with terrorism becoming a perennial threat to the state.[165] The country had to address the enormous influx of refugees from neighbouring Afghanistan—with some figures estimating over a million displaced Afghanis have taken in Pakistan—and the rise of violent extremism within its own borders. In response the Pakistani state—more specifically its military—has often invoked emergency powers, using terrorism as the pretext;[166] echoing the civil-military imbalance, emergency measures have also been imposed extra-legally by military leaders, with Musharraf's November 3, 2007, declaration of a state of emergency being a notable example.[167]

In 2015 the Pakistani legislature enacted the 21st Amendment to the Pakistani Constitution, excluding the application of articles 8(1) and (2) of the Constitution to a series of military-related statutes, thereby excluding the exercise of military powers from civilian oversight and allowing for the trial of civilian suspects of terrorism in military courts.[168] These clauses of the Constitution prevent the promulgation and application of laws which contravene the rights the Constitution confers—i.e., the 'fundamental rights' including due process protections and the right to life, and excluding these provisions effectively enabled a military-sympathetic legislature to exclude the corpus of military law from constitutional rights protections. A further attempt to curtail opposition—or even critique—of the powerful military came in September 2020, when the government proposed a bill to the legislative assembly imposing criminal sanctions on anyone who "ridicules, brings into disrepute or defames the Armed Forces of Pakistan or a member thereof . . . ".[169] While the bill has yet to materialize as law, and has faced a degree of nominal opposition, its imprecision lends itself well to chilling any form of public critique or resistance to military interference into civilian affairs. More recently, significant amendments have been made to the [Pakistan Army Act, 1952] by way of the Pakistan Army (Amendment) Act, 2023 to criminalize the 'defamation' of the country's armed forces, effectively criminalizing the intranational critique of the country's armed forces, their personnel, and their associated concerns. Additionally, through the proposed Official Secrets (Amendment) Bill, 2023, Pakistan's intelligence agencies would have been granted extraordinary, sweeping powers to warrantlessly conduct raids, confiscate property, and arrest citizens for breach of the instrument's provisions. Over the course of its passage through Parliament's legislative houses the bill came under harsh criticism for its "draconian" nature and was referred to the Senate Standing Committee for review despite which it passed in the face of strong opposition from both the opposition benches as well as from members of the ruling coalition government. The Official Secrets (Amendment) Act 2023 was passed with the amendments recommended by the Senate, significantly, this includes removal of the clause that would have otherwise granted sweeping powers to the intelligence agencies to conduct raids and make arrests without warrants.

Granting the military wide-ranging emergency powers and exceptional protections is particularly problematic within a pluralist federal system like Pakistan's, where the risk of abuse of such powers to the detriment of minority communities is far greater, particularly those minority communities that are already marginalized and disenfranchised by the majority as well as the military.[170] Such communities, already operating at the margins of the Pakistani polity, are often characterized as either 'fair game' for abuse at the hands of the military, owing to historical tensions between these communities and the political centre, or do not loom large enough in the public consciousness to warrant much sympathy from larger, more influential elements of the Pakistani polity.[171] Ethnicities or religious minorities which have historically failed to achieve significant representation in the civilian political leadership or bureaucracy are often treated as subject groups or colonized peoples;[172] the most visible example of which is the pre-1971 differential treatment accorded to the Bangladeshis, which culminated in the 1971 war and the secession of Bangladesh. Even today the Pakistani army remains disproportionately Punjabi and Pashtun, with ethnic groups such as the Balochis largely excluded. This ethnic exclusion has exacerbated the discord caused by military operations conducted in the former Tribal areas, with minorities alleging human rights violations at the behest of the armed forces.[173] These campaigns, such as Zarb-E-Azb, have not only raised serious human rights concerns, but have also inordinately impacted the collective group rights for populations internally displaced due to conflict.[174]

In the context of the military's leveraging of its particular conception of religiosity, and its potential for repressive state action against minority groups, it is necessary to discuss Pakistan's Ahmadi minority as a case study of such military oppressiveness.[175] In 1974 Prime Minister Zulfiqar Ali Bhutto promulgated an amendment to the Pakistani Constitution declaring Ahmadis to be non-Muslims,[176] despite the fact that this contravenes the fundamental freedom to practice religion guaranteed under article 20 of the Constitution.[177] Further to this, Zia-ul-Haq implemented separate electorates before the 1985 elections, requiring Ahmadis to register as and vote for non-Muslims, therefore barring them from active political participation.[178] This is significant as by isolating this minority group from freely voting and contesting in elections, the Zia regime amalgamated an erstwhile Muslim group with other religious minorities—such as Hindus, Sikhs, and Christians—diluting and fracturing the voting power of all such groups.

The military has also been accused of interfering in civilian elections, including the 2018 general elections,[179] and more recent by-elections.[180] This political engineering, a reflection of colonial-era 'divide and rule' policies employed by the British colonial presence, has allowed the military to ensure its interests are served without directly engaging in the messy business of overtly running the state. Capitalizing on ethnic and religious differences, these intrusions have resulted in the further polarization of civilian participants in politics and the emboldening of religious fundamentalist parties such as the Tehreek-e-Labaik,[181] and highlight the growing challenges to fundamental rights—including freedoms of personal, religious, and political expression—presented by the country's armed forces. This, in turn, further erodes the civilian polity's ability to push back against intrusion by the armed forces in a vicious cycle and paves the way for future transgressions by the military.

Successive military tenures in Pakistan have attempted to institute local government mechanisms to centralize power further, impacting the organic development of grassroots democracy, with formalized local government infrastructures replacing the informal, pre-independence panchayat systems.[182] Upon the institution by Ayub Khan of martial law,

> the military government immediately set about purging the political system of politicians through the promulgation of Public Offices (Disqualification) Order in March 1959. Owing to the lengthy procedure and limited scope of PODO, it was followed only a few months later by EBDO, Elective Bodies (Disqualification) Order, which was applicable to any person who had held any public office or position including membership of any elective body in the country. Thus about 6,000 politicians and officials were disqualified under EBDO, or EBDOed in the parlance of the time.[183]

To reinstate the local governance system Ayub Khan introduced the system of 'Basic Democracies' in 1960, to further consolidate power and introduce a 'party less political system'.[184] 'Basic Democrats' were elected at the local government level to form the Electoral College, which re-elected Ayub Khan as president and lent his regime significant support and legitimacy.[185] This "consolidation of power, designed to serve and benefit various military regimes . . . has tainted the very concept of local democracy in Pakistan".[186]

In 1979 Zia also adapted a local government model with a view towards centralizing power by bypassing provincial governments.[187] Following the fourth military takeover, the Musharraf regime similarly instituted a devolution plan, which established a three-tiered local government system[188] which effectively blunted the impact of provincial concerns in the electoral processes; while Musharraf's local government system held some degree of promise, the fact that it had been implemented under military rule—in the absence of functional national and provincial governments—poisoned the attempt in the eyes of the polity.[189] In addition to a degree of broader centralization, specific areas such as the police, irrigation, higher education, and planning and development were not devolved to the local level but instead retained by the centre.[190] Taj and Baker note:

> (a)s such, the Musharraf government may have sought to bolster itself by empowering local governments who would then lend their support to the regime. Second, the Musharraf government might have sought to entrench the power of the federal governments through the bureaucracy (which it could control). As the government had oversight of the funds necessary to deliver public goods, it was able to manipulate the elected representatives who were supposed

to hold executives to account. As such, the reforms allowed the federal government to secure greater control of Pakistan.[191]

Following its fourth experience with military rule, the 18th Amendment was signed into law by President Zardari in 2010,[192] pursuant to which the President no longer controlled the appointment of judges or senior military officials without the aid of the elected Prime Minister. The 18th Amendment can thus be viewed as an effort to resist the ever-increasing encroachment of the military upon civilian affairs, and an attempt to bring parity in civil-military relations.[193] The 18th Amendment, however, does not—and arguably cannot—guarantee that the Pakistani military will not continue to influence domestic politics. Not only does the civilian government continue to have limited say in the development of the military budget and policies,[194] it also lacks real independence in the determination and application of national foreign policy due to domestic security threat perceptions presented by India and Afghanistan—less than friendly states on Pakistan's eastern and western borders.[195]

The 18th Amendment also fails to address the issue of disparity of representation and does little to tackle the persistent centralization of power at the federal level.[196] Even in a hypothetical democratic utopia this consolidation raises concerns *vis-à-vis* the apportionment of powers and resources at the provincial and local levels; in the Pakistani context this also carries with it the uncomfortable sentiment that such a concentration of power at the centre renders it easier for co-option by the military. Further, since its promulgation, there have been increasingly strident calls to reverse or revise the 18th amendment to allow the civilian government to exercise more control over budget allocation,[197] though these calls have yet to develop any measure of significant traction.

The 18th Amendment can thus be viewed as an—arguably—ambitious attempt by civilian political elites to curb the burgeoning influence of the military on civilian affairs, to decentralize executive state power and, in doing so, render the state less susceptible to military capture. This represented an attempt by intranational consociationalist forces and provincial elites, targeted at the military immediately preceding an extended period of direct military rule, to empower the provinces at the expense of the federal centre. The amendment's implementation, however, has left the state with more problems than those it solved. Many of the powers devolved to the provinces—such as criminal justice, human rights implementation, and energy policy—have been poorly exercised, often due to disparities in provincial capacities to affect these policies. This has resulted in hindered international reporting on international treaty compliance—including on human rights issues, inconsistent—and often inadequate—provincial budgetary allocations, patchy promulgation of enabling provincial legislation, and the exacerbation of provincial asymmetries and the further entrenchment of ethnic ascription in political activity, among other serious issues. Though the 18th amendment was a correction, Pakistan's federal architecture is in dire need of authentic, grassroots federalism as opposed to the top-down devolution wrought by the amendment; while the state remains inordinately centralized and the provinces still require significant empowerment, such cannot come at the expense of the effectiveness of national responses, particularly in areas impacted by the state's international legal obligations.

Over the course of Pakistan's post-independence history, the nature of the military's role within it has ranged from minimal influence through entrenched political channels to overt control through military intervention.[198] Despite receiving the largest part of the national budget, the military has also become a commercial juggernaut within the Pakistani economy.[199] The diversification of its economic interests has allowed the military to become the strongest commercial enterprise within Pakistan, which it naturally furthers through its military, political, and sociocultural clout.[200] Further, numerous significant bureaucratic positions are allocated to retired senior military personnel, with many others serving on the boards or as chairmen of important public- and private-sector organizations.[201] As a result, retired generals and brigadiers have—upon leaving active service—assumed control of key civilian positions.[202] During the Zia regime international lending institutions such as the IMF and the World Bank issued a number of loans to Pakistan, part of the west's cultivation of the military regime in light of the Soviet incursion into neighbouring Afghanistan. Today a not-inconsiderable percentage of the national budget goes towards servicing this debt; the lion's share of what remains is allocated to the military as part of the defence budget,[203] with the insufficient remainder trickling down for social welfare programs such as health care and education.[204] Pakistan's financial policies have since been largely dictated by foreign financial institutions, which have increasingly come to espouse an extreme, neoliberal position.[205]

Pakistan's armed forces benefited from this pivot towards predatory neoliberal policies not only during the periods of direct military rule, but subsequently as well, leveraging its position as the dominant state institution—with its uncontested monopoly over intra-national violence—to transform itself into the largest and most successful corporation in Pakistan, further weakening civilian institutions.[206] The perpetuation of these neoliberal practices has given rise to massive food and water insecurity within Pakistan, with negligible levels of human development and tremendous oppression of disenfranchised elements of the polity—the rural poor in particular. This disaffection—and the tremendous scale it is occurring on—and the sacrifice of the already-inadequate welfare structures in place have left a vacuum readily filled by Islamic fundamentalist forces[207]—something not inherently unique to the Pakistani context, but which has seen expression across the Muslim world; the failure of state institutions to address the core needs of their polities leaves fertile soil for extremism—religious or otherwise—to fester, and the rise of Islamic extremism in Pakistan—and elsewhere—can be directly attributed to these neoliberal praxes.

The steady march of neoliberalism, coupled with the ever-increasing power imbalance in favour of the military if left unchecked, will severely impact the rights of Pakistanis—of minorities in particular (further elaborated upon in chapter 4) by reducing the space within which to effect distributive justice and realize these groups' collective minority rights.[208] The current situation is already untenable, and there seems little hope if present trends are allowed to play out to their inevitable conclusion. The downward spiral in Pakistan's civil-military power equilibrium and the steady, unimpeded encroachment by the military beyond its domain necessitates a revised CMR approach, with fundamental, structural changes to Pakistan's existing politico-legal framework required to address this civil-military asymmetry and ensure the autonomy of civilian governmental institutions.

CIVIL-MILITARY IMBALANCE AND COMMUNAL DEMOCRATIC NORMS

The military has ruled Pakistan directly for over thirty of its seventy-year history. It is not only the strongest institution within Pakistan - the recipient of a significant and ostensibly disproportionate chunk of the national budget - but is also the most affluent commercial enterprise within the country. Aside from this, significant bureaucratic positions are often taken up by retired military personnel, with senior ex-servicemen from the institution also occupying major roles as chairmen or board members of some seminal public and private sector organizations. The military's involvement in China's economic agenda in Pakistan through the China-Pakistan Economic Corridor (CPEC) further compounds the army's negative socioeconomic role. It's control over - and involvement with—the CPEC projects and investments have meant the further suppression of minority voices, such as Pashtuns and Balochis, who not only feel that they are disempowered in these projects but are particularly resentful of the Punjabi-dominated armed force's usurpation of the economic gains. All these factors deepen the inequitable distributive divide against the civilian population generally but most acutely against the underrepresented ethnicities and minorities.

Throughout Pakistan's history, frequent military interventions have led to disruptions in democratic apparatuses; these coups are then justified on the basis of the “doctrine of necessity” through the judiciary, which further undermines the system of democratic checks and balances upon autocratic use of power. The country’s powerful military has also subverted democratic processes by distorting electoral functions, often ‘engineering’ elections to support certain political alliances, who are then expected to prioritize and serve the interests of the army.

In addition, the military’s attempts at establishing local governments without allowing party affiliations in Pakistan were extraneous to the very concept of local democracy, as they had the aim of consolidating power at the center to further cement their autocratic rules. These local governments have, more often than not, been used to bypass functional provincial governments, which eventually served the purpose of retaining power within the top brass of the army establishment.

The military’s composition has also been one that negatively impacts the protection of collective group rights and the state of multiculturalism in Pakistan (see chapter 1). With Punjabi hegemony consistently displayed within the military’s top ranks, it is no surprise the military has suppressed separatist movements and ethnic minorities, like the ones initiated by the Baluchis and Pashtuns. The military’s use of religion to overwhelm political rhetoric has also resulted in the suppression of certain religious minorities, particularly Ahmadis. Another way in which the military has compromised multicultural values is by attempting to create a narrative, through its media-savvy Inter Service Public Relations company, that promotes a false unitary national identity of speaking a common language (Urdu) and belonging to a common ideological frontier (Sunni Muslim). This alienates minority ethnicities and religions—for example, the Shi’a Muslim community—and has, in the past, also led to the Bengalis feeling disenfranchised and discriminated against.

The following section will recommend prescriptions to address the various issues at the heart of civil-military imbalance in Pakistan. These recommendations for positive change are developed to be indigenously viable and are intended to address not only the symptoms of the military’s burgeoning power but also the underlying tensions and frictions extant in Pakistan’s diverse socio-cultural and politico-legal context which facilitated the military’s rise to dominance, to ensure that the proposed remedial measures inhere within the state’s organization.

PRESCRIPTIONS FOR CIVIL MILITARY RELATIONS

The preceding section comprehensively outlines the means and methods utilized by Pakistan’s strong military to impinge upon the relatively weaker civilian institutions which were unable to maintain or foster democracy in Pakistan. As a result of this military prominence in the Pakistani state and society, the state itself has trended towards heavy-handedness in its use of violence against both external and internal threats, which holds implications for minority groups perceived—or presented—to be 'allied' with these hostile forces.[209] Much like the Jewish population was scapegoated by the Nazi-era German state, minority groups—particularly religious minorities, being perceived or presented as 'non-Muslim', are 'other-ized' and rendered into convenient scapegoats to excuse failures of the state; while this ascription of blame or fault to these already-disenfranchised groups may initially be limited to the state and its institutions—such as the military, subsequently this predisposition permeates civil society, further pushing these communities to the political periphery.

The norm of civilian supremacy would thus require constitutional protection to effect internal order and civil liberties in a way which prevents the military from using excessive force without concomitant adequate government oversight. This alone may, however, not go far enough; as posited by Huntington, weak civilian institutions may enable or encourage ambitious civilian leaders to enlist the military to come to power, thereby eroding democracy and providing the military with inroads into the halls of civilian power.[210] As a result, constitutional provisions asserting civilian supremacy alone prove insufficient in the absence of similarly strong civil institutions which seek to confine the military to the barracks.[211]

In the absence—or compromise by the military—of such institutions, as discussed in the earlier sections of this chapter, the professionalization of the military[212] may lead it to assume the role of the principal, rather than the agent.[213] This, subsequently, leads to the possibility of the military, formally or informally, exercising effective control[214] or accreting *de facto* political power.[215] It is thus necessary for all stakeholders—the military, the political elite, and the citizenry—to agree on the composition of the officer corps, the recruitment and style of the military, and the political decision-making process.[216] It is through such an agreement that a convergence of the civilian and military institutions may emerge as a solution for inter-institutional frictions.[217] This concordance, and the collaborative framework built upon it, can only be agreed to through consultative dialogue between the civilian institutions (including the legislature, judiciary, civil bureaucracy, and armed forces). To this end a binding and authoritative legal instrument, establishing a national oversight council and clearly delineating the individual areas of competence and roles of stakeholders, with mechanisms to address potential issues which may arise in each area of national significance, can be prepared outlining the bases for constructive consultative dialogue to take place.

A system of government is needed which cultivates strong civilian institutions.[218] This may be achieved through a localized centripetal parliamentary system of government, as opposed to the present presidential-parliamentary hybrid.[219] As demonstrated in the case of Pakistan, presidential systems can allow for a concentration of power, and rule by decree; such systems might have the ability to respond well in emergency situations or to counter threats, but this very characteristic has—in the Pakistani context—been used by the military as a pretext to co-opt power through the use of various emergency powers and ordinances.[220] Linz argues that parliamentary systems are more conducive to fostering stable democracies, especially for countries, such as Pakistan, with pre-existing deep socio-cultural rifts.[221] This is supported by the fact that parliamentary systems are less likely than presidential or mixed systems to rely on emergency measures,[222] lending Linz's thesis a nontrivial degree of weight in contexts such as Pakistan's.[223]

The use of these emergency powers by the military has led to the consolidation of power in the centre, generating friction in and between federal and provincial structures.[224] This, in turn, has prompted and exacerbated inter-provincial issues, which have even resulted in particular minority groups being singled out for oppressive treatment.[225] In Pakistan's recent past, the peoples most affected by expressions of military violence—primarily counterterrorism and secessionist-suppression campaigns—have come from the 'smaller' provinces of Khyber Pakhtunkhwa and Baluchistan, who are also subjected to ethnic profiling and 'preventative' incarceration under special laws.[226] Granting the centre emergency power undermines the consensual nature of the relationship between the subunits, and between these federating units and the centre upon which federalism is predicated.[227] However, absent outright civil war or armed conflict, these concerns may, instead, be circumvented by requiring consent from, or granting veto powers to, the federal subunits affected by such declarations of emergency or military intervention within their territory, allowing the federating units to maintain their autonomy in times of peace.

To this end there needs to be constitutionalized emergency powers provisions regulating the use of these emergency powers, incorporating the necessary safeguards for when the military is required to bring its monopoly on violence to bear. These could include a) a legislative majority agreeing to the declaration of an emergency; b) an emergency constitution in operation for the duration of the crisis; c) the formation of committees under this emergency constitution in which opposition parties can play a role in military oversight; and d) a judiciary able to review the declaration of an emergency and executive actions taken during it.[228]

In addition to delivering on governance and developing adequate policies for the social welfare of the masses, which—in turn—reduces the space within which inter-communal resentment may fester, the legislature also must reinvigorate its powers to scrutinize the actions of the security apparatus via parliamentary committees.[229] While parliamentary committees do exist for oversight on issues such as human rights, the CPEC, and defence, the role of these committees needs to be bolstered through constitutional reform. For instance, while the Parliamentary Committee on National Security was established in 2019 to oversee the transition, the prosecution of extremism-related offences from military courts to civilian courts through criminal justice reform,[230] the committee still lacks any stakeholders or experts on criminal justice reform to assist with monitoring or facilitating this transition.

Seeing the military's control over the judiciary throughout Pakistan's history, another essential criterion to address the civil-military asymmetry is an independent judiciary, fully empowered to conduct the necessary checks and balances on the military where required. For instance, in the face of rising extremist violence, Pakistan instituted military courts—on the pretext of a weak and 'lenient' criminal justice system—to try civilians for a host of political crimes on the basis of terrorism without them providing the requisite levels of due process protections to the accused.[231] It becomes imperative, therefore, to strengthen both the civilian criminal justice and law enforcement systems[232] through procedural reform to limit the need for and reliance upon military courts.[233] More specifically, while it may not be possible to limit the application of military courts to trials of 'hardened terrorists'—though that term itself eludes clear and necessary definition—section 7.2.3 of the 1952 Pakistan Army Act should be amended to accord the convicted the right to appeal the decision of a military court before the civilian superior judiciary.[234]

In a similar vein, the corpus of precedents historically justifying the grant and use of emergency powers by the military requires serious reconsideration; to do so, the Pakistani courts must be empowered to make free and fair determinations on the cases before them, without fear of facing personal or professional consequences for their decisions, or out of excess concern for the principle of *stare decisis*. While the value of judicial precedent in a common law legal system as a means of ensuring predictability and consistency of legal outcomes cannot be overstated, given the volume of case law justifying and legitimizing the grant and use by the executive—including the military—of emergency powers has had a disproportionately chilling effect on the broader democratic context of the country. Whether this change is affected through judicial reform, increased judicial protections, or greater transparency, the arbiters of Pakistan's legal system must be able to render their judgements without pressures from political or military leadership.

Further, while the effects of the 18th amendment's curbing of the executive's role in judicial appointments will take time to become more pronounced, the potential increase in relative judicial autonomy is nonetheless a net positive.[235] This judicial independence granted by the 18th amendment might provide a useful starting point in effecting institutional and systemic reform in Pakistan's judicature, strengthening this pillar of the state to institutionalize checks and balances for the military,[236] not only within the appellate courts but the subordinate judiciary as well.

A key feature in Pakistan's constitution are the provisions for the civilian government to call upon the military to act in aid of civil power.[237] These provisions need to be revisited, given the wide array of ways in which the military may—and historically has—abuse(d) the powers vested in them through these provisions. This concern has come into sharp distinction following the inception of the United States' 'global war on terror,' where—in Pakistan for example—the military adopted an enhanced and pervasive role within the state using the threat of terrorism as its pretext. This imbalance was further compounded by the promulgation of a series of draconian legislative instruments—passed under pressure from the military—which essentially allow Pakistan's armed forces, 'acting in aid of civil powers,' to target citizens in restive or underdeveloped regions of the country under the cover of law with near impunity. To this end the Pakistani military was further empowered through the Actions (in Aid of Civil Power) Regulations, 2011 (AACPR) and the Protection of Pakistan Act, 2014 (PPA).[238] The former conferred powers on the military during counter-insurgency campaigns to detain individuals, seize property, and punish 'miscreants'.[239] It was employed by the military in its conduct of extensive military operations against extremists in the Swat Valley and other Provincially Administered Tribal Areas (PATA), including against the insurgents who attacked Nobel laureate Malala Yousafzai.[240] The fact that the civilian government has called upon the military to address the threat of terrorism is inherently problematic; in other parts of the world such offences are prosecuted against by civilian law enforcement agencies, with the presumption being that the military is a defence against external or existential threats to the state. For instance, the US Posse Comitatus Act expressly forbids the use of the armed forces for law enforcement operations, unless expressly authorized to do so by an Act of Congress or the Constitution.[241]

With the merger of these former tribal areas into the province of KP, it becomes increasingly necessary for the civilian courts and law enforcement to exert their jurisdiction, and for the elected legislature to redefine the emergency powers of the military; while these regions may have represented Pakistan's 'Wild West'—a position originally taken by the British colonial imposition which saw them as being too much trouble to formally annex—this has only served to disenfranchise their populations, freeing the military from the mundane concerns of 'due process' or 'civil liberties'. Their incorporation into one of the provinces brings the former tribal areas into the mainstream constitutional framework and is a step in the right direction; however, so long as the military is empowered to act as a policing force, the underlying concern of military excesses will persist, regardless of the targeted region's geographical or constitutional proximity to the centre.

In balancing the civilian-military relationship, the military's domestic actions towards promoting internal order must not be allowed to lead to further violence. The Pakistani armed forces' perspective on Baluchistan—as a subject region or colony—has encouraged a heavy-handed approach to its peoples. This, in turn, has precipitated a significant and long-running secessionist movement in the region, one which has courted—and been courted by—foreign states including India and Iran. One of the safeguards instituted to forestall this antipathy may be to ensure that the military deployed to a particular area, especially an area consisting of ethnic minorities or other underrepresented groups, is representative of the respective majority ethnicity of that region.[242] This would require reforms to the recruitment processes of the military, fostering an even more centripetal military adequately reflective of not only the diversity of Pakistan itself, but—in that specific context—of minorities of the region within which the force is operating. Legislative reform may be needed to achieve this goal, with provisions dealing with military recruitment to remove any barriers to recruitment for ethnic or other minority groups. The military leadership should similarly be diversified to ensure greater representation of historically disenfranchised and underrepresented groups in the armed forces' top brass. Policies emphasizing diversity management should also be instituted into the organizational ethos of Pakistan's armed forces, to attract a more diverse force and sustain this ethnic diversity.[243] Increased diversity would not only prevent any particular ethnic group from inordinately influencing the institution as a whole—or any deployment thereof, but would also ameliorate the 'other-ization' of disenfranchised and underrepresented groups, moderating or precluding any excesses the military may commit.

Taking attempts to decentralize further, the 18th Amendment must be implemented more stringently, enabling provinces with the necessary expertise to manage the new technical subjects devolved under the 18th Amendment and indirectly keep the military at bay. While the amendment had the effect—on paper—of devolving several technical subjects to the provincial domain, in practice since its promulgation few provinces have either the capacity or the appetite to assume the burden. For example, while labour law is one of the subjects that now falls within the legislative and executive competencies of the provincial government, most provinces continue to apply the federal legal and regulatory regime to labour issues within their borders, even though the labour realities across the provinces differ significantly. Encouraging and enabling the provinces to adopt these responsibilities would not only ensure better outcomes but would also draw down the previously-consolidated power from the military and the centre to the provincial—and potentially local—levels. To strengthen democratic institutions and electoral processes—with a view towards improving collective minority representation—it is also imperative to break up the power-oligopolies currently wielded by the country's military and the larger ethnic and religious groups. To do so, it is necessary to create more provinces, by splitting up the existing ones, to break the power of the dominant regional majority parties—which organize themselves on ethnic lines almost exclusively—and to encourage new alliances and collaboration across ethnic divides.[244]

Finally, to achieve a meaningful and sustainable balance between civilian and military institutions, it is important for the government to realign economic policies to counter the 'Milbus'[245] and the prevailing neoliberal policies—including under the CPEC—which bolster military unilateralism.[246] While a military should, in the conduct of its operations, be left free enough to prosecute its campaigns as effectively as possible, the Pakistani military's tremendous war chest—in the form of its inordinate share of the national budget and its far-flung commercial enterprises—lends it a degree of autonomy and independence that cannot be checked by the civilian government. Speaking more specifically to the CPEC project, and the neoliberal policies instituted under its rubric, the Parliamentary Committee on CPEC must be more proactive in reviewing any actions and projects envisioned by the CPEC authority[247]that could adversely impact the provinces, as well as the collective rights of the peoples—including the minority groups—of these provinces. The legislature must not pass any legislation that would, in any way, reduce the role of the Ministry of Planning Development and Special Initiatives in overseeing and regulating CPEC and its associated projects.[248] Furthermore, to ensure civil-military symmetry, the military needs to be gradually divested of its significant commercial interests, to close off any economic channels available to it which remain independent of civilian oversight.[249]

Realigning civil military relations is crucial to achieving political, economic, and social prosperity within a state. Much of the present hardships Pakistan is undergoing can be attributed—directly or otherwise—to the inordinate role the military has played in the country's history. The military needs to remain within its trusted and professional role, rather than operating almost as the state itself, and the civilian government and its institutions must equip themselves with the tools required to apply checks and balances on the military and must possess the appetite to maintain them.

ISPR-led campaigns disseminating the image of the army as Pakistan's national hero fall flat in the face of the resentment sections of the public have over the unequal distribution of resources and budgetary allocations, the unjustified intrusions into their spaces, and the overbearing and ubiquitous presence of the armed forces in every city nationwide, with the military conversely enjoying exclusive access to generous amenities, perks, immunity from censure, and tangible economic windfalls. This imbalance is obvious and promises to become even more stark if mega-projects like the CPEC are disproportionately driven by the military leadership. By continuing to operate in its self-serving, neo-colonial manner, the Pakistani military continues to perpetuate—and aggravate—ethnic and provincial grievances associated with the CPEC, deepening inter-communal friction, and eroding the framework of political federalism in Pakistan.

NOTES

1. Peter D. Feaver, "Civil-military relations 1." *Annual Review of Political Science* 2.1 (1999): 211–41.
2. *Ibid.*
3. *See* Alexander Hamilton, James Madison and John Jay, *The federalist papers*. Oxford University Press, 2008, No. 26, No. 47, No. 48, and No. 51.
4. David Easton cited in Veena Kukreja, *Civil-Military Relations in South Asia: Pakistan, Bangladesh, and India*. Sage publications, 1991, 18. *See also* Veena Kukreja, "Civil-Military Relations in Developing Countries." *India Quarterly* 45, no. 2/3 (1989): 154–92, 154.
5. *Ibid.*
6. *See* Samuel P. Huntington, *The soldier, and the state: The theory and politics of civil–military relations*. Harvard University Press, 1981.
7. Peter D. Feaver, *Armed servants: Agency, oversight, and civil-military relations*. Harvard University Press, 2009.
8. Rebecca L. Schiff, *The military and domestic politics: A concordance theory of civil-military relations*. Routledge, 2008.
9. Morris Janowitz, *The professional soldier: A social and political portrait*. Simon and Schuster, 2017.
10. Mark D. Mandeles, Review of Huntington, Soldier and State, Conference paper, May 2009.
11. *See supra* note 6.
12. *See supra* note 10.
13. *See supra* note 6, chapter 4. *See also* Carnes Lord, "On military professionalism and civilian control." *Joint Force Quarterly* (2015): 70–74. Huntington asserts that the key to achieving a healthy civil-military balance lies in "objective civilian control," whereby the military is conceded independence and discretion to establish military professionalism in areas specific to the military. This "objective civilian control" is offered in return for non-interference in civilian decision-making. In contrast to "objective civilian control," "subjective civilian control" occurs where political

forces directly interfere and monitor "non-professional" military forces (for e.g. civilian militias).

14. *See supra* note 6, 83–84.

15. Edgar Kiser, "Comparing varieties of agency theory in economics, political science, and sociology: An illustration from state policy implementation." *Sociological Theory* 17.2 (1999): 146–70.

16. *See supra* note 1.

17. *See supra* note 7.

18. *Ibid.*

19. *Ibid.*

20. Peter D. Feaver, "Crisis as Shirking: An Agency Theory Explanation of the Souring of American Civil-Military Relations." *Armed Forces & Society* 24.3 (1998): 407–34.

21. *See supra* note 7.

22. *See supra* note 8.

23. *See supra* note 9.

24. *See supra* note 9, at 418.

25. *Ibid.*

26. *See supra* note 9.

27. *See* Daron Acemoglu and James A. Robinson, *why nations fail: The origins of power, prosperity, and poverty*. Currency, 2012.

28. Daron Acemoglu and James A. Robinson, "De facto political power and institutional persistence." *American Economic Review* 96.2 (2006): 325–30, 326.

29. Michael C Desch, *Civilian control of the military: The changing security environment*. JHU Press, 2008.

30. Russell F. Weigley, "Civilian Control of the Military: The Changing Security Environment." (2001): 196–98.

31. *See supra* note 29, at p. 87.

32. *Ibid. See also* supra note 30.

33. Thomas C. Bruneau and Florina Christiana Matei, eds., *The Routledge Handbook of Civil-Military Relations*. Routledge, 2013, 14.

34. *Ibid.* at 28.

35. *Ibid.*

36. Jeffrey W. Donnithorne, *Culture Wars: Air Force Culture and Civil-Military Relations*. Air Univ Maxwell Afb Al Air Force Research Inst, 2013, 12.

37. *See supra* note 33, at. 17–18,

38. *Ibid.* at 31.

39. *Ibid.* at 30.

40. *Ibid.* at 32.

41. *Ibid.*

42. Verena Gruber, "Revisiting Civil-Military-Relations Theory." *Small Wars Journal* (2015). *See also supra* notes 6 and 9.

43. David Pion-Berlin, "Informal Civil—Military Relations in Latin America: Why Politicians and Soldiers Choose Unofficial Venues." *Armed Forces & Society* 36.3

(2010): 526–44. *See generally* David Pion-Berlin, ed., *Civil-military relations in Latin America: New analytical perspectives*. Univ of North Carolina Press, 2003.

44. *See supra* note 42.

45. BTI 2020 Pakistan Country Report, accessed on June 27, 2021, <https://www.bti-project.org/en/reports/country-report-PAK-2020.html>.

46. Frederick M Nunn, "Foreign influences on the South American military: Professionalization and politicization." *The Soldier and the State in South America*. Palgrave Macmillan, London, 2001. 13–37.

47. *Ibid.*

48. *Ibid.* at 15.

49. *Ibid.* at 16.

50. *Ibid.* at 17.

51. Paul Cammack, "In Permanent Retreat? The Modest Future Role of the Armed Forces in South America." *The Soldier and the State in South America*. Palgrave Macmillan, London, 2001. 175–93, 175.

52. *See infra* note 118, "Pakistan: Civil-Military Relations in a Post-Colonial State.".

53. *See supra* note 46, at 17.

54. *Ibid.* at 19.

55. *Ibid.*

56. *Ibid.* at 25.

57. *Ibid.* at 21.

58. *Ibid.* at 35.

59. Paul E. Lenze Jr., *Civil–Military Relations in the Islamic World*. Lexington Books, 2016, 62.

60. Robert Springborg, "Learning from failure: Egypt." *The Routledge Handbook of Civil-Military Relations*. Routledge, 2012, 105.

61. Sinan Ciddi, *Kemalism in Turkish politics: the Republican People's Party, secularism, and nationalism*. Routledge, 2009.

62. Kasra Aarabi, "Beyond Borders: The Expansionist Ideology of Iran's Islamic Revolutionary Guard Corps." *Tony Blair Institute for Global Change* (2020).

63. *Ibid.*

64. Alex Vatanka, "Iran's Use of Shi 'I Militant Proxies. Ideological and Practical Expediency Versus Uncertain Sustainability." *Middle East Institute Policy Paper* 5 (2018): 22.

65. 'Profile: Iran's Revolutionary Guards', *BBC* (Jan 3, 2020), accessed on June 27, 2021, <https://www.bbc.com/news/world-middle-east-47852262>.

66. *See generally* Vali Nasr, "Military rule, Islamism and democracy in Pakistan." *The Middle East Journal* 58.2 (2004): 195–209. The Pakistan military has historically used the Islamic banner, rallied through the populist Islamic political parties of the time, to justify its own agendas and legitimize its monopoly of violence.

67. *See supra* note 59, at 126.

68. Veena Kukreja, "Pakistan's Army from an Institutional Pressure Group to Final Arbiter in Governance." *Indian Journal of Public Administration* 61.3 (2015): 576–583, p.581.

69. *Ibid.*

70. *See supra* note 59, at p.55.

71. *See supra* note 68, at p.583.

72. Harris Samad, 'The United States must end its contradictory Pakistan policy,' *The Atlantic Council* (29 Jan 2020), accessed on June 27, 2021, <https://www.atlanticcouncil.org/blogs/new-atlanticist/the-united-states-must-end-its-contradictory-pakistan-policy/>.

73. Mohammad Ayub Khan,"The Pakistan American Alliance," *Foreign Affairs* (Jan, 1964), accessed on27, 2020 <https://www.foreignaffairs.com/articles/asia/1964-01-01/pakistan-american-alliance>.

74. *See supra* note 72.

75. *See infra* notes 197 and 200.

76. 'Pakistan National Human Development Report 2020,' *United Nations Development Programme*, (6 Apr 2021), p.113, accessed on June 27, 2021, <https://www.pk.undp.org/content/pakistan/en/home/library/human-development-reports/PKNHDR-inequality.htm>.

77. *See supra* note 33.

78. *Ibid.*

79. *See generally* Husain Haqqani, *Pakistan: Between mosque and military*. Carnegie endowment, 2010.

80. *Ibid.*

81. *Ibid.*

82. Najiyah Khan, "Civil-military relations: A case study of Pakistan." (2010), 33.

83. David Smith, 'Civil-Military Relations in Pakistan: Positive Evolution or More of the Same?,' *Stimson Centre* (4 Feb 2020), accessed on June 27, 2021, <https://www.stimson.org/2020/civil-military-relations-in-pakistan-positive-evolution-or-more-of-the-same/>.

84. *See supra* note 45.

85. *Ibid.*

86. *See supra* notes 6, 7, 8 and 9.

87. *See infra* note 202.

88. *See* Hamza Alavi, "The state in post-colonial societies Pakistan and Bangladesh." *New Left Review* 74 (1972): 59.

89. John L. Esposito, Tamara Sonn, and John O. Voll, *Islam and democracy after the Arab Spring*. Oxford University Press, 2015, p.83.

90. Timothy Besley and James A. Robinson, "Quis custodiet ipsos custodes? Civilian control over the military." *Journal of the European Economic Association* 8.2–3 (2010): 655–663.

91. Andreas Musolff, "The reception of antisemitic imagery in Nazi Germany and popular opinion-Lessons for today." *Analysing fascist discourse. European fascism in talk and text* (2013): 56–72, p.67.

92. *Ibid.*

93. *Ibid. See also* Robert D. Kaplan, 'Looking the World in the Eye,' *The Atlantic* (Dec. 2001), accessed on July 5, 2021 <https://www.theatlantic.com/magazine/archive/2001/12/looking-the-world-in-the-eye/302354/>.

94. S.E. Finer, *The Man on Horseback: The Role of the Military in Politics*. 2nd ed. London: Printer Publishers, 1988.

95. *See supra* note 29.

96. *Ibid.*

97. *See Hasan* Rizvi, *Military, state, and society in Pakistan*. Springer, 2000.

98. *See supra* note 7.

99. *See supra*-27.

100. *See supra* note 8.

101. *Ibid.*

102. Zufiqar Ali questions the cultural neutrality of concordance theory, believing that there is a contradiction in Schiff's application of the concordance theory; according to Ali, this contradiction arises in her emphasis on the need to account for cultural complexities and differences across different contexts while, simultaneously, employing a standardized model of three partners and four indicators not derived from the particular cultural context or a case study thereof to which it is being applied to, in order to understand it. Schiff's primary response to this critique is that concordance theory emphasizes the role of "dialogue" among three partners and presumes no civil-military model, demonstrating that there is no superimposition of a particular model but that this model will instead be shaped, depending upon the context, by how that dialogue between the parties plays out. Secondly, for Schiff, all cultures possess three partners and four indicators, expressed differently in a manner consistent with their indigenous forms. Ali contends that while the theory relies heavily on the aspect of a "dialogue" among the three partners, this dialogue does not play a decisive role in shaping civil-military relations where the relationship between the three partners is unequal, as is the case in Pakistan where the power exerted by the polity and political elite is significantly outweighed by that of the military establishment.

103. *See supra* note 59, p.82.

104. Rebecca L. Schiff, "Concordance Theory in Pakistan: Response to Zulfiqar Ali," *Armed Forces & Society* 42, no. 1 (2016): 226–234, p. 227.

105. For instance, Zulfiqar Ali contests Schiff's idea that the Pakistani military coups of 1958, 1977, and 2009 were not a result of discordance, arguing instead that they were, in fact, a result of concordance. Repeated invitations extended by the civilian leadership for military intervention in politics, particularly to address Bengali numerical superiority in the legislature, illustrates how—in the Pakistani context—political leaders sought to leverage the influence of the military in erstwhile non-military contexts. *See* Zulfiqar Ali, "Contradiction of Concordance Theory: Failure to Understand Military Intervention in Pakistan," *Armed Forces & Society* 40, no. 3 (2014): 544–567, 556–557. Additionally, public opinion was—and remains—largely in favor of the military in general and coups in particular, illustrated by several polls and surveys. Zulfiqar Ali, "Pakistan, Military Coup, and Concordance: Four Objections to Schiff," *Armed Forces & Society* 42, no. 2 (2016): 463–469. p.465). Ali's second point of divergence from the concordance theory is that identifying only three relevant partners in determining the civil-military dynamic in Pakistan is inadequate, arguing instead that the US government's engagement, particularly with the Pakistani military, has made it an active determinant of how civil-military relations

pan out in Pakistan. Ali also posits that, given the key roles the judiciary and media play in determining the outcomes of Pakistani civil-military relations, these should also be considered as partners (p.466). He thus emphasizes how the standard three-partner approach can be significantly critiqued, if not refuted entirely, when applied to cultural contexts other than that which it originated in. Schiff takes the position that the scope of civil-military theory involves an assessment of intranational factors, as opposed to regional or international ones, and thus such an examination should not include the US as an actor.

106. Ejaz Hussain, another South-Asian scholar, refutes Ali's position, arguing in support of Schiff by pointing out the lack of reliability and the empirical flaws extant in much of the survey data relied upon by Ali. *See* Ejaz Hussain, "Failure to Understand Military Intervention in Pakistan: A Rejoinder," *Armed Forces & Society* 44, no. 2 (2018): 368–378, 374, 375; 371.

107. *See supra* note 105. In this regard, Ali's contention with concordance theory has him questioning the significance of the four indicators over which civil-military disagreements may occur. For Ali, these factors are inadequate and too over-simplistic to be able to account for military coups in such a diverse array of cultural contexts, and he highlights how other geostrategic factors are crucial in providing a holistic account of military coups.

108. *Ibid.*

109. Aasim Sajjad Akhtar, "The China-Pakistan Economic Corridor Beyond the Rule of Capital?" *Monthly Review—An Independent Socialist Magazine* 70.2 (2018): 34–48.

110. *See supra* note 9.

111. Faseeh Mangi, 'Soft coup' warning as Pak's army chief meets business leaders on economy', *Business Standard* (4 Oct 2019), accessed on June 27, 2021, <https://www.business-standard.com/article/international/soft-coup-warning-as-pak-s-army-chief-meets-business-leaders-on-economy-119100300669_1.html>.

112. *See supra* note 68, at p.582.

113. *See infra* note 126.

114. *See infra* note 200.

115. *See generally* Saeed Shafqat, et al., *Pakistan's Political Parties: Surviving Between Dictatorship and Democracy*. Georgetown University Press, 2020. To counter the control exercised by the military as principal over political parties as agents, political parties have also shown some form of resistance to gain power and effect these relations of functional subordination.

116. Yasser Latif Hamdani, 'Jinnah as Governor General and Democracy,' *Criterion Quarterly* Vol 8 No.1 (18 Sep 2013), accessed on June 27, 2021, <https://criterion-quarterly.com/jinnah-as-governor-general-and-democracy/>.

117. 'The 1857 uprising', *The News International* (5 May 2007), accessed on June 27, 2021, <https://www.thenews.com.pk/archive/print/53946-the-1857-uprising>.

118. Ejaz Husain, "Pakistan: Civil-Military Relations in a Post-Colonial State." *Pcd journal* 4.1–2 (2012): 113–146. *See also* Tan Tai Yong, The Garrison State: Military, Government and Society in Colonial Punjab, 1849–1947. Vol. 8. Sage, 2005.

119. *Ibid.* "Pakistan: Civil-Military Relations in a Post-Colonial State," at p.126. ("This civil-military integration was a planned mechanism to prevent the recruiting districts being influenced by nationalist politics of the post-war period. In other words, the British authorities were instrumental in the creation of praetorian oligarchy. Thus, during the inter-war period (1919–1939), the Punjab Soldiers Board functioned as an institutional part of the district administration.").

120. *Ibid.* at 125. ("The 'Punjabicisation' of the colonial military initiated the recruitment of Punjabi Sikhs, Punjabi Muslims and Pathans of north India—the military districts—into the restructured Bengal Army.").

121. Veena Kukreja, "Ethnic Diversity, Political Aspirations and State Response: A Case Study of Pakistan." *Indian Journal of Public Administration* 66.1 (2020): 28–42, 34. ("Punjab is referred to as the 'big older brother' in NWFP, Sindh and Baluchistan. It is not surprising that such thoughts have been internalised in people's psyche as the federating units other than Punjab are still referred to as chotai soobe, that is, smaller provinces.").

122. *Ibid.* at 35. ("The central government charges a much lower price for Baluchistan gas than for gas produced in other provinces and pays lower royalties. Sui gas is extracted under the direct control of the Pakistani armed forces and interfering with access to the gas had rapidly been a goal of Baluch insurgents.").

123. *See* Dr Gulshan Majeed and Dr Rehana Saeed Hashmi, "Baloch Resistance during Zulfiqar Ali Bhutto's Era: Causes and Consequences." *South Asian Studies* 29.1 (2020). *See also* supra note 121. ("The Baluchs' demands included raising the royalty for gas piped out of Baluchistan, increase in the recruitment of Baluchs in the Federal Services, paramilitary forces, and the army and a freeze in the construction of new military cantonments in Baluchistan, the renewed conflict was related to the development of Gwadar Port in the province. The unwarranted brutal killing of Nawab Akbar Khan Bugti triggered ethno-national insurgency in Pakistan's severely strained federal structure.").

124. 'How CPEC Left Behind the People of Gwadar,' *The Diplomat* (30 June, 2020), accessed on June 27, 2021 <https://thediplomat.com/2020/06/how-cpec-left-behind-the-people-of-gwadar/>. ("For instance, in 2018, one of the China-Pakistan Economic Corridor's development schemes—a 19-kilometer expressway providing a direct link for cargo traffic to and from Gwadar Port, connecting it with Makran Coastal Highway—once more stirred conflict. The expressway blocked 4.3 kilometers of the coastline, cutting off the old neighborhoods and limiting the access of fishing boats to the sea, resulting a new wave of protests by the local population").

125. 'Historical aspect of Pashtun nationalism,' *The Nation* (19 Jan 2020), accessed on June 27, 2021, <https://nation.com.pk/19-Jan-2020/historical-aspect-of-pashtun-nationalism>.

126. *See* Madiha Afzal, "Why is Pakistan's military repressing a huge, nonviolent Pashtun protest movement?" *BROOKINGS* (7 Feb, 2020),on June 27, 2021 <https://www.brookings.edu/blog/order-from-chaos/2020/02/07/why-is-pakistans-military-repressing-a-huge-nonviolent-pashtun-protest-movement/>. *See also* 'Pashtun movement leader: "Pakistani army is afraid of our popularity,"' *DW* (6 May 2019),

accessed on June 27, 2021, <https://www.dw.com/en/pashtun-movement-leader-pakistani-army-is-afraid-of-our-popularity/a-49069682>.

127. 'Why Pakistan's army is targeting the MQM party,' *DW* (23 Aug, 2016), accessed on June 27, 2021 <https://www.dw.com/en/why-pakistans-army-is-targeting-the-mqm-party/a-18708521>. ("Arif Jamal . . . says in a DW interview that one of the key objectives of the Pakistani military is to weaken mainstream political parties to increase their control on government and civilian institutions.").

128. *See Supra* note 59, at pg 78.

129. *See* Neil Stewart, "Divide and rule: British policy in indian history." *Science & Society* (1951): 49–57.

130. *See supra* note 82, at 23. *See also* Ayesha Siddiqa, "Pakistan military ethnic balance in the Armed Forces and problems of Federalism." *Manekshaw Paper No* 39 (2013): 149–162.

131. *See supra* note 121.

132. *Ibid.* at 31.

133. *See supra* note 59, at 86–88.

134. *Ibid.*

135. Christophe Jaffrelot ed., *Pakistan at the Crossroads: Domestic Dynamics and External Pressures*. Random House India, 2016.

136. *See supra* note 59, at 82.

137. *Ibid.*

138. *Supra note* 118.

139. *Ibid.*

140. *Supra* note 59, at 89.

141. Francis Fukuyama, 'Samuel Huntington's Legacy,' *Foreign Policy* (6 Jan 2011), accessed on June 27, 2021, <https://foreignpolicy.com/2011/01/06/samuel-huntingtons-legacy/>.

142. *See supra* note 118.

143. *See supra* note 59, at 90.

144. *Ibid.* at 93.

145. *Ibid.* at 91.

146. *Ibid.* at 95

147. *See supra* note 123, "Baloch Resistance during Zulfiqar Ali Bhutto's Era: Causes and Consequences."

148. 'Bhutto and the 1977 coup,' *The News* (9 July 2017), accessed on June 27, 2021, <https://www.thenews.com.pk/tns/detail/563623-bhutto-1977-coup>. ("When Bhutto held second general elections in March 1977 . . . what was not certain was if PPP would get two-third majority so that he could change the country's constitution to his taste. To achieve that, Bhutto unleashed police, FSF, and ISI to cow down and scare away the opposition candidates first from filing their papers for election and then from running electoral campaign. Consequently, the PPP unbelievably secured 77 per cent of National Assembly seats, far more than desired for two-third majority, which led to the opposition parties' boycott of elections for provincial assemblies."). *See also* 'Pakistan's Black Day', *The Diplomat* (8 July 2016), accessed on June 27, 2021, <https://thediplomat.com/2016/07/pakistans-black-day/>.

149. *Supra note* 59, at 97.

150. 'Pakistan's Islamization—before and after dictator Zia-ul Haq,' *DW* https://www.dw.com/en/pakistans-islamization-before-and-after-dictator-zia-ul-haq/a-19480315. ("Pakistani decision makers have found religious extremists a natural choice for alliance/usage as tools of foreign policy due to, a) its own religious identity basis; b) perception of India as a Hindu state which has not accepted Pakistan as an independent state; c) The United States also considered Islamic forces as good allies during the Cold War against the Soviets; and d) the centrist, post-colonial state dominated by the military has always considered secular, nationalist and democratic forces a challenge to its hold on power.").

151. *See* PAK. PEN. CODE, ch. XV, Sections 295-B, 295-C, 298-A, 298-B, and 298-C. *See also* Siddique, Osama, and Zahra Hayat. "Unholy speech and holy laws: Blasphemy laws in Pakistan-controversial origins, design defects, and free speech implications." *Minn. J. Int'l L.* 17 (2008): 303.

152. *See supra* note 59, at 102–108.

153. Zahid Hussain. 'THE LAST COUP," *DAWN NEWS* (13 Oct 2019), accessed on June 27, 2021, <https://www.dawn.com/news/1510272>.

154. In 2000 Chief Justice Saeeduzzaman Siddiqui of the Supreme Court declared the coup unlawful and unconstitutional, but mysteriously retired immediately after issuing this judgment. The judge who replaced Siddiqui was quick to revert this decision, announcing that the coup was indeed within the rubric of the constitution and the law.

155. *See supra* note 59, at 97.

156. 'President assents 17th Amendment,' *DAWN NEWS* (1 Jan 2004), accessed on June 27, 2021, <https://www.dawn.com/news/390611/president-assents-17th-amendment>.

157. *See supra* note 59, at 111.

158. *Ibid.* at 112.

159. 'Pervez Musharraf resigns as president of Pakistan,' *The Guardian* (18 Aug 2008), accessed on June 27, 2021, <https://www.theguardian.com/world/2008/aug/18/pakistan>.

160. Frederic Grare, "Pakistan's foreign and security policies after the 2013 general election: the judge, the politician and the military." *International Affairs* 89.4 (2013): 987–1001.

161. Backed by foreign powers (including the US and Saudi Arabia), Zia's era is one of many illustrations of how unabated military dictators have often utilized national security and Islamic religious values to accumulate power to subvert and eradicate Western liberal values and suppress religious minorities. *See* 'Zia-ul-Haq and the "Islamization" of Pakistan's Public Universities,' *The Diplomat* (28 March 2017), accessed on June 27, 2021 <https://thediplomat.com/2017/03/zia-ul-haq-and-the-islamization-of-pakistans-public-universities/>.

162. In the immediate aftermath of military coups, the Supreme Court has always declared them to be legal mostly on a supra-constitutional basis and relying on the doctrine of necessity. *See The State Vs. Dosso & Others* (PLD 1958 SC (PAK.) 533).

163. *See Begum Nusrat Bhutto vs. Chief of Army Staff and Federation of Pakistan* PLD 1977 SC 657. *See also* Hamid Khan, Constitutional and Political History of Pakistan (2nd edn, Oxford University Press 2009), 326. On the question of influence on the judges in this particular instance, it is reasonable to suggest that the judiciary was biased in favor of the military regime because they had been reconstituted by Zia upon the promulgation of a Provisional Constitutional Order (PCO), according to which members of the judiciary had accepted ab initio the lawful authority of the regime and recognized it as the new legislature.

164. The Constitution was, however, silent on what exactly constituted an "emergency," but the power granted to the President—the head of the executive –was used to weaken democratic processes and promote personal and institutional self-interests.

165. *See generally* Sikander Ahmed Shah, "War on terrorism: Self defense, operation enduring freedom, and the legality of US drone attacks in Pakistan." *Wash. U. Global Stud. L. Rev.* 9 (2010): 77.

166. 'Is Pakistan's outgoing army chief Raheel Sharif worthy of praise?,' *DW* (25 Dec, 2016), accessed on June 27, 2021 <https://www.dw.com/en/is-pakistans-outgoing-army-chief-raheel-sharif-worthy-of-praise/a-36521719>. ("Pakistan's army chief Raheel Sharif used the terrorism pretext to consolidate the military's supremacy in his country. Experts say his successor will continue the same policy of undermining the civilian rule."). *See also* CONST. of PAK Art. 232–235.

167. Saba Naveed Shaikh, 'Emergency and Security Laws Pakistan' *South Asians for Human Rights* (25 Feb, 2011), accessed on June 27, 2021 <www.southasianrights.org/wp-content/uploads/2009/10/Security-Laws-Report-Pakistan-Final.pdf>. Significantly, Article 236(b) of the Constitution of Pakistan bars the judiciary from reviewing a constitutional proclamation of emergency. A key judicial safeguard then is not available during times of emergency to check the executive. The Pakistani Supreme Court has nevertheless attempted to reclaim a role in this process in the Musharraf Treason Trial. *See Sindh High Court Bar Association v Federation of Pakistan* PLD [2009] SC 879. Salman Masood. 'Musharraf Decree in '07 Was Illegal, Court Rules' *The New York Times* (31 Jul, 2009), accessed on June 27, 2021 <https://www.nytimes.com/2009/08/01/world/asia/01pstan.html>.

168. *See* CONST. of PAK.—21st Amendment. 'Parliament passes 21st Constitutional Amendment, Army Act Amendment,' *DAWN* (6 Jan 2015), accessed on June 27, 2021, <https://www.dawn.com/news/1155271>.

169. According to the Statement of Object and Purposes shared with the bill, the bill was proposed to "prevent hatred and disrespectful behaviour against the Armed Forces . . . ," requiring "(s)trict action . . . (to) be taken against those bringing disrepute to the Armed Forces institution(s) . . . " This act has now been passed by the National Assembly Standing Committee on Interior, *see* 'NA panel approves bill against intentional disrespect for forces', *DAWN* (8 Apr 2021), accessed on June 27, 2021, <https://www.dawn.com/news/1617040>.

170. *See generally* Tayyab Mahmud, "Freedom of Religion & (and) Religious Minorities in Pakistan: A Study of Judicial Practice." *Fordham Int'l LJ* 19 (1995): 40.

171. *See supra* note 82, at 23.

172. *See supra* note 126. ("Pakistan's military—increasingly emboldened and powerful vis-à-vis the country's civilian institutions—has said publicly that it has had enough of the PTM, telling the protesters their "time is up." While the group has mostly been allowed to hold protests, it has also been maligned relentlessly as full of traitors, charged with a colonial-era sedition law (which criminalizes disloyalty, contempt, hatred, and disaffection for the state), and labelled agents of 'enemy governments,' alternatively India and Afghanistan.").

173. *Ibid.* ("The movement alleges grave human rights violations by Pakistan's military against Pashtuns in the country's northwest. It says that Pashtuns have been the target of violence at the hands of both the Taliban and the Pakistani military for two decades. The movement claims that the military has killed innocent civilians in its operations against the Pakistani Taliban, and that it needs to answer for "missing persons.").

174. Sajad Rasool and Zahid Anwar, "Operation Zarb-e-Azb, IDPs, and the Life in Camps." *Review of Human Rights* 5.1 (2019): 33–54. *See also* Chapter 1.

175. *See generally* "The Paradoxes of Ahmadiyya Identity: The Legal Appropriation of Muslimness and the Construction of Ahmadiyya Difference," in Naveeda Khan (ed)., *Beyond Crisis: A Critical Second Look at Pakistan.*Routledge, 2010.

176. CONST. of PAK—Second Amendment (1974). *See also* Nadeem F. Paracha, 'The 1974 ouster of the 'heretics': What really happened?' *DAWN* (21 Nov 2013), accessed on June 27, 2021. <https://www.dawn.com/news/1057427>.

177. CONST. of PAK - Art. 20.

178. 'Pakistan: Ensure Ahmadi voting rights,' *Human Rights Watch* (28 Jun 2018), accessed on June 27, 2021, <https://www.refworld.org/docid/5b87de574.html>. ("Elections held in 1985 under the military dictatorship of President Gen. Muhammad Zia-ul-Haq reversed universal voting rights and introduced a system of separate electorates that required non-Muslims to register as a separate category and vote for non-Muslim candidates. To vote, the Ahmadis had to register as non-Muslims. Since then, Ahmadis have in practice been denied the right to vote in local, provincial, and national elections.").

179. 'Pakistan's Sham Election,' *Foreign Affairs* (27 Jul, 2018), accessed on June 27, 2021 <https://www.foreignaffairs.com/articles/pakistan/2018-07-27/pakistans-sham-election>. ("Second, the result was predetermined by Pakistan's powerful army, which engaged in electoral malfeasance for months leading up to the election . . . The army was hell-bent upon securing Khan's victory and even encouraged political parties with overt ties to terrorist groups to field several hundred candidates.").

180. 'NA-249 recount will strengthen people's trust in electoral process,' *The Express Tribune* (4 May, 2021), accessed on June 27, 2021 <https://tribune.com.pk/story/2298160/na-249-recount-will-strengthen-peoples-trust-in-electoral-process>. ("The demand for keeping election material, including ballot boxes, ballot papers, counter foils and forms in possession of military was meant to prevent any doubt of tampering the documents.").

181. 'Pakistan protests: Why the Islamist TLP party is now a major political force', *DW* (15 Apr 2021), accessed on June 27, 2021, <https://www.dw.com/en/pakistan-protests-why-the-islamist-tlp-party-is-now-a-major-political-force/a-57214719>.

("Observers say that if the TLP threat goes unchallenged, it will increase Pakistan's international isolation. Haqqani said the country's establishment, the military, has "historically used Islamist groups to strengthen Pakistan's anti-India narrative.").

182. Ali Cheema, Asim Ijaz Khwaja, and Adnan Khan, "Decentralization in Pakistan: Context, content and causes." (2005), 1. (" . . . a rudimentary local government system did exist in the rural areas. This was the system of village panchayats (literally council of five) which performed administrative, judicial, and sometimes developmental functions.").

183. *Ibid.* at 5.

184. *Ibid.* ("BDs were used by Ayub to legitimize his essentially unitary new Presidential Constitution (1962), which gave effective state power to the armed forces through the office of the President. The 1962 constitution explicitly linked the office of the President to the newly created local bodies by declaring the 80,000 Basic Democrats as the Electoral College for the election of the President and national and provincial assemblies."). *See also* Razia Musarrat and M. Salman Azhar, "Decentralization Reforms in Pakistan During Ayub and Zia Era." Journal of Public Administration and Governance 2.1 (2012): 123–133, pp 125–126, outlining the justification for the BD system: ("a) To limit the role of the urban political presentation; b) To increase the rural political participation; c) To equalize the political power of urban and rural representation; d) To decentralize the political power structure but only in downward direction e) To centralize and strengthen the political power in the office of the President; f)To minimize the role and the impact of the traditional political parties; g) To develop a political party less political system; h) To control the overall political system; i) To establish a strong presidential system of government; j) To dilute the concentration of political power up to an easily manageable level; k) To create rural leadership; l) To create a grand assembly at national level; [and] m) To use it for the social integration."). *See also* Kunal Mukherjee, "Ayub Khan's Basic Democracy and Political Continuity in Contemporary Pakistan." *India Quarterly* 72.3 (2016): 268–277.

185. Tariq Ali, *Pakistan: Military Rule or People's Power*. London: Jonathan Cape (1970), 132.

186. 'Democracy at the local level,' *DAWN NEWS* (4 Mar 2021), accessed on June 27, 2021, <https://www.dawn.com/news/610768/democracy-at-the-local-level>.

187. Local Government Ordinance 1979. *See also* Syed Shahid Zaheer Zaidi, "Local Government Under Army Rule: A Comparative Analysis of Zia ul Haq and Pervez Musharraf Local Government System." (2019). ("rural areas had three government levels: union council, tehsil council and district council. . . . Although politically important they were not complemented by any further decentralization of federal or provincial administrative functions or financial powers to the local level.").

188. *See supra* note 182.

189. *Ibid. See also* Aamer Taj and Keith Baker, 'Multi-Level Governance and Local Government Reform in Pakistan, *Progress in Development Studies* (2018), 3. ("The Musharraf era reforms were strikingly similar to previous reforms enacted by the military government of Ayub Khan in the 1960s and Zia-ul-Haque in 1979 . . .

the structures created by the Musharraf government have remained at the heart of Pakistani local government.").

190. *Ibid.* at 16. ("These departments remained under the administrative domain of provincial bureaucracy. This is consistent with a legacy of centralised control through a civil military bureaucracy.").

191. *Ibid.* at 28.

192. Constitution (Eighteenth Amendment) Act, 2010.

193. Catherine Yang, "Ending Dictatorship: Pakistan's Eighteenth Amendment." *Harvard International Review* 32.2 (2010): 10. ("This amendment was intended to devolve power from the federal executive to the National Assembly—one of the bicameral bodies of the federal legislature—and the provincial assemblies.").

194. *Ibid.*

195. Aqil Shah, "Where is foreign policy made in Pakistan's democracy?," *East Asia Forum* (12 Oct 2018), accessed on June 27, 2021, <https://www.eastasiaforum.org/2018/10/12/where-is-foreign-policy-made-in-pakistans-democracy/>.

196. 'Provincial Autonomy,' *DAWN* (18 Dec 2020), accessed on June 27, 2021, <https://www.dawn.com/news/1596395>. ("The government's decision to 'devise a mechanism to hold provinces accountable' for how they spend money they receive as their share from the federal tax pool under the NFC award is at best illogical and at worst lacks a constitutional basis.").

197. Ayesha Siddiqa,' Why is Pakistan spending so much money on defence amid COVID-19?', *Al Jazeera* (1 Jul 2020), accessed on June 27, 2021, <https://www.aljazeera.com/opinions/2020/7/1/why-is-pakistan-spending-so-much-money-on-defence-amid-covid-19>. ("Khan's government, in collusion with the military, is desperately trying to take control of more funds at a time when provincial governments are struggling to meet the most basic needs of their constituents. There is a consistent effort to undo the 18th amendment to the country's 1973 constitution, which gives financial autonomy to the provinces and reduces the federal government's share.").

198. Veena Kukreja, *Contemporary Pakistan: Political processes, conflicts, and crises*. Sage, 2003.

199. *Ibid. See also* Chapter 4.

200. *See generally* Ayesha Siddiqa, *Military Inc.: Inside Pakistan's military economy*. Penguin Random House India, 2017, 1. ("Milbus refers to military capital that is used for the personal benefit of the military fraternity, especially the officer cadre, but is neither recorded nor part of the defence budget. In this respect, it is a completely independent genre of capital. Its most significant component is entrepreneurial activities that do not fall under the scope of the normal accountability procedures of the state, and are mainly for the gratification of military personnel and their cronies . . . in most cases the rewards are limited to the officer cadre . . . The top echelon of the armed forces who are the main beneficiaries of Milbus justify the economic dividends as welfare provided to the military for their services rendered to the state.").

201. Khan, Jamshed, and Asmat Ullah Wazir, Civil-Military Imbalance in the Administration of Pakistan: A Case Study of Musharraf Era. Rep. Vol. VI: The Dialogue, 2011.

202. 'Pakistan: Why is the military taking over civilian posts?,' *DW* (2 May, 2021), accessed on June 27, 2021 <https://www.dw.com/en/pakistan-why-is-the-military-taking-over-civilian-posts/a-56473442>. ("Even diplomatic positions, which have largely been held by civilians since Pakistan's independence from British rule in 1947, have been taken over by the generals. . . . Besides the mission in Riyadh going back to a general, ambassadors in Brunei, Jordan, Syria, Sri Lanka, Ukraine, the Maldives, Nigeria and Libya are retired armed forces officers . . . There is a widespread perception in the country that politicians and civilian bureaucracy are incompetent and corrupt, whereas the military is efficient and well-organized.").

203. *See supra* note 197. ("The military is still getting a large share of the nation's resources because of its gradual usurpation of power and decades-long dominance of the state apparatus. By claiming more and more funds in the name of "national security" the military is simply trying to grab greater political, economic, and social space for itself to the detriment of millions of struggling Pakistani citizens. The army chief is already a member of the top economic decision-making body, and military officers dominate most institutions.").

204. *See supra* note 197.

205. 'Is IMF backing away from Neoliberalism.' *The Express Tribune* (Sep 4, 2016), accessed on June 27, 2021, <https://tribune.com.pk/story/1175968/imf-backing-away-neoliberalism>.

206. *See supra* note 135, at 24–49.

207. Raja Masood Ashraf, "Neoliberal dispositif and the rise of fundamentalism: the case of Pakistan." *J Int Glob Stud* 3.1 (2011): 21–31.

208. Mishele Ijaz, "Growth versus Development: The case of China Pakistan Economic Corridor." (2018). 47. ("In the midst of the construction on Gwadar, live the indigenous fishing community, who have seen the port change hands since its acquisition from Oman. They have experienced displacement, seen ecological degradation, and fear loss of livelihood as the infrastructure boom in Gwadar continues to ignore their plight."). James C. Mulvenon, a specialist on the Chinese military, noted the similarities between the Pakistani Military Business (Milbus) and what had been until 1998 the heavy involvement of the Chinese People's Liberation Army (PLA) in the Chinese economy. In China's case, Mulvenon observed, the Milbus clearly distorted the country's overall economic development, but in certain sectors, such as telecommunications, PLA commercial activities also had a positive role in fostering development. *See also* supra note 200.

209. *See supra* note 126.

210. Samuel P. Huntington, "Reforming civil military relations." *Civil-Military Relations and Democracy* (1996), 10–11.

211. Michael Desch, "Threat environments and military missions." *Civil-Military Relations and Democracy* (1996): 12–29.

212. *See supra* note 6.

213. *See supra* note 7.

214. *See supra* note 135, at 24–49.

215. *See supra* note 28.

216. *See supra* notes 8 and 104.

217. *See supra* note 9. Morris Janowitz, "The Social Demography of the All-Volunteer Force." *Annals of the American Academy of Political Science* 406 (1973): 86–93.

218. Juan J. Linz, 'The Virtues of Parliamentarism' in Larry Diamond and Marc F. Plattner, eds. *The global resurgence of democracy*. Journal of Democracy Book, 1996.

219. *Ibid.*

220. This is illustrated by Musharraf's imposition of a state of emergency during his Presidency through the concentration of power rather than parliamentary approval.

221. *See supra* note 218.

222. Arend Lijphart, *Patterns of democracy: Government forms and performance in thirty-six countries*. Yale University Press, 2012, 128–129.

223. *See supra* note 135. *See also* Donald Horowitz, 'Comparing Democratic Systems' in Diamond, Larry, and Marc F. Plattner, eds., *The global resurgence of democracy*. Journal of Democracy Book, 1996.

224. Susan H. Williams, 'States of Emergency and Federalism: An exploration for the implications for constitutional design,' 759.

225. *Ibid.*

226. 'Pashtun Tribes Stage Unprecedented Protest in Pakistan,' *The Diplomat* (8 Feb 2018), accessed on June 27, 2021, <https://thediplomat.com/2018/02/pashtun-tribes-stage-unprecedented-protest-in-pakistan/>; 'Baloch separatist leader Harbiyar Marri among 13 booked for Chinese consulate attack,' *DAWN NEWS* (7 Dec 2018), accessed on June 27, 2021, <https://www.dawn.com/news/1447419>.

227. *Ibid.*

228. Bruce A. Ackerman, *Before the next attack: preserving civil liberties in an age of terrorism*. Yale University Press, 2006, 77.

229. 'Parliament's Role in Pakistan's Democratic Transition,' *Crisis Group* (18 Sep 2013), accessed on June 28, 2021, <https://www.crisisgroup.org/asia/south-asia/pakistan/parliament-s-role-pakistan-s-democratic-transition>.

230. 'Parliamentary Committee on National Security formed,' *The News* (27 Apr 2019), accessed on June 28, 2021, <https://nation.com.pk/27-Apr-2019/parliamentary-committee-on-national-security-formed>.

231. Pakistan's New Antiterror Law Gives Security Forces Unprecedented Power,' *TIME* (3 Jul, 2014), accessed on June 28, 2021 <https://time.com/2953028/pakistan-counterinsurgency-law-protection-of-pakistan-bill>. The current legal framework in Pakistan arguably allows for the militarization of the state. Today, the armed forces in Pakistan under the colour of law can arrest and sentence civilians under their own codes of conduct without providing necessary due process. In extreme cases they can also shoot civilians on sight. Such measures can be taken all over Pakistan on the premise of fighting terrorism or safeguarding national sovereignty and integrity.

232. *See generally* 'Military Overreach in Brazil and Pakistan: When the Generals Become the Judges' in Kyle, Brett J., and Andrew G. Reiter, *Military Courts, Civil-Military Relations, and the Legal Battle for Democracy: The Politics of Military Justice*. Routledge, 2020.

233. 'Military Injustice in Pakistan,' *Briefing Paper ICJ*, (January 2019), accessed on June 28, 2021 <https://www.icj.org/wp-content/uploads/2019/01/Pakistan-military-courts-Advocacy-Analysis-brief-2018-ENG.pdf>. 'Pakistan: as military courts lapse, Government must prioritize reform of the criminal justice system,' *ICJ* (1 Apr, 2019), accessed on June 28, 2021 <https://www.icj.org/pakistan-as-military-courts-lapse-government-must-prioritize-reform-of-the-criminal-justice-system/>. Following the political unrest precipitated by the arrest of former Prime Minister Imran Khan on 9th May 2023, key military installations were targeted by protesters (including the Corps Commander's residence in Lahore and the General Head Quarters in Rawalpindi). Mass arrests followed, with several civilian protestors now being tried before military tribunals; *see* Baqir Sajjad, 'Undermining Justice: Court-Martialing Civilians in Pakistan,' *Wilson Centre* (Jun 05, 2023), accessed on August 08, 2023, <https://www.wilsoncenter.org/blog-post/undermining-justice-court-martialing-civilians-pakistan>. The Apex court is presently hearing petitions filed by ex-premier Khan and others on the constitutionality of trying civilians in military courts. During the proceedings the Chief Justice of Pakistan remarked that "the military will not be allowed to take any illegal steps"; *see* 'Military trials for civilians: Pakistan court says won't allow army to take "illegal steps,"' *Arab News* (Aug 03, 2023), accessed on August 08, 2023, <https://www.arabnews.com/node/2349086/pakistan>.

234. *See* Pakistan Army Act, 1952. ACT XXXIX OF 1952, s.7. *See also* 'The sun has set on Pakistan's military courts—here's why it should never rise again', *DAWN NEWS* (6 Mar 2017), accessed on June 28, 2021, <https://www.dawn.com/news/1306792>. ("According to the PAA (1952) those convicted by military courts can only appeal in the Military Appellate Tribunal. However, convicts can have decisions of the military courts 'reviewed' by civilian courts under Section 7.2.3 of the PAA.").

235. 'Independence of Pakistan's Judiciary is Under Threat,' *The Wire* (8 May, 2019), accessed on June 28, 2021 <https://thewire.in/south-asia/pakistan-judiciary-faizabad-justice-isa>. ("The resolution to remove Justice Qazi Faez Isa for 'criticising the army and the ISI' in his Faizabad case verdict shows 'there are clamps on freedom of speech within the judiciary.'"). The Presidential reference against Justice Faiz Isa was quashed by the Supreme Court. 'Justice Isa reference tainted with mala fide in law: SC,' *The Express Tribune* (23 Oct, 2020), accessed on June 28, 2021 <https://tribune.com.pk/story/2269636/justice-isa-reference-tainted-with-mala-fide-in-law-sc>.

236. The more-recent 2007 Lawyers Movement that culminated in the ouster of Musharraf is proof of how much force and influence this institution can bring to bear, coupled with populist sentiment.

237. CONST. of PAK—Art. 245.

238. Actions (in Aid of Civil Power) Regulation, 2011; Protection of Pakistan Act, 2014.

239. *Ibid. See* Sadaf Aziz, *The Constitution of Pakistan: A Contextual Analysis*. Bloomsbury Publishing, 2018, 211.

240. 'Pakistan: Countering Militancy in PATA' *Crisis Group* Report No. 242 (15 Jan 2013), accessed on June 28, 2021, accessed on June 28, 2021, <https://www.crisisgroup.org/asia/south-asia/pakistan/pakistan-countering-militancy-pata>.

241. Charles Doyle, "The Posse Comitatus Act and Related Matters: the use of the military to execute civilian law." LIBRARY OF CONGRESS WASHINGTON DC CONGRESSIONAL RESEARCH SERVICE, 2000.

242. *See* Susan H. Williams, 'States of Emergency and Federalism: An exploration for the implications for constitutional design,' 759. An example may be the deployment of the Frontier Corps or the Balochistan Regiment in Balochistan and the Gilgit Scouts in Gilgit, instead of a predominantly Punjabi force. Furthermore, a parliamentary system of government should be given constitutional protection to foster strong civilian institutions which would not be easily overpowered by the military. This system would require an independent judiciary capable of reviewing all executive actions, be they civil or military, without fear of retribution.

243. *See generally* K.N. Kamarck, "Diversity, inclusion, and equal opportunity in the armed services: background and issues for congress. Congressional Research Service. 2016." (2019).

244. Krzysztof Trzcinski, "Centripetal Federalism." (2020), ("After the army took power in 1966, centripetal federalism began to take shape in Nigeria. In 1967, after the four regions were replaced by 12 states, the three largest ethnic groups found themselves living in as many as seven of the new territorial units. As Horowitz points out, this, along with the de-legalization by the army of ethnic parties, freed the smaller ethnic groups from the control of regionally dominant groups . . . ").

245. *See supra* note 200.

246. 'The Pakistan Army's Belt and Road Putsch,' *Foreign Policy* (26 Aug, 2020), accessed on June 28, 2021 <https://foreignpolicy.com/2020/08/26/the-pakistan-armys-belt-and-road-putsch/>. (" . . . there's also indication that the Army has tried to use Bajwa and CPEC as Trojan horses to claim a greater share of power back from the civilian government. Last month, Pakistan's Express Tribune reported on proposed legislation that would have radically enhanced the powers of the CPEC Authority . . . The draft legislation would have cut Pakistan's Planning Commission—which has served as the country's chief economic policy development body since the 1950s—out of the picture on CPEC, giving the CPEC Authority sole power to conceive and develop the projects. . . . In other words, the CPEC Authority, effectively controlled by the Army, would exercise control over a large percentage of the country's development budget . . . The CPEC Authority could potentially even supersede the powers of the prime minister.").

247. *See* China Pakistan Economic Authority Act, 2020, accessed on June 28, 2021, <www.na.gov.pk/uploads/documents/1612267873_350.pdf>. The CPEC Authority was established by the China Pakistan Economic Authority Act, 2020, and has a total of nine members, including the chairman (currently retired military general Asim Saleem Bajwa).The authority has been established for the coordination, monitoring and evaluation, planning, facilitating and enforcement of CPEC projects.

248. Ministry of Planning Development & Special Initiatives, accessed on 27 June 2021, <https://www.pc.gov.pk/web/ministry>. ("The Planning Commission [denoted as PC] is a financial and public policy development institution of the Government of Pakistan. The Commission comes under the Ministry of Planning, Development and Reforms. The Planning Commission undertakes research studies and state policy

development initiatives for the growth of national economy and the expansion of the public and state infrastructure of the country in tandem with the Ministry of Finance [MoF].")

249. Zain Hussain Shah, "Escaping Pakistan's Pernicious Military-Business Conglomerate: An Obstacle to Sustained Growth," *Crossfire KM* (1 Jul 2020), accessed on June 28, 2021, <https://www.crossfirekm.org/articles/escaping-pakistans-pernicious-military-business-conglomerate-an-obstacle-to-sustained-growth>. ("In 1998, during China's economic liberalization, the People's Liberation Army (PLA) was ordered by the Communist Party to divest from the service industry entirely, as the state sought to build an efficient, merit-based economy, run by civilian experts who could be held accountable."). *See also* Yezid Sayigh, 'Sudan's Military Companies Go Civilian: How the Recent Divestment Agreement Can Succeed', *Carnegie Middle East Centre* (23 Apr 2021), accessed on June 28, 2021, <https://carnegie-mec.org/2021/04/23/sudan-s-military-companies-go-civilian-how-recent-divestment-agreement-can-succeed-pub-84374>.

BIBLIOGRAPHY

Aarabi, Kasra. "Beyond Borders: The Expansionist Ideology of Iran's Islamic Revolutionary Guard Corps." *Tony Blair Institute for Global Change* (2020). https://institute.global/sites/default/files/2020-01/IRGC percent20Report percent2027012020.pdf

Acemoglu, Daron, and James A. Robinson. "De facto political power and institutional persistence." *American economic review* 96, no. 2 (2006): 325–330.

Ackerman, Bruce A. *Before the next attack: preserving civil liberties in an age of terrorism*. Yale University Press, 2006.

Actions (in Aid of Civil Power) Regulation, 2011.

Afzal, Madiha. "Why is Pakistan's military repressing a huge, nonviolent Pashtun protest movement?" *BROOKINGS,* February 7, 2020. https://www.brookings.edu/blog/order-from-chaos/2020/02/07/why-is-pakistans-military-repressing-a-huge-nonviolent-pashtun-protest-movement/.

Ahmed, Asad A. "The Paradoxes of Ahmadiyya Identity: Legal Appropriation of Muslim-ness and the Construction of Ahmadiyya Difference." In *Beyond Crisis*, pp. 295–336. Routledge India, 2012.

Akhtar, Aasim Sajjad. "The China-Pakistan Economic Corridor Beyond the Rule of Capital?" *MONTHLY REVIEW—AN INDEPENDENT SOCIALIST MAGAZINE* 70, no. 2 (2018): 34–48. https://monthlyreview.org/2018/06/01/the-china-pakistan-economic-corridor/.

Alavi, Hamza. "The state in post-colonial societies Pakistan and Bangladesh." *New left review* 74 (1972): 59.

Ali, Tariq. "Pakistan: Military Rule or People's." *Power* (1970): 196–97.

Ali, Zulfiqar. "Contradiction of concordance theory: Failure to understand military intervention in Pakistan." *Armed Forces & Society* 40, no. 3 (2014): 544–567.

Ali, Zulfiqar. "Pakistan, Military Coup, and Concordance: Four Objections to Schiff." *Armed Forces & Society* 42, no. 2 (2016): 463–469.

Aziz, Sadaf. *The Constitution of Pakistan: A Contextual Analysis*. Bloomsbury Publishing, 2018.

"Baloch separatist leader Harbiyar Marri among 13 booked for Chinese consulate attack." *DAWN,* December 7, 2018. https://www.dawn.com/news/1447419.

Begum Nusrat Bhutto v Chief of Army Staff PLD [1977] SC 657.

Besley, Timothy, and James A. Robinson. "Quis custodiet ipsos custodes? Civilian control over the military." *Journal of the European Economic Association* 8, no. 2–3 (2010): 655–663.

"Bhutto and the 1977 coup." *The News*, July 9, 2017. https://www.thenews.com.pk/tns/detail/563623-bhutto-1977-coup.

BTI 2020 Pakistan Country Report. https://www.bti-project.org/en/reports/country-report-PAK-2020.html.

Cammack, Paul. "In Permanent Retreat? The Modest Future Role of the Armed Forces in South America." In *The Soldier and the State in South America*, pp. 175–193. Palgrave Macmillan, London, 2001.

Cheema, Ali, Asim Ijaz Khwaja, and Adnan Khan. "Decentralization in Pakistan: Context, content and causes." *Content and Causes (April 2005)* (2005).

China Pakistan Economic Authority Act, 2020. www.na.gov.pk/uploads/documents/1612267873_350.pdf.

Ciddi, Sinan. *Kemalism in Turkish politics: the Republican People's Party, secularism, and nationalism*. Routledge, 2009.

CONST. of PAK. (Second Amendment), 1974.

CONST. of PAK. (Eighteenth Amendment) Act, 2010.

CONST. of PAK. (Twenty-First Amendment), 1973.

CONST. of PAK. Art. 20.

CONST. of PAK Art. 232–235.

CONST. of PAK Art. 236(b)

CONST. of PAK. Art. 245.

"Democracy at the local level." *DAWN,* March 4, 2021. https://www.dawn.com/news/610768/democracy-at-the-local-level.

Desch, Michael C. *Civilian control of the military: The changing security environment*. JHU Press, 2001.

Desch, Micheal C. "Threat environments and military missions." In Diamond, Larry, and Marc F. Plattner, eds. *Civil-military relations and democracy*. JHU Press, 1996.

Donnithorne, Jeffrey W. *Culture Wars: Air Force Culture and Civil-Military Relations*. AIR UNIV MAXWELL AFB AL AIR FORCE RESEARCH INST, 2013.

Doyle, Charles. "The Posse Comitatus Act and Related Matters: the use of the military to execute civilian law." LIBRARY OF CONGRESS WASHINGTON DC CONGRESSIONAL RESEARCH SERVICE, 2000. https://apps.dtic.mil/sti/pdfs/ADA463090.pdf.

Esposito, John L., Tamara Sonn, and John O. Voll. *Islam and democracy after the Arab Spring*. Oxford University Press, 2015.

Feaver, Peter D. "Civil-military relations 1." *Annual review of political science* 2, no. 1 (1999): 211–241.

Feaver, Peter D. "Crisis as shirking: An agency theory explanation of the souring of American civil-military relations." *Armed Forces & Society* 24, no. 3 (1998): 407–434.

Feaver, Peter. *Armed servants: Agency, oversight, and civil-military relations*. Harvard University Press, 2009.

Finer, S.E. *The Man on Horseback: The Role of the Military in Politics*. 2nd ed. Printer Publishers, 1988.

Fukuyama, Francis. "Samuel Huntington's Legacy." *Foreign Policy*, January 6, 2011. https://foreignpolicy.com/2011/01/06/samuel-huntingtons-legacy/.

Grare, Frederic. "Pakistan's foreign and security policies after the 2013 general election: the judge, the politician and the military." *International Affairs* 89, no. 4 (2013): 987–1001.

Gruber, Verena. "Revisiting Civil-Military-Relations Theory." *Small Wars Journal* (2015).

Hamdani, Yasser Latif. "Jinnah as Governor General and Democracy." *Criterion Quarterly* Vol 8 No.1, September 18, 2013. https://criterion-quarterly.com/jinnah-as-governor-general-and-democracy/.

Hamilton, Alexander, James Madison, and John Jay. *The federalist papers*. Oxford University Press, 2008. No. 26, No. 47, No. 48, and No. 51.

Haqqani, Husain. *Pakistan: Between mosque and military*. Carnegie endowment, 2010.

"Historical aspect of Pashtun nationalism." *The Nation* January 19, 2020. https://nation.com.pk/19-Jan-2020/historical-aspect-of-pashtun-nationalism.

Horowitz, Donald. 'Comparing Democratic Systems' in Diamond, Larry, and Marc F. Plattner, eds., *The global resurgence of democracy*. Journal of Democracy Book, 1996.

"How CPEC Left Behind the People of Gwadar." *The Diplomat* June 30, 2020. https://thediplomat.com/2020/06/how-cpec-left-behind-the-people-of-gwadar/.

Huntington, Samuel P. "Reforming Civil Military Relations." In *Civil-Military Relations and Democracy*, 10–11. 1996.

Huntington, Samuel P. *The soldier and the state: The theory and politics of civil–military relations*. Harvard University Press, 1981.

Hussain, Ejaz. "Failure to Understand Military Intervention in Pakistan: A Rejoinder." *Armed Forces & Society* 44, no. 2 (2018): 368–378.

Hussain, Ejaz. "Pakistan: Civil-military relations in a post-colonial state." *Pcd journal* (2012): 113–146.

Hussain, Zahid. "THE LAST COUP." *DAWN,* October 13, 2019. https://www.dawn.com/news/1510272.

Ijaz, Mishele. "Growth versus Development: The case of China Pakistan Economic Corridor." (2018).

"Independence of Pakistan's Judiciary is Under Threat." *The Wire,* May 8, 2019. https://thewire.in/south-asia/pakistan-judiciary-faizabad-justice-isa.

"Is IMF backing away from Neoliberalism." *The Express Tribune*, September 4, 2016. https://tribune.com.pk/story/1175968/imf-backing-away-neoliberalism.

"Is Pakistan's outgoing army chief Raheel Sharif worthy of praise?" *DW*, December 25, 2016. https://www.dw.com/en/is-pakistans-outgoing-army-chief-raheel-sharif-worthy-of-praise/a-36521719.

Jaffrelot, Christophe. *Pakistan at the Crossroads: Domestic Dynamics and External Pressures*. Random House India, 2016.

Janowitz, Morris. "The social demography of the all-volunteer armed force." *The ANNALS of the American Academy of Political and Social Science* 406, no. 1 (1973): 86–93.

Janowitz, Morris. *The professional soldier: A social and political portrait*. Simon and Schuster, 2017.

Kamarck, Kristy N. "Diversity, inclusion, and equal opportunity in the armed services: Background and issues for Congress." Library Of Congress Washington DC, 2019.

Kaplan, Robert D. "Looking the World in the Eye." *The Atlantic*, Dec 2001. https://www.theatlantic.com/magazine/archive/2001/12/looking-the-world-in-the-eye/302354/.

Khan, Hamid. *Constitutional and political history of Pakistan*. Oxford University Press, USA, 2005.

Khan, Jamshed, and Asmat Ullah Wazir. "Civil-Military Imbalance in the Administration of Pakistan: A Case Study of Musharraf Era." *Dialogue (Pakistan)* 6, no. 2 (2011).

Khan, Mohammed Ayub. "The Pakistan-American Alliance: Stresses and Strains." *Foreign Affairs* 42, no. 2 (1964): 195–209.

Khan, Najiyah. "Civil-military relations: A case study of Pakistan." (2010). UNLV Theses, Dissertations, Professional Papers, and Capstones, 2010. 880. http://dx.doi.org/10.34917/2228992.

Kiser, Edgar. "Comparing varieties of agency theory in economics, political science, and sociology: An illustration from state policy implementation." *Sociological Theory* 17, no. 2 (1999): 146–170.

Kukreja, Veena. "Ethnic diversity, political aspirations and state response: A case study of Pakistan." *Indian Journal of Public Administration* 66, no. 1 (2020): 28–42.

Kukreja, Veena. "Ethnic diversity, political aspirations and state response: A case study of Pakistan." *Indian Journal of Public Administration* 66, no. 1 (2020): 28–42.

Kukreja, Veena. *Contemporary Pakistan: Political processes, conflicts, and crises*. Sage, 2003.

Kukreja, Veena. *Civil-Military Relations in South Asia: Pakistan, Bangladesh, and India*. Sage publications, 1991.

Lenze Jr, Paul E. *Civil–Military Relations in the Islamic World*. Lexington Books, 2016.

Lijphart, Arend. *Patterns of democracy: Government forms and performance in thirty-six countries*. Yale University Press, 1999.

Linz, Juan J. "The Virtues of Parliamentarism." In Diamond, Larry, and Marc F. Plattner, eds. *The global divergence of democracies*. JHU Press, 2001.

Local Government Ordinance, 1979.

Lord, Carnes. "On military professionalism and civilian control." *Joint Force Quarterly* 78, no. 3 (2015): 70–74.

Mahmud, Tayyab. "Freedom of Religion & (and) Religious Minorities in Pakistan: A Study of Judicial Practice." *Fordham Int'l LJ* 19 (1995): 40.

Majeed, Dr Gulshan, and Dr Rehana Saeed Hashmi. "Baloch Resistance during Zulfiqar Ali Bhutto's Era: Causes and Consequences." *South Asian Studies* 29, no. 1 (2020).

Mandeles, Mark D. Review of Huntington, Soldier and State, Conference paper, May 2009. https://www.researchgate.net/publication/236857961_Review_of_Huntington_Soldier_and_the_State.

Mangi, Faseeh. "Soft coup' warning as Pak's army chief meets business leaders on economy." *Business Standard*, October 4, 2019. https://www.business-standard.com/article/international/soft-coup-warning-as-pak-s-army-chief-meets-business-leaders-on-economy-119100300669_1.html.

Masood, Salman. "Musharraf Decree in '07 Was Illegal, Court Rules." *The New York Times*, July 31, 2009. https://www.nytimes.com/2009/08/01/world/asia/01pstan.html.

Matei, Florina Cristiana, Carolyn Halladay, and Thomas C. Bruneau, eds. *The Routledge handbook of civil-military relations*. Routledge, 2021.

Ministry of Planning Development & Special Initiatives. Accessed June 27, 2021. https://www.pc.gov.pk/web/ministry.

"Military Injustice in Pakistan." *Briefing Paper ICJ*, January 2019. https://www.icj.org/wp-content/uploads/2019/01/Pakistan-military-courts-Advocacy-Analysis-brief-2018-ENG.pdf.

"Military trials for civilians: Pakistan court says won't allow army to take 'illegal steps", *Arab News*, August 03, 2023. https://www.arabnews.com/node/2349086/pakistan.

Mukherjee, Kunal. "Ayub Khan's basic democracy and political continuity in contemporary Pakistan." *India Quarterly* 72, no. 3 (2016): 268–277.

Musarrat, Razia, and Muhammad Salman Azhar. "Decentralization Reforms in Pakistan During Ayub and Zia Era." *Journal of Public Administration and Governance* 2, no. 1 (2012): 123–133.

Musolff, Andreas. "The reception of antisemitic imagery in Nazi Germany and popular opinion—Lessons for today." In *Analysing Fascist Discourse*, pp. 66–82. Routledge, 2013.

"NA panel approves bill against intentional disrespect for forces." *DAWN* April 8, 2021. https://www.dawn.com/news/1617040.

"NA-249 recount will strengthen people's trust in electoral process." *The Express Tribune*, May 4, 2021. https://tribune.com.pk/story/2298160/na-249-recount-will-strengthen-peoples-trust-in-electoral-process.

Nasr, Vali. "Military rule, Islamism and democracy in Pakistan." *The Middle East Journal* 58, no. 2 (2004): 195–209.

Nunn, Frederick M. "Foreign influences on the South American military: Professionalization and politicization." In *The Soldier and the State in South America*, pp. 13–37. Palgrave Macmillan, London, 2001.

Pakistan Army Act, 1952, Act XXXIX of 1952, section 7.

"Pakistan Penal Code." In *Chapter XV*, Sections 295-B, 295-C, 298-A, 298-B, and 298-C.

Paracha, Nadeem F. "The 1974 ouster of the 'heretics': What really happened?" *DAWN,* November 21, 2013. https://www.dawn.com/news/1057427.

Pion-Berlin, David. "Informal Civil—Military Relations in Latin America: Why Politicians and Soldiers Choose Unofficial Venues." *Armed Forces & Society* 36, no. 3 (2010): 526–544.

Protection of Pakistan Act, 2014.

"Pakistan National Human Development Report 2020." *United Nations Development Programme*, April 5, 2021, p.113. https://www.pk.undp.org/content/pakistan/en/home/library/human-development-reports/PKNHDR-inequality.htm.

"Pakistan protests: Why the Islamist TLP party is now a major political force." *DW*, April 15, 2021. https://www.dw.com/en/pakistan-protests-why-the-islamist-tlp-party-is-now-a-major-political-force/a-57214719.

"Pakistan: Countering Militancy in PATA." *Crisis Group* Report No. 242, January 15, 2013. https://www.crisisgroup.org/asia/south-asia/pakistan/pakistan-countering-militancy-pata.

"Pakistan: Ensure Ahmadi voting rights." *Human Rights Watch*, June 28, 2018. https://www.refworld.org/docid/5b87de574.html.

"Pakistan: Why is the military taking over civilian posts?" *DW*, May 2, 2021. https://www.dw.com/en/pakistan-why-is-the-military-taking-over-civilian-posts/a-56473442.

"Pakistan's Black Day." *The Diplomat,* July 8, 2016. https://thediplomat.com/2016/07/pakistans-black-day/.

"Pakistan's New Antiterror Law Gives Security Forces Unprecedented Power." *TIME*, July 3, 2014. https://time.com/2953028/pakistan-counterinsurgency-law-protection-of-pakistan-bill.

"Pakistan's Sham Election." *Foreign Affairs*, July 27, 2018. https://www.foreignaffairs.com/articles/pakistan/2018-07-27/pakistans-sham-election.

"Parliament passes 21st Constitutional Amendment, Army Act Amendment." *DAWN*, January 6, 2015. https://www.dawn.com/news/1155271.

"Parliament's Role in Pakistan's Democratic Transition." *Crisis Group*, September 18, 2013. https://www.crisisgroup.org/asia/south-asia/pakistan/parliament-s-role-pakistan-s-democratic-transition.

"Parliamentary Committee on National Security formed." *The News*, April 27, 2019. https://nation.com.pk/27-Apr-2019/parliamentary-committee-on-national-security-formed.

"Pashtun movement leader: 'Pakistani army is afraid of our popularity.'" *DW*, May 6, 2019. https://www.dw.com/en/pashtun-movement-leader-pakistani-army-is-afraid-of-our-popularity/a-49069682.

"Pashtun Tribes Stage Unprecedented Protest in Pakistan." *The Diplomat*, February 8, 2018. https://thediplomat.com/2018/02/pashtun-tribes-stage-unprecedented-protest-in-pakistan/.

"Pervez Musharraf resigns as president of Pakistan." *The Guardian,* August 18, 2008. https://www.theguardian.com/world/2008/aug/18/pakistan.

"President assents 17th Amendment." *DAWN NEWS,* January 1, 2004. https://www.dawn.com/news/390611/president-assents-17th-amendment.

"Profile: Iran's Revolutionary Guards." *BBC News*, January 3, 2020. https://www.bbc.com/news/world-middle-east-47852262.

"Provincial Autonomy." *DAWN*, December 18, 2020. https://www.dawn.com/news/1596395.

"PTI challenges 30-day deadline in foreign funding case." *DAWN*, April 21, 2022. https://www.dawn.com/news/1686064.

Raja Ph D, Masood Ashraf. "Neoliberal Dispositif and the Rise of Fundamentalism: The Case of Pakistan." *Journal of International and Global Studies* 3, no. 1 (2011): 2.

Rasool, Sajad, and Zahid Anwar. "Operation Zarb-e-Azb, IDPs, and the Life in Camps." *Review of Human Rights* 5, no. 1 (2019): 33–54.

Reiter, Andrew G. "Military overreach in Brazil and Pakistan: When the generals become the judges." In *Military Courts, Civil-Military Relations, and the Legal Battle for Democracy*, pp. 159–196. Routledge, 2020.

Rizvi, Hasan. *Military, state, and society in Pakistan*. Springer, 2000.

Robinson, James A., and Daron Acemoglu. *Why nations fail: The origins of power, prosperity, and poverty*. London: Profile, 2012.

Sajjad, Baqir. 'Undermining Justice: Court-Martialing Civilians in Pakistan,' *Wilson Centre* June 05, 2023. https://www.wilsoncenter.org/blog-post/undermining-justice-court-martialing-civilians-pakistan.

Samad, Harris. "The United States must end its contradictory Pakistan policy." *The Atlantic Council*, January 29, 2020. https://www.atlanticcouncil.org/blogs/new-atlanticist/the-united-states-must-end-its-contradictory-pakistan-policy/.

Sayigh, Yezid. "Sudan's Military Companies Go Civilian: How the Recent Divestment Agreement Can Succeed." *Carnegie Middle East Centre* April 23, 2021. https://carnegie-mec.org/2021/04/23/sudan-s-military-companies-go-civilian-how-recent-divestment-agreement-can-succeed-pub-84374.

Schiff, Rebecca L. "Concordance Theory in Pakistan: Response to Zulfiqar Ali." *Armed Forces & Society* 42, no. 1 (2016): 226–234.

Schiff, Rebecca L. *The military and domestic politics: A concordance theory of civil-military relations*. Routledge, 2008.

Shafqat, Saeed, Philip Jones, Tabinda M. Khan, Tahir Naqvi, Anushay Malik, Johann Chacko, Asad Llaqat et al. *Pakistan's Political Parties: Surviving Between Dictatorship and Democracy*. Georgetown University Press, 2020.

Shah, Aqil. "Where is foreign policy made in Pakistan's democracy?" *East Asia Forum* October 12, 2018. https://www.eastasiaforum.org/2018/10/12/where-is-foreign-policy-made-in-pakistans-democracy/.

Shah, Sikander Ahmed. "War on terrorism: Self-defence, operation enduring freedom, and the legality of US drone attacks in Pakistan." *Wash. U. Global Stud. L. Rev.* 9 (2010): 77.

Shah, Zain Hussain. "Escaping Pakistan's Pernicious Military-Business Conglomerate: An Obstacle to Sustained Growth." *Crossfire KM*, July 1, 2020. https://www.crossfirekm.org/articles/escaping-pakistans-pernicious-military-business-conglomerate-an-obstacle-to-sustained-growth.

Shaikh, Saba Naveed. "Emergency and Security Laws Pakistan." *South Asians for Human Rights*, February 25, 2011. www.southasianrights.org/wp-content/uploads/2009/10/Security-Laws-Report-Pakistan-Final.pdf.

Shams, Shamil. "Pakistan's Islamization - before and after dictator Zia-ul Haq." *DW*, August 17, 2016. https://www.dw.com/en/pakistans-islamization-before-and-after-dictator-zia-ul-haq/a-19480315.

Siddiqa, A. "Why is Pakistan spending so much money on defence amid COVID-19." *Al Jazeera*, July 1, 2020. https://www.aljazeera.com/opinions/2020/7/1/why-is-pakistan-spending-so-much-money-on-defence-amid-covid-19.

Siddiqa, Ayesha. "Pakistan military ethnic balance in the Armed Forces and problems of Federalism." *Manekshaw Paper No* 39 (2013): 149–162.

Siddiqa, Ayesha. *Military Inc.: Inside Pakistan's military economy*. Penguin Random House India, 2017.

Siddique, Osama, and Zahra Hayat. "Unholy speech and holy laws: Blasphemy laws in Pakistan-controversial origins, design defects, and free speech implications." *Minn. J. Int'l L.* 17 (2008): 303.

Sindh High Court Bar Association v. Federation of Pakistan PLD [2009] SC 879.

Smith, David. "Civil-Military Relations in Pakistan: Positive Evolution or More of the Same?" *Stimson Centre*, February 4, 2020. https://www.stimson.org/2020/civil-military-relations-in-pakistan-positive-evolution-or-more-of-the-same/.

Springborg, Robert. "Learning from Failure: Egypt." In *The Routledge Handbook of Civil-Military Relations*, 105–116. Routledge, 2012.

State v Dosso PLD [1958] SC 533.

Stewart, Neil. "Divide and rule: British policy in indian history." *Science & Society* (1951): 49–57.

Taj, Aamer, and Keith Baker. "Multi-Level Governance and Local Government Reform in Pakistan." *Progress in Development Studies* (2018): 3.

"The Presidential Reference against Justice Faiz Isa was quashed by the Supreme Court." *The Express Tribune*, October 23, 2020. Accessed June 28, 2021.

Trzcinski, Krzystof. "Centripetal Federalism." (2020).

"The 1857 uprising." *The News International*, May 5, 2007. https://www.thenews.com.pk/archive/print/53946-the-1857-uprising.

"The Pakistan Army's Belt and Road Putsch." *Foreign Policy*, August 26, 2020. https://foreignpolicy.com/2020/08/26/the-pakistan-armys-belt-and-road-putsch/.

"The sun has set on Pakistan's military courts—here's why it should never rise again." *DAWN,* March 6, 2017. https://www.dawn.com/news/1306792.

Vatanka, Alex. "Iran's Use of Shi 'I Militant Proxies. Ideological and Practical Expediency Versus Uncertain Sustainability." *Middle East Institute Policy Paper* 5 (2018): 22.

Weigley, Russell F. "Civilian Control of the Military: The Changing Security Environment." (2001): 196–198.

"Why Pakistan's army is targeting the MQM party." *DW*, August 23, 2016. https://www.dw.com/en/why-pakistans-army-is-targeting-the-mqm-party/a-18708521.

Williams, Susan H. "States of Emergency and Federalism: An exploration for the implications for constitutional design." (Unpublished paper on file with author).

Yang, Catherine. "Ending Dictatorship: Pakistan's Eighteenth Amendment." *Harvard International Review* 32, no. 2 (2010): 10.

Zaidi, Syed Shahid Zaheer. "Local Government Under Army Rule: A Comparative Analysis of Zia ul Haq and Pervez Musharraf Local Government System." (2019). https://iiste.org/Journals/index.php/JEDS/article/view/47213.f

"Zia-ul-Haq and the 'Islamization' of Pakistan's Public Universities." *The Diplomat*, March 28, 2017. https://thediplomat.com/2017/03/zia-ul-haq-and-the-islamization-of-pakistans-public-universities/.

Chapter 4

Chinese Expansionism and the Impact of Chinese Investments in Pakistan

Neoliberalism, China's Belt and Road Initiative and Unpacking the Chinese–Pakistan Economic Corridor

INTRODUCTION

This chapter commences with the trajectory of neoliberalism in the context of the non-Western, postcolonial world. Beginning with a brief overview of the origins, manifestations, and evolution of neoliberal theory, the chapter delineates the ways in which the doctrine has economically, socially, and politically impacted the societies in which it has been expressed. These dynamics are examined through critiques of neoliberalism emerging from the left, and by factoring key observations emerging from the Third World Approaches to International Law (TWAIL). Specifically focusing on neoliberalism as practiced by China, the chapter examines how this economic and political order fundamentally differs from classical, Western notions of neoliberalism. The Belt and Road Initiative (BRI) is examined as a global investment project, with its roots in Chinese expansionism, and so this chapter makes important observations on how the countries involved in the project, including Pakistan, are inevitably importing Chinese economic policies, in the hopes of achieving the high economic growth and rapid development promised under the Initiative.

This experiment, regarded by some as a novel form of imperialism under the guise of inclusive growth, is however not without its costs and implications upon local arenas within participant countries. In complex multicultural societies like Pakistan, the unconsidered unilateral adoption of such investment policies and plans has led to the dilution of several democratic rights—such as distributive justice, local governance, and collective minority rights—as well as communitarian values, exacerbating pre-existing sociocultural frictions within the country. Specifically, this chapter analyses the ways in which the CPEC—one of the most visible projects under the BRI—is affecting Pakistan's internal economic, political and socio-cultural climate exacerbating inequalities, considering the country's relatively weak governance structures, its administrative failures, its complicated civil-military relationship, and its inter-communal divides.

The chapter concludes by making certain prescriptions aimed at mitigating the negative consequences of the adoption of exploitative policies, focusing instead on sustainable ways in which the state can equip itself against such outcomes such as spiralling into debt traps; experiencing local discontent and its mismanagement resulting in increased alienation between local communities; environmental degradation; and unsustainable and inefficient economic investments such as the poorly executed and regulated SEZs.

AN OVERVIEW OF NEOLIBERALISM

The earliest origins of the term *neoliberalism* can be traced to the late 1930s, when it was used at the 1938 Walter Lippman conference held in Paris.[1] Francois Denord, explaining Louis Rougier's terminology, states: "(b) eing neoliberal is thus about standing apart from 'orthodox liberalism' and standing against 'planned economy,' while still allowing the state to intervene, provided that its action remains subordinate to the market."[2] From this inception, the subsequent evolution of neoliberalism—and its ensuing political, economic, and social ramifications—needs to be contextualized as a doctrinal response to leftist state policies.[3] As Gregory Albo notes:

> (i)t is important to recall that the initial political initiative in response to the crisis of the 1970s was seized by the Left. It came in the form of an array of strategies for reflation, redistribution, and socialization: the Meidner Plan in Sweden, the civil rights mobilization for the Humphrey-Hawkins Full Employment Bill in the US, the left-nationalist turn in Canada, the Bennite Left in Britain, Euro-communism, and revolutionary and nationalist upheavals across the South. Neoliberalism was the policy of those who recognized that these movements and cadres needed to be crushed.[4]

For Noam Chomsky, neoliberalism's advancement as a developmental agenda can be associated most explicitly with the Thatcher-Regan political era, and has since then grown to dominate the global political order.[5] One of the ideology's most distinguished apologists, Friedrich A. Hayek, strongly promoted limited state intervention under neoliberal frameworks.[6] While he embraced the role of the state as a provider for the community in his 'Constitution of Liberty,' he also set certain preconditions for a more restricted state role. Viewing the functioning of these institutions as a prerequisite to the ideas of 'freedom' and 'liberty' (interchangeable terms for Hayek), Hayek's emphasis, however, remains on individual liberty and free markets.[7]

Proponents of the neoliberal project have lauded the establishment of international non-governmental institutions, such as the World Bank (WB) and the International Monetary Fund (IMF), which for critics operate to proselytize and propagate neoliberal policy. Characterized as 'progressive institutions' these were "created at Bretton Woods in 1944, their mandate was to help prevent future conflicts by lending for reconstruction and development and by smoothing out temporary balance of payments problems. They had no control over individual government's economic decisions nor did their mandate include a license to intervene in national policy."[8]

Yet for critic's accession by the Global South to the neoliberal norms established through and pushed by these institutes has led to a severe deconstruction of not just institutional frameworks but has also caused and contributed to "divisions of labour, social relations, welfare provisions, technological mixes, ways of life, and attachments to the land."[9]

Neoliberal theory advances a political economic framework underpinned by free markets, free trade, and individual and private property rights.[10] In this context, the state must restructure itself to limit its own role in the economy and society in favour of that of the private sector, with theorists in this space presenting the 'neoliberal model' as a lower threshold of state regulation *vis-à-vis* greater stability in economic policy.[11] Similarly, competition—and its promotion—often takes centre stage in the propagation and maintenance of neoliberal power structures, given the norms efficacy at minimizing the role of the public sphere through the privatization of services which, in turn, serves to promote market competition for enhanced profits.[12] Another structural element of the ideology has been the reallocation and consolidation of wealth and capital upwards to the higher economic strata of society, a corollary of 'Reaganomics' emphasis on 'trickle-down economics' where economic dividends are encouraged to accrue to society's wealthiest elements in the belief that part of this wealth will 'trickle down' to society's lower economic strata as a second-order effect thereof; this consolidation of wealth in the hands of domestic economic elites, however, comes at significant cost to other elements of society—particularly its labour class.[13]

Neoliberal theory has developed—and its influence has grown—over the 1970s and 1980s to now be categorized as an extension or evolution of classical western liberal thought. The ideology ostensibly serves to further exacerbate socioeconomic inequalities in weaker democracies and economies, adversely impacting weakening ecosystems and communities and eroding flagging collective rights to local governance by empowering domestic socioeconomic elites. Against this backdrop, this chapter will seek to explore the impact of the CPEC—and its associated projects—on Pakistan's diverse sociocultural fabric.

David Harvey, one of neoliberalism's strongest critics, describes a neoliberal state as one that "acts only on behalf of certain segments of society, particularly the capitalist class";[14] given the inherent inequalities in postcolonial states, a neoliberal economy—and its classist preferences—serves to exacerbate these socioeconomic disparities in Global Southern states, widening these pre-existing divides. Harvey thus remains sceptical of Western globalization, underpinned as it is by neoliberal principles and in light of the neoliberal state's destructive capacity;[15] he characterizes Western globalization as a political project furthered by the "corporate capitalist class [who] felt intensely threatened both politically and economically towards the end of the 1960s into the 1970s . . . [and who] desperately wanted to launch a political project that would curb the power of labour."[16] Tugrul Keskin further elaborates upon this 'neoliberal scepticism' as: "(s)weatshops, occupations, wars, military regimes, and human rights violations in the developing countries are all somehow tied to post colonialism within the neoliberal trend,"[17] underlining the toxicity of neoliberal doctrine as expressed in developing, non-Western countries, where poverty—as a corollary of historical colonialism—remains rampant, and thus the workforce is already vulnerable to further exploitation under the auspices of these newer, neoliberal norms.

As per Harvey, neoliberalism "has swept across the world like a vast tidal wave of institutional reform and discursive adjustment, entailing much destruction, not only of prior institutional frameworks and powers, but also of divisions of labor, social relations, welfare provisions, technological mixes, ways of life, attachments to the land, habits of the heart, ways of thought, and the like."[18]

The inherent elements of neoliberalism (and those of its modified forms) have succeeded in co-opting, retaining, and reinforcing 'class power,' serving to preserve and reinforce pre-existing class divisions and disparities.[19] While discussing neoliberalism's effects on the instigation and propagation of intergroup frictions—such as classism or racism—Noam Chomsky questions the limited role of the state expected under neoliberal doctrine in aiding and abetting these disparities, raising the concern that if state regulation and power is minimized, where exactly does decision-making occur? In a 2017 interview, Chomsky noted that:

> when you impose socioeconomic policies that lead to stagnation or decline for most of the population, undermine democracy, remove decision-making out of popular hands, you're going to get anger, discontent, fear take all kinds of forms. And that's the phenomenon that's misleadingly called "populism."[20]

These considerations become even more pertinent in postcolonial states, such as Pakistan, where the military plays an oversized role within the state and domestic politics to fill existing political and economic vacuums,[21] and where historical tensions persist among a socioculturally diverse polity.

Gregory Albo critiques the burgeoning global neoliberal ethos from a socialist perspective, regarding it as a "more aggressive western imperialism," used to advance economic and military intervention around the globe;[22] stressing that neoliberalism presented itself as "a relentless voice of dissent to Keynesianism and the welfare state."[23] Essentially regarding it as a tool of the "ruling-class political programme"[24] to entrench and organize power and control amongst "leading cadres"[25] of professionals, Albo notes that the ideology further empowered this class to upgrade and order their professions around the evolving capitalist structures. Over time, neoliberalism became internalized within key state institutions that govern public policy and national economic trends—even impacting the practices and norms of unions and civil society organizations—culminating in the perpetuation of power, control, and economic strength among the "leading cadres" while other segments of society remain, at best, at the periphery of any developmental gains.[26] Describing how neoliberalism has altered the very foundations of the ways in which financial decisions relating to infrastructure, investments and industrialization are made, Albo notes that the

> change that has occurred has often been described as a 'hollowing-out of the state', as welfare and redistributive functions are 'downloaded' to local governments and a range of policies to support the internationalization of capital and protect private property rights are 'uploaded' to international state agencies and multinational blocs. . . . 'Hollowing out' is, however, a quite misleading image. It especially misses the authoritarian hardening of the central state and the reorganization of its administrative apparatus.[27]

This 'hollowing-out' of the state's apparatus reinforces a more general trend wherein neoliberalism's successes seem to be directly proportional to the consolidation of power within the state's centre; the more state apparatuses are shaped to strengthen the central state's autonomy to enforce neoliberal policies, the more relentlessly neoliberal reforms are seen to disregard social justice, regulation, and centralization, thereby extending "peoples' dependence on the market in all aspects of daily life."[28] This highlights a poignant reality in developing states, such as Pakistan, where access to the market is inordinately predicated upon one's preceding access to opportunities, such as education and basic welfare; these opportunities—and one's access to them—are dependent in turn on the existence and efficacy of key state welfare structures that the imposition of neoliberal norms seemingly is progressively eroding.

Wendy Brown incisively analyses neoliberalism's undoing of liberal democracy and the welfare state.[29] According to Brown, approaches to neoliberal policy in the Global South have become increasingly worrying, with such states moving to prioritize their economies over other considerations, and with democratic norms and the welfare of their people no longer being considered—even superficially—as high a priority.[30] Furthermore, given that all states have to operate within certain resource constraints, the prioritization of revenue and profit generation results in decreased state attention towards subsidies, welfare, health care, and education among other social and cultural essentials. This, in turn, accentuates class divides within the state, with disadvantaged and marginalized individuals pushed further into the peripheries of society. As inequality worsens, these underprivileged groups—who must divert even more of their time and energy towards meeting their immediate wants and needs—often deprioritize participation in political and democratic processes, further excluding them from meaningful participation in the state's governance mechanisms. At a more micro level, neoliberalism's negative impacts are also borne by individuals in such societies, forced to divert their attention away from creative and critical experiences—including their engagement with the state's political processes—and instead invest increasingly in behaviours and practices which maximize their economic returns; thus, according to Brown if people are not educated and critically aware, democracy ends up being little more than a sham.[31] As will be further explored in the proceeding sections, multi-billion-dollar infrastructure projects, such as the CPEC, have undermined local labour laws and displaced indigenous communities in Pakistan, with the federal government and the armed forces showing little respect for political, social and economic rights of communities so affected.[32] In doing so, these neoliberal projects generate economic windfalls for privileged elements of Pakistani society, while further disenfranchising already-marginalized groups. These latter groups, already having to devote much of their limited time, resources, and energies towards subsistence, are left unable to organize socially effectively and meaningfully and politically and are thus further relegated to the peripheries of Pakistan's society and its power centres.

Doctrinally, for many scholars, neoliberalism has not remained a static concept but has instead rapidly evolved as it plays out in different contexts beyond its Western points of origin. In China, for example, the central role of the state in promoting and ensuring economic development with neoliberal features is inimical to classical forms of neoliberalism. Drawing upon the Chinese experience some developing countries, in Latin America for example, have leaned towards greater central autonomy, often adopting unorthodox policies to facilitate access to alternative sources of financing, aid, and trade.[33] Richard Sandbrook notes that, in response to these new patterns of behaviour, major financial institutions such as the World Bank began shifting "from a market-fundamentalist 'Washington Consensus' to an increasingly variegated and more centrist 'Post-Washington Consensus'."[34] In his book *Reinventing the Left in the Global South: The Politics of the Possible*, Sandbrook responds to these arguably newer variants of neoliberalism from a leftist perspective, stressing that "the Left offers an alternative vision of development in the Global South, distinct from the inclusive growth or social liberalism of the Post-Washington Consensus with which it is sometimes confused."[35]

In this context it is crucial to revisit Karl Polanyi's 'Double movement" model, as presented in his seminal work *The Great Transformation*,[36] where he speaks of a 'countermovement' that arises in response to capitalist forces attempting "to expand the scope and influence of self-regulating markets. On the other side has been the movement of protection—the initiatives, again by a wide range of social actors, to insulate the fabric of social life from the destructive impact of market pressures. What we think of as market societies or 'capitalism' is the product of both of these movements; it is an uneasy and fluid hybrid that reflects the shifting balance of power between these contending forces."[37] This 'countermovement' therefore attempts to 're-embed' the economy within society by introducing measures such as labour protection laws and tariffs; premised primarily on the inherent and persistent inconsistencies within capitalism,[38] as per Polanyi, this model proposes that neoliberalism has increased the commodification of everything, including culture and nature, which might previously have otherwise been 'public' goods. In casting these hitherto public goods as commodities, neoliberalism operates to place them out of reach of all but select participants in the domestic political and economic apparatuses, with those disenfranchised within—or by—the state denied access to these historically-accessible resources.

Polanyi, in his piece titled 'The great transformation' argues that a 'free'—i.e., self-regulating market—as espoused and beatified by neoliberal doctrine—cannot exist independently from the socioeconomic context within which it operates.[39] Rather than being able to serve as a social order itself, neoliberalism's free market instead operates parasitically, relying upon a pre-existing economic and social regime—and its enforcement capabilities—to function itself. In the specific context of China, the country's free market leveraged the not-inconsiderable resources and coercive capabilities of the pre-existing Chinese state to effect and enforce outcomes desirable by the market, legitimizing state intervention—otherwise contrary to classical liberal thought—in the pursuit of the desired economic and second-order social results. In so doing, China effectively made the policy decision to prioritize its economic objectives above the social and welfare interests of its people, a policy since cohered into what is now being termed as 'Neoliberalism with Chinese Characteristics' (see discussion in section IV below).

Sandbrook employs a version of Polyani's "double movement model" to address the problems plagued by the Left in its reaction to the development of neoliberal doctrines in the Global South.[40] Modifying Polanyi's model to allow the Left to address the pressing need of disembedding the economy from society, Sandbrook applies a "developmental paradigm,"[41] proposing dynamic policy shifts (or "bundles of policies") focused on "equal freedom, social solidarity and participatory democracy."[42] Polyani believes that dominant institutions critically inform, or even mold, human perceptions and dispositions; consequently, Sandbrook posits that if the dominant policy framework changes from neoliberalism-driven policies to Sandbrook's "developmental paradigm," the challenges faced by the Global South today can well be addressed.[43] Perceiving neoliberalism as a waning influence, with its decline leaving space within which to explore alternative doctrines, Sandbrook believes that the time is ripe for a paradigm shift.[44]

THE IMPACT OF NEOLIBERAL PRACTICES ON COMMUNITARIANISM

As neoliberalism grows and takes root in a society, it is seen to have a foundationally deleterious effect on communitarian values. Specifically: when individual rights, capitalism, and competition are prioritized, this raises fundamental questions regarding domestic notions of moral solidarity and political community—and more poignantly – how one goes about building or preserving a common national identity without simultaneously stifling or erasing pre-existing religious and cultural diversity. Kymlicka's work explores a way through which diverse cultures can coexist, one which engenders a sense of communitarian belonging and while preserving and promoting peoples' individual freedom to define their values, and the ways in which such communities and their ideals are politically evaluated and legitimized.[45] Western political thought recognizes and allows for the creation of community values, practices and forums, but is often criticized because it politically avows the state to remain culturally neutral, which can often encourage majoritarianism instead, thereby stifling cultural diversity and freedom;[46] neoliberalism takes this a step forward by preferring to leave determinations of typically communal matters to a "cultural marketplace"[47] instead. Conversely, communitarians argue that "the preferability of different ways of life should be a matter of political advocacy and state action,"[48] as opposed to the orthodox stance of the state remaining neutral in such matters, and the neoliberal stance of such being left to the "cultural marketplace."[49]

According to Communitarians, once individuals begin to 'distance' themselves from the community's shared form of existence, they also begin to lose a sense of responsibility or social justice. What results as a consequence is, as Kymlicka puts it, a "legitimation crisis," where "citizens are asked to sacrifice more and more in the name of justice, but they share less and less with those for whom they are making sacrifices."[50] This worry is echoed by Charles Taylor, who believes that the increasing focus on individuality over collective decision-making may eventually erode the legitimacy of the democratic order, essentially removing the underpinning sense of solidarity within citizens.[51] Whereas Western states have, over time, built a narrative of nationhood—garnering solidarity and legitimacy through the diffusion of a national language, national symbols and holidays, and the gradual dispensation of a common history, literature, and heritage—the experience of introducing solidarity has remained far more challenging in non-Western, postcolonial states.[52]

Particularly in the case of Pakistan, any notion of a shared nationhood or sense of national solidarity has been continuously beset by an array of racial and ethnic considerations, with these sociocultural groups either demonstrating outright secessionist tendencies or, at the very least, rejecting conventional ideologies of nationhood to opt instead for a more "multicultural" conception of the collective political community. In this context it is therefore not viable for Pakistan to first construct a narrative of national solidarity, as some Western states have done, and to diffuse this understanding of a shared national identity gradually, including those communities subscribing to the state's narrative in the state's processes while excluding those expressing their dissent towards this constructed notion of a shared Pakistani collective identity.

Rather than embracing multiculturalism and recognizing the sociocultural autonomy of such minority groups, neoliberalism contributes instead to the dilution of these shared communitarian values, dictating a form of cultural assimilation which is necessarily political, or state-led. Rather than embracing multiculturalism, and respecting and accommodating ethno-cultural diversity, neoliberalism seems to discourages sociocultural 'deviance' from the state-imposed norm, compelling ethnic, religious, and cultural minorities to conform as closely as they are able to the cultural hegemony of the dominant cultural groups in the state.[53] In the Pakistani context one of the ways in which this 'cultural homogenization' has been effected has been through the adoption of Urdu as the national language, relegating the other regional languages to the private sphere, something which extends even to the country's dominant Punjabi ethnic group, whose own language—along with the other languages—is not part of formal school curricula. To cite a starker historical example: the Bhasha Andolôn, which advocated for the recognition and use of Bengali in then-East Pakistan considering state policy imposing Urdu as the *lingua franca* of the Bengali-majority East Pakistan. This political movement, initially rooted as it was in the struggle for recognition and enfranchisement of the Bengali language, was the precursor to other Bengali nationalist movements, laying the foundations for ethnic nationalist sentiments which—in turn—precipitated the secession of East-Pakistan and the formation of Bangladesh.

Given Pakistan's sobering experiences with suppressing cultural expression, and how such suppression, in the name of imposing a unified—and unifying—national cultural consensus, instead spurred the successful secession and independence of East-Pakistan—now Bangladesh—should give pause to present attempts, by way of the imposition of neoliberal policies, to forcibly homogenize Pakistani culture at the expense of the country's distinct sociocultural groups.

THIRD WORLD APPROACHES TO INTERNATIONAL LAW AND NEOLIBERAL AGENDAS

In the absence of strong institutional and economic frameworks, post-independence Pakistan has been compelled to adopt the neoliberal agenda advanced by international financial organizations such as the International Monetary Fund (IMF) and the World Bank (WB). The following section will explore the expansion and evolution of the neoliberal project in South Asia, the adaptation of neoliberal agendas in TWAIL theory, and neoliberalism's impacts on development, wealth redistribution, economic inequality, poverty, and the ensuing exacerbation of inter-ethnic conflict.

Certain non-western, South Asian countries have undertaken neoliberal reforms on the pretext of improving efficiency and productivity, and for promoting economic growth. This was affected through an attempt to adopt the neoliberal characteristics of prioritizing market competitiveness not only economically, but politically and socially as well. However, like China, most non-western countries have also retained heavy state regulation, a distinctly non-neoliberal trait.

Asian states have, as core to their sovereign governmental instrumentalities, taken as Aihwa Ong puts it, "exceptions" to classical neoliberal policies, to specifically exclude (certain sections of the polity that are denied protections), or include ("a positive decision to include selected populations and spaces as targets of calculated choices and value orientation associated with neoliberal reform").[54] This exclusionary logic is still neoliberal in nature—it is market-driven, and often implemented at palpable costs to ethnographic constructs, and notions of citizenship and solidarity—but it also possesses the non-neoliberal characteristic of being state-driven. These policies have created, as Ong puts it, "new forms of inclusion, setting apart some citizen subjects, and creating new spaces that enjoy extraordinary political benefits and economic gain."[55] Ong distinguishes between two distinct state policy strategies coexisting within neoliberal strategy: "technologies of subjectivity" and "technologies of subjection,"[56] which help differentiate between progressive neoliberalism as contrasted with divisive and segregated progress. As per Ong, technologies of subjectivity encompass policies enabling individual citizens otherwise faced with unstable market choices to optimize their respective choices, competitiveness, and efficiencies, through forms of self-engineering and modes of individual betterment such as the provision of health care, the acquisition of skills, expert education, and systems that encourage entrepreneurship and other critical means of capital accumulation and self-animation.[57] By contrast, technologies of subjection focus instead on optimizing productivity, often without consideration to the costs of such gains to certain compromised or disenfranchised segments of the population.[58] An example of this would be the creation of growth hubs like the SEZ's, and the consequent "fortressization" of such spaces, that permit access to the space only to specialized actors who, in turn, enrich the hub in specific, state-determined ways.[59] This state-within-a-state enables the state to circumvent processes and systems that would otherwise hinder the hub's ability to freely compete at the global market level.[60] Such practices often disregard local sensitivities and the pre-existence of multiple ethnic, national, or cultural identities, pushing smaller—less influential—groups further to the state's socioeconomic peripheries. As Ong frames it: "(w)hile technocrats embrace business agendas and legitimize ideals of human talent and self-enterprise, many ordinary people remain ambivalent and sceptical about market criteria and its assault on collective values and community interests."[61]

Placing an overarching emphasis on market competitiveness is thus deeply problematic, particularly for societies that are multicultural, multilingual, and multi-ethnic. An inordinate focus on market competitiveness contributes to the dilution of the fraternity required for social solidarity and cohesion, deepening class divides and socioeconomic disparities. India, for example, began implementing neoliberal reforms in 1992, employing slogans like "One Nation, One Market" to engender support for the reforms. Today, the richest 1 percent of Indians own 51.5 percent of the country's wealth, while the poorest 60 percent own 4.7 percent.[62] It must be noted that the overall improvement in national economic conditions has ensured, characteristically, a broad improvement in domestic poverty rates, generally operating to uplift large segments of the Indian population up and out from abject poverty; this uplift, however, pales in comparison to the relative wealth disparities that this economic growth has precipitated.

In India, as per Sarah Joseph, neoliberalism has had the inevitable consequence of diluting liberal, democratic values.[63] For example, large development projects have dislocated people and destroyed pre-existing local social and economic arrangements; the neoliberal dispensation towards these 'obstacles' involves individual compensation and relocation, which is often inadequate in the face of the negative consequences of being uprooted in this manner. Typically smaller, more disenfranchised groups—already susceptible to inordinate state intervention—those displaced to pave the way for these megaprojects are often pushed to the peripheries of the Indian sociocultural context. Individual compensation is also small comfort in comparison to the loss of such groups' means of subsistence—such as historical agricultural or pastoral lands—which are often difficult if not impossible to reacquire with the state-sanctioned compensation. While these projects benefit the state economically, the individuals dislocated as a result are mostly excluded from the project's accrued benefits,[64] and India—historically organized as a welfare state—now finds itself grappling with the fallout of this neoliberalist "inclusive growth" on the fabric of Indian society, social justice, and access to opportunities.[65]

The impact of neoliberalism in these societies clearly comes at the heavy cost of undermining liberal and democratic values, and creating and perpetuating severe economic imbalances, in what were already inherently weak democracies and economies. These circumstances contribute to the disenfranchisement of large segments of the indigenous population, eroding the common factors which would engender a shared sense of national unity, culminating in the fracturing of the polity. This, in turn, is followed by the rise of 'nationalist' sentiments, with nationalist assertions being made to suppress discontent. Speaking on the rise of nationalism globally and in India in particular, Noam Chomsky notes that "when you impose socioeconomic policies that lead to stagnation or decline for most of the population, undermine democracy, remove decision-making out of popular hands, you're going to get anger, discontent, fear take all kinds of forms. And that's the phenomenon that's misleadingly called 'populism'."[66] These trends become increasingly worrying in ethnically fragmented societies such as Pakistan, where democratic norms are already relatively underdeveloped.[67]

In liberalizing markets, neoliberalism fails to foresee the damage these "unleashed market forces" have on pre-existing society, institutions, and the environment.[68] Sandbrook identifies five key negative effects of "neoliberal development doctrine in the regions of its greatest influence: Latin America and Africa."[69] The first effect appears as economic market crashes and high rates of unemployment, leading to and exacerbating poverty.[70] Secondly, contrary to classical neoliberal precepts, the emphasis on removing state regulation from the market conversely contributes to increased market volatility, precipitating recessions and economic declines. The third serious impact of these market conditions is 'growing inequality.' As Sandbrook notes: "concentrated income and wealth, in turn, translate into disproportionate political influence, which allows the wealthy to manipulate tax and other policies to advance their interests."[71] Therefore, growing inequality also translates to increasing discontent and decreasing social cohesion within societies.[72] These divided societies, in turn, result in a further weakening of democratic norms and an increase in conflicts between sociocultural groups in diverse, multi-ethnic countries such as Pakistan.[73] Fourthly, further exacerbating circumstances arising due to neoliberalism take the form of ecological and environmental degradation, which severely and inordinately affect populations already vulnerable to climate change and economies—and communities—reliant on agriculture, an impact that we also anticipate worsening in Pakistan under the CPEC project.[74] Lastly, Sandbrook underlines the nexus between neoliberal policies and the ensuing outcomes leading to conflicts;[75] in states such as Pakistan, where the establishment and maintenance of a unifying national identity is tenuous at best, and where sociocultural identities—such as religion ascription and ethnic identity—often prove stronger than any shared national sentiment, the negative impacts of neoliberalism become far more pronounced. Having considered the wide-ranging impact neoliberalism has on the economic standing, the environment and the sociopolitical rights of a particular state and its citizenry, it comes as no surprise that these impacts can quickly give rise to internecine tensions and conflicts, and prove especially difficult to address for countries that have historically been plagued with inter-ethnic violence.[76] These impacts of neoliberalism as identified by Sandbrook have also been felt strongly in Pakistan. As per the UNDP's Pakistan National Human Development Report 2020, there is a massive income inequality between the rich and the poor.[77] The report's findings note:

> with the widening wealth inequality, access to services, and income generation, translate into a negative long-term impact on human development. The poorest 1 percent of the population holds only 0.15 percent of national income, compared to the richest 1 percent, which held 9 percent of national income in 2018–2019.[78]

This growing inequality also contributes to increasing ethnic tension and in Pakistan's case, the rise of religious extremism.[79] As will be subsequently discussed in greater detail, Pakistan has also recently been engulfed by the

Chinese model of economic expansionism by way of the CPEC infrastructure. There are growing concerns regarding the increase in the country's international debt, the aggravation of political tensions between provinces by the outcomes—both positive and negative—of the initiative, and the harm caused to the environment and local communities by CPEC projects.[80] The proceeding section will therefore explore China's growth model and its evolution under the Belt and Road Initiative, while the final section will examine the model's impacts on Pakistan more specifically under the China Pakistan Economic Corridor and its associated projects.

NEOLIBERALISM WITH CHINESE CHARACTERISTICS

Post 1978, China made a distinct shift in its politico-economic systems; the Communist Party came into power with an agenda to transition the Chinese economy away from Maoism and towards a model focused on capitalistic economic growth that closely resembled neoliberalism.[81] As discussed above, however, Beijing did not mechanistically implement quintessentially Western neo-liberal policies; instead, China sought to adapt the doctrine in a perceptively different way: expressed as a kind of Chinese socialism, or as Anastas Vangeli describes it, State Neoliberalism.[82]

David Harvey comprehensively overviews the Chinese approach to neoliberalism characterized by a selective implementation of the classical neoliberal model which initially generated broad economic uplift, but which eventually resulted in the capitalist concentration and consolidation of power, as is the case with neoliberal agendas in general. Harvey notes: "(b)y taking its own peculiar path towards 'socialism with Chinese characteristics' or, as some now prefer to call it, 'privatization with Chinese characteristics,' it managed to construct a form of state-manipulated market economy that delivered spectacular economic growth (averaging close to 10 percent a year) and rising standards of living for a significant proportion of the population for more than twenty years. But the reforms also led to environmental degradation, social inequality, and eventually something that looks uncomfortably like the reconstitution of capitalist class power."[83]

One fundamental point of divergence between China's approach to neoliberalism and more traditional, Western constructions of the doctrine, is that while neoliberalism with Chinese characteristics, a termed coined by David Harvey, embraces the central role of the market—much like classic neoliberalism—the Chinese model also emphasizes the role the state plays in controlling the economy, albeit in a distinctly authoritarian manner.[84] By prioritizing the ideal of economic growth and development, the China of the post-reform era integrated itself within neoliberal globalization, while its state-interventionist strategies and policies simultaneously contradicted the classical neoliberal view towards state-market relations.[85] Classical neoliberalism required the state to simply create and maintain an institutional framework that supported the neoliberal preconditions of strong private property rights, free markets, and free trade. However, as Harvey notes, "(t)he outcome in China has been the construction of a particular kind of market economy that increasingly incorporates neoliberal elements interdigitated with authoritarian centralized control."[86]

Another point of distinction between Chinese and classical approaches to neoliberalism, is the former's disregard—and arguable outright suppression—of the private sector. The private sector plays a robust and critical role in classic neoliberal capitalist economies; by contrast, however, the Chinese state's confusing policies on private ownership and entrepreneurship, which some scholars mark as "deliberately vague," are distinctly anti-capitalist.[87]

While some elements of the Chinese neoliberal experience have evolved over time, there nonetheless remain certain core components which have remained fundamental to the model. Firstly, the Chinese prioritized four main modernizations: industry, education, science, and defence, with reforming these sectors considered the primary impetus towards growth.[88] These reforms sought to stimulate competition between various State-Owned Enterprises, where the bulk of the Chinese economy operated and thrived. As Huang notes in his seminal work on Chinese Capitalism, private entrepreneurship was viewed askance by the Chinese state and its political representatives in China's financial hub, Shanghai.[89] Huang argues that post-1980s' rural China flourished under distinctly neoliberal growth trends cantered around being competitively market-driven and apolitical, and encouraging private ownership and entrepreneurship. These trends were, he argues, ostensibly reversed in the Chinese government's reforms post the 1990s, led by strong state-led policies and reforms primarily geared at revamping State-Owned Enterprises, and FDI liberalization, all of which brought the focus of economic expansion to the urban front.[90] Essentially, Huang asserts that China's economic successes were more due to allowing access to efficient institutions outside of China, rather than creating its own functional institutions.[91] Other reforms instituted by the Chinese state post-1990 aimed at encouraging innovation and growth, through the devolution of political-economic power from the centre to the localities and regional heads and by introducing market pricing.[92] These policies had the dual result of encouraging individual and local initiatives to take the lead in innovation and establishing growth, while simultaneously avoiding confrontation between locals and the centre.

Against this backdrop, Huang's accounts of the Chinese state's inimical role in rural economic growth, and his subsequent attribution of the economy's growth path to private entrepreneurship's ability to circumvent the system, enjoy a significant degree of credibility.[93] China's state policies, particularly its quasi-neoliberal ordering of its economic apparatus, have nonetheless also contributed significantly towards the country's rise and present pre-eminence in the global economic system.

Further, by opening itself up to foreign trade and investment, China attracted joint ventures which not only brought in the foreign reserves subsequently used to bolster its efforts to support strong internal growth, but also attracted much needed technology transfers.[94] This exercise was, however, nonetheless still conducted under the rubric of the Chinese putative neoliberal model; and as Harvey notes:

> foreign direct investment kept the power of the capitalist class ownership offshore and made it easier for the Chinese state to control. Barriers were erected to foreign portfolio investment, which limited the powers of international finance capital over the Chinese state. There was a reluctance to permit forms of financial intermediation other than the state-owned banks—such as stock markets and capital markets—which deprived capital of one of its key weapons vis-a-vis state power.[95]

In doing so, not only was there a determined effort on the part of the Chinese state to ensure that no other power compromised its power, there was also a deliberate attempt to keep the structures of state ownership intact while only liberating managerial autonomy.[96] Eventually, monetary policy came to be the principle means by which the Chinese state retained control over its economy, reintroducing competitiveness between locally-produced goods and imports by way of readjusting foreign exchange rates to move towards an eventually unified rate, to ensure positive economic outcomes for the country.[97]

Simultaneously, regional development zones were created as hubs of economic growth and development, initial renderings of the urban growth zones where each sector of the economy was organized in line with the state's plans, which specified budgets, output targets, and assigned inputs.[98] State-owned banks essentially existed for providing these zones investment loans and grants outside of the state specified budgets.[99]

Originally, SOE's ran a comprehensive welfare and pension system (colloquially known as the "iron rice bowl—or the State's guarantee of a livelihood");[100] over time, however, welfare arrangements and other social welfare provisions were internalized within the regional development zones, with these benefits coming to be conditional upon residency permits within the sector.[101] Essentially, this excluded the rural population while largely benefiting urbanites, the state bureaucracy, and party officials. When domestic protests were raised[102] decrying rising inequality, the Chinese state's authoritarian response made it evident that its agenda was limited only to the boosting and developing the economy, and that it largely unconcerned with the progression of the human, democratic, or civil rights domestically.[103]

China's developmental model, driven by a strong state and its regulated monetary policies, places the bulk of its focus on attracting foreign direct investment, developing a robust export economy, and micromanaging economic activity through its urban financial hubs, to which the country's exponential economic growth over the past forty years can largely be attributed. Joshua Cooper Ramo coined the phrase 'Beijing Consensus' to describe the developmental model adopted by the Chinese, a model which has since gained traction in other Central and South Asian states as well.[104] Developed by the Chinese as an alternative to the "Washington Consensus"[105] discussed above,[106] China has—in pursuit of the Beijing Consensus—founded the Asian Infrastructure Investment Bank (AIIB) and holds a 30 percent stake therein, with commentators believing that by providing developmental lending to other developing countries in Asia, the AIIB extends Beijing's financial and diplomatic reach, and counterbalances leverage previously exerted by Washington and its allies.[107]

Having established the broad parameters for Chinese expansionism, the following section will explore the damaging nature and adverse impacts of the developmental model, considering how the doctrine—under the rubric of the BRI—has been critiqued as an attempt by Beijing at developing regional—if not global—hegemony.

Chinese Expansionism and the One Belt and Road Initiative

With the launch of the Belt and Road Initiative, Chinese expansionism and global investment strategy have taken a much broader, almost 'neocolonial' approach. Since the launch of China's One Belt One Road (OBOR), functionally 'the Belt and Road Initiative (BRI)'—part of which is the China-Pakistan Economic Corridor (CPEC)—it is becoming increasingly necessary to examine what Chinese economic expansionism means for countries in the region that are actively participating in projects related to the BRI, such as Pakistan, as well as those invariably experiencing second-order effects of the project. Against this backdrop, it is crucial to glean insight into how China conducts its offshore economic projects, and to assess whether and how the nature of Chinese intervention differs across the different states the BRI intersects with.

Keeping in view the magnitude of the OBOR, and the non-trivial amounts to be invested by Beijing on the various projects under the initiative, it is likely to have hugely transformative and long-term geopolitical implications for the regions involved.[108] As such, the Belt and Road Initiative represents China's contemporary approach towards garnering greater regional and global political influence, securing access to energy and natural resources, and expanding its consumer markets and trade networks. Crucially, as most of the investments made to partner countries will come in the form of loans and not grants, if a country were to default on its payments, this could potentially result in Chinese ownership of another state's resources as well as control of its power sector and natural resources.[109] Described as 'Debt-Trap Diplomacy,' the lattermost has become a major point of concern—particularly from western commentators—regarding Beijing's potential co-option of critical infrastructure of foreign states.

The BRI can thus be viewed as an ever-evolving—and expanding—project, with varying interpretations and applications by participating countries. Given the initiative's ambitious scope, and the variety of the schemes falling within its rubric, it necessarily prompts an equally varied response from other states—whether participants in the BRI itself or those likely to experience second- or third-order effects. Underpinning the entirety of the discourse around—and state responses to—the project, however, is the pervasive influence of neoliberalism with Chinese characteristics, which informs the BRI and projects conducted under its auspices. The Chinese presence in Africa, for instance, has had far-reaching social and geopolitical implications for the continent, and a booming economy due to enhanced development has not been the most apparent outcome.[110] The past two decades have seen a massive increase in China-Africa trade relations,[111] and a large percentage of the funds made available to African partner countries has been in the form of development loans.[112] In the case of Sri Lanka's debt payment default, the Hambantota port had to be leased out to China for a ninety-nine-year period, which lends credence to concerns that China is attempting to colonize Africa, there were concerns that China could take over Kenya's Mambosa port if they defaulted on debt payments.[113] Although these concerns regarding the Mambosa port have been allayed by the authorities,[114] Kenya refuses to disclose loan contract details for the Chinese built SGR railway project, citing breach of a bilateral agreement and national security concerns.[115] Furthermore, due to the steady expansion by China into various development sectors across the world, a substantial amount of global infrastructural work is being carried out by Chinese firms and Chinese workers, causing issues of discrimination against local workers.[116] Against this backdrop it is clear that international Chinese lending cannot thus be considered free of added external costs; instead, they must be viewed not only in terms of the financial terms of the loans themselves, but also through the lens of the broader geopolitical consequences of such arrangements.[117]

An evaluation of the immense Chinese diaspora also suggests a form of neo-colonialism being expressed in parts of Africa.[118] This approach seems to be built on the Chinese expansionist model's embedded interests in developing a global hegemony through overseas investment in soft and hard infrastructure projects.[119] Despite China's portrayal of the BRI as an opportunity to "focus on the fundamental issue of development, release the growth potential of various countries and achieve economic integration and interconnected development and deliver benefits to all," a closer look reveals a broader, geostrategic agenda being implemented through the economic control and influence netted by China by way of BRI projects.[120] These neo-colonial aspirations are also evinced through China's growing military influence in Africa and South Asia.[121] Thus far, China has gained access to around fifteen ports in the region, ranging from Cambodia to Pakistan. Pakistan's port at Gwadar provides a strategic base for the expression of Chinese interests in the region and has been a source of concern for unfriendly neighbouring countries such as India.[122] These factors are likely to have various impacts on the socioeconomic and geopolitical landscape in Pakistan which will be explored at greater length in the following section of this chapter.

As explained in the preceding sections, China's approach towards neoliberalism significantly departs from historical, classical understandings of the doctrine. Similarly, there are certain points of divergence that serve to distinguish the Chinese international geostrategic presence from classical colonialism. Unlike the latter, the Chinese rise to international power has largely been achieved through the foreign expansion of the Chinese economic model, "that is driven by capital, resource acquisition and technology."[123] The asymmetry between China and the several African countries with which it engages also calls into question the ability of such underdeveloped nations to maintain their sovereignty in both domestic and foreign policy.[124] Complicity from state governments and domestic political elites in favour of external Chinese interests also serves to compromise the social, economic, and environmental rights of citizens of these countries.[125]

China's colonial footprint is also seen advancing in the North African regions of Egypt, Algeria, and Morocco. China's earlier diplomatic support for countries—such as Algeria—in their anti-colonial struggles has now developed into economic and strategic support, with concomitant expressions of Chinese regional interests.[126] In particular, China's Comprehensive Strategic Partnerships (CSPs) with Algeria and Egypt

> reflects the major role these states play in the MENA region, as well as the fact that these are its two key bilateral relationships in the region in terms of trade, arms sales, and infrastructure projects. In turn, China has become the top trading partner for both Egypt and Algeria.[127]

As in the case of other African states, China's economic and trade support is often backed by expressions of its 'soft' and 'hard power.'[128] Recurring features of the former include the use of Chinese labour, 'debt trap diplomacy,' neo-colonialism, and strategic partnerships between Chinese and indigenous academic elites. As Jacobs notes

> (t)he cases of Pakistan, Sri Lanka, and Ecuador have been cited as particularly disastrous in terms of Chinese debt and failed projects. While each of these countries has its own unique economic challenges, Chinese debt has given Beijing oversized influence in all of them, sometimes with disastrous consequences.[129]

However, it is China's 'hard power,' connected with its diplomatic and defence efforts, that is even more disconcerting when on display.[130] For instance, in addition to increasing weaponization and arms exports from China to these regions, economic advances could be used as tools for surveillance and monitoring.[131]

A direct and highly visible corollary of China's 'foreign' expansionism into regions and states engaged under the 'Belt and Road' project is the concomitant erosion of indigenous expressions of liberal norms, economic and social rights, and democratic values. China's "all-inclusive" approach to financing deals with African nations without any pre-set conditions, as opposed to the United States and European countries which apply stricter conditions to investments and ostensibly prefer to deal with "transparent and accountable democracies."[132] With dwindling investment from Europe and the United States, China's grants, aid and loans with generous repayment schedules is quite appealing to African states.[133] However, the rising debt of African nations under the BRI questions the accuracy of the BRI being "a win-win model of cooperation," as well as the fact that Chinese initiatives under the project are more broadly aimed at working in tandem with local needs.[134] While China can be said to work with states in need of international assistance or developmental or economic uplift, the fact remains that engaging with the antidemocratic regimes governing such states often only serves to perpetuate them. Under the garb of its "non-interference" policy, China has been known to turn a blind-eye to corruption and malpractice in recipient countries.[135] As Virginia Marantidou and Brad Glosserman note: "Beijing touts this as a virtue of Chinese policy, contrasting its condition-free lending with that of Western countries and international financial institutions, all which demand compliance with good governance practices before providing funds." China justifies these policies in the name of its "non-interference policy," arguing that Beijing has no right to intervene in the internal affairs of recipient states. China's official policy on aid explains that

> when providing assistance, it adheres to the principles of not imposing any political conditions, not interfering in the internal affairs of the recipient countries,

> and fully respecting their right to independently choose their political systems and models of development. (In fact, recipients of Chinese aid must accept conditions such as the use of Chinese companies—a demand that isn't uniquely Chinese—and promise to adhere to the One-China policy, both of which could be considered interference in domestic affairs.)[136]

Further, neoliberalism with Chinese characteristics' indifference towards democratic norms or socioeconomic rights—often finds fertile ground amidst the political and economic elites indigenous to China's BRI partner states, further entrenching such elites into the domestic sociopolitical landscape.

Given the need for proximity to natural resources (such as in the case of industrial and energy projects), Chinese developmental engagement often results in the dislocation and environmental encroachment on land historically inhabited by local communities.[137] These projects are often implemented by bribing local officials, directly undermining norms of distributive justice, grassroots democracy, and the rule of law.[138] China's influence has also risen through its direct ownership of large percentages of external debt in this region,[139] leading several African countries to cancel or postpone projects over their concerns relating to environmental compliance, labor standards, heightened 'debt trap' concerns, and disagreements with Chinese authorities over revenue sharing.[140] Consequently, BRI projects have received considerable push back from local communities in several BRI partner African states such as Nigeria, Kenya, Uganda, and Ghana.[141]

Similarly, in the context of the CPEC, China is unconcerned with Pakistan's local political climate, complaints of resource and power grabbing by Punjabi elites, environmental degradation, or displacement of—and subsequent protest by—local communities by huge infrastructure development projects, issues that will be discussed in greater detail in the proceeding sections. Pakistani political elites have historically leveraged religious and ethnic identity considerations to gain political advantage; this practice has—in turn—served to foster persistent and systemic inequities between members of these various religious and ethnic groups in areas such as access to national resources and technologies of development. Deploying identity concerns in this manner, and the disparities arising as a result, has led to certain cultural markers being used to identify and disunite, rather than cohere, the community, fostering resentment and distrust towards "dominant" sociocultural groups—the Punjabi ethnic group or the Sunni Muslim religious sect in the case of Pakistan. These trends towards increased divisiveness are brought into sharper distinction by the fact that Pakistan has historically had a relatively weak system of governance, making it easier for China to dictate policies and outcomes without regard for local sensitivities and cultural anomalies.[142] By strategically courting or co-opting these dominant sociocultural groups in its

BRI partner state, China has been able to realize its economic and developmental goals without needing to engage in any meaningful manner with the communities most impacted by these initiatives, and to insulate itself from any real political consequences thereof. By contrast, China appears to have several strategic advantages over Pakistan: it is politically more united, far stronger economically, and its approach so far has been to retain control of project execution to the greatest extent possible, focusing less on cooperation and conflict resolution, and more on expediting progress and bypassing hurdles autocratically and non-transparently. This asymmetry, and the way it is expressed in China's realization of Pakistan-specific BRI projects, questions democratic sovereignty, particularly at the grass-roots level, and overlooks Pakistan's dire need—which admittedly predated China's CPEC aspirations—to address the existing and emerging needs of entire communities disenfranchised, as well as those disrupted or dislocated by development projects. Indeed, questions also remain unanswered regarding collective minority protections, or inclusive economic growth—where access to development and growth opportunities seem to be limited to the religious and/or ethnic majority groups.

NEOLIBERALISM AND CPEC IN PAKISTAN

This section will explore the adaptation of the neoliberal project to the Pakistani context, and the evolution and modification of this model under Chinese expansionism in the region and specifically through the China Pakistan Economic Corridor. The privatization of State-Owned enterprises and the overhaul of the economic infrastructure through various projects will also be evaluated to determine the impact of these economic models in the local context and specifically upon the rights of minority populations and groups, which damages political federalism. Additionally, Pakistan has created "Special Economic Zones" in furtherance of CPEC-related projects, modelled after Special Economic Zones established in China.[143] This section will explore some of the ways in which these zones have negatively impacted communal democratic norms—such as self-governance and political accountability—and the socioeconomic rights of local communities.

In any event, it is becoming increasingly difficult to accept the vision that China presents, i.e., that of the BRI creating a space of mutual benefit and non-interference. For instance, in Pakistan pre-existing ethnic and regional divides are already deepening due to the policies surrounding the implementation of the CPEC, and Pakistan's heavily problematic and divisive civil-military relationship—and the concomitant political asymmetry between the country's powerful military and its civilian governance infrastructure—is being exacerbated by China's agenda, which supports the state's interventionist strategies—expressed in Pakistan's case through its military's institutional effectiveness—to facilitate the implementation of CPEC project goals.[144]

The following section will look at the introduction, implementation, and evolution of neoliberal policies in the Pakistani context.

The Neoliberal Experiment in Pakistan

By the 1970s, neoliberal agendas were apparently being imposed on the developing world and the Global South through international organizations such as the World Bank, the International Monetary Fund, and the World Trade Organization. Pakistan's postcolonial, sociopolitical structure, heavily influenced by Western imperialism, adapted its initial neoliberal economic policies during the Zia era (1977–1988) and entered into its first financial arrangement with the IMF in 1980.[145] Consequently, in the proceeding decades, the Pakistani state has begun down a downward spiral through limiting its role "in the economic sphere both as a producer of goods and services and as a regulator of the corporate sector."[146]

Previously, under Ayub Khan's regime, the state had assumed a role as facilitator for the accumulation of capital by incentivizing private entrepreneurs through a 'Western' model to be implemented and steered by the bureaucratic elite.[147] This model provided the increase in economic growth as promised but, as Hassan Gardezi writes: "the regime of low wages and neglect of distributive justice aggravated mass poverty and inequality across social and regional lines. These disparities fuelled a popular uprising against the Ayub regime."[148] These policies, as well as subsequent ones implemented up until the 1990s, led to "growth without development," and "overall economic growth of the country but it has failed in promoting social and institutional development because of the elite domination, social polarisation and ethnic divisions."[149]

This neoliberal experiment ostensibly served to compound the concentration of power in the hands of domestic elites, and heightened pre-existing ethnic and interprovincial tensions within the country, with this trajectory continuing across successive terms of three major political parties, through the privatization of state-owned enterprises, amnesty schemes for the rich, and policies favouring particular elite classes in both the agricultural and industrial sectors of the economy, resulting in the elite capture of power in Pakistan with very little resources left to allocate towards human development.

To cite a specific example of the corrosive effect neoliberal forces have had on Pakistan, a series of democratically elected governments have, over time, privatized much of the domestic educational sector in a bid to justify cuts in public spending,[150] a policy which persisted through periods of autocratic rule when—during the Musharraf regime—incentives to keep educational spending low did not change. The elected Sharif and military Musharraf governments both opted to support welfare activities initiated by Islamic networks—another excuse to justify state inactivity in the sector, and to pass what would otherwise be state functions off on to private actors. As a result of these policies, the state's inability to provide free or subsidized quality education has resulted in a significant uptick in madrassah—or religious seminary—enrolment.[151] This set of circumstances has given rise to a number of problems: firstly, in the absence of formal education, most students passing out from madrasahs are unable to secure jobs in the skilled labour segments of Pakistan's workforce, rendering them unable to secure a liveable standard of income and pushing them into poverty. Secondly, madrassah's are known to promote arch-conservative, and radicalized perspectives on Islam, ideologies which later manifest as violent extremism.[152] Lastly, control over millions of madrassah students give the religious political parties and outfits a significant amount of leverage and bargaining power against the government.[153] In the absence of meaningful participation by the state in the domestic educational sector, the vacuum left as an adverse impact of neoliberal policies has been filled by Pakistan's political right, consequently reducing the space and scope within which progressive forces and values can flourish.

It would be useful to highlight this point generally as well, that in Pakistan, successive neoliberal policies have been met with hostility in the form of Islamization, where religious seminaries have played a crucial and highly active role in terms of securing socioeconomic rights in the country, often in the face of neoliberal trends in the country's politico-economic development. Given the significant emphasis the Pakistani polity places on religion and religious identification, elements of external ideologies—such as neoliberalism—have been pushed back against by elements of the country's Muslim conservatives. With the state ceding its role as guarantor of socioeconomic rights and provider of welfare benefits, partly because of neoliberal policies, it has left vacant spaces within which such groups can operate; this, in turn, arranges the country's religious right as a counterpoint to the ostensibly secular state architecture, and empowers the bloc—often to the detriment of religious and sexual minorities extant in the country.

The CPEC advances Chinese expansionism under the rubric of the broader BRI, promoting development and infrastructure projects in poorer countries and—to facilitate the implementation and operational success of these initiatives—inculcating exploitative Chinese business norms in these states; China's engagement is also predominantly limited to political and economic elites in these BRI partner states, further deemphasizing the stakes and roles held by more marginalized groups in these societies. In the Pakistani context, which has already seen decades of neoliberal policies erode liberal and social welfare norms in the country, the introduction of neoliberalism with Chinese characteristics has further weakened the state's social welfare architecture. To compound the negative impacts of these Chinese foreign investment facilitation policies, given that much of the project financing under the BRI—including that of the CPEC—is through Chinese lending, these countries are then saddled with long-term Chinese debt,[154] with the potential for China to 'repossess' the projects so financed if the host state is unable to meet its debt repayment obligations. Given that many of these states—including Pakistan—are already underdeveloped economies, there persists the credible risk that all of Pakistan's efforts towards realizing the 'game-changer'—as CPEC is described by Pakistan's political leadership—could yield little more than another Chinese strategic asset. Precedent for such can be found in China's well-documented take-over of the Hambantota Port in Sri Lanka, as well as—more recently—a major port situated in Greece.[155] These circumstances are further complicated by the state's fiscal deficit, which prevents it from accumulating enough resources to be transferred to lower income, or economically disenfranchised groups within the state. With widespread unemployment, underemployment, and poverty, the working class is often forced to work at rates that fall well below the prescribed employment rates—which themselves may arguably be inadequate—causing greater hardships and fomenting discontent amongst this significant segment of the population.[156]

As highlighted by Abrahim Shah, neoliberalism's diminishment of the state's role in society and the economy leaves the individual to fend for themselves, with limited to no social security and public support; vulnerable sections of Pakistani society and the country's weaker provinces are more severely impacted by an unregulated market and unemployment, and can expect little—if any—assistance from the state,[157] creating an environment conducive to inter-group resentment and socioeconomic tensions towards the political and economic elites favoured by successive governments and military regimes, much of which is consolidated in the province of Punjab.[158] These tensions, in turn, contribute to a weakening of federalism in states such as Pakistan, and the next section will provide a brief overview of the unfolding of the CPEC infrastructure and the impact of Chinese investment on political federalism in Pakistan.

The Impact of Chinese Investment and CPEC on Political Federalism and Generating Inequalities in Pakistan

Pakistan's colonial legacy and ensuing socio-political makeup, and the country's approaches to federalism and civil-military relations have been discussed at length in Chapters 1 through 3 of this work. It is, however, important to highlight specific grievances of the provinces towards the centre to evaluate how the CPEC infrastructure can impact federalism in Pakistan.

Pakistan suffers from a historically weak federal structure due to its ethnically divided political and physical context.[159] There is a strong feeling of hostility towards the dominant Punjab province by the smaller provinces of Sindh, Khyber-Pakhtunkhwa, and Balochistan.[160] In the evolving circumstances under CPEC, Balochistan is also the most strategically significant due to the Gwadar port as the terminus of the BRI—and its subordinate projects such as CPEC—in Pakistan.[161] The Baloch people nonetheless continue to be politically and financially marginalized, which has led to a sustained increase and persistence in intra-provincial violence directed towards the centre and towards Punjabi settlers in Balochistan.[162] Balochi political marginalization is further compounded by the province's lack of control over the wealth of its significant natural and mineral resources,[163] with the federal government thus far having failed to meaningfully invest in the development of basic infrastructure in the region. The following section will outline the progression of CPEC and its adverse impacts on communal democratic values and political federalism in the country, considering the inter-provincial frictions arising because of the project.

The China Pakistan Economic Corridor

The CPEC is valued above sixty-five billion dollars, predominantly in the form of loans and grants from the Chinese government for the completion of a series of infrastructural and commercial projects in Pakistan linked to: (1) the transportation sector—building a vast network of highways and roads spanning over two thousand kilometres, and upgrading and improving the national railways system; (2) the energy sector—setting up renewable and fossil fuel energy power generation plants; the establishment and operationalization of several coal mines to cater to coal-fired power plants; and the construction of numerous oil, petroleum, and gas (including liquid gas) pipelines which will connect to similar pipelines in other regional countries; and (3) the port and shipping sector—primarily in developing Gwadar's deep sea Port and its associated facilities.

The CPEC also includes other associated projects, including the construction of an international airport at Gwadar; the creation of industrial estates and technology parks; the laying of fibre optic links; and the construction of numerous bridges, interchanges, city subways, and bus lines. The whole route between CPEC's two commercial terminuses is planned to be covered by the SEZs modelled on similar zones set up internally within China—which are spaces unencumbered by many domestic laws and exempt from a variety of taxes (e.g. income, corporate income tax, and sales tax) and duties (e.g., duty-free import, custom duty, and stamp duty) in the short and medium term—and in limited cases—in perpetuity, for the purpose of facilitating energy generation and the free production and movement of goods.[164] Most of these schemes will be situated and function within the aforementioned special economic zones in Pakistan created under the Special Economic Zones (SEZ) Act, (2012)[165] and governed under the Special Economic Zones (Amendment) Act, 2016 and the Special Economic Zones Rules (2013).[166] Under the Act, provincial Special Economic Zone Authorities will directly monitor provincial SEZs and retain the right to acquire private land through eminent domain processes under the Land Acquisition Act, 1894 (I of 1894).[167]

In the recent past, the last PTI government sought to complete projects and SEZs already underway with the aim to promote local businesses and generate employment. The politicization of these—and related—projects and SEZs by domestic political actors has drawn attention away from how these initiatives could benefit the public, focusing instead on significantly less important extraneous factors. For instance, the Khan government had selected to establish a SEZ in the Khyber-Pakhtunkhwa province to appease his political base in the province, despite Beijing's interest in other regions.[168]

All things considered, the SEZs may have the potential to contribute towards poverty alleviation within the region they are established in, primarily by generating employment opportunities and raising wages, and by uplifting living standards through the construction of teaching facilities and hospitals to cater to the populations working in the zones. These positives, however, are often specific to the region hosting the SEZ itself; further, these need to be considered considering the not-inconsiderable negative impacts these zones have on broader Pakistani society.

Resistance from locals threatened with being displaced from their homes and livelihoods to make way for CPEC projects, and the concomitant failure of the state to incorporate these—and other—local concerns, have resulted in project sites becoming heavily militarized, exacerbating the divide between the affected communities and the state.[169] Additionally, China's frustrations over project delays and Pakistan's dense array of bureaucratic red tape have led the former to either autocratically disregard prescribed procedures, relying on the ease with which these zones can be turned into a 'state within a state,' or to autonomously negotiate procedures that are in its own interests, regardless of the interests of locals.[170] Another complication lies for areas like Azad Jammu and Kashmir and Gilgit Baltistan, which are not classified as provinces of Pakistan, and exist instead as federally administered areas, or 'disputed territories.' This characterization further alienates them from the federal centre, which decides the fate of the people and the SEZ's that fall within these regions but remains detached from the on-ground realities and sentiments of these communities. Provincial and local governments are better equipped and are more proximally located to monitor and administer the functioning of SEZs within their territories, while remaining politically accountable to residents of these regions; by contrast, zones falling within areas remotely managed by the centre are more prone to looser management, corruption, and failures to accommodate local concerns—essentially leaving a vacuum that is readily misappropriated by the strong establishment presence in Pakistan.

With regards to CPEC projects, Chinese policy has predominantly been to rely on Chinese workers brought in to supply labour, with the intention being to consolidate payments and technical facility within Chinese-owned institutions. This propensity is compounded by the indigenous lack of skilled labour, which compromises employment opportunities and further depresses wages for locals who have sacrificed their existing livelihoods and have had their way of life upended to establish these zones. While the SEZs may generate some benefits for the local communities they directly impact, it is therefore nonetheless important, to counter the attendant negatives of these enclaves by safeguarding the rights of local communities and preserving municipal governance mechanisms that are otherwise being compromised under CPEC. Recommendations to this effect will be explored in greater detail in the prescriptions section of this chapter.

Another major negative outcome of neoliberal policies and approaches to development appears in the form of environmental degradation. Both neoliberalism and its contested Chinese variant fundamentally do not entertain the capacity to make cost-benefit analyses that factor in important values like safeguarding welfare concerns, the long-term costs to the environment and the right of future generations to enjoy a viable ecosystem, or even the human costs associated with achieving certain developmental goals. Characterized as 'externalities,' social or environmental concerns—being relatively difficult to quantify in the immediate to short terms—are often disregarded outright in neoliberal calculi. Considering Pakistan's reliance on its agricultural sector, and its unenviable position as one of the top ten countries most vulnerable to climate change,[171] neoliberalism's apparent indifference to environmental 'externalities'—and the hidden costs of neoliberal policies—becomes increasingly critical for a state already struggling to accommodate the needs of its poorest citizens.[172] Yet in spite of these grave environmental risks, there is still no clear and uniform policy in place to conduct environmental impact assessments (EIAs) before initiating projects under CPEC, particularly energy projects.[173] CPEC projects present three principal environmental concerns: (1) the direct rise of air pollution due to planned coal-powered energy projects; (2) deforestation due to the construction of major road networks stretching from Kashghar, China, to Gwadar, Pakistan; and (3) vehicle emissions from increased road traffic as a result of the completion and operationalization of this road infrastructure. Attempts at quantifying this last concern have described its impact in alarming terms, with the "Karakorum Highway (one of the primary road projects envisioned under the CPEC) . . . expected to carry up to 7000 trucks per day that will release up to 36.5 million tons of CO_2."[174] As Ahmad Rafay Alam notes:

> Pakistani cities already suffer from toxic air pollution resulting from the diesel, petrol, furnace oil and coal that we consume as a non-industrial economy. Pakistan's air-quality crisis will be worsened by the coal-fired power plants that comprise a substantial portion of CPEC's first phase. And if the government doesn't crack down on the poor-quality diesel and petroleum products available in the country, the ageing trucks on the planned Khunjerab–Gwadar highway will remain a major contributor to this public health crisis.[175]

These environmental concerns are extrinsic to the neoliberal calculus as the doctrine is famed to concern itself fundamentally with increasing productivity through free market competition and does not factor in the damage to the environment as a functional costs of such production to outweigh the objectives of growth. Neoliberalism with Chinese characteristics is arguably even worse, as it is an expression of—and relies upon—the state's own ignorance of or disregard towards policies and practices the state itself puts in place to safeguard the environment and the welfare of its citizenry, all in the interests of uninhibited economic growth.

CPEC's intersection with Pakistan's agricultural economy will also be a determining factor in gauging the potential impacts of this Chinese intrusion into Pakistan. Agriculture is often referred to as the 'backbone' of Pakistan's economy, contributing 18.5 percent to the GDP and employing 38.5 percent of the total domestic labour force.[176] While technological advances can be of immense value to the agriculture sector in terms of increased yields and greater efficiencies, the environmental sustainability of these projects remains a concern, and as the sector is intertwined with a number of other sectors in the economy, any negative impacts on agriculture will contribute to increased social inequity.[177] In this context, the CPEC framework has identified at least eighteen agricultural projects worth around Rs. eighty-three billion.[178] China's interests in the sector stems principally from its need to import huge amounts of food and commodities from the United States, Australia, Russia, and Brazil to cater to its large population, significantly increasing the associated costs; by contrast, China's investments into Pakistan's agricultural sector will be far more feasible for future imports.[179] Another reason for Chinese interest in Pakistan's agriculture sector is more strategic; as Asim Sajjad Akhter notes:

> (a)s far as China is concerned, Pakistan's comparative advantage is in agriculture, and improving infrastructure and technical expertise while reducing waste in the sector will directly complement the modernization of agriculture in Xinjiang and other parts of western China. In the context of (Beijing's) relatively undisguised policy of promoting migration by Han Chinese to the underdeveloped and sparsely populated western provinces, some of which have become hotbeds of minority unrest, the utility of Pakistan's agricultural sector becomes even clearer.[180]

Another impact of CPEC on Pakistani agriculture has been the appropriation of arable land for the establishment of SEZs. As outlined in an online report by GRAIN:

> (i)n Balochistan, more than 15,300 hectares of land will be taken under the Kachhi Canal Development project, while in Peshawar, farmers have been protesting since 2015 against the development of the Northern Bypass Road that is taking their homes and farmland without compensation. . . . In the last two years, fisherfolk in the Gwadar area have held strikes and large demonstrations against the development of the Gwadar port and the industrial complex under CPEC. A 19-kilometre expressway which provides a direct link for cargo traffic to and from Gwadar Port, is blocking 4.3 kilometres of the coastline—cutting off old fisherfolks' neighbourhoods and limiting the access of fishing boats to the sea. This has sparked waves of protests among the local population.[181]

The loss of historical and ancestral agricultural lands—often in exchange for inadequate or sometime no recompense—cripples pre-existing indigenous agricultural economies and societies, disenfranchising large groups, and pushing them either into abject poverty or towards militant resistance.

While Pakistan's agricultural sector is in dire need of investment—in terms of both financing and technological advancement—such inputs cannot come at the expense of sections of the polity already engaged in—and dependent upon—the sector. While Pakistan—and China—should seek to improve the technologies applied and effect scientific exchange *vis-a-vis* agriculture, the Pakistani state cannot legitimately sacrifice the rights of its citizens already working in the sector; nor the rights of its labour force—especially should they be rendered 'obsolete' because of such 'modernization.' Left entirely to the devices of the Chinese investment projects, these rights will never be safeguarded, as China has historically been apathetic to concerns that otherwise threaten to slow the pace of its progress. It is imperative for Pakistan that it constructs its own economic growth objectives, distinct from those advocated by Chinese project sponsors as being in the mutual interests of the countries, which must be democratically inclusive and reflective of threats to Pakistan's land or its people in the long run. An excessive focus on the agricultural sector in Pakistan has been demonstrated, in China's interests, but this focus may have opportunity costs for Pakistan in the form of land, food, or ecological objectives that better cater to the needs of the Pakistani people. For instance, Pakistan is one of the main contributors to global methane emissions and has committed internationally[182] to reduce its impact on global warming by cutting down on its pollutant output. However, with its vast agriculture sector primarily to blame for the emissions, it is unclear how Pakistan will be able to uphold its international commitments, particularly if it is also being pressured by China to expedite the further expansion of its agricultural sector without first focusing on enacting effective policies and protections to make the sector more ecologically efficient.[183]

Beyond its domestic effects, another potential impact of CPEC with grave potential ramifications will be the project's second-order effects on the regional geopolitical and security context. While the unsettled security situation in Balochistan—and its port at Gwadar—will be explored in greater detail below, it is also critical to consider the Gilgit-Baltistan region. Given its proximity to Central Asia, and as the point of entry for the CPEC 'belt and road' into Pakistan, Gilgit-Baltistan is in a key geostrategic location in terms of regional connectivity, its relation to the CPEC and its associated projects, and as a security stronghold.[184] This critical site, however, has historically been relegated to the margins of Pakistani policymaking, with China instead seeking to exploit its resources in a manner likely to leave thousands among the local populace unemployed. Due to its semi-autonomous status, the Gilgit-Baltistan region has consistently been excluded as a key stakeholder from the CPEC negotiations, arguably due to the fact that—as touched upon earlier—the region is not considered to be a 'province,' and thus lacks any meaningful representation at Pakistan's political centre, and will likely also be left out when it comes time to recoup any financial benefits from CPEC projects. As Hamna Tariq writes:

> (g)radually, locals realized that Islamabad's promise of 1.8 million jobs to revitalize the region was a façade; instead, China had planned to send 400,000 construction workers to Gilgit-Baltistan at the expense of local labor. China has almost exclusively profited off the people and resources of the region—the Government of Pakistan cancelled licenses of local miners to allow Chinese developers exclusive control over mining activities and reportedly displaced thousands of residents without plans for rehabilitation. Pakistan has turned a blind eye to China's exploitations in Gilgit-Baltistan and strategic support for the cause of Kashmir at large.[185]

This increasingly neo-colonial approach represents a clear departure from China's stated "non-interference" policy, demonstrating its clear intent to bolster its geopolitical power in Ladakh, to which both China and India share competing claims. This increased Chinese presence in and control over Gilgit-Baltistan, and Pakistan's acceptance—if not outright support—will likely result in heightened tensions between Pakistan and India.[186]

Pakistan's smaller provinces have suspected—and accused—the larger province of Punjab of intending to essentially appropriate the CPEC, and that, too, at their expense,[187] with the formers' political leadership questioning whether their provinces' historical neglect would be perpetuated under CPEC.[188] Sindh, Balochistan and KPK have justly demanded greater inclusion, transparency, and parity within the allocation of CPEC projects—and their associated benefits[189]—and it is essential to ensure that these provinces—and their peoples—are considered equal stakeholders and beneficiaries of the CPEC as a whole. Otherwise even progressive and beneficial steps towards economic development in these provinces may be politically spun as harmful and exploitative, potentially compromising the entire project, and—at the very least—reducing its narrative legitimacy.[190]Against this backdrop, Boni and Adeney have argued that there is a disconnect between the devolution ordained by the Eighteenth Amendment to Pakistan's Constitution, which decentralized institutions, and CPEC's centripetal nature,[191] establishing that the 'early harvest' CPEC projects planned for the initiative's initial phases demonstrate that most projects are being completed in Sindh and Punjab, with those in Balochistan and KP lagging behind.[192]

CPEC is a neoliberal initiative focused on attracting investments and profit maximization that mandates the creation and implementation of a supra-constitutional legal regime that only protects capital invested through the project.[193] This legal framework operates to undermine national and local labour and civil rights, fails to protect Pakistan's migrant labourers, and is displacing scores of local communities while misappropriating their ancestral lands.[194] CPEC's adverse impacts are disproportionality being borne by smaller ethnic communities, already politico-economically marginalized, and not in a realistic position to either inure themselves to the project's negative outcomes or to push back against it. This last point is particularly concerning because domestically, the Pakistani Army has taken complete ownership of protecting this project at all social and political costs and has hence displayed zero tolerance for any political discontentment that may stall the implementation of the CPEC.[195]

Following the passage of the Eighteenth Amendment to the Constitution of Pakistan (1973), all residual powers not explicitly enumerated in the Federal Legislative List of the Fourth Schedule—and thus falling within the exclusive purview of the federal government—have devolved to the respective provinces.[196] This was an attempt to appease the smaller provinces that felt that the dominant province of Punjab—and its Punjabi majority ethnic group—was abusing the pre-existing constitutional framework and its own inordinate influence over the federal government to its sole benefit.[197] These fears, however, have not been allayed and the smaller provinces continue to fear a complete appropriation of the CPEC project and its benefits by Punjab and the federal government, which remains controlled by the Punjabi elite.[198]

With regards to legal disputes arising under the CPEC, the courts of Pakistan have limited jurisdiction in allaying grievances raised by the smaller provinces. For instance, an Article 184 (2) challenge against the federal government by any province would be futile and lacking legal significance, as even a favourable judgment rendered in favour of a province will only be declaratory in nature.[199] It is also extremely unlikely that the apex court would accept jurisdiction under Article 184 (3) over the planning or implementation of the CPEC as no vested, individual (fundamental), right would have been directly infringed under the Constitution.[200] Even if the Court were to entertain such a case it would in all likelihood find the matter non-justiciable, either because of exclusions under the political question doctrine or because the CPEC links directly with foreign relations and treaties, matters over which the federal government retains exclusive authority. From a legal perspective therefore, it seems that the current ordering of the Constitution precludes all smaller provinces of Pakistan from successfully challenging—directly or indirectly—federal authority over the planning or implementation of the CPEC. It is also important to note here that with rising foreign lawsuits against Chinese companies, China has established a set of "Belt and Road" courts to settle disputes arising under the Belt and Road Initiative and which might be adopted as a mechanism to address disputes arising out of CPEC.[201]

CPEC has thus become a major obstacle to a harmonious operation of ethnic federalism in Pakistan; the existing constitutional framework essentially allows the populous province of Punjab to pass any federal legislation, or to veto any bill tabled by another province, on CPEC and over connected fiscal measures or policies due to its absolute majority in both houses of parliament. In a similar vein, the fact that the Senate has equal representation from all the provinces is inconsequential due to the constitutional exclusion of the Senate to exercise oversight and powers over matters pertaining to foreign relations and fiscal policy. In any case, because Punjab enjoys an absolute majority of votes in both houses, regardless of the political parties amongst which this majority is distributed, it will effectively perform the constitutional role otherwise envisioned for the Council of Common Interests (CCI)[202] and formulate the relevant policy or regulation, eroding the putative role of the CCI to resolve inter-provincial disputes.[203]

This alarming trajectory of Pakistani legal and political development demonstrates the facility with which neoliberal structures can consolidate power within the state and, in Pakistan's case, accentuates the involvement and control of the military over otherwise civilian affairs through the CPEC. Much like in China's case, this translates into the suppression of minority rights, local self-governance, and the socioeconomic disenfranchisement of groups outside of the domestic elites. Against this background, mega-projects aimed at exploiting the natural resources and strategic location of the provinces are a cause for further contention between the provinces and centre.[204] This contention also overshadows the CPEC and the Gwadar port development, the latter of which specifically highlights the international politics and security challenges associated with the CPEC. With increasing Chinese interest in Gwadar's development, Baloch nationalists have recently directed attacks at Chinese workers.[205] As Abdul Basit writes: "Sindhi and Baloch ethno separatist groups perceive China as a neocolonial power usurping their resources and partnering with their primary adversary, the Pakistani state, to worsen their already abysmal socioeconomic condition." This was clearly articulated in the Baloch Liberation Front's claiming responsibility for shooting at Chinese nationals in Karachi: "(i)n the garb of development projects, China is not only colluding with the Pakistani state in plundering the Baloch resources but assisting in the Baloch community's persecution as well."[206]

In addition to China's 'debt trap diplomacy,' discussed in reference to Northern Africa in the preceding section, it is also crucial to note how China has now become Pakistan's greatest creditor, giving it substantial influence over the country's economic policies.[207] This is particularly troubling given that it renders Pakistan increasingly vulnerable to further Chinese neoliberal exploitation. By employing a language of development, carrying with it the promise of economic growth and poverty alleviation, it is easy to disguise China's self-serving objectives as being for Pakistan's greater good; even more so if China's hegemonic extra-territorial neoliberal policies, such as promoting resource extraction for profit maximization, are particularly tailored to fulfil the demands of—and for the benefit of—Chinese elites back home. Most troubling is the fact that this is not Pakistan's first experience with such exploitation; over the course of the British colonial regime, an estimated forty-five trillion dollars' worth of value was expropriated by colonial authorities from South Asia for the benefit of British elites,[208] and China's neoliberal dispossession of present-day Pakistan's resources seems to eerily mimic the latter's colonial experiences. Similarly couched in benevolent, almost patronizing, terms, the British colonial regime's plundering of South Asia's wealth allowed it to leverage considerable resources in its empire-building efforts throughout the world, even drawing upon the Indian subcontinent's labour pool to facilitate the establishment and operation of colonies elsewhere, and to conscript the same to prosecute Britain's wars. Pakistan has already drawn painful lessons from its time as a British colony and needs to draw upon this historical experience to ensure its sovereignty is not similarly compromised in pursuit of the Chinese neoliberal agenda, and that it is able to benefit from the gains of Chinese investment equally and equitably in Pakistan—including the CPEC and its associated projects.

A major concern for Pakistan's public, economists, and analysts in general has been the near-complete lack of transparency in the conduct of CPEC negotiations, with crucial documents and agreements signed between Pakistan and China still being kept highly confidential years after they have been concluded, and the projects envisioned thereunder being brought online. Following the initiation of the CPEC and the signing of its related MOU's, China pledged to invest over sixty-two billion dollars into Pakistan,[209] yet there remains no real clarity or transparency regarding this proposed investment. In an effort to alleviate concerns regarding the project, the Long-Term Plan (LTP), a document detailing the mechanics of the project, was released in a far more abbreviated form in December 2017,[210] and while the document provides some a degree of insight indicating the focus of the project towards Pakistan's agricultural sector, infrastructure, and water resources, it fails to address pressing issues associated with the implementation of the project. In fact, as Akhtar notes,

> (w)hile the document makes boilerplate overtures to Pakistan's economic and social development, it can overall be read as a not very subtle assertion of China's regional interests—especially the drive to gain market access for Chinese firms and develop China's vast western interior via the transportation routes to be built under the CPEC plan.[211]

Rather than addressing these concerns, the document instead raises new ones relating to China's own geostrategic interests beyond Pakistan's borders, interests which may not necessarily align with Pakistan's.

Recognizing China's focused approach under CPEC, and its efforts at confronting the United States' hegemony and rebalancing geopolitics in the region, is critical for Pakistan. The CPEC has aggravated internal issues in Pakistan's already-weak federal and legal frameworks, and Pakistan's current secrecy on the minutiae of the Project's execution only serves to confound matters, and ward off constructive input and analysis from relevant quarters and key stakeholders, both domestic and international: at present it is next to impossible to determine with any degree of certainty just how (im)balanced the terms and conditions of the project arrangements are, and in case of a conflict between the parties, there is no effective system in place for dispute resolution—formal or otherwise. For a project that has, to date, involved Chinese investment more than sixty-five billion dollars, the second phase of which involves around twenty-seven projects in a broad array of sectors,[212] it is difficult to believe that no formal, institutional mechanisms for dispute resolution exist. Interestingly, however, this is exactly what Chinese foreign direct investment regimes promote: closed door, state-to-state interactions, with no systems in place for transparency, accountability, democratic feedback, or legal support.

Once the projects under CPEC were underway, various security concerns arose, both in Pakistan (against Chinese workers) and within China, prompting China to reconsider its policy towards the security situation in Pakistan and the region.[213] To make up for this loss in trust, Pakistan increased the militarization of project sites, a response which often did not sit well with the local populace, and which further weakened Pakistan's already damaged political federalism.

Nonetheless, the CPEC presents a valuable opportunity for Pakistan to progress, provided that the country's present political apparatus and its military are willing to do so. This assertion, however, comes with an essential caveat: the country must navigate a space to effectively articulate its own interests, without being pressured into rash decisions by an increasingly impatient and autocratic China. It must employ a more transparent policy when it comes to the particulars of agreements on CPEC projects, to attract cogent feedback on safeguarding its own interests in a manner more conducive to both its own geostrategic and socioeconomic realities, while ensuring that these projects do not become a Trojan horse for Chinese hegemonic aspirations.

CHINESE FOREIGN DIRECT INVESTMENTS AND THEIR IMPACT ON COMMUNAL DEMOCRATIC NORMS IN PAKISTAN

China's economic agendas in Pakistan—while ostensibly aimed at mutually benefiting the two countries—has certain negative impacts on Pakistan's complex sociopolitical and cultural landscape. China's developmental projects, largely relating to the CPEC, involve the displacement and land acquisition of the local communities that reside in the affected areas. This impacts these communities' historical and cultural associations with these lands and, to make matters worse, the compensations they receive in lieu of these sacrifices are barely calculated at market value. This not only exacerbates distributive injustice, but also negates multiculturalism by gradually eroding the historical and social ties these communities have with their local professions and their land.

A further compounding factor is that the implementation rights of these projects are often achieved through bribing relevant officials, which is problematic not only because the project is then implemented by the richest bidder instead of the most competent, but also because it severely compromises the rule of law and consequent accountability structures. The workings of SEZ's in Pakistan, for example, have shown how these spaces become fortresses of economic activity—with access to the Zone allowed only to specific actors that will benefit the project in specific ways—often to the blatant disadvantage of local labour and expertise. In addition to this, the 'state-within-a-state' that is created within the SEZ's allows China to conduct operations with near impunity: it autonomously negotiates procedures that are in its own interest, often overriding local priorities, and evading the protections accorded to them by local laws and municipal oversight. To further compound these disadvantages, the machinery and technological equipment imported from China to operate within these Zones often run exclusively in the Chinese language, thereby not only deepening the alienation locals feel towards such projects, but also predicating progress upon developing basic know-how in a foreign language, which takes a toll on the local community's right to its own language's development and expression. Thus, while the Zones are applauded for bringing economic prosperity to the region, local communities who have made space for such projects often find themselves at the periphery of the economic gains and are left without explanations for the assault on their collective values and community interests.

Particularly in Pakistan, we see that the military incorporated and the Punjabi elite, capture the lion's share of the economic gains accruing through CPEC—which additionally negatively impacts the social distribution of economic benefits to other provinces, and minority ethnicities. Essentially, the aims of China's interactions in Pakistan are so focused on economic growth, that those sections of the community that can subscribe to this agenda are included in economic gains, while those sections of the community—particularly minorities—who are not able to conform as closely to this economic hegemony are excluded from the wealth calculus.

It is with this context in mind, that we move on to prescriptions to help Pakistan carve out its unique economic space whilst simultaneously determining how best to proceed with the huge dividends promised by the CPEC.

PRESCRIPTIONS

The preceding section has sought to explore the CPEC and its potential adverse impacts on democratic values, communal and civil rights, and the environment, within the broader setting of political federalism in Pakistan. This section will now aim to propose targeted prescriptions aimed at tackling the inequalities manifesting under CPEC, and to avert their negative impacts on Pakistan's political federalism.

Firstly, the transfer and exchange of knowledge and technology is envisioned as an important component of the CPEC umbrella.[214] I have already identified the negative impact of neoliberal policies on Pakistan's educational system, where the state's abdication of its responsibility resulted in the education system's co-option by religious seminaries. To rectify its failures, and to wrest back control over large parts of the country's educational infrastructure, the federal government must support the provincial governments to supplement budgets for educational spending and encourage enrolment in conventional public schools. The federal and provincial governments must also work with the Higher Education Commissions to reserve quotas for students from Balochistan, the interior of Sindh, Southern Punjab, and Khyber-Pakhtunkhwa (particularly from the newly merged districts formerly part of the FATA) to receive education at Chinese universities through exchange programs. This education and vocational training would serve a dual purpose by providing a skilled labour force for implementing and leading projects under CPEC, while simultaneously effecting the transfer of necessary technical skills and expertise previously monopolized by the Chinese labour force employed on CPEC projects in Pakistan and creating a cosmopolitan 'class' of peoples familiar with Chinese culture and language, who would be able to leverage these skills in other similar projects.

Secondly, as discussed in preceding sections, keeping in view Pakistan's mounting circular debt, paired with high-interest Chinese loans, the secrecy in project contracts and "hidden Chinese loans" are a cause of concern that needs to be addressed.[215] It is imperative that the relevant institutional infrastructure be reformed to curb corruption and improve governance, transparency, and accountability. Tax reforms must be introduced to implement redistributive policies aimed at decreasing economic inequality and funding domestic public infrastructural and welfare works, that must also cover the projects falling under the CPEC, or those established within Special Economic Zones, which presently, enjoy a onetime exemption on custom duties and taxes on imports, as well as further exemptions from income tax on production for the first ten years of their operation.[216] These serve only to facilitate and enrich economic elites already engaged in, and benefiting from, the institution of such projects, and tax 'incentives' such as these further compound inequality, poverty, and discontent.[217]

Thirdly, the state must revisit its land acquisition policies, as ensuring local ownership—or retention and protection of ownership—of property will empower locals in a manner which would insulate them to a degree from the ill effects of Chinese investments and acquisitions in Pakistan. The first step in establishing SEZs is through the acquisition of land, largely using the state's coercive power of eminent domain. Even if the land has been acquired through more—relatively—equitable means, such as through a private deal, or a public-private partnership, clear policies are required that holistically cover the process to ensure an equitable outcome for the local communities affected by the procurement. The current Pakistani legal framework relating to eminent domain is archaic, dating back to the colonial period, and is easily abused—particularly considering mercurial and flexible descriptions of what constitutes a "public good." A truly libertarian execution of the laws of eminent domain would recognize the value of private ownership: "(p)roperty being an inviolable and sacred right, no one can be deprived of it unless the public necessity plainly demands it, and upon condition of a just and previous indemnity."[218] Instead, in Pakistan a more Hobbesian execution of the law is observed—beginning with a ruling oligarchy's determination of what constitutes a "public good," and ending at valuing the land at its basic market rate which fails to account for additional values associated with the land by its present owners, such as the community's means of livelihood being inextricably linked to the land, and generational sociocultural or religious associations and landmarks that the zone otherwise replaces.[219] The state must realize that the happiness and contentment of communities that are making sacrifices for projects under the CPEC is essential for the successes of the CPEC in Pakistan,[220] which should involve a critical review of the ways in which the powers of eminent domain are executed, and a robust revisiting of the kinds of compensations, relocation, and rehabilitation provided to indigenous communities. The Pakistani state's current strategies of responding to local dissent and alienation with heavier militarization and crackdowns needs to be fundamentally reversed,[221] with the state recognizing the community's ties to the land and seeking to adequately and equitably redress any forcible appropriation thereof. CPEC's Long Term Plan (2017–2030) was formulated without seeking sufficient input from local leaders, members of the business community, or members of the community affected by the CPEC,[222] even though the plan would invariably have an inordinate impact on these groups. It is imperative, thus, that the state revisit this attitude, and should constitute a regulatory body that ensures equitable land acquisition and compensation, factoring in elements such as loss of livelihood in addition to the bare market value of land, and providing sustainable resettlement programs that appropriately and effectively assimilate the affected into their new territories and communities —a process which should also include the provision of the means necessary to broaden or transition their skill sets and means of livelihoods. These actions will go a long way towards ensuring the collective rights of marginalized or weaker sections of society impacted by land acquisitions under CPEC and human displacement resulting therefore thereof.

In a similar vein, there is a dire need to revisit Pakistan's labour policy with respect to employment within CPEC projects. For instance, Egypt had a clear policy on foreign labour employment in the Chinese project undertaken in the Suez region: one Chinese work permit was allowed per nine Egyptians in employment.[223] Pakistan needs to follow suit with a clear and comprehensive labour policy, whose implementation should be ensured by the local governments or by duly appointed administrative committees. If China continues to prefer bringing its own labour to work in Pakistan on CPEC projects, and in the absence of a clear policy from Pakistan in this regard, most employment opportunities generated by the initiative will not benefit local communities as they ought to. As touched upon previously, reports from Kenya suggest the creation of Chinese enclaves—described as "a small kingdom in which Kenyan workers are being discriminated against"—where the bulk of lucrative employment opportunities remain consolidated in Chinese hands.[224] To forestall this eventuality, Pakistan needs to ensure that its own citizenry is adequately represented—and thus benefits from participation—in CPEC projects, not only to ensure gainful employment of its citizenry but also to facilitate the transfer of technical skills and knowledge from Chinese labourers to the domestic labour pool. Additionally, existing labour laws under the Industrial Relations Act, 2011 (IRA) need to be enforced, particularly those pertaining to protecting workers' union memberships, rights and working conditions, and safety measures.[225]

Further, it is imperative that the state develops a good governance strategy, followed by frequent onsite inspections, to ensure that the SEZ's are operating according to the comprehensive stipulated rules and regulations. Currently, the SEZ's in Pakistan are unable to realize their maximum productivity—or even demonstrate positive growth—due to poor regulation, political influence over key matters, and exploitative rent-seeking behaviour from industrialists.[226] Widespread corruption interferes with the productive workings of the SEZ's, and a lack of accountability within local governments and administrative authorities leads to the laws and regulations not being followed and implemented as they ought to. A key feature of a successful SEZ is decentralized decision-making and implementation, where the administrative committee—usually selected by the local government—monitors and oversees the management of the zone, including allocating land usage and economic and social development within. This committee must be appointed by merit, and not political leverage, and its decisions must truly be decentralized, in the interest of the zone and the people and investors constituting it. A sure way to attract investors is to assure them of transparent policies and their uniform application, secure financial regimes, and a conducive institutional environment. Incentives provided to industries have to be closely tied to sustainable, demonstrable, and efficient standards; the current circumstances are inexcusable, where subsidies are perpetuated out of sheer political pressure and leverage, and where corruption is so pervasive that it remains unclear who the true beneficiaries of the subsidies are.[227]

The government also must ensure the implementation of the Eighteenth Amendment in relation to governance issues which arise in the provinces by way of the imposition of neoliberal policies. At present, though the Eighteenth Amendment allows greater financial and legislative autonomy to the provinces, the CPEC is modelled along 'state-to-state' lines, thereby strengthening the role of the federal government *vis-a-vis* the project.[228] It is therefore necessary to accord the provinces greater involvement in CPEC projects to develop and sustain consensus on key project issues, and to prevent the negative impacts of such projects on an already-strained federal structure. The strengthening of federalism through a centripetal model will also mean reining in the power of the executive—and particularly the military—when it comes to development under CPEC; this necessarily also includes the CPEC Authority (now the secretariat), which was established through an ordinance (bypassing the National Assembly and the Senate), and which can otherwise seriously undercut the powers of the provinces in relation to CPEC-related matters.[229]

Additionally, Environmental Impact Assessments must be made mandatory and be made public for foreign developmental projects, and for energy projects, industrial zones, and infrastructure projects under CPEC. This transparency will allow for local communities to have some ownership and say—and an awareness of at the very least—in the implementation of these projects as key stakeholders, thereby realizing democratic norms through local self-governance mechanisms as envisioned under the Eighteenth Amendment. Further, while EIAs and resettlement policies feature in CPEC land use plans, these plans do not provide for nor substantively address climate change concerns, sustainable development, or other environmental safeguards. The Ministry for Climate Change and the Pakistan Environmental Protection Agency must be mandated to review and vet CPEC projects before they are initiated, assessing the broader environmental impact or potential degradation of water bodies around industrial zones. Additionally, as both the Pakistani and Chinese governments have expressed the will to shift to renewable energy resources, Pakistan must leverage this political will to transition to a low-carbon SEZ model and adopt green policy initiatives that include green financing and climate mitigation plans, as well as incentivizing and encouraging this shift.[230] These initiatives will help mitigate the negative ecological impacts of Chinese investments on the environment and climate, as expressed through the CPEC projects.

The Federal and Provincial governments must also collaborate, with the relevant federal ministries and provincial departments working together to devise a cohesive agricultural reform policy that stresses the use of green technology in future innovations and projects. With regards to CPEC projects, development frameworks should be revised and amended to include mandatory parallel reforestation in areas where the ecosystem is otherwise disturbed by new infrastructure networks. Reforestation will also serve to inure waterfront areas from flash floods, and, through water retention and carbon capture, help mitigate other climate-related emergencies such as water scarcity and gas emissions. In addition to importing the latest technological advances from China—and rather than having them largely be consolidated in the hands of imported Chinese labour—the government and other key stakeholders must also engage in and incentivize training local communities in techniques such as water conservation, crop rotation, and designating fenced land for grazing.[231] Furthermore, through applying scientific research conducted in China, the Pakistani government should develop and disseminate crop varieties that are high-yielding and use less water. Given that a nontrivial section of Pakistan's population is engaged in the agricultural sector, the livelihoods of the rural population working on agricultural lands must be safeguarded. To do so, it is imperative that they receive similar technical and vocational training. Pakistan can cooperate with China in this regard to integrate training and educational programs for the former's rural population to familiarize them in contemporary and efficient agricultural practices.

Further, Pakistan's civilian and military leadership must both involve all other key stakeholders—including regional actors—when formulating national foreign policy. As outlined above, Chinese expansionism through its financing structures, has a broader aim to effect Chinese hegemony in the region. With the United States' withdrawal from and return of the Taliban regime in Afghanistan, the security dynamics of the region are in a state of flux,[232] with China, Iran, and even Russia sharing a vested interest in seeing a stable Afghanistan.[233] Domestic and foreign stakeholders must therefore work together to prevent a Taliban-governed Afghanistan from turning into an ungoverned space, which would mean regional political instability, increased threats due to terrorism—particularly along the porous borders Pakistan and Iran share with Afghanistan, security threats (including to ongoing CPEC projects), and the increased likelihood of a new refugee influx from Afghanistan into its neighbouring countries.[234] Collaborative efforts should be directed to increasing regional trade, people-to-people exchanges, technology and expertise transfers, and devising partnerships and programs that can be used to direct humanitarian aid and resources towards the socio-economic uplift of Afghans and to mitigate the adverse effects of neoliberalism which could otherwise exacerbate deprivation and socioeconomic disparities which—in turn—contribute towards extremism and conflict.

CONCLUSION

This chapter traces the evolution of neoliberalism from a free-market model to one that has since been adapted to specific regions, and which has a direct nexus with domestic politics, geopolitics, and—more recently—a form of neo-colonialism. Neoliberalism's failures have prompted criticism from various leftist powers; however, these powers have failed to produce and implement viable alternatives to tackle the doctrine's adverse effects. The void left by this lack of a viable alternative to the doctrine has greatly impacted regions such as Africa, resulting in the impacted states struggling under billions of dollars in foreign debt, rampant corruption, successive military regimes, and a severe weakening of forms of distributive justice, the rule of law, and basic human rights. These distressed countries, often with extremely weak or non-existent democratic structures, are then left with no choice but to comply with foreign interventionist regimes.

Amidst the international turmoil left in the wake of neoliberalist policies, China has successfully remodelled its domestic policies, leading to significant growth in its economy, progress towards poverty alleviation, and development. The Chinese model was so successful that China is now able to invest both through its private and public sectors in foreign jurisdictions. As we've discussed at length in section 2, this ambitious goal is being achieved through the BRI, perceived as a golden opportunity for autocratic and semi-autocratic regimes, where the stringent conditions attached with Western funding and loans cannot otherwise be fulfilled. The already-compromised position of these countries, however, has resulted in severe harms effected on their local populations and fiscal systems, with similar effects manifesting in Pakistan as well under the rubric of the CPEC.

To ensure the successful—and equitable—implementation of the CPEC, and for Pakistan to reap the project's advertised financial and socioeconomic benefits, the federal government must find political solutions and arrangements to alleviate legitimate concerns held by minority groups in the country and to take their interests into account. Locally, government policy and funds allocation must be directed towards the social and economic uplift of vulnerable populations, with the goal being to effect poverty alleviation, economic growth, and welfare guarantees for the entire populace. Further, as outlined in the prescriptions section above, the government must work to counter the effects of CPEC on local communities, domestic labour laws, the environment, and the national and local economies. Furthermore, it must also work on devising a holistic foreign policy to prevent any spill-over effects due to the evolving geopolitics in the region. The state must generate viable solutions to minimize and address its increasing debts; prevent and discourage the flouting of domestic laws in the SEZs; develop and implement policies for the protection and uplift of the domestic labour force; ensure that displaced communities are socially and productively re-assimilated and relocated; and monitor and minimize the negative impacts of such mega-projects on the climate, working with local governments to develop and institute environmentally sustainable strategies for local, provincial, and national growth and productivity. Pakistan must put in constructive thought and action into deriving the maximum benefits accruable from the CPEC, in a manner that does not irreparably harm its geopolitical standing, nor compromise its sovereignty and its economy in the long-term by becoming a neo colonized state that is exploitable by foreign powers such as China to further their own economic and strategic interests.

NOTES

1. François Denord, "The Origins of Neoliberalism in France. Louis Rougier and the 1938 Walter Lippmann Conference." *Le Mouvement Social* 195.2 (2001): 9. *See also* Michael A. Peters, "The early origins of neoliberalism: Colloque Walter Lippman (1938) and the Mt Perelin Society (1947)." *Educational Philosophy and Theory* (2021): 1–8.
2. *Ibid.*
3. Gregory Albo, "Neoliberalism and the Discontented." *Socialist Register* 44 (2008), p. 356.
4. *Ibid.*
5. Noam Chomsky, *Profit over people: Neoliberalism and global order*. Seven Stories Press, 1998. *See supra* note 3 at 356. ("Neoliberal policies of wage compression, cuts in social programmes and export-led growth in liberalized markets were adopted in one country after another, whatever party was in power. Neoliberalism was no longer limited to a set of ideas promulgated by revanchist intellectuals or a political strategy of 'market populist' parties of the New Right.").
6. Stephen Metcalf, "Neoliberalism: the idea that swallowed the world," *The Guardian* (Aug 18, 2017), accessed on March 10, 2022, <https://www.theguardian.com/news/2017/aug/18/neoliberalism-the-idea-that-changed-the-world>. ("Hayek's was a total worldview: a way of structuring all reality on the model of economic competition. He begins by assuming that nearly all (if not all) human activity is a form of economic calculation, and so can be assimilated to the master concepts of wealth, value, exchange, cost—and especially price. Prices are a means of allocating scarce resources efficiently, according to need and utility, as governed by supply and demand. For the price system to function efficiently, markets must be free and competitive.").
7. *See generally* Friedrich August Hayek, *The constitution of liberty*. University of Chicago Press, 2011.

8. Susan George, “A short history of neoliberalism.” *Conference on Economic Sovereignty in a Globalising World*. Vol. 24. 1999.

9. David Harvey. “Neo-liberalism as creative destruction.” *Geografiska Annaler: Series B, Human Geography* 88.2 (2006): 145–58.

10. David Harvey, *A brief history of neoliberalism*. Oxford University Press, USA, 2007.

11. Thomas I. Palley, “From Keynesianism to neoliberalism: Shifting paradigms in economics.” *Neoliberalism: A critical reader* 268 (2005).

12. Ruth Cohen, *Alien Invasion: How the Harris Tories Mismanaged Ontario*. Insomniac Press, 2009, 189. (“The whole point of privatisation is neither economic efficiency nor improved services to the consumer but simply to transfer wealth from the public purse—which could redistribute it to even out social inequalities—to private hands. In Britain and elsewhere, most privatised company shares are now in the hands of financial institutions and very large investors.”).

13. *Ibid.* at 190. (“America is one of the most unequal societies on earth, but virtually all countries have seen inequalities increase over the past twenty years because of neo-liberal policies. UNCTAD published some damning evidence to this effect in its 1997 Trade and Development Report based on some 2600 separate studies of income inequalities, impoverishment, and the hollowing out of the middle classes.”).

14. Tugrul Keskin, “Book Review of a Brief History of Neoliberalism.” *Societies Without Borders* 4 (1) (2009): 94–95, 94.

15. *Ibid.* at 95. (“Harvey claims that neoliberalism entails creative destruction and has shaped the current division of labor, social relations, welfare provisions, technological mixes, and ways of life and thought. Neoliberalism has damaging social effects on society other than just economic ramifications. The meaning of concepts such as freedom, democracy, and human rights has also changed negatively.”).

16. Bjarke Skærlund Risager, “Neoliberalism is a political project: An interview with David Harvey.” *Jacobin* (Jul 23, 2016), accessed on March 10, 2022, <https: //www.jacobinmag.com/2016/07/david-harvey-neoliberalism-capitalism-labor-crisis -resistance/>.

17. *Ibid.*

18. *See supra* note 9 at 145.

19. *Ibid.*

20. Christopher Lydon, ‘Noam Chomsky: Neoliberalism Is Destroying Our Democracy,’ *Nation* (Jun 17, 2017) accesssed on March 3, 2022,>https://www.thenation.com/article/archive/noam-chomsky-neoliberalism-destroying-democracy/>.

21. *See supra* note 5.

22. *See supra* note 3 at 2.

23. *Ibid.* at 3. From here, Albo states that neoliberalism grew into a larger movement that was gradually becoming entrenched within state institutions and civil society: (“By the 1990s it became a far broader project of regulating social life through market imperatives and incorporated within it the Third Way strategies of ‘progressive competitiveness’ that accepted the parameters imposed by the current distribution of income and assets, and by world markets. Neoliberalism had become the political

form in which political and social relations are reproduced at the local as well as the national level of the state, and across the international state system.")

24. *Ibid.*

25. *Ibid.* at 2.

26. *Ibid.* at 2. ("The programme of neoliberalism may well be discredited and the numbers of discontented growing. But, as far as the balance of political power is concerned, this has not yet shifted in a way that allows anyone—least of all political militants—to speak honestly about a period 'after neoliberalism.'").

27. *Ibid.* at 6.

28. *Ibid.* at 6.

29. Wendy Brown, "Neo-liberalism and the end of liberal democracy." *Theory & event* 7.1 (2003).

30. Wendy Brown, *Undoing the Demos: Neoliberalism's Stealth Revolution*. MIT Press, 2015.

31. *Ibid.*

32. Siegfried O Wolf, *The China-Pakistan Economic Corridor of the Belt and Road Initiative*. Springer International Publishing, 2020. *See also* "China-Pakistan Economic Corridor: Opportunities and Risks." *International Crisis Group*, Report No 297. 29 Jun. 2018, accessed on March 10, 2022, <https://www.crisisgroup.org/asia/south-asia/pakistan/297-This china-pakistan-economic-corridor-opportunities-and-risks>.

33. Richard Sandbrook, *Reinventing the left in the global south: The politics of the possible*. Cambridge University Press, 2014, 3.

34. *Ibid.* at 2–3.

35. *Ibid.* at 7–8. He highlights that: ("Although I concentrate on progressive experiments at the national level, I do not ignore alternatives at the global and local levels. I emphasize the national arena because it remains the most inclusive level at which solidarity can most readily be mobilized behind a vision of equal freedom, solidarity, and democracy. Cosmopolitanism, the sense of obligation one feels for people beyond one's national borders, remains rudimentary. However, at the national level, the global neoliberal order constrains the Left by restricting the autonomy of national policy making and by locking in various neoliberal arrangements through multilateral and bilateral treaties and agreements. A realistic progressive national strategy must thus include (in addition to some protectionist measures) a complementary regional or global component—to change the global order or construct regional buffers and alliances. Also, many significant experiments in equitable cooperation have developed at the local level. Nevertheless, I suggest, few of these local experiments can survive without a sympathetic regional or national government.").

36. *See generally* Karl Polanyi, *The great transformation.* Vol. 2. Boston: Beacon Press, 1944.

37. Fred Block, "Polanyi's double movement and the reconstruction of critical theory." *Revue interventions économiques. Papers in political economy* 38 (2008).

38. *See supra* note 36.

39. *Ibid.*

40. *See supra* note 33 at 8. ("An inherent conflict at the heart of capitalism—a double movement—presents progressive forces with difficult choices. On the one

hand, a liberal 'movement,' inspired by the ideal of the productive and liberating self-regulating market, seeks to achieve this end by 'disembedding' the economy from restrictive social norms and regulations. Yet this movement is doomed to failure because the liberal project is 'utopian,' in the sense of impossible, owing to the devastation unleashed by any attempt to realize it. On the other hand, this social and environmental devastation inevitably arouses a disparate 'countermovement' of societal protection to mitigate the damage—by re-instituting institutional and normative checks on market forces or abolishing [some] markets altogether. But, Polanyi contends, the countermovement, in seeking to protect society by 're-embedding' economy in society, unavoidably interferes with the logic of the market system. By undermining the conditions for efficient, productive, and interconnected markets, the countermovement unintentionally instigates an economic crisis that, in countries with weak political institutions, leads to an associated political crisis. Whatever solution the Left chooses to deal with this dilemma stakes out a route strewn with deadly pitfalls.").

41. *Ibid.* at 27–28. Sandbrook uses the term *development paradigm* to describe how the leftist vision goes beyond the Post-Washington Consensus in responding to neoliberal capitalism.

42. *Ibid.* at 28.

43. *Ibid.* ("The paradigm, therefore, sets the agenda for decision makers; once dominant, it excludes policies that are inconsistent with its assumptions about the world. A development paradigm covers a broader range of policy instruments than other policy paradigms but serves the same purpose. The Left's development vision, I argue, is not only distinctive but plausibly addresses the challenges of the Global South today.").

44. *Ibid.* at 29. ("In the case of neoliberal doctrine, these failures include both lackluster economic performance in the 1980s and 1990s and major economic crises, especially the Great Recession of 2008–9. Exogenous events may also erode support, such as, in the case of neoliberalism, the rise of state-capitalist China, the association of neoliberalism with United States imperialism [especially in Latin America] and the allure of heterodox experiments [such as in Chávez's Venezuela or contemporary Uruguay].").

45. Will Kymlicka, "Community and multiculturalism." *A companion to contemporary political philosophy* (2017): 463–77.

46. *Ibid.*

47. *Ibid.*

48. *Ibid.* at 470. In this context, state action is simply the role it plays in ensuring sufficient options: ("The state thereby acts to ensure that there are sufficient options, but the evaluation of these options occurs outside the state, through the choices of private individuals.").

49. *Ibid.* at 470–71.

50. *Ibid.*

51. *Ibid. See also* Charles Taylor and Taylor Charles, *Philosophical papers: Volume 2, philosophy, and the human sciences*. Cambridge University Press, 1985, 225. Taylor suggests a return to the "politics of the common good," where the common ends

behind the politics of the common good must be accepted as legitimate to all members of the community, regardless of their social groupings.

52. *Ibid.*

53. *See supra* note 45 at 475.

Interestingly, critics of multiculturalism state that accommodation of diversity and embracing ethnic individuality will eventually lead to a dilution of solidarity and nationhood and erode the legitimacy that supports a democratic welfare state. Therefore, either way, it has been argued that hardlining state policies towards either end of the liberalism/multiculturalism spectrum leads to a loss of national solidarity and, consequently, a dilution of state legitimacy. This is what Kymlicka calls "the progressive's dilemma": "we need multiculturalism to make liberal nationalism legitimate, but multiculturalist reforms may weaken the bonds of nationhood and hence its ability to secure stability and solidarity." *See also* Brian Barry, *Culture, and equality: An egalitarian critique of multiculturalism*. Harvard University Press, 2002; Will Kymlicka, "Solidarity in diverse societies: Beyond neoliberal multiculturalism and welfare chauvinism." *Minorities and Populism—Critical Perspectives from South Asia and Europe*. Springer, Cham, 2020. 41–62.

54. Aihwa Ong, *Neoliberalism as exception*. Duke University Press, 2006, 5.

55. *Ibid.* Specifically ("Rather than taking neoliberalism to be a tidal wave of market driven phenomena that sweeps from dominant countries to smaller ones, we could more fruitfully break neoliberalism down into various technologies: the kind of political exceptions that deviate from the established norm.").

56. *Ibid.*

57. *Ibid.*

58. *Ibid.*

59. *Ibid.* at 7. ("For example, in southeast and east asia, zoning technologies have carved special spaces to achieve strategic goals in regulating groups in relation to market forces. The spatial concentration of strategic political, economic, and social conditions attract foreign investment, technology transfer and international expertise to zones of high growth; these are isolated 'ecosystems' or hyper growth zones. Special Economic Zones [SEZs] or Special Administrative Regions [SARs] carve out special spaces for labor markets, investment opportunities and administrative freedom, typified by special taxation and investment schemes, urban budgets, infrastructural development, and some degree of autonomous rule [or variegated or graduated sovereignty].").

60. *Ibid.* Ong mentions that these hubs can successfully circumvent state policies or market practices that can hinder or slow growth, especially ("escaping, for example, the restraints of socialism in China, or in other Southeast Asian contexts, the lethargic administrative systems, bureaucratic delays, and cultural or religious impediments.")

61. *Ibid.*

62. Sarah Joseph, "Neoliberal reforms and democracy in India." *Economic and Political Weekly* (2007): 3213–18.

63. *Ibid.*

64. *Ibid.*

65. *Ibid.*

66. *See supra* note 20.

67. *See* Chapter 2 (this volume).

68. *See supra* note 33. *See generally* Karl Polanyi, "The great transformation: The political and economic origins of our time" (1944).

69. *See supra* note 33 at 64.

70. *Ibid.* at 65. ("Since 1997, Latin America, East Asia, Russia, and Turkey have suffered devastating financial crises. Latin America recovered in the first half of the 1990s but then foundered. Argentina and Uruguay underwent a severe economic crisis in 2001. Growth continued to stagnate in sub-Saharan Africa, despite policy and institutional reforms and high levels of foreign aid since the early 1980s.").

71. *Ibid.* at 78.

72. *Ibid.* at 73.

73. *Ibid.* ("Perceived horizontal inequalities among ethnic, religious, racial, or regional groups, if unresolved, can lead to civil war or ethnic cleansing. Vertical inequalities, on the other hand, divide the population on a class or quasi-class basis, leading to populist outbursts [peasant wars, urban riots, millenarian movements, or tax revolts], or even revolutions.").

74. *Ibid.* at 81. ("Climate change is wreaking its most detrimental effects on the poor in the poorest countries of the Global South.. . . Flooding represents a major threat to the concentrated populations that reside in low-lying areas with marshy soil and poor water drainage, as for example in Bangladesh. The vast semi-arid areas of sub-Saharan Africa and the tropical region of Latin America are undergoing exceptionally high rates of warming and drying."). *See infra* note 174.

75. *See supra* note 33 at 95. ("The low-income countries are most vulnerable to political violence. . . their governments have limited institutional resources to counteract disorder through mounting safety nets, resolving conflicts and applying force; their economic and social infrastructure is limited and dilapidated; and they typically suffer from localized unrest or incipient armed conflicts. Neoliberal policies, when refracted through weak political institutions, foment serious challenges to governments.").

76. Geoff Brown, 'Pakistan: failing state or neoliberalism in crisis?' *International Socialism* (Apr 4, 2016), accessed on March 10, 2022, <isj.org.uk/pakistan-failing-state-or-neoliberalism-in-crisis/>.

77. 'Human Development Report 2020: Massive income inequality among rich and poor,' *News International* (Apr 7, 2021), accessed on March 10, 2022, <https://www.thenews.com.pk/print/816040-human-development-report-2020-massive-income-inequality-among-rich-and-poor#:~:text=The%20gap%20was%20larger%20during,economy%20witnessed%204%20percent%20growth>.

78. *Ibid.*

79. 'Neoliberalism and poverty,' *News International* (May 26, 2018), accessed on March 10, 2022, <https://www.thenews.com.pk/print/321437-neoliberalism-and-poverty> ("the rise of religious extremism in the era of economic growth during the dictatorial regime of Pervez Musharraf, despite all his secular overtures, hints at the failure of the neoliberal economic growth model in curbing excruciating disparities and relative poverty. When national governments adopt economic policies without a

consultative democratic process, they are doomed to fail in addressing the poverty and underdevelopment.").

80. 'Pakistan's Growing Problem with Its China Economic Corridor,' *United States Institute for Peace* (May 26, 2021) <https://www.usip.org/publications/2021/05/pakistans-growing-problem-its-china-economic-corridor>.

81. Isabella Weber, "Origins of China's contested relation with Neoliberalism: Economics, the World Bank, and Milton Friedman at the dawn of reform." Global perspectives 1.1 (2020).

82. *See* Anastas Vangeli, 'The Normative Foundations of the Belt and Road Initiative,' in Shan, Wenhua, Kimmo Nuotio, and Kangle Zhang, eds., *Normative Readings of the Belt and Road Initiative*. London: Springer International Publishing, 2018.

83. *See supra* note 10 at 122. For David Harvey, neoliberalism 'with Chinese Characteristic' avoided the 'shock therapy' approach to privatization promoted by the IMF and World Bank and therefore managed to avoid economic meltdowns associated with those programs. In fact, the state was able to consolidate power and control market policy by giving the population economic growth.

84. *See supra* note 81.

85. *Ibid.* ("China has not pursued the core policies of full-fledged price, trade, and financial liberalization and privatization.").

86. *See supra* note 10 at 120.

87. *See* Yasheng Huang, *Capitalism with Chinese characteristics: Entrepreneurship and the state*. Cambridge University Press, 2008, 8. ("One of the most important—if not the most important—hallmarks of a market economy are the role and magnitude of the private sector. However, as in so many other areas of the Chinese economy, there is no straightforward answer to this seemingly direct question about the size of the Chinese private sector. The reason is that the Chinese style of reforms has spawned many firms that have fundamentally confusing and often deliberately vague ownership structures. After sorting through some definitional complications, I show that the size of the Chinese private economy, especially its indigenous component, is quite small. Using fixed-asset investment as a measure of policy, I show that the policy treatment of the indigenous private sector deteriorated substantially in the 1990s as compared with the 1980s. This policy reversal is the most important reason why China's transition to capitalism remains incomplete 30 years after the reforms began.").

88. *See supra* note 10 at 120.

89. *See supra* note 87, preface. Ix–x. ("That corporate success in China requires a combination of Chinese management and foreign legal status is probably the cleanest illustration of the massive distortions in China's business environment—that this is a system that has imposed a straitjacket on the domestic private sector.").

90. *Ibid.* ("Capitalism with Chinese characteristics is a function of a political balance between two Chinas—the entrepreneurial, market-driven rural China vis-a-vis the state-led urban China. In the 1980s, rural China gained the upper hand, but, in the 1990s, urban China gained the upper hand. Although China made notable progress in the 1990s in terms of FDI liberalization and reforms of state-owned enterprises (SOEs), this book assigns greater weight to the rural developments in determining the

overall character and the pace of China's transition to capitalism. When and where rural China has the upper *hand,* Chinese capitalism is entrepreneurial, politically independent, and vibrantly competitive in its conduct and virtuous in its effects. When and where urban China has the upper hand, Chinese capitalism tends toward political dependency on the state and is corrupt.").

91. *Ibid.* at 6.

92. *See supra* note 10 at 121.

93. *See supra* note 87 at 6. ("To put it another way, China's success has less to do with creating efficient institutions and more to do with permitting access to efficient institutions outside of China. . . . China is unique in that some of its capable entrepreneurs have the option of accessing one of the most efficient financial markets and legal institutions in the world [Hong Kong]. But here is an important policy implication. It would be futile for other developing countries to emulate China's domestic financial and legal institutions and practices to achieve economic growth.").

94. *See supra* note 10 at 121.

95. *Ibid.* at 123.

96. *Ibid.*

97. *Ibid.* at 123–24.

98. *Ibid.* at 125.

99. *Ibid.* at 125.

100. *Ibid.* at 125.

101. *Ibid.*

102. *Ibid*. at 123. For example, the Tiananmen Square incident of 1989, where the state violently cracked down by massacring protesting students.

103. *Ibid.* at 126.

104. Joshua Cooper Ramo, *The Beijing consensus*. London: Foreign Policy Centre, 2004.

105. Since 1989, when economist John Williamson first conceived of the economic and policy recommendations known as the Washington Consensus, this Consensus became generally accepted as the most effective model by which developing nations could spur growth. Embracing ideals of free-market capitalism, which included open trade policies, privatization, and deregulation, the Washington Consensus provided a prescription for development in the Third World.

106. Wei Pan, *Western system versus Chinese system*. East Asian Institute, National University of Singapore, 2010.

107. He Li, "The Chinese model of development and its implications." *World Journal of Social Science Research* 2.2 (2015): 128.

108. Anja Manuel, "China is quietly reshaping the world," *Atlantic* (2017), accessed on March 10, 2022, <https://www.theatlantic.com/international/archive/2017/10/china-belt-and-road/542667/>; *See also* Axel Dreher et al., 'Aid, China, and Growth: Evidence from a New Global Development Finance Dataset,' *AIDDATA*, Working Paper 46 (October 2017), accessed on March 10, 2022, <docs.aiddata.org/ad4/pdfs/WPS46_Aid_China_and_Growth.pdf>. In comparison to the post–World War II Marshall fund (which is calculated at some eight hundred billion dollars in today's GDP values), the OBOR has already spent an estimated amount of

around three hundred billion dollars in its initial stages, whereas China has plans to spend over one trillion dollars over the next decade.

109. *Ibid.* 'China Is Quietly Reshaping the World'; *See also* 'How the Silk Road plans will be financed,' *Financial Times*, May 10, 2016, accessed on March 10, 2022, <https://www.ft.com/content/e83ced94-0bd8-11e6-9456-444ab5211a2f>.

110. *See generally* Howard W. French, *China's second continent: How a million migrants are building a new empire in Africa*. Vintage, 2014; François Lafargue, "China's presence in Africa," *China perspectives* 2005.61 (2005); 'China in Africa: What's the Real Story?'*Diplomat* (April 11, 2017), accessed on March 10, 2022, <https://thediplomat.com/2017/04/china-in-africa-whats-the-real-story/>.

111. 'China in Africa,' *Council for Foreign Relations* (Jul 12, 2017), accessed on March 10, 2022, <https://www.cfr.org/backgrounder/china-africa>. This interest in Africa came with the rapid growth in China's middle class and the need for China to secure resources and energy supplies to support its rapid industrialization process. China continues to rely on Africa for its oil and gas needs; it has also expanded into the mining industry, and the manufacturing, agriculture, and telecommunications sectors. Alongside boosting trade, China has provided loans through various channels; however, these activities have been criticized widely by civil rights organizations and the Western media because of an apparent disregard for human rights violations in Africa.

112. *Ibid.* 'China in Africa.' As Eleanor Albert notes: ("Chinese financing comes often in the form of loans and credits provided by the People's Bank of China, the China Development Bank, the Export-Import Bank of China, and the China-Africa Development Fund. Between 2000 and 2014, Chinese banks, contractors, and the government loaned more than $86 billion to Africa, according to SAIS-CARI. Angola, the Democratic Republic of Congo [DRC], Ethiopia, Kenya, and Sudan were the top recipients. However, these large loans are beginning to raise questions about debt loads in African countries, showing indications of a potential debt crisis.").

113. "China signs 99 year lease on Sri Lanka's Hambantota port," *Financial Times*(Dec 11, 2017), accessed on March 10, 2022, <https://www.ft.com/content/e150ef0c-de37-11e7-a8a4-0a1e63a52f9c>. *See also* Abhishek Mishra. "A Chinese-built port in the Indian Ocean: The story of Kenya's Lamu port," *Observer Research Foundation* (Jun 1, 2021), accessed on March 10, 2022, <https://www.orfonline.org/expert-speak/a-chinese-built-port-in-the-indian-ocean-the-story-of-kenyas-lamu-port/>;'China's Port Expansion in Africa,' *Council on Foreign Relations* (Jul 29, 2021), accessed on March 10, 2022, <https://www.cfr.org/blog/chinas-port-expansion-africa>.

114. 'Kenya: China Cannot Seize Port of Mombasa if Debt Default Occurs,' *Maritime Executive* (Mar 16, 2021), accessed on March 10, 2022, <https://www.maritime-executive.com/article/kenya-china-cannot-seize-port-of-mombasa-if-debt-default-occurs>.

115. 'Kenya is refusing to release the loan contracts for its Chinese-built railway,' *Quartz Africa* (Jan 20, 2022), accessed on March 10, 2022, <https://qz.com/africa/2115070/kenya-refuses-to-release-contracts-for-china-debt/>. ("Built at a cost of more than $4.7 billion, the standard-gauge railway [SGR] is Kenya's most expensive

infrastructure project. Since its inception, the project has been marred by accusations of being overpriced and damaging to the environment. It's also been criticized for being highly unprofitable.").

116. *See supra* note 111. ("African workers have also begun to fault Chinese companies for unfair labor practices, including disputes over wages and working conditions. Beijing has 'less and less' ability to control these companies, says Ian Taylor, a professor at Scotland's University of St. Andrews, thus undermining China's official stance promoting Chinese investment in Africa as 'win-win.' Zambiahas experienced civil strife in response to an influx of Chinese companies; in 2012, the country witnessed protests and even deaths of Chinese mine managers.").

117. Yun Sun, "China's aid to Africa: monster or messiah." *Brookings East Asia Commentary* 75 (2014). ("In exchange for most Chinese financial aid to Africa, Beijing requires that infrastructure construction and other contracts favour Chinese service providers: 70 percent of them go to 'approved,' mostly state-owned, Chinese companies, and the rest are open to local firms, many of which are also joint ventures with Chinese groups. In this sense, China's financing to Africa, including aid, creates business for Chinese companies and employment opportunities for Chinese laborers, a critical goal of Beijing's Going Out strategy.").

118. 'Chinese return from Africa as migrant population peaks,' *Financial Times* (Aug 28, 2017), accessed on March 10, 2022, <https://www.ft.com/content/7106ab42-80d1-11e7-a4ce-15b2513cb3ff. An estimated one million migrants of Chinese origin resided across Africa by 2013.

119. 'How Will the Belt and Road Initiative Advance China's Interests?' *China Power* (May 8, 2017), accessed on March 10, 2022, <https://chinapower.csis.org/china-belt-and-road-initiative/>.

120. *Ibid.* ("To support the BRI, Beijing has injected massive amounts of capital into Chinese public financial institutions, such as the Chinese Development Bank [CDB] and the Export-Import Bank of China [EXIM]. These banks enjoy low borrowing costs, as their bonds are treated like Chinese government debt with very low interest rates and they have access to lending from the People's Bank of China, allowing them to lend cheaply to Chinese companies working on BRI projects."). *See also supra* note 107.

121. *Ibid.* ("In a move that clearly demonstrated these objectives, construction of China's first ever overseas military base officially began on the African continent in April of 2016. Located on the coast of Djibouti, the naval base is located less than ten miles away from US AFRICOM, the United States' largest African military base, and it offers China strategic access to the Red Sea and Indian Ocean.") *See also* "'Significant' consequences if China takes key port in Djibouti: U.S. general," REUTERS (Mar 7, 2018), accessed on March 10, 2022, <https://www.reuters.com/article/us-usa-china-djibouti/significant-consequences-if-china-takes-key-port-in-djibouti-u-s-general-idUSKCN1GI2V0>. ("In a letter to U.S. Defense Secretary Jim Mattis, Byrne said he was concerned about China's influence in Djibouti and the impact it would have on U.S. military and intelligence assets. Djibouti is strategically located at the southern entrance to the Red Sea on the route to the Suez Canal. Marine General Thomas Waldhauser, the top U.S. military commander overseeing troops in Africa,

said that if China placed restrictions on the port's use, it could affect resupplying the U.S. base in Djibouti and the ability of Navy ships to refuel there.").

122. 'One Belt, One Road, One Happy Chinese Navy,' *Foreign Policy* (Apr 17, 2018), accessed on March 10, 2022, <foreignpolicy.com/2018/04/17/one-belt-one-road-one-happy-chinese-navy/>. ("Chinese ports at the top of the Bay of Bengal, in Sri Lanka, and in Pakistan essentially fence in India, its traditional rival. If sporadic Chinese port calls by destroyers and submarines in recent years were enough to make Indian naval planners look east, the prospect that China's Silk Road business deals could give the Chinese navy greater staying power in the neighbourhood is ringing more alarm bells.").

123. Alyaa Wagdy el-Shafei and Mohamed Metawe, "China drive toward Africa between arguments of neo-colonialism and mutual-beneficial relationship: Egypt as a case study." *Review of Economics and Political Science* (2021).

124. M. Chan and Mary Madeleine Edel, "China in Africa: A Form of Neo-Colonialism?" *Yerepouni News* (2018).

125. *Ibid.* ("Zambia under the presidency of Michael Sata represents a compelling case in point which illustrates the dangers of economic dependency for state sovereignty as decried by Nkrumah. After winning the 2011 presidential elections upon the labelling of Chinese businesses as neo-colonialists and the promise of stricter regulations of trade practices, Michael Sata has been left powerless in face of increasing Chinese firms lobbying and threat of closing crucial economic operations. This effectively resulted in the Sata government backing down on major tax reforms.").

126. Adel Abdel Ghafar and Anna Jacobs, *Beijing Calling: Assessing China's Growing Footprint in North Africa*. Brookings Doha Center, 2019. ("China engages in two main types of 'partnership diplomacy' in the MENA region: strategic partnerships [SPs] and comprehensive strategic partnerships [CSPs].").

127. *Ibid.*

128. *Ibid.* ("While China's growing commercial presence in North Africa has seen many successes, it also has problematic aspects. Notable among these is the exploitation of cheap Chinese labor to build Chinese-funded construction projects. Chinese projects have been criticized over 'questionable labor practices,' and questions have been raised as to how much these construction projects actually support local labor markets or promote shared economic prosperity.").

129. *Ibid.* ("In Ecuador, for example, the case of the $19 billion Coca Codo Sinclair dam, financed by China, has become a national scandal. The dam faced structural and operational issues before it even opened, environmental impact studies were woefully inadequate, and top Ecuadorian officials who signed the deal have been imprisoned on bribery charges.").

130. *Ibid.* ("The two major North African military powerhouses—Egypt and Algeria—are among the top buyers of Chinese weapons. According to CSIS's China Power project, 'Northern African countries are the primary destination of Chinese weapons [in Africa], constituting 42 percent of Chinese exports to the continent.'").

131. *Ibid.* (These concerns stem from the precedent set by BRI projects in South Asia, such as the Hambantota port in Sri Lanka, where Sri Lankan officials claimed

that the Chinese insisted on an intelligence-gathering component that would monitor all traffic through the port.)

132. Venkateswaran Lokanathan, "China's Belt and Road Initiative: Implications in Africa." *Observer Research Foundation Brief* 395 (2020).

133. *Ibid.*

134. *Ibid.* ("The public debt in Sub-Saharan Africa has risen from 34 percent in 2013 to 53 percent in 2017. China owns 72 percent of Kenya's external debt, which stands at US$50 billion. Over the next three years, Kenya is expected to pay US$60 billion to the China Exim Bank alone. . . . China claims to have adopted a pragmatic approach—what it calls a 'win-win cooperation' model, in its economic investments abroad. However, in most cases, particularly in Africa, it appears to be benefiting more from its investments compared to the host countries. While most of the projects that China is pursuing in Africa under the BRI do help create infrastructure, industry, and connectivity across the continent, they are immensely beneficial for Chinese companies in utilising its overcapacity and bringing labour and materials into Africa. The skilled labour in industrial projects is mostly from China, with a few African locals taking up low-end employment.").

135. Marantidou, V., and B. Glosserman, "China's double standard? Fighting corruption at home, turning a blind eye abroad." PacNet No. 13, *Pacific Forum.* Center for Strategic and International Studies (CSIS). 2015.

136. *Ibid.* ("China's foreign assistance funds [excluding government-sponsored investments] during the period 2010–2012 reached $14.41 billion with 51.8 percent pouring into Africa. Top recipients of Chinese aid in Africa have been Angola, the Democratic Republic of Congo, and Ethiopia, countries plagued by corruption, weak governance structures, and instability.").

137. *See infra* note 141.

138. *Ibid. See also* Alexander Demissie, Moritz Weigel and Tang Xiaoyang, "China's Belt and Road Initiative & Its Implications for Africa," *Worldwide Fund Kenya*, December 2016.

139. *Ibid.*

140. Anthony Kleven, "Belt and Road: colonialism with Chinese characteristics," *Interpreter, Lowy Institute* (May 6, 2019); Agatha Kratz, Allen Feng, and Logan Wright, "New Data on the 'Debt Trap' Question," *Rodium Group* (Apr 29, 2019); Bill Ide, Joyce Huang, "Caution, Cancellations, Protests as Concerns Grow on China's Belt and Road," *Voice of America* (Oct 15, 2018).

141. *See supra* note 132. ("In Tanzania, over 2,000 people were forced to relocate, leading to protests that resulted in the suspension of the Bagamoyo Port and an attached industrial zone by the Tanzanian government in July 2016. In Madagascar, local protests began in October 2016 after their land was affected, and the demolition of a church and a school was proposed to accommodate mining activities by a Chinese enterprise Jiuxing Mines. Currently, local fishermen are protesting China's US$2.7 billion investment in the country's blue economy. In Kenya, local protests erupted in fall 2016 in the area around Voi, over a 6-km elevated section of the planned Mombasa–Nairobi Standard Gauge Railway Line that was supposed to cross Nairobi national park; consequently, the Kenyan government paused its construction.

A coal power plant in Lamu Island announced in 2015, to be financed with a US$ 900 million loan from Industrial and Commercial Bank of China has been halted, despite vocal support from the Kenyan government, due to local protests over environmental and economic viability concerns. An investigation by *The Standard*, one of Kenya's largest news organisations, has concluded that Chinese nationals have created a small kingdom in which Kenyan workers are being discriminated against.").

142. Khanindra Ch. Das, "The making of one belt, one road and dilemmas in South Asia." *China Report* 53.2 (2017): 125–42.

143. *See supra* notes 57–59.

144. Maham Hameed, "The politics of the China—Pakistan economic corridor." *Palgrave Communications* 4.1 (2018): 1–10.

145. Hussain H Zaidi, 'Neoliberal economics: the challenge within,' *News International* (Jul 21, 2018), accessed on March 10, 2022, <https://www.thenews.com.pk/print/344278-neoliberal-economics-the-challenge-within>. ("An Extended Fund Facility arrangement with the International Monetary Fund [IMF], which committed the government to pursuing the star neoliberal policies of deregulation, trade liberalisation, and cutting back on fiscal deficit. The Zia regime, understandably, also upended the flagship nationalisation policy of Z A Bhutto. The sixth five-year programme, which was introduced in 1983, for the first time described export-led growth as a principal policy objective. It was also during the Zia era that a managed floating exchange rate system was put in place. Thus, the stage was set for Pakistan to fully embrace neoliberal economics.").

146. *Ibid.*

147. Hassan N. Gardezi and Soofia Mumtaz, "Globalisation and Pakistan's dilemma of development [with comments]." *Pakistan Development Review* (2004): 423–40.

148. *Ibid.* at 3–4. ("Economic growth as measured by the rate of increase in Gross National Product [GNP] was accelerated from an average of 3.1% in 1950s to 6.8% in 1960s, reaching a record high of 10% over the year 1969–70.5.").

149. Dr Aamer Taj, Dr Muhammad Nouman, and Dr Saleem Gul, "The dynamics of international political economy relationships and its influence on the process of democratisation, institution building and national governance structure in Pakistan." *South Asian Studies* 30.1 (2020).

150. Tariq Thachil, "Neoliberalism's two faces in Asia: Globalization, educational policies, and religious schooling in India, Pakistan, and Malaysia." *Comparative Politics* 41.4 (2009): 473–94. In particular, the democratic government of Pakistan Political Party (PPP) slashed educational spending to expand their patronage channels and the Sharif government followed suit since elite supporters of Pakistan Muslim League-N had no interest in improving the educational sector.

151. Zia Ur Rehman, "Pakistani madrassas: an indispensable institution, a worry for the state," *TRT World* (May 20, 2019), accessed on March 10, 2022, <https://www.trtworld.com/magazine/pakistani-madrassas-an-indispensable-institution-a-worry-for-the-state-26787>.

152. *Ibid.* ("The Pakistani government, mainly under pressure from the international community, has continuously been making efforts to regulate madrassas—some

of them are accused of promoting radical ideologies and having links with terrorist networks—and bring them under the government's control.").

153. Syed Fazl-E-Haider, "Pakistan's extremist dilemma," *Lowy Institute* (Apr 26, 2021), accessed on March 10, 2022, <https://www.lowyinstitute.org/the-interpreter/pakistan-s-extremist-dilemma>. As Syed Fazl-e-Haider notes: ("This is not a first-time incident—Pakistan's governments in the past have been coerced by Islamists, but what is different this time is the government's mishandling of the TLP protest and miscalculation of its popular support across the country for the sensitive issue it raised. . . . While the political and security scenario across the region appears to be in a state of flux with the future of Afghanistan in question, the rise of TLP is a particularly local phenomenon. And how the government chooses to proceed now will have lasting implications.").

154. Mark Green, 'China's Debt Diplomacy,' *Foreign Policy* (25 Apr 2019), accessed on March 10, 2022, <https://foreignpolicy.com/2019/04/25/chinas-debt-diplomacy/>. According to a study by the International Monetary Fund (IMF), ("from 2013 to 2016, China's contribution to the public debt of heavily indebted poor countries nearly doubled from 6.2 percent to 11.6 percent.").

155. 'How China Got Sri Lanka to Cough Up a Port,' *New York Times* (25 Jun 2018), accessed on February 23, 2022, <https://www.nytimes.com/2018/06/25/world/asia/china-sri-lanka-port.html>.

156. 'Over 60% workers paid below minimum wage,'*Express Tribune* (Apr 4, 2021), accessed on March 10, 2022, <https://tribune.com.pk/story/2293067/over-60-workers-paid-below-minimum-wage>.

157. Abrahim Shah, 'Cost of Neoliberalism,' *DAWN* (Jul 30, 2021), accessed on March 10, 2022, <https://www.dawn.com/news/1637735/cost-of-neoliberalism>.

158. Huma Yusuf, 'The Other Threat to Pakistan,' *New York Times* (Apr 2, 2014), accessed on March 10, 2022, <https://www.nytimes.com/2014/04/03/opinion/the-other-threat-to-pakistan.html>. ("Pakistan's elites, political, bureaucratic, and military have long hailed from Punjab and shaped the country's policies to the province's advantage.... Also, the government and the military have long allotted prime agricultural land and urban real estate in other parts of Pakistan to Punjabi officers and senior bureaucrats. Punjab itself is not a monolith. Some of the province's southern districts are among the country's poorest, and their inhabitants have grudges of their own against Lahore-based politicians. . . . These resentments animate the politics of Pakistan's other provinces and threaten national unity. A separatist movement in Baluchistan taps grievances against Punjabis it says are exploiting Baluch gas and mineral resources to spur industrial growth in Punjab. It also rejects efforts by the predominantly Punjabi military to suppress Baluch nationalists. Killings of Punjabi 'settlers'— often schoolteachers and civil servants—by Baluch separatists are a brutal expression of this.").

159. *See supra* note 67.

160. *See generally* Veena Kukreja, "Ethnic Diversity, Political Aspirations and State Response: A Case Study of Pakistan." *Indian Journal of Public Administration* 66.1 (2020): 28–42.

161. Sadia Ashraf and Aisha Shahzad, "Federalism and provincial autonomy in Pakistan: A case of Balochistan." *Pakistan Social Sciences Review* 4.3 (2020): 25–35. ("It is producing 17% of Pakistan's total gas but consuming only two percent of it and the rest of the gas is provided to other provinces. They are receiving not more than 24% of the due royalties for supplying gas. Baloch people also express strong resentment on federal government projects like Gwadar port, CPEC and Saindak copper projects. They claim to receive only two percent out of 48% shares.").

162. 'Pakistan: The Worsening Conflict in Balochistan,' *Crisis Group*, Report 119/ Asia (14 Sept 2006), accessed on March 10, 2022, <https://www.crisisgroup.org/asia/south-asia/pakistan/pakistan-worsening-conflict-balochistan>.

163. 'Balochistan: The State versus the Nation,' *Carnegie Endowment for International Peace* (Apr 11, 2013), accessed on March 10, 2022, <https://carnegieendowment.org/2013/04/11/balochistan-state-versus-nation-pub-51488>.

164. 'Balochistan to sign economic zone deal with China: Official,' *Express Tribune* (11 November 2015), accessed on March 10, 2022, <http://tribune.com.pk/story/989188/balochistan-to-sign-economic-zone-deal-with-china-official/)>.

165. The Special Economic Zones Act, 2012. *See also* The Special Economic Zones (Amendment) Act 2016.

166. Special Economic Zones Rules, 2013.

167. Land Acquisition Act (1 of 1894) art. 10 (4): Each SEZ Authority may acquire land in its respective Province in accordance with the Land Acquisition Act, 1894 (I of 1894).

168. 'What Pakistan's Relationship With China Tells Us About The Belt And Road Initiative' (June 8, 2021), accessed on March 10, 2022, <https://gandhara.rferl.org/a/pakistan-china-belt-and-road-initiative/31296850.html>.

169. International Crisis Group. *China-Pakistan Economic Corridor: Opportunities and Risks*. International Crisis Group, 2018, accessed on March 10, 2022, <https://www.crisisgroup.org/asia/south-asia/pakistan/297-china-pakistan-economic-corridor-opportunities-and-risks>.

170. Ishrat Hussain, 'CPEC & Pakistani Economy: An Appraisal,' *Centre of Excellence China Pakistan Economic Corridor*, accessed on March 10, 2022, <cpec.gov.pk/brain/public/uploads/documents/CPEC-and-Pakistani-Economy_An-Appraisal.pdf>.

171. Global Climate Risk Index 2021, OCHA, accessed on March 10, 2022, <https://reliefweb.int/report/world/global-climate-risk-index-2021>.

172. 'Pakistan 5th most vulnerable country to climate change, reveals German watch report,' *DAWN* (Jan 16, 2020), accessed on March 10, 2022, <https://www.dawn.com/news/1520402>.

173. Ahmad Rafay Alam, 'Why don't CPEC projects factor in the climate crisis?' *China Dialogue* (Jan 3, 2020), accessed on March 10, 2022, <https://chinadialogue.net/en/business/11750-why-don-t-cpec-projects-factor-in-the-climate-crisis/>.

174. Kouser Shahzad and Abdul Subhan, "Uncovering Pakistan's environmental risks and remedies under the China-Pakistan economic corridor." *Environmental Science and Pollution Research* 27.5 (2020): 4661–63, 4661. *See also* 'CPEC—challenges and solutions,' *Express Tribune* (Apr 18, 2018), accessed on March 10, 2022,

<https://tribune.com.pk/story/1688108/6-cpec-challenges-solutions>. ("Currently, about 2,000 trucks running on both sides emit 793.2 tons in and a total of 5,826.2 tons of CO2 from cargo vehicles per day. In future 9,508.8 tons of CO2 will be emitted per day in G-B territory and a total of 69,914.4 tons of CO2 will be emitted into the atmosphere along the entire route in a single day.").

175. *Ibid.*

176. 'Agriculture is backbone of economy: PM,' *Nation* (Jan 25, 2021), accessed on March 10, 2022, <https://nation.com.pk/25-Jan-2021/agriculture-is-backbone-of-economy-pm>.

177. Ammar Junaid Asghar et al., "The Critical Junction between CPEC, Agriculture and Climate Change." *Centre for Chinese Legal Studies LUMS*, accessed on March 10, 2022, <https://ccls.lums.edu.pk/sites/default/files/user376/the_critical_junction_between_cpec_agriculture_and_climate_change.pdf>.

178. 'Rs83bn projects identified to modernise agriculture sector under CPEC,' *Daily Times* (May 19, 2021), accessed on March 10, 2022, <https://dailytimes.com.pk/758032/rs83bn-projects-identified-to-modernize-agriculture-sector-under-cpec/>.

179. *Ibid.* ("The seven projects to be executed by PARC included promotion of cherry cultivation on commercial Scale in Gilgit-Baltistan for taping the export potential to China, adding that this project would be completed within five years with an estimated cost of Rs, 1,200 million, he added.")

180. Aasim Sajjad Akhtar, 'The China-Pakistan Economic Corridor: Beyond The Rule of Capitalism,' *Monthly Review* (2008), <https://monthlyreview.org/2018/06/01/the-china-pakistan-economic-corridor/>.

181. 'Unmasking the China-Pakistan Economic Corridor,' *GRAIN* (May 12, 2021), accessed on March 10, 2022, <https://grain.org/en/article/6669-unmasking-the-china-pakistan-economic-corridor>. *See also* Roots for Equity and Pakistan Kissan Mazdoor Tehreek (PKMT), 'Peshawar Northern Bypass, pushing farmers to further destitution,' *PAN AP* (2020), accessed on March 10, 2022, <https://files.panap.net/resources/No-Land-No-Life-Land-Conflicts-and-Struggles-in-Asia.pdf>;Mariyam Suleman,'How CPEC Left Behind the People of Gwadar,' *Diplomat* (Jun 2020), accessed on March 10, 2022, <https://thediplomat.com/2020/06/how-cpec-left-behind-the-people-of-gwadar/>; Ghulam Nabi et al., "China–Pakistan Economic Corridor (CPEC): an alarming threat to the biodiversity of Northern Pakistan." *Biodiversity and Conservation* 26.12 (2017): 3003–04.

182. For example, the Global Methane Pledge, initiated by the United States and the EU, to which Pakistan became signatory in October 2021. Sana Jamal, 'Pakistan Joins Global Pledge to Cut Methane Emissions,' *Gulf News* (Oct 11, 2021), accessed on March 10, 2022, <https://gulfnews.com/world/asia/pakistan/pakistan-joins-global-pledge-to-cut-methane-emissions-1.82880575>.

183. *Ibid.* ("Pakistan is now among the 24 new signatories to join the pledge, led by the US and EU, to slash planet-warming methane emissions by 30 per cent by the end of the decade. World leaders are galvanizing rapid climate action ahead of the COP26 climate conference in Glasgow later this month. . . . Detailing the sources of methane emissions, the PM's aide said that the countries represent a range of different methane emissions profiles, and in Pakistan, the agriculture sector is considered as a

major source that emits a significant quantity of the highly climate-potent odourless gas.").

184. Hamna Tariq, 'Gilgit-Baltistan: China's Golden Opportunity,' *Stimson* (Oct 8, 2020), accessed on March 10, 2022, <https://www.stimson.org/2020/gilgit-baltistan-chinas-golden-opportunity/>.

185. *Ibid.*

186. *Ibid.* ("However, China and Pakistan's capacity to project collective power through Gilgit-Baltistan could complicate the current stand-off as India will now need to consider a territorial dispute on two fronts—Ladakh and Gilgit—which might weaken India's morale to respond on either front. Also, it could be that Pakistan is attempting to grant Beijing greater access to the region, as Gilgit and Ladakh are only separated by the Siachen Glacier. Stationing forces in Gilgit-Baltistan, which is not an uncommon practice historically, could widen China's vantage point. China's presence in a territory with provincial status may receive less scrutiny, thus China could station troops in the region in the event of a border standoff with India. Furthermore, even if China does not use the region as a military base, provincial status could cement China's stronghold in the region with the expedition of CPEC projects previously halted because of Gilgit-Baltistan's disputed status.")

187. 'Khattak threatens "extreme step" over CPEC project,' *DAWN* (Jan 1, 2016), accessed on March 10, 2022, <http://www.dawn.com/news/1230034>.The former chief minister of Khyber Pakhtunkhwa (KP) Pervez Khattak reproached both the federal and the Punjab governments in claiming that the western route of the CPEC, which traverses KP, has been restricted only to roads whereas all the major development projects associated with the CPEC dealing with investment and energy—fibre optic links, railway tracks, gas and oil pipelines, etc.—are being planned by the federal government on the eastern route, which primarily will pass through Punjab.

188. Filippo Boni and Katharine Adeney, "The Impact of the China-Pakistan Economic Corridor on Pakistan's Federal System: The Politics of the CPEC." *Asian Survey* 60.3 (2020): 441–65, 441.

189. *Ibid.* In January 2016, Pervez Khattak, KP's chief minister, asked that CPEC's route be discussed in parliament and the Council of Common Interests (CCI), stating that ("his province had not been awarded a single penny [from the CPEC] ...and that he had now lost trust in the federal government.")

190. *Ibid.* at 449. Energy projects in Balochistan under CPEC, according to Michael Kugelman could ("pour more fuel on the fire as it undertakes large-scale infrastructure development and natural resource extraction, thereby playing right into the hardened historical narratives of Baluch [Baloch] insurgents.").

191. *Ibid.* at 441.

192. *Ibid.* at 443.

193. 'China sidelines Pakistan govt, manipulates law to acquire control over democratic, economic system,' *ANI News* (Aug 3, 2020), accessed on March 10, 2022, <https://www.aninews.in/news/world/asia/china-sidelines-pakistan-govt-manipulates-law-to-acquire-control-over-democratic-economic-system-report20200803094424/>.

194. 'Over 2,500 families displaced to make way for economic corridor,' *Express Tribune* (Jan 3, 2017), accessed March 10, 2022, <https://tribune.com.pk/story/1283421/2500-families-displaced-make-way-economic-corridor/>.

195. Srijan Shukla, 'Under pressure from China, Pakistan Army has taken institutional control over CPEC,' *Print* (Dec 17, 2019), accessed on March 10, 2022, <https://theprint.in/world/under-pressure-from-china-pakistan-army-has-taken-institutional-control-over-cpec/336634/>.

196. Christophe Jaffrelot. *The Pakistan paradox: instability and resilience*. Oxford University Press, 2015.

197. Asma Jahangir, 'Strengths and pitfalls,' *DAWN* (Apr 16, 2010), accessed on March 10, 2022, <http://www.cfr.org/pakistan/dawn-strengths-pitfalls/p21930>.

198. Theodore P. Wright, "Center-periphery relations and ethnic conflict in Pakistan: Sindhis, Muhajirs, and Punjabis." *Comparative Politics* 23.3 (1991): 299–312. *See also* Charles H. Kennedy. "Policies of ethnic preference in Pakistan." *Asian Survey* 24.6 (1984): 688–703.

199. *See* CONST. of PAK. Art. 184(2). The Supreme Court of Pakistan (SCP) enjoys no executory authority in disputes between the provinces, or between the provinces and the federal government. Under Article 184 (2), the SCP can only exercise declaratory jurisdiction when adjudicating these kinds of disputes but lacks the authority to implement its judgments or entertain cases where the non-implementation of its orders thereof is alleged.

200. *See* CONST of PAK. Art 184(3). Historically, this inability of the SCP to effect or implement its judgments has, at times, led provinces to cloak their legal challenges against the federal government, by indirectly facilitating individual citizens to file lawsuits against the federal government under Article 184 (3), for violations of constitutional fundamental rights of public importance—a clause under which the Supreme Court does possess executory jurisdiction.

201. 'China's "belt and road" courts move is innovative,' *Pinsent Masons* (Jul 03, 2018), accessed on March 10, 2022, <https://www.pinsentmasons.com/out-law/analysis/chinas-belt-and-road-courts-innovative>.

202. The CCI, created in 1973, is a constitutional body meant "to harmonize federal-provincial relations and conform to the spirit of federalism." It is tasked with resolving power-sharing disputes between the federation and the federating units and includes both provincial and federal representation. CCI decisions are through majority voting, but if a provincial government or the federal government is dissatisfied with its decision, either of them can refer the matter to the parliament, which then decides through a joint vote of both houses, the outcome of which has binding authority. *See* Ahmed Mahmood Zahid, 'Institutional Analysis of Council of Common Interests,' *UNDP*(Dec 2013), accessed on March 10, 2022, <http://www.pk.undp.org/content/dam/pakistan/docs/Democratic%20Governance/Federalism/CCI%20Manual%20(1).pdf>.

203. *See* Mahendra Prasad Singh and Veena Kukreja, *Federalism in South Asia*. Routledge, 2014, 225.

204. Yogesh Gattani, "The Resilience of Baloch Insurgencies: Understanding the Fifth Period." (2021). ("For instance, while the province contributes to nearly

$1.4 billion USD in a year through gas revenues, it receives only $116 million USD from the government in royalty. Similarly, the Saindak project, operated by the Chinese, provides only two per cent of the total profit for the Baloch while it expropriates eighty per cent and gives eighteen per cent to Pakistani federal government.").

205. 'Why Terrorists Will Target China in Pakistan,' *Foreign Policy* (Aug 21, 2021), accessed on March 10, 2022, <https://foreignpolicy.com/2021/08/27/why-terrorists-will-target-china-in-pakistan/>.

206. *Ibid.*

207. 'Pakistan's Growing Problem with its China Economic Corridor,' *USIP* (May 26, 2021), accessed on March 10, 2022, <https://www.usip.org/publications/2021/05/pakistans-growing-problem-its-china-economic-corridor>. ("According to documents released by Pakistan's finance ministry, Pakistan's total public and publicly guaranteed external debt stood at $44.35 billion in June 2013, just 9.3 percent of which was owed to China. By April 2021, this external debt had ballooned to $90.12 billion, with Pakistan owing 27.4 percent—$24.7 billion—of its total external debt to China, according to the International Monetary Fund [IMF].").

208. Jason Hickel, 'How Britain stole 45 trillion from India,' *Al Jazeera* (Dec 19, 2018), accessed on March 10, 2022, <https://www.aljazeera.com/opinions/2018/12/19/how-britain-stole-45-trillion-from-india>. ("Prior to the colonial period, Britain bought goods like textiles and rice from Indian producers and paid for them in the normal way—mostly with silver—as they did with any other country. But something changed in 1765, shortly after the East India Company took control of the subcontinent and established a monopoly over Indian trade. Here's how it worked. The East India Company began collecting taxes in India, and then cleverly used a portion of those revenues [about a third] to fund the purchase of Indian goods for British use. In other words, instead of paying for Indian goods out of their own pocket, British traders acquired them for free, 'buying' from peasants and weavers using money that had just been taken from them.") *See generally* Shubhra Chakrabarti and Utsa Patnaik, eds., *Agrarian and Other Histories: Essays for Binay Bhushan Chaudhuri*. Tulika Books, 2017.

209. 'Growth, not development: The China-Pakistan Economic Corridor,' *Daily Times* (Jun 13, 2018), accessed on March 10, 2022, <https://dailytimes.com.pk/253077/growth-not-development-the-china-pakistan-economic-corridor/>.

210. 'CPEC Long Term Plan,' *DAWN* (Nov 2, 2017), accessed on March 10, 2022, <https://www.dawn.com/news/1367767>.

211. *See supra* note 180.

212. 'CPEC Phase-2: China pledges investment of billions of dollars in seven new sectors,' *Pakistan Today* (Feb 7, 2022), accessed on March 10, 2022, <https://www.pakistantoday.com.pk/2022/02/07/cpec-phase-2-china-pledged-investment-of-billions-of-dollars-in-seven-new-sectors/>.

213. *See* Andrew Small, *The China Pakistan axis: Asia's new geopolitics*. Random House India, 2015.

214. CPEC AUTHORITY Ministry of Planning, Development, & Special Initiatives, accessed on March 10, 2022, <cpec.gov.pk/project-details/83>. *See also* 'Education, a core aspect of the China Pakistan Economic Corridor,' *OBOR Europe* (Nov

9, 2019), accessed on March 10, 2022, <https://www.oboreurope.com/en/education-cpec-ehsaas/>. ("China and Pakistan are cooperating in the field of education in Baluchistan with the establishment of vocational training centres. According to the Chinese ambassador, about fifty professional institutes are being created in this province alone. Students from the Baluchistan province also received scholarships to study in China. These agreements are not limited to Baluchistan. Today, nearly 28,000 Pakistani students are enrolled in Chinese universities, being the third largest contingent after South Koreans [50,600 students] and Thais [28,603 students] in Chinese universities.").

215. 'Most loans under CPEC at commercial rates: report,' *DAWN* (Sep 30, 2021), accessed on February 23, 2022, <https://www.dawn.com/news/1649227>. ("However, they often benefit from an explicit or implicit form of government liability protection . . . the government has issued sovereign guarantees in some cases. This means the national exchequer will repay the loans if non-government borrowers fail to generate sufficient revenue to meet their financial obligations.").

216. Special Economic Zones (Amendment) Act, 2016, accessed on March 10, 2022, <https://senate.gov.pk/uploads/documents/1570772186_280.pdf>.

217. 'Understanding CPEC: Without tax reform economic growth will simply increase inequality,' *LSE BLOGS*, accessed on March 10, 2022, <https://blogs.lse.ac.uk/southasia/2017/06/15/understanding-cpec-without-tax-reform-economic-growth-will-simply-increase-in-equality/>. ("In the first decade of twentieth century, France, Germany, and the United States had a similar tax-to-GDP ratio. These statistics changed in the wake of the First and Second World Wars. The elites were forced to pay higher taxes. 'In the wake of these shocks,' Thomas Piketty suggests, 'western elites finally gave in to the kind of social and tax reforms that they had denied prior 1914.'")

218. French Declaration of the Rights of Man and of the Citizen of 1789.

219. 'Maqpon Das Village in Gilgit—Owners reluctant to surrender Land for CPEC,' *DAWN* (Mar 17, 2017), accessed on March 10, 2022, <https://www.dawn.com/news/1321025>.

220. Shahid Mahmood, Muazzam Sabir and Ghaffar Ali, "Infrastructure projects and sustainable development: Discovering the stakeholders' perception in the case of the China–Pakistan Economic Corridor." *PloS one* 15.8 (2020). ("Results reveal that with respect to the relationship between land acquisition and dissatisfaction with a CPEC project, the level of dissatisfaction is 2.45 times higher when land is acquired by force or when compensation for the land is perceived to be inadequate by the local people. Individuals favour economic zones and development projects over road projects; the likelihood of being dissatisfied is approximately nine times greater in regions without economic zones than that in regions with such zones. Similarly, when no development project is allocated to a community, the probability of dissatisfaction of the local people is about 7.6 times greater. In addition, expectations of poor financial outcomes for CPEC projects cause significant dissatisfaction and are a source of tension among the local people.").

221. *See supra* note 169.

222. *Ibid.*

223. Karim Khan, Krim Khan, and Saba Anwar, "Special economic zones (SEZs) and CPEC: Background, challenges and strategies." *Pakistan Development Review* (2016): 203–16, 219.

224. 'Kenya must face up to rising claims of racial discrimination by Chinese against locals,' *Quartz* (Oct 15, 2018), accessed on March 10, 2022, <https://qz.com/africa/1423930/kenya-must-deal-with-chinese-racial-discrimination/>.

225. *Supra* note 225.

226. *Ibid.* at 205.

227. *Ibid.* at 219. ("Many Pakistani industries has been protected and pampered for too long and the result, in many cases, is that even after decades of protection, these industries stay small, inefficient, without scale economics and are not able to export. Even today, the car, sugar, textile, and flour industries are subsidised. There have been very few years in our history that these industries have not been subsidised. They are given protection dispensations at will. They are given subsidised land in industrial estates. They are given insider deals in privatisation. These types of protection have three problems. First, subsidies are very hard to remove once given, especially in places where governments are weak, are captured by elites and/or are open to interest group activities. Second, interest groups coalesce around the issue of subsidies and lobby for their continuation. Third, these interest groups are willing to spend a good fraction of the subsidy in ensuring the continuation of the subsidy and in weak states, where corruption is invasive; it is hard to resist the offers.").

228. 'Pakistani military in charge, provinces sidelined in a revived CPEC,' *Eco-Business* (Oct 6, 2020), accessed on March 10, 2022, <https://www.eco-business.com/news/pakistani-military-in-charge-provinces-sidelined-in-a-revived-cpec/>.

229. 'With Military at the Helm, CPEC Fuels Centre-Province Tensions in Pakistan,' *Wire* (Oct 8, 2020), accessed on March 10, 2022, <https://thewire.in/south-asia/cpec-china-pakistan-military-belt-and-road-initiative>. ("Adeney said both China and the army feel that a centralised authority will be more capable of pushing through the objectives of CPEC. 'But for CPEC to be a success and to bring the Pakistani people along with it, it is vitally important that the CPEC Authority includes the provinces in its decision-making procedures,' she warned. Her research, carried out with Filippo Boni, shows a higher completion rate of CPEC projects in Punjab and Sindh compared with historically marginalised provinces such as Balochistan, Khyber Pakhtunkhwa and Gilgit-Baltistan.") The CPEC Authority has now been reorganized, with the CPEC secretariat being revived within the Ministry for Planning and Development, *see* "PM gives nod to abolish CPEC Authority," *Express Tribune* (Aug 18, 2022), <https://tribune.com.pk/story/2371790/pm-gives-nod-to-abolish-cpec-authority>.

230. Hina Aslam, "CPEC & Environmental Sustainability," *South Asian Voices* (20 July, 2021), accessed on 23 February, 2022, <https://southasianvoices.org/cpec-environmental-sustainability/>. *See also* Hina Aslam, Maaz Sakib, and Amna Sandhu, "SEZs for Sustainable Development in Pakistan: Building on the Lessons from China." (2019), accessed on March 10, 2022, <https://think-asia.org/bitstream/handle/11540/11373/SEZsforSustainableDevelopmentinPakistan.pdf?sequence=1>.

231. *See supra* note 177 at 5. ("In Ethiopia, for example, with the help of the Chinese government, sustainable technologies and practices like crop-rotation and

designated, fenced land for grazing have been used, partially developed out of the Chinese aid for Ethiopia and its agriculture.")

232. Elizabeth Threlkeld and Grace Easterly, "Afghanistan-Pakistan Ties and Future Stability in Afghanistan." (2021).

233. James Landale. "Afghanistan: What rise of Taliban means for Pakistan," *BBC News* (Sep 3, 2021), accessed on March 10, 2022, <https://www.bbc.com/news/world-asia-58443839>.

234. Zahir Sherazi. "Will Afghanistan's powerful neighbours engage the Taliban?" *Al Jazeera* (Oct 16, 2021), accessed on March 10, 2022, <https://www.aljazeera.com/opinions/2021/10/16/will-afghanistans-powerful-neighbours-engage-the-taliban>.

BIBLIOGRAPHY

"Agriculture is backbone of economy: PM." *Nation*, January 25, 2021. https://nation.com.pk/25-Jan-2021/agriculture-is-backbone-of-economy-pm.

Akhtar, Aasim Sajjad. "The China-Pakistan Economic Corridor Beyond the Rule of Capital?" *MONTHLY REVIEW-AN INDEPENDENT SOCIALIST MAGAZINE* 70, no. 2 (2018): 34–48. https://monthlyreview.org/2018/06/01/the-china-pakistan-economic-corridor/.

Alam, Ahmad Rafay. "Why don't CPEC projects factor in the climate crisis?" *China Dialogue*, January 3, 2020. https://chinadialogue.net/en/business/11750-why-don-t-cpec-projects-factor-in-the-climate-crisis/.

Albo, Gregory. "Neoliberalism and the Discontented." *Socialist Register* 44 (2008).

Asghar, Ammar Junaid, Amna Mahnoor Cheema, Muhammad Ibrahim Hameed, and Syed Qasim. "The Critical Junction between CPEC, Agriculture and Climate Change." (2021). https://ccls.lums.edu.pk/sites/default/files/user376/the_critical_junction_between_cpec_agriculture_and_climate_change.pdf.

Ashraf, Sadia, and Aisha Shahzad. "Federalism and provincial autonomy in Pakistan: A case of Balochistan." *Pakistan Social Sciences Review* 4, no. 3 (2020): 25–35.

Aslam, Hina, Maaz Sakib, and Amna Sandhu. "SEZs for Sustainable Development in Pakistan: Building on the Lessons from China." (2019). https://think-asia.org/bitstream/handle/11540/11373/SEZsforSustainableDevelopmentinPakistan.pdf?sequence=1.

Aslam, Hina. "CPEC & Environmental Sustainability." *South Asian Voices,* July 20, 2021. https://southasianvoices.org/cpec-environmental-sustainability/.

"Balochistan to sign economic zone deal with China: Official." *Express Tribune*, November 11, 2015. http://tribune.com.pk/story/989188/balochistan-to-sign-economic-zone-deal-with-china-official/.

"Balochistan: The State versus the Nation." *Carnegie Endowment for International Peace*, April 11, 2013. https://carnegieendowment.org/2013/04/11/balochistan-state-versus-nation-pub-51488.

Barry, Brian. *Culture and equality: An egalitarian critique of multiculturalism.* Harvard University Press, 2002.

Block, Fred. "Polanyi's double movement and the reconstruction of critical theory." *Revue interventions économiques. Papers in political economy* 38 (2008).

Boni, Filippo, and Katharine Adeney. "The impact of the China-Pakistan economic corridor on Pakistan's federal system: The politics of the CPEC." *Asian Survey* 60, no. 3 (2020): 441–65.

Brown, Geoff. "Pakistan: failing state or neoliberalism in crisis?" *International Socialism: A Quarterly Review of Socialist Theory* 150 (2016).

Brown, Wendy. "Neo-liberalism and the end of liberal democracy." *Theory & event* 7, no. 1 (2003).

Brown, Wendy. *Undoing the demos: Neoliberalism's stealth revolution*. Mit Press, 2015.

Chakrabarti, Shubhra, and Utsa Patnaik. "*Agrarian and other histories: essays for Binay Bhushan Chaudhuri*." (2017).

Chan, M., and Mary Madeleine Edel. "China in Africa: A Form of Neo-Colonialism?" *Yerepouni News* (2018). https://www.e-ir.info/2018/12/02/china-in-africa-a-form-of-neo-colonialism/.

"China in Africa." *Council for Foreign Relations*, July 12, 2017. https://www.cfr.org/backgrounder/china-africa.

"China in Africa: What's the Real Story?" *Diplomat*, April 11, 2017. https://thediplomat.com/2017/04/china-in-africa-whats-the-real-story/.

"China sidelines Pakistan govt, manipulates law to acquire control over democratic, economic system." *ANI News*, August 3, 2020. https://www.aninews.in/news/world/asia/china-sidelines-pakistan-govt-manipulates-law-to-acquire-control-over-democratic-economic-system-report20200803094424/.

"China signs 99-year lease on Sri Lanka's Hambantota port." *Financial Times*, December 11, 2017. https://www.ft.com/content/e150ef0c-de37-11e7-a8a4-0a1e63a52f9c.

"China's Port Expansion in Africa." *Council on Foreign Relations,* July 29, 2021. https://www.cfr.org/blog/chinas-port-expansion-africa.

"China-Pakistan Economic Corridor: Opportunities and Risks." *International Crisis Group*, 2018. https://www.crisisgroup.org/asia/south-asia/pakistan/297-china-pakistan-economic-corridor-opportunities-and-risks.

"China-Pakistan Economic Corridor: Opportunities and Risks." *International Crisis Group*, 2018. https://www.crisisgroup.org/asia/south-asia/pakistan/297-china-pakistan-economic-corridor-opportunities-and-risks.

"China's 'belt and road' courts move is innovative." *Pinsent Masons*, July 03, 2018. https://www.pinsentmasons.com/out-law/analysis/chinas-belt-and-road-courts-innovative.

"Chinese return from Africa as migrant population peaks." *Financial Times*, August 28, 2017. https://www.ft.com/content/7106ab42-80d1-11e7-a4ce-15b2513cb3ff. An estimated one million migrants of Chinese origin resided across Africa by 2013.

Chomsky, Noam. *Profit over people: Neoliberalism and global order*. Seven Stories Press, 1998.

Cohen, Ruth. *Alien Invasion: How the Harris Tories Mismanaged Ontario*. Insomniac Press, 2009.

CPEC AUTHORITY Ministry of Planning, Development, & Special. Initiativescpec.gov.pk/project-details/83.
"CPEC—challenges and solutions." *Express Tribune,* April 18, 2018. https://tribune.com.pk/story/1688108/6-cpec-challenges-solutions.
"CPEC Long Term Plan." *DAWN,* November 2, 2017. https://www.dawn.com/news/1367767.
"CPEC Phase-2: China pledges investment of billions of dollars in seven new sectors." *Pakistan Today*, February 7, 2022. https://www.pakistantoday.com.pk/2022/02/07/cpec-phase-2-china-pledged-investment-of-billions-of-dollars-in-seven-new-sectors/.
Das, Khanindra Ch. "The making of one belt, one road and dilemmas in South Asia." *China Report* 53, no. 2 (2017): 125–42.
Demissie, Alexander, Moritz Weigel and Tang Xiaoyang. "China's Belt and Road Initiative & Its Implications for Africa." *Worldwide Fund Kenya*, December 2016. https://www.tralac.org/images/docs/11316/chinas-belt-and-road-initiative-and-its-implications-for-africa-wwf-kenya-december-2016.pdf.
Denord, François. "The Origins of Neoliberalism in France. Louis Rougier and the 1938 Walter Lippmann Conference." *Le Mouvement Social* 195, no. 2 (2001): 9.
Dreher, Axel, Andreas Fuchs, Bradley Parks, Austin Strange, and Michael J. Tierney. "Aid, China, and growth: Evidence from a new global development finance dataset." *American Economic Journal: Economic Policy* 13, no. 2 (2021): 135–74.
el-Shafei, Alyaa Wagdy, and Mohamed Metawe. "China drive toward Africa between arguments of neo-colonialism and mutual-beneficial relationship: sprinas a case study." *Review of Economics and Political Science* (2021).
Fazl-E-Haider, Syed. "Pakistan's extremist dilemma." *Lowy Institute*, April 26, 2021. https://www.lowyinstitute.org/the-interpreter/pakistan-s-extremist-dilemma.
French Declaration of the Rights of Man and of the Citizen of 1789.
French, Howard W. *China's second continent: How a million migrants are building a new empire in Africa*. Vintage, 2015.
Gardezi, Hassan N., and Soofia Mumtaz. "Globalisation and Pakistan's dilemma of development [with comments]." *Pakistan Development Review* (2004): 423–40.
Gattani, Yogesh. "The Resilience of Baloch Insurgencies: Understanding the Fifth Period." *E-International Relations.*
George, Susan. "A short history of neoliberalism." In *Conference on Economic Sovereignty in a Globalising World*, vol. 24, 26. 1999.
Ghafar, Adel Abdel, and Anna Jacobs. "Beijing Calling: Assessing China's Growing Footprint in North Africa." *Brookings Doha Center*, 2019. https://www.brookings.edu/research/beijing-calling-assessing-chinas-growing-footprint-in-north-africa/.
"Global Climate Risk Index 2021." *OCHA.* https://reliefweb.int/report/world/global-climate-risk-index-2021.
Green, Mark. "China's Debt Diplomacy." *Foreign Policy*, April 25, 2019. https://foreignpolicy.com/2019/04/25/chinas-debt-diplomacy/.
"Growth, not development: The China-Pakistan Economic Corridor." *Daily Times*, June 13, 2018. https://dailytimes.com.pk/253077/growth-not-development-the-china-pakistan-economic-corridor/.

Hameed, Maham. "The politics of the China—Pakistan economic corridor." *Palgrave Communications* 4, no. 1 (2018): 1–10.
Harvey, David. "Neo-liberalism as creative destruction." *Geografiska Annaler: Series B, Human Geography* 88, no. 2 (2006): 145–58.
Harvey, David. *A brief history of neoliberalism*. Oxford University Press, USA, 2007.
Hayek, Friedrich August. *The constitution of liberty*. University of Chicago Press, 2011.
Hickel, Jason. "How Britain stole 45 trillion from India." *Al Jazeera*, December 19, 2018. https://www.aljazeera.com/opinions/2018/12/19/how-britain-stole-45-trillion-from-india.
"How China Got Sri Lanka to Cough Up a Port." *New York Times,* June 25, 2018. https://www.nytimes.com/2018/06/25/world/asia/china-sri-lanka-port.html.
"How CPEC Left Behind the People of Gwadar." *Diplomat* June 30, 2020. https://thediplomat.com/2020/06/how-cpec-left-behind-the-people-of-gwadar/.
"How the Silk Road plans will be financed." *Financial Times*, May 10, 2016. https://www.ft.com/content/e83ced94-0bd8-11e6-9456-444ab5211a2f.
"How Will the Belt and Road Initiative Advance China's Interests?" *China Power*, May 8, 2017. https://chinapower.csis.org/china-belt-and-road-initiative/.
Huang, Yasheng. *Capitalism with Chinese characteristics: Entrepreneurship and the state*. Cambridge University Press, 2008.
"Human Development Report 2020: Massive income inequality among rich and poor." *News International,* April 7, 2021. https://www.thenews.com.pk/print/816040-human-development-report-2020-massive-income-inequality-among-rich-and-poor#:~:text=The percent20gap percent20was percent20larger percent20during, economy percent20witnessed percent204 percent20percent percent20growth.
Hussain, Ishrat. "CPEC & Pakistani Economy: An Appraisal," *Centre of Excellence China Pakistan Economic Corridor*. cpec.gov.pk/brain/public/uploads/documents/CPEC-and-Pakistani-Economy_An-Appraisal.pdf.
Ide, Bill, and Joyce Huang. "Caution, Cancellations, Protests as Concerns Grow on China's Belt and Road." *Voice of America* 15 (2018). https://www.voanews.com/a/caution-cancellations-protest-concerns-grow-china-belt-road/4614103.html.
Jaffrelot, Christophe. *The Pakistan paradox: Instability and resilience*. Oxford University Press, 2015.
Jahangir, Asma. "Strengths and pitfalls." *DAWN*, April 16, 2010. http://www.cfr.org/pakistan/dawn-strengths-pitfalls/p21930.
Jamal, Sana. "Pakistan Joins Global Pledge to Cut Methane Emissions." *Gulf News*, October 11, 2021. https://gulfnews.com/world/asia/pakistan/pakistan-joins-global-pledge-to-cut-methane-emissions-1.82880575.
Joseph, Sarah. "Neoliberal reforms and democracy in India." *Economic and Political Weekly* (2007): 3213–18.
Kennedy, Charles H. "Policies of ethnic preference in Pakistan." *Asian Survey* 24, no. 6 (1984): 688–703.
"Kenya is refusing to release the loan contracts for its Chinese-built railway." *Quartz Africa*, January 20, 2022. https://qz.com/africa/2115070/kenya-refuses-to-release-contracts-for-china-debt/.

"Kenya must face up to rising claims of racial discrimination by Chinese against locals." *Quartz,* October 15, 2018. https://qz.com/africa/1423930/kenya-must-deal-with-chinese-racial-discrimination/.

"Kenya: China Cannot Seize Port of Mombasa if Debt Default Occurs." *Maritime Executive* March 16, 2021. https://www.maritime-executive.com/article/kenya-china-cannot-seize-port-of-mombasa-if-debt-default-occurs.

Keskin, Tugrul. "A brief history of neoliberalism." *Societies Without Borders* 4, no. 1 (2009): 94–95.

Khan, Karim, and Saba Anwar. "Special economic zones (SEZs) and CPEC: Background, challenges and strategies." *Pakistan Development Review* (2016): 203–16.

"Khattak threatens 'extreme step' over CPEC project." *DAWN*, January 1, 2016. http://www.dawn.com/news/1230034.

Kleven, Anthony. "Belt and Road: colonialism with Chinese characteristics." *Interpreter* (2019). https://www.lowyinstitute.org/the-interpreter/belt-road-colonialism-chinese-characteristics.

Kouser, Shahzad, and Abdul Subhan. "Uncovering Pakistan's environmental risks and remedies under the China-Pakistan economic corridor." *Environmental Science and Pollution Research* 27, no. 5 (2020): 4661–63.

Kratz, Agatha, Allen Feng, and Logan Wright. "New Data on the 'Debt Trap' Question." *Rodium Group*, April 29, 2019. https://rhg.com/research/new-data-on-the-debt-trap-question/.

Kukreja, Veena. "Ethnic diversity, political aspirations and state response: A case study of Pakistan." *Indian Journal of Public Administration* 66, no. 1 (2020): 28–42.

Kymlicka, Will. "Solidarity in diverse societies: Beyond neoliberal multiculturalism and welfare chauvinism." In *Minorities and populism–critical perspectives from South Asia and Europe*, 41–62. Springer, Cham, 2020.

Kymlicka, Will. "Community and multiculturalism." *A companion to contemporary political philosophy* (2017): 463–77.

Lafargue, François. "China's presence in Africa." *China perspectives* 2005, no. 61 (2005).

Land Acquisition Act (1 of 1894) Art. 10 (4).

Landale, James. "Afghanistan: What rise of Taliban means for Pakistan." *BBC News*, September 3, 2021. https://www.bbc.com/news/world-asia-58443839.

Li, He. "The Chinese model of development and its implications." *World Journal of Social Science Research* 2, no. 2 (2015): 128.

Lokanathan, Venkateswaran. "China's belt and road initiative: Implications in Africa." *Observer Research Foundation Brief* 395 (2020). https://www.orfonline.org/research/chinas-belt-and-road-initiative-implications-in-africa/.

Lydon, Christopher. "Noam Chomsky: Neoliberalism Is Destroying Our Democracy." *Nation*, June 17, 2017. https://www.thenation.com/article/archive/noam-chomsky-neoliberalism-destroying-democracy/.

"Maqpon Das Village in Gilgit—Owners reluctant to surrender Land for CPEC." *DAWN*, March 17, 2017. https://www.dawn.com/news/1321025.

Mahmood, Shahid, Muazzam Sabir, and Ghaffar Ali. "Infrastructure projects and sustainable development: Discovering the stakeholders' perception in the case of the China–Pakistan Economic Corridor." *Plos one* 15, no. 8 (2020): e0237385.

Manuel, Anja. "China is quietly reshaping the world." *Atlantic*, 2017. https://www.theatlantic.com/international/archive/2017/10/china-belt-and-road/542667/.

Marantidou, V., and B. Glosserman. "China's double standard? Fighting corruption at home, turning a blind eye abroad." In *PacNet No. 13, Pacific Forum. Center for Strategic and International Studies (CSIS)*. 2015. https://www.files.ethz.ch/isn/189192/Pac1513.pdf.

Metcalf, Stephen. "Neoliberalism: the idea that swallowed the world." *Guardian*, August 18, 2017. https://www.theguardian.com/news/2017/aug/18/neoliberalism-the-idea-that-changed-the-world.

Mishra, A. "A Chinese-built port in the Indian Ocean: The story of Kenya'a Lamu port." *Observer Research Foundation* (2021). https://www.orfonline.org/expert-speak/a-chinese-built-port-in-the-indian-ocean-the-story-of-kenyas-lamu-port/.

"Most loans under CPEC at commercial rates: report." *DAWN*, September 30, 2021. https://www.dawn.com/news/1649227.

Nabi, Ghulam, Suliman Khan, Shahid Ahmad, Ahsan Khan, and Rabeea Siddique. "China–Pakistan Economic Corridor (CPEC): an alarming threat to the biodiversity of Northern Pakistan." *Biodiversity and Conservation* 26, no. 12 (2017): 3003–04.

"Neoliberalism and poverty," *News International* (May 26, 2018), accessed on March 10, 2022 <https://www.thenews.com.pk/print/321437-neoliberalism-and-poverty>.

"One Belt, One Road, One Happy Chinese Navy." *Foreign Policy*, April 17, 2018. foreignpolicy.com/2018/04/17/one-belt-one-road-one-happy-chinese-navy/.

Ong, Aihwa. *Neoliberalism as exception: Mutations in citizenship and sovereignty*. Duke University Press, 2006.

"Over 2,500 families displaced to make way for economic corridor." *Express Tribune*, January 3, 2017. https://tribune.com.pk/story/1283421/2500-families-displaced-make-way-economic-corridor/.

"Over 60 percent workers paid below minimum wage." *Express Tribune*, April 4, 2021. https://tribune.com.pk/story/2293067/over-60-workers-paid-below-minimum-wage.

"Pakistan 5th most vulnerable country to climate change, reveals German watch report." *DAWN*, January 16, 2020. https://www.dawn.com/news/1520402.

"Pakistan: The Worsening Conflict in Balochistan." *Crisis Group*, Report 119/Asia, September 14, 2006. https://www.crisisgroup.org/asia/south-asia/pakistan/pakistan-worsening-conflict-balochistan.

"Pakistan's Growing Problem with its China Economic Corridor." *USIP*, May 26, 2021. https://www.usip.org/publications/2021/05/pakistans-growing-problem-its-china-economic-corridor.

"Pakistan's Growing Problem with its China Economic Corridor." *USIP*, May 26, 2021. https://www.usip.org/publications/2021/05/pakistans-growing-problem-its-china-economic-corridor.

"Pakistani military in charge, provinces sidelined in a revived CPEC." *Eco-Business*, October 6, 2020. https://www.eco-business.com/news/pakistani-military-in-charge-provinces-sidelined-in-a-revived-cpec/.

Palley, Thomas I. "From Keynesianism to neoliberalism: Shifting paradigms in economics." *Neoliberalism: A critical reader* 268 (2005).

"Peshawar Northern Bypass, pushing farmers to further destitution." *PAN AP*, 2020. https://files.panap.net/resources/No-Land-No-Life-Land-Conflicts-and-Struggles-in-Asia.pdf.

Peters, Michael A. "The early origins of neoliberalism: Colloque Walter Lippman (1938) and the Mt Perelin Society (1947)." *Educational Philosophy and Theory* (2021): 1–8.

"PM gives nod to abolish CPEC Authority." *Express Tribune,* August 18, 2022. https://tribune.com.pk/story/2371790/pm-gives-nod-to-abolish-cpec-authority.

Polanyi, Karl. *The Great Transformation: The Political and Economic Origins of Our Time.* 1944.

Ramo, Joshua Cooper. *The beijing consensus*. London: Foreign Policy Centre, 2004.

Rehman, Zia Ur. "Pakistani madrassas: an indispensable institution, a worry for the state." *TRT World*, May 20, 2019. https://www.trtworld.com/magazine/pakistani-madrassas-an-indispensable-institution-a-worry-for-the-state-26787.

Risager, Bjarke Skærlund. "Neoliberalism is a political project: An interview with David Harvey." *Jacobin Magazine* (2016). https://www.jacobinmag.com/2016/07/david-harvey-neoliberalism-capitalism-labor-crisis-resistance/.

"Rs83bn projects identified to modernise agriculture sector under CPEC." *Daily Times*, May 19, 2021. https://dailytimes.com.pk/758032/rs83bn-projects-identified-to-modernize-agriculture-sector-under-cpec/.

Sandbrook, Richard. *Reinventing the left in the global south: The politics of the possible*. Cambridge University Press, 2014.

Sherazi, Zahir. "Will Afghanistan's powerful neighbours engage the Taliban?" *Al Jazeera*, October 16, 2021. https://www.aljazeera.com/opinions/2021/10/16/will-afghanistans-powerful-neighbours-engage-the-taliban.

Shah, Abrahim. "Cost of Neoliberalism." *DAWN*, July 30, 2021. https://www.dawn.com/news/1637735/cost-of-neoliberalism.

Shukla, Srijan. "Under pressure from China, Pakistan Army has taken institutional control over CPEC." *Print*, December 17, 2019. https://theprint.in/world/under-pressure-from-china-pakistan-army-has-taken-institutional-control-over-cpec/336634/.

"Significant' consequences if China takes key port in Djibouti: U.S. general." *REUTERS*, March 7, 2018. https://www.reuters.com/article/us-usa-china-djibouti/significant-consequences-if-china-takes-key-port-in-djibouti-u-s-general idUSKCN1GI2V0.

Singh, Mahendra Prasad, and Veena Kukreja. *Federalism in South Asia*. Routledge India, 2014.

Small, Andrew. *The China Pakistan axis: Asia's new geopolitics*. Random House India, 2015.

Sun, Yun. "China's aid to Africa: monster or messiah." *Brookings East Asia Commentary* 75 (2014). https://www.brookings.edu/opinions/chinas-aid-to-africa-monster-or-messiah/.

Taj, Dr Aamer, Dr Muhammad Nouman, and Dr Saleem Gul. "The dynamics of international political economy relationships and its influence on the process of democratisation, institution building and national governance structure in Pakistan." *South Asian Studies* 30, no. 1 (2020).

Tariq, Hamna. "Gilgit-Baltistan: China's Golden Opportunity." *Stimson*, October 9, 2020. https://www.stimson.org/2020/gilgit-baltistan-chinas-golden-opportunity/.

Taylor, Charles, and Taylor Charles. *Philosophical Papers: Volume 2, Philosophy, and the Human Sciences*. Cambridge University Press, 1985, 225.

Thachil, Tariq. "Neoliberalism's two faces in Asia: Globalization, educational policies, and religious schooling in India, Pakistan, and Malaysia." *Comparative Politics* 41, no. 4 (2009): 473–94.

Threlkeld, Elizabeth, and Grace Easterly. "Afghanistan-Pakistan ties and Future stability in Afghanistan." *United States Institute of Peace*, 2021. https://www.usip.org/publications/2021/08/afghanistan-pakistan-ties-and-future-stability-afghanistan.

"Understanding CPEC: Without tax reform economic growth will simply increase inequality." *LSE BLOGS*. https://blogs.lse.ac.uk/southasia/2017/06/15/understanding-cpec-without-tax-reform-economic-growth-will-simply-increase-in-equality/.

"Unmasking the China-Pakistan Economic Corridor." *GRAIN*, May 12, 2021. https://grain.org/en/article/6669-unmasking-the-china-pakistan-economic-corridor.

Vangeli, Anastas. "The normative foundations of the Belt and Road Initiative." In *Normative readings of the belt and road initiative*, 59–83. Springer, Cham, 2018.

Weber, Isabella. "Origins of China's contested relation with Neoliberalism: Economics, the World Bank, and Milton Friedman at the dawn of reform." *Global Perspectives* 1, no. 1 (2020).

Wei, P. A. N. "Western system versus Chinese system." *University of Nottingham Contemporary China Centre Briefing Series* 61 (2010): 9. https://www.nottingham.ac.uk/iaps/documents/cpi/briefings/briefing-61-chinese-western-system.pdf.

"What Pakistan's Relationship with China Tells Us About the Belt and Road Initiative." June 8, 2021. https://gandhara.rferl.org/a/pakistan-china-belt-and-road-initiative/31296850.html.

"Why Terrorists Will Target China in Pakistan." *Foreign Policy*, August 21, 2021. https://foreignpolicy.com/2021/08/27/why-terrorists-will-target-china-in-pakistan/.

"With Military at the Helm, CPEC Fuels Centre-Province Tensions in Pakistan." *Wire*, October 8, 2020. https://thewire.in/south-asia/cpec-china-pakistan-military-belt-and-road-initiative.

Wolf, Siegfried O. *The China-Pakistan Economic Corridor of the Belt and Road Initiative*. Springer International Publishing, 2020.

Wright, Theodore P. "Center-periphery relations and ethnic conflict in Pakistan: Sindhis, Muhajirs, and Punjabis." *Comparative Politics* 23, no. 3 (1991): 299–312.

Yusuf, Huma. "The Other Threat to Pakistan." *New York Times*, April 2, 2014. https://www.nytimes.com/2014/04/03/opinion/the-other-threat-to-pakistan.html.

Zahid, Ahmed Mahmood. "Institutional Analysis of Council of Common Interests." December 2013. http://www.pk.undp.org/content/dam/pakistan/docs/Democratic percent20Governance/Federalism/CCI percent20Manual percent20(1).pdf.

Zaidi, Hussain. "Neoliberal economics: The challenge within." *News International*, July 21, 2018. https://www.thenews.com.pk/print/344278-neoliberal-economics-the-challenge-within.

Conclusion

April 10 marks an historic day for Pakistan: it was on this day in 1973 that the country's parliament approved the Constitution of the Islamic Republic of Pakistan, considered to this day to be the supreme law of the land. It was also on this day, forty-nine years later, that—for the first time in the country's parliamentary history—a highly contentious vote of no confidence was successfully cast against an elected government.[1] The response to this event has polarized the country, with some celebrating it as a victory for constitutionalism while others lamenting it as a collapse of parliamentary democracy in the country. These events, and the context within which they unfolded, provide a rich tapestry within which to further contextualize and examine the prescriptions proposed in the preceding chapters of this work. Prior to this analysis, a brief synopsis of these recent political developments will serve to unpack and study these prescriptions in a real-world—and arguably real-time—context.

Conducting a vote of no confidence against an incumbent prime minister is the constitutionally enshrined right of the opposition.[2] The circumstances that surrounded this particular motion, however, were far more opaque: former Prime Minister Imran Khan had alleged that the motion moved against him was the result of an international conspiracy—a foreign attempt at regime change due to Khan's independent foreign policy decisions not sitting well with a certain western superpower.[3] This claim, he said, is bolstered by the overt political 'horse-trading' that took place before the vote of no confidence, with some of the ruling coalition's members—including members of Khan's cabinet—defecting to join the assorted political opposition groups banding together under the umbrella of the Pakistan Democratic Movement (PDM), giving the PDM the numbers needed to successfully vote Khan out.[4] To substantiate his allegations of foreign interference in Pakistan's internal politics, Khan relied heavily on a purported diplomatic cable, which he claims threatened Pakistan with "difficulties" should Khan's government continue to hold office.[5] An internationally sponsored regime change, Khan claimed, was an insult not only to Pakistan's sovereignty but to its democratic processes as well, and domestic actors furthering this "international conspiracy" have violated their constitutional oaths to protect Pakistan from foreign interference and to ensure its independence and internal democratic processes are not compromised. In an eleventh-hour attempt to forestall the vote, Khan's government closed the parliamentary session during which the vote was to be conducted and attempted to dissolve the National Assembly, announcing fresh general elections.[6]

In response to these events the Supreme Court of Pakistan took immediate *suo moto* notice of the matter to assess the constitutionality of the Khan government's actions, with a five-member bench unanimously declaring Khan's actions as illegal and unconstitutional and ordering the national assembly to reconvene in order to complete the voting process against the prime minister.[7] Minutes prior to the expiration of the court-stipulated time within which the parliamentary session was to cast the vote, Khan—as expected—lost his majority in Parliament and was ousted by the PDM. Following this ouster, Khan conducted dozens of nationwide anti-government rallies—displaying his political strength and popularity with the masses. The theme for these rallies was common: decrying the Sharif governments' feeble attempts at stabilizing an economically, socially, and politically volatile country, and asking for fresh general elections. Khan faced many challenges during this time: the PDM placed deliberate hurdles to restrict and contain his rallies, they conducted strategic crackdowns on his political workers and associated, even surviving an assassination attempt on his person.[8] Importantly however, Khan was able to secure key victories in the by-elections that followed: with his party installed in government in Punjab and KPK, he was able to further his narrative that the government that replaced his was not a popular one, but was "imported"—once again solidifying his demand for fresh elections.[9] When this show of strength did not succeed in getting the PDM government to conduct elections, Khan resorted to more desperate measures: he dissolved two out of four of the Country's assemblies—in Punjab and KPK, both led by his party.[10] He hoped that this would force the PDM government to announce immediate general elections, because the Constitution of Pakistan demarcates that fresh elections must be held within ninety days of the dissolution of an assembly. The Supreme Court of Pakistan repeatedly endorsed this view, in a landmark judgment which stipulated that the PDM government must publish a date for elections within the time stipulated by the Constitution, and then again when it ruled against the Election Commission of Pakistan (ECP), after the ECP announced that the elections were to be delayed from the constitutionally stipulated date.[11] However, even these judicial pronouncements from the country's apex courts did not guarantee the conduct of timely elections as they should have, becoming yet another example of how the separation of powers in Pakistan fails to serve the main purpose it is meant for: to ensure that no institution oversteps its boundaries. In traditional conceptions of a governmental trichotomy of powers, such as the archetype upon which Pakistan's own governance structure is based, the judiciary must necessarily rely upon the executive to abide by and enforce its decrees; in the Pakistani context, however, the executive—often coopted directly or indirectly by the country's armed forces—has historically enjoyed preeminence over both the legislature as well as the judiciary, often compelling the latter to subsequently ratify or legitimize executive excesses. The ECP's delayed conduct of elections is merely the most recent, visible expression of the general disregard state actors—particularly within the executive branch of government—evince for the judiciary.

This recounting of recent political events is, however, missing the clandestine yet significant role played by Pakistan's influential military establishment: popularly considered to have played a key role in bringing Khan to power in the first place, the military was seen in the weeks prior to these events to have abandoned their support of his government. For example, Khan's visit to Russia on the eve of the latter's invasion of Ukraine—ostensibly the turning point of the recent souring of relations with the United States—seemed at the time to have the full support of Pakistan's armed forces. Subsequent statements from the country's top brass, however, contended that Russia's aggressive actions were inconceivable at the time of the visit, leaving Pakistan in a diplomatically embarrassing situation. Statements such as these, however, lack real justificatory power given that the international community had, prior to Russia's incursion into Ukraine, been emphatically expressing their concerns of an imminent invasion, with the United States making its views on Pakistan's planned visit to Russia particularly explicit.[12] An overwhelming majority of the international community took a clear position against Russia's actions in Ukraine; despite this near-universal condemnation, however, Pakistan seemed to maintain a peculiar neutrality and when the matter was deliberated upon in the UN General Assembly Pakistan, along with China and India, abstained from registering a protest against the war.[13] Tellingly, however, days before the vote succeeded against Khan, the Pakistani Chief of Army Staff condemned Russia's invasion of Ukraine, describing the incursion as "a huge tragedy,"[14] distinctly at odds with Pakistan's diplomatic position on the matter.

This estrangement between the military and Khan's party was also reflected in the May 9th attacks (2023): countrywide protests, conducted by Khan's party and its supporters, which took a sour turn when the protesters attacked, damaged, and destroyed certain key sites that hold military significance. As noted earlier in the introduction—Pakistan's military has shown, several times in the past, how it is entirely capable of deterring and preventing entry into its cantonment areas, and so the fact that protestors were allowed to even come near these sites begs the question: did the military orchestrate these events to dampen Khan's political strength, disband his core political advisory committee, intimidate his supporters, and gain another opportunity to glorify the personal sacrifices it has made for the country?[15]

Having thus established an estrangement between Khan's party and Pakistan's armed forces,[16] it is easier to contextualize the events taking place in the minutes before the vote of no-confidence was confirmed against Khan: unprecedently both the Supreme Court of Pakistan and the Islamabad High Court, rushed to open their doors shortly before midnight on the night the parliamentary session was to conclude the vote. Ostensibly, the only reason the courts would open at such an unusual hour—and in such haste—is for the Supreme Court to hold Khan in contempt of court for not conducting the vote as mandated,[17] and for the High Court to nullify any orders that might come from Khan's office to replace the Chief of Army Staff.[18] Most exceptionally, none of these claims had actually even materialized, and the courts were summoned to open their doors to preemptively hear cases on issues that had not yet even arisen. In light of Pakistan's judicial history, where the country's courts have repeatedly rendered decisions affirming political interference on the part of the armed forces, the courts' prompt—and anticipatory—intervention prior to Khan's ouster is arguably demonstrative of yet another instance of the military coopting the judiciary to further its political interests and consolidate its power.[19] Another example of this is the Islamabad District and Sessions Court and the Election Commission of Pakistan's decisions in Khan's "Toshakhana" case: where the ousted premier was charged with corruption involving state gifts during his term, condemning him to a fine, three years of imprisonment, and—of course—disbarring him from contesting in election for a term of five years.[20] This cooption of the judicial branch is not entirely unique to Pakistan: a review of states such as Egypt, Iran, and Turkey demonstrates the risks of a country's military's attempts to wield power by subverting democratic norms and exploiting political and judicial institutions.[21]

Therefore, a key takeaway for Pakistan lies in the pressing need for judicial independence and exercising constitutional restraint when dealing with political crises such as the one the country is presently undergoing. The Supreme Court's decision to dismiss the deputy speaker's ruling and restore the National Assembly to proceed with the vote of no-confidence against Khan, though legally tenable, can be best termed as the most conservative approach—consolidating the push towards effecting regime change, rather than moving the needle towards general elections instead. This latter option would have arguably been the more appropriate and democratic solution to what was clearly a crisis of politics, where political strong-arming was on clear display in light of defections between the parties. Additionally, the preemptive judicial activism seen shortly before Khan's ouster severely damaged the judiciary's reputation as an apolitical and independent institution; instead, it seemed that the courts were responding to instructions from the country's military establishment, which wanted to ensure that Khan was voted out.[22] This was another example—in a long line of similar decisions—of Pakistan's judiciary rendering verdicts that perversely worked to undermine judicial independence in the country. The judiciary must actively assume and take ownership of its role as the protector of democratic processes and institutions in Pakistan—and vociferously defend its ability to act as such; an independent and powerful judiciary is a *sine qua non* for the existence of a robust federation, underpinning the rule of law and constitutionalism while minimizing the possibility of illegal political adventurism.

Another important conclusion arising out of these events is the fact that the civil-military imbalance that exists within Pakistan repeatedly allows the military to collude with other institutions, such as the judiciary, to repress the democratic process. In this particular instance, Pakistan's military also used the PDM—a coalition of opposition political parties—to further its agenda; having withdrawn support from Khan's government, the establishment placed its weight squarely behind the PDM.[23] In point of fact, it has even been argued that the Election Commission of Pakistan has also been coopted by the military by way of the judiciary: under the Constitution of Pakistan the ECP's is exclusively required to conduct elections within three months of the dissolution of assemblies—as moved by the PTI—and yet it has squarely been denied the opportunity to perform its constitutional role of conducting general elections in the prescribed time.[24]

The military establishment in Pakistan has displayed a *modus operandi* of working behind the scenes and off the record. What it did not expect, in this particular case, was such significant pushback from Khan's camp. In the weeks following his ouster, Khan has conducted massive crowd-pulling events, clearly demonstrating his popular support. This, coupled with the fact that the military's undemocratic interference has—in this instance —been brought to light, has put the military politically on the defensive, and it appears that political divisions and alliances have emerged even within the upper echelons of armed forces. Regardless, it has become clear, not only in the internal political arena in Pakistan, but—due to Khan's immense populist appeal—to the public at large as well, that the military has manipulated the weaknesses of Pakistan's parliamentary system (*vis-à-vis* horse-trading) to orchestrate regime change. What has really forced Pakistan's armed forces to adjust their strategy for political involvement, however, has been Khan's populist appeal; though largely perceived as a sacred cow the Pakistan's military, in setting itself in opposition to Khan, cannot afford to risk eroding its own populist support and have its image as the nation's savior tainted.

Khan's populist narrative against corruption, and his indirect allusions to the military to internally reflect and to rectify its mistakes, all serve to place significant pressure on the armed forces to realign their interests, either in support of Khan's independent regime, or to take its proverbial "hat" out of the political "bag."[25]

Pakistan's military, as discussed earlier in this work, is significantly invested in several domestic industries, enabling it to provide a range of private sector goods and services—including housing, construction, food goods, and certain other services—at prices often lower than the market's. For the first time, however, it seemed that a civilian government was providing these essential goods and services at a public level; for example, Khan's government tackled cartels of sugar producers—something that even caused Khan to lose support with a major sugar baron, previously one of his major financial backers.[26] But on a larger scale these events demonstrate how—without precedent—a civilian government was infiltrating the spaces within which the military had previously enjoyed inordinate influence—if not a complete monopoly—over, yet another reason why the military has been forced to rethink its approach to political interventionism.

A closer examination of Khan's populist appeal shows that, prior to the motion of no-confidence against him, his policy approach was being critiqued domestically as being detrimental to Pakistan's international diplomacy efforts, with elite moderates also not appreciating his policies that indulged the country's religious right. From the outset Khan's political narrative has seemed to revolve around a familiar mix of religious rhetoric and anti-Americanism and, before his untimely acquittal from government, Khan seemed to have lost a degree of popular favor due to his continuous pandering to elements of Pakistan's religious fundamentalist bloc. Much like preceding politicians, Khan's politics have leaned heavily towards leveraging religiosity for political advantage—a strategy mirroring his political predecessors and one which has served to disunite, rather than cohere, Pakistan's polity. However, as soon as his own cabinet members defected to oust his government, Khan began to spin a populist narrative of regime change, fomenting and leveraging latent anti-imperialist sentiments within the Pakistani polity. Both strategies have served to further destabilize the tenuous balance maintained in Pakistan's political status quo, and the mass resignations of all PTI parliamentarians following Khan's ouster have left a huge political vacuum in the country's senior political leadership, one that will rapidly be filled in the interregnum by the remaining political actors ordered stringently around ethnic or religious lines, as is currently—and has historically been—the case in Pakistan's largely consociational-federalist structure.

Following his ouster, however, Khan has managed to amass a significant support base from across the country. Contrary to the current array of parties who have historically derived their influence directly from their links to particular ethnicities or provinces—thereby projecting a consociationalist system of politics[27]—Khan's party seems to draw support from a more diverse cross-section of the country. His party's work regarding social programs has been substantial, including the Ehsaas Programme targeted at poverty alleviation;[28] the provision of free health services under the Sehat Sahulat Program;[29] the Naya Pakistan Housing and Development Authority aimed at providing lower cost housing;[30] and the establishment and operationalization of the National Command and Operation Center (NCOC),[31] which coordinated national efforts to effectively control the spread of COVID-19. The salient feature of all these programs was that they were tailored not to suit any particular ethnic group or province, but were instead designed to be implemented nationwide. To cite the NCOC's work as an example, provinces were not seen to be competing with one other to achieve greater COVID-19 responses, but rather COVID-19 responses were determined and applied uniformly at the federal level: Khan relied on local governments to enforce "smart lockdowns" depending on where the spread of the virus was more pernicious, regardless of where outbreaks occurred. This policy effectively controlled the spread of the virus, while minimizing the regional impacts on the economy by shutting down entire cities or regions.[32]

Additionally, Khan's current narrative, focused on national sovereignty and dignity, seems to cohere across ethnic and provincial boundaries. A clear local centripetalist tendency can be observed in Khan's politics,[33] resonating strongly with the polity across Pakistan's various demographic groups. Khan's ouster represents a prime and topical example of how much Pakistan's present consociational-federalist framework has done to fracture its polity into smaller, hyper-factionalized and polarized political groups, which—in this case—have only united under the PDM aegis in order to achieve the sole aim of dismissing Khan's government. While Pakistan's two major dynastic political parties,[34] with deep-rooted histories of mutual resentment, have united to overwhelm Khan through sheer weight of numbers, it is unlikely that there will be inclusive, amicable and lasting agreement on the formation of a federal cabinet or the conduct of federal policy in the proceeding months.

Since Khan's ouster the various factions of the PDM hitherto arrayed against him began to maneuver in order to contest elections—presently scheduled for early 2024 by the ECP; fault lines began to appear within the PDM, with the major political parties comprising the bloc—the PPP and the PML(N)—sharply diverging in their policies and rhetoric. The appointment of the caretaker cabinet—principally tasked under the 1973 Constitution and Election Act with guaranteeing the conduct of free, fair, and transparent elections—was a particular point of contention, with the PPP vehemently contesting the nomination of a PML(N) stalwart and former PML(N) finance minister Ishaq Dar as caretaker prime minister.[35] While the PML(N) backed down and nominated Anwaar ul Haq Kakar – also aligned with the PML(N) though not a member of the party's former cabinet – the rift between the PPP and the PML(N), the two largest parties comprising the PDM bloc, has continued to widen. The PDM government dissolved on the 9th of August, 2023 – almost a week prior to the original date of the 14th the PDM itself set;[36] arguably leaving the country in a precarious state with an underperforming economy, skyrocketing inflation, and an uncertain foreign policy. During and since its tenure the PDM – and the various political factions comprising it – have come under fire from various sectors, not least of which has been the PPP itself. Despite being a major coalition partner, the PPP has since taken pains to distance itself from the PDM and its record in government, levying serious criticisms over the coalition's handling of the economy in particular in an attempt to reposition itself before the elections scheduled for early 2024.

The ouster of Khan's government – which had previously enjoyed significant grassroots support – and the highly visible and tumultuous manner in which it occurred harkened back to previous periods of Pakistan's history, where elected civilian governments were more likely than not forced out of power and prevented from completing their terms in office. The PPP government of 2008 through 2012 – the first in Pakistan's history to complete a full term in office – appeared to represent a divergence from the previous decades post-independence, where civilian governments were brought down before their time, by way of either direct military intervention or through political infighting; Khan's dismissal and the subsequent PDM tenure appear to represent a regression to the historically turbulent *status quo* of civilian politics, where the country's well-established military was able to leverage factional differences to weaken civilian institutions and promote its own interests. That similar patterns of political behavior are being expressed is cause for concern, with the military already having taken advantage of the PDM's precarious political footing to effect the promulgation of amendments to the corpus of Pakistan's criminal justice statutes – most significantly by effectively criminalizing domestic critique of the institution.

As discussed in chapter 1, the polarization within and between the various political factions extant in Pakistan serves to dilute their overall political influence, both enabling the military's political maneuvering and adventurism as has most recently been observed during the tenure of the PDM government, as well as consolidating the political dominance of larger demographic groups. In the present context, this dilution of political power is evinced not only through the military's overt involvement in orchestrating this regime change but also in the fact that the party replacing the ruling government draws most of its political strength from the province of Punjab. Presently the brother of the Prime Minister preceding Khan has taken up the country's premiership, with the new Prime Minister's son being appointed as Punjab's Chief Minister, further consolidating the province's – and by extension the Punjabi ethnic group's – stranglehold over domestic politics. By contrast, a centripetalist federalist arrangement would work to attenuate the influence exerted by these more significant socio-cultural groups, diminishing the political effect of domestic majoritarianism and – as a corollary – reducing the political capital the country's historically powerful military enjoys. However, as discussed in preceding chapters, the realization of a localized form of centripetalist federalism in Pakistan would require major structural constitutional modifications that would deeply impact the country's current political landscape, such as by altering the current number, status, and powers of the existing federating units; reforms to the parliamentary election format; and the institution of effective forms of local governance.

One of Khan's unfulfilled promises remains his work on the development of a more robust local government elections system, which – if completed – would have provided a foundation for ensuring greater inclusivity and accountability at the grass roots level. After having rolled out his plan in KPK, he was planning to branch out into Punjab;[37] starting with the creation of local village councils, Khan's plan envisaged direct elections to populate these councils, stressing that candidates need not be members of any political party in order to contest elections,[38] and foresaw direct elections at the tehsil level under similar terms. This would have served to not only engender grass roots connectivity and responsiveness, boosting targeted development for each locality, but would also have provided for new leadership options. In urban settings Khan suggested having a directly elected mayor, one who would form a cabinet of professionals to assist in the management of the city.[39] Had this plan been allowed to come to fruition, it would have significantly contributed towards establishing a functional and coherent system of elected local governments, with the aim of strengthening the foundations of democratic federalism in Pakistan. Democratically representative local governments promote communitarianism by valuing and prioritizing local choices, and by allowing communities to elect representatives that are more relatable, transparent, accessible, and responsive to their particular needs and concerns. Incentivizing the development of cross-communal or -ethnic electoral bases and rewarding popularity across a diverse array of communities would have promoted a localized form of centripetalism, further deemphasizing the exclusionary political role ethnicity has come to play in the country.

Khan's achievements in promoting a stronger local government system, together with his aforementioned successes in social welfare schemes, and his opposition to historical reliance on dynastic and ethnically driven politics in Pakistan, may arguably be contributing to his current rise in popularity. At present he seems to be enjoying the status of a presidential head of government, forcing the opposition to cooperate in a more centripetalist way in order to push back against Khan's politics. If this wave of populism continues, Pakistan may be headed towards a political revolution of sorts, as the political solution the country seems to be presently yearning for is a shift towards the local centripetalist framework that Khan seems to be advocating.

Another perspective for reflection and analysis arises out of the confluence of domestic and international politics. Preliminarily, it appears that Pakistan has become a battleground for competing neoliberal interests: the US bloc, with its historical and vested geopolitical and strategic interests in Pakistan, set against the Chinese bloc, with its economic adventurism in the form of the CPEC and associated development projects. While Khan and his cabinet seemed to lean toward the China and Russia bloc, hoping to secure national economic security on more equitable terms,[40] the Pakistani military – which has historically aligned itself with and enabled US interests in the region – likely would have been displeased with Khan's government resisting the pressure to conform to Western expectations. Although, as discussed in chapter 4, the military holds significant economic interests in CPEC projects, it is nonetheless unwilling to completely alienate US interests – particularly in light of the long-standing patronage it has enjoyed since the Soviet invasion of neighboring Afghanistan. Regardless of whether or not the present regime change was orchestrated by the US, it nonetheless appears that Pakistan's politically influential military establishment has ceased to support a government that was no longer taking its cues from the armed forces.[41] When Khan's government began to develop and follow its own agenda, particularly when such contradicted Western expectations from Pakistan, the country's top brass was seen to, once again, subvert the country's internal democratic political processes.[42] This is telling in light of the Pakistani military's historic domestic role as kingmaker, and it is arguable that the armed forces – noting Khan's growing policy independence – acted to stymie his party's continued political activities. Khan's political narrative of driving Pakistan's sovereignty and integrity through maintaining an independent and self-serving foreign policy challenged Western neoliberal forces,[43] and it is through this lens that Khan discusses Islamophobia; pushes back against allowing drone attacks through its airspace or on its territory;[44] highlights the perils of accepting loans from IMF and other institutions that provide foreign funding;[45] and justifies visiting Russia on the eve of its declaring war to secure crucial energy and wheat deals – despite international pressure to condemn and withdraw from such arrangements. This, inadvertently, has become a simplistic way in which to present and fight against imperialistic influences and pressures that have historically plagued Pakistan.

Even in defeat, Khan's most laudable accomplishment has arguably been his exposure – however unintentional – of the structural weaknesses existing at every level of Pakistan's democratic machinery – be it the limited accountability of elected officials due to their detachment from grass roots support; the skewed civil-military relationship, where the military's involvement and investment in civilian democratic processes has been demonstrated; the country's weak judiciary, unable – or unwilling – to preserve the democratic expression of the polity's political will; or even the pressing need to move towards a local centripetalist framework, as Khan seems to be gearing towards. Should Khan be given another chance at forming his government in Pakistan, he might even be successful in moving the country towards a constructive majoritarian system along Presidential lines, similar to the system presently en vogue in the US. Inadvertently, Khan may pressure parties to change their narratives from ethnic or regional appeals to more nationalistic discourses, simply in order to survive in the new political arena he is creating.

Pakistan has historically had an unpleasant courtship with Presidential systems: historically, Pakistan's military dictators have retained presidential status in order to entrench their own vested interests and powers, retaining the power to unilaterally dissolve parliament[46] and organizing the state's governance architecture in such a way as to ensure a servile, party-less local government contrasted to the military-led federal government.[47] Given Pakistan's constitutional history, replete with instances of 'military presidencies', the only way a presidential system can lead to organic, democratic, and representative change in Pakistan's politics is if such change originates at the grassroots level, coming from the bottom up. To do so would require invigorating the local government system, which ideally should be party based and ordered around smaller federating units collaborating with one another and the central government. The country's 'deep state' or 'establishment' exerts significant influence over domestic politics – often through proxy candidates or by leveraging the country's feudal, landholding elites – undermining local politics, which are so convoluted that an individual often cannot vote for their preferred candidate. A directly elected presidential system – where the electee is directly beholden to the electorate – could, however, significantly curtail this influence, enabling a populist leader to accede sufficient power to effect broader, more impactful change, particularly *vis-à-vis* the country's unelected elites – such as its civilian bureaucracy, military, and feudal landholders. This form of direct representation at the highest echelons of power could also blunt the impact the country's ethnic federal organization presently has upon domestic politics. An empowered head of state, one directly elected and thus enjoying an irrebuttable mandate from the polity, might thus be able to effect change without having to court – and thus compromise with – entrenched elites. To cite a recent, specific example, former premier Imran Khan enjoys the type of grassroots support desired under such a model, though it remains to be seen whether he will be able to leverage this support to effect meaningful change – particularly when he himself has been dogged by rumors of close ties to the entrenched establishment.

Having smaller federating units would work to dilute the inordinate impact ethnicity has on political organization in Pakistan, serving to constrain – if not reverse entirely – the existing consociationalist trend of having the provincial government system essentially tending almost exclusively to the needs of specific ethnic groups represented by their corresponding political parties. Splitting the existing provinces – organized almost exclusively along ethnic lines – into smaller federating units would deemphasize the political traction ethnic identity presently enjoys, ordering them instead around multi-party based elected local governments. This, in turn, would ameliorate interethnic frictions, strengthen public service delivery, engender greater transparency and accountability in government mechanisms, check the elite capture of resources, and foster development opportunities at a grassroots level.

Given the complex geopolitical context that Pakistan provides – with competing notions of neoliberalism vying for fertile ground within – it has become a matter of utmost importance that the country puts its own house in order. Existing at a geostrategic flashpoint and caught between a fraught relationship with the colonial west and the burgeoning might of neighboring China, Pakistan's overreliance on sociocultural divisions as the basis for organizing and conducting its political affairs represents a clear existential threat to the country's continued existence. Desperate times call for desperate measures, and the times have never been other than desperate for Pakistan.

NOTES

1. 'Imran Khan ousted as Pakistan's PM after vote,' *BBC News* (Apr 10, 2022), accessed on April 19, 2022 <https://www.bbc.com/news/world-asia-61055210>.

2. CONST. of PAK. Art. 95.

3. 'PM Imran says 'foreign-funded conspiracy' out to topple his govt, claims to have evidence in writing,' *DAWN News* (Mar 27, 2022), accessed on April 19, 2022 <https://www.dawn.com/news/1682104>.

4. This political defection was challenged by Khan before the Supreme Court of Pakistan through a Presidential Reference seeking the court's interpretation of Article 63-A on parliamentarians' defections and asking the court to impose a lifetime ban on the defecting ministers. While observing that a violation of Article 63-A does not amount to treason, the court stated that if one no longer has allegiance to one's party, it is certainly more 'honorable' to resign one's position and re-contest their election through their desired party's by-elections, than to defect. This approach by the Supreme Court demonstrates the court backtracking from its earlier activist approach taken in relation to the vote of no confidence against Imran Khan; *see* 'Article

63-A: '"Is disloyalty to party not dishonesty?" asks SC judge,' *DAWN News* (Apr 20, 2022), accessed on April 23, 2022 <https://www.dawn.com/news/1685945>.

5. Khan's contentions have since gained validity since this cable that he refers to - essentially a diplomatic cypher narrating details of U.S officials recommending to Pakistani diplomats that removing Khan from office is a prerequisite of future Pak-US cooperation - was leaked by a news agency. Ryan Grim, Murtaza Hussain, "SECRET PAKISTAN CABLE DOCUMENTS U.S. PRESSURE TO REMOVE IMRAN KHAN," *The Intercept* (Aug 09, 2023), accessed on August 12, 2023 <https://theintercept.com/2023/08/09/imran-khan-pakistan-cypher-ukraine-russia/>.

6. 'President Alvi dissolves National Assembly on PM Imran's advice,' *DAWN News* (Apr 3, 2022), accessed on April 19, 2022 <https://www.dawn.com/news/1683230>.

7. 'Imran Khan: Pakistan court rules no-confidence vote block is illegal,' *BBC News* (Apr 8, 2022), accessed on April 19, 2022 <https://www.bbc.com/news/world-asia-60978798>.

8. "Pakistan's ex-PM Imran Khan was shot: What, where and why?," *Al Jazeera* (Nov 3, 2022), accessed on August 12, 2023 <https://www.aljazeera.com/news/2022/11/3/pakistan-ex-pm-imran-khan-was-shot-what-where-and-why>.

9. Ayaz Gul, "Ousted Pakistan PM Khan Sweeps Key By-Election," *Voice of America* (Oct 12, 2022), accessed on August 12, 2022 <https://www.voanews.com/a/ousted-pakistan-pm-khan-sweeps-key-by-election/6793241.html>.

10. Abid Hussain, 'Another Khan party-led provincial assembly dissolved in Pakistan,' *Al Jazeera* (Jan 18, 2023), accessed on August 12, 2023 <https://www.aljazeera.com/news/2023/1/18/another-khan-party-led-provincial-assembly-dissolved-in-pakistan>.

11. Abid Hussain, "Pakistan's Supreme Court orders Punjab election on May 14," *Al Jazeera* (Apr 4, 2023), accessed on August 12, 2023 <https://www.aljazeera.com/news/2023/4/4/pakistan-top-court-says-punjab-election-delay-unconstitutional>.

12. 'US reacts to PM Imran Khan's Russia visit amid Ukraine conflict,' *Geo News* (Feb 24, 2022), accessed on April 23, 2022 https://www.geo.tv/latest/401195-us-reacts-to-pm-khans-visit-to-moscow.

13. 'Why The Russian Invasion of Ukraine Has Galvanized the International Community,' *Geopolitical Monitor* (Mar 1, 2022) <https://www.geopoliticalmonitor.com/why-the-russian-invasion-of-ukraine-has-galvanized-the-international-community/>. ("China and India, two of Russia's closes allies, abstained from a resolution tabled by the US and Albania that condemned the Russian invasion of Ukraine in the UN Security Council. The resolution called for Russia to immediately withdraw its forces from Ukrainian territory and to reverse its recognition of the regions of Donetsk and Lugansk as independent."). *See* 'Pakistan abstains from voting against Russia at UNGA,' *The News* (Mar 3, 2022), accessed on April 25, 2022 https://www.thenews.com.pk/print/938140-pakistan-abstains-from-voting-against-russia-at-unga; 'General Assembly resolution demands end to Russian offensive in Ukraine,' *UN News* (Mar 2, 2022), accessed on April 25, 2022 <https://news.un.org/en/story/2022/03/1113152>.

14. 'Day before Imran's no-trust vote, Pakistan army chief condemns Ukraine war, cosies up to West,' *The Print* (Apr 2, 2022), accessed on April 23, 2022 <https://theprint.in/world/day-before-imrans-no-trust-vote-pakistan-army-chief-condemns-ukraine-war-cosies-up-to-west/899570/>.

15. Shah Meer Baloch, Hannah Ellis-Peterson, "Pakistan internet cut as violence erupts after arrest of ex-PM Imran Khan," *The Guardian* (May 09, 2023), accessed on August 13, 2023 <https://www.theguardian.com/world/2023/may/09/pakistan-former-pm-imran-khan-arrested-in-islamabad>; "Imran terms May 9 mayhem bid to eliminate PTI", *The Express Tribune* (May 20, 2023), accessed August 13, 2023 <https://tribune.com.pk/story/2417736/imran-terms-may-9-mayhem-bid-to-eliminate-pti>.

16. In a recent interview, Pakistan's newly-ousted Information Minister revealed that if ties had not been weakened between Khan's party and the country's military establishment, Khan's government would still be in power. 'PTI would still be in power if ties with establishment weren't fragile: Fawad,' *The Express Tribune* (Apr 21, 2022), accessed on April 23, 2022 <https://tribune.com.pk/story/2353495/pti-would-still-be-in-power-if-ties-with-establishment-werent-fragile-fawad>.

17. *See infra* note 22.

18. *Ibid. See also* 'Imran Khan threatened to impose martial law, documents suggest,' *The Guardian* (Apr 10, 2022), accessed on April 24, 2022 <https://www.theguardian.com/world/2022/apr/10/imran-khan-threatened-to-impose-martial-law-documents-suggests-pakistan-elections-army>.

19. The military in Pakistan has historically relied on the judiciary to legalize coups on a supra-constitutional basis by relying on the doctrine of necessity. *See The State Vs. Dosso & Others* (PLD 1958 SC (PAK.) 533. *See also Begum Nusrat Bhutto vs. Chief of Army Staff and Federation of Pakistan* PLD 1977 SC 657 and Chapter 3 (this volume).

20. 'Pakistan's Imran Khan sentenced to three years in prison, arrested,' *Al Jazeera* (Aug 5, 2023), accessed on August 12, 2023 <https://www.aljazeera.com/news/2023/8/5/pakistan-court-sentences-ex-pm-imran-khan-to-3-years-in-prison-state-tv>;'Jailed ex-premier Imran Khan barred from Pakistan politics for 5 years,' *Reuters* (Aug 8, 2023), accessed on August 12, 2023 <https://www.reuters.com/world/asia-pacific/pakistan-ex-pm-imran-khan-challenges-his-conviction-high-court-lawyer-2023-08-08/>.

21. In Egypt, the military or 'deep state' has historically held power by co-opting the judiciary in order to legitimize authoritarian regimes. For instance, the January 25th revolution against Hosni Mubarak in 2011 was followed by an extended 'interim' rule and consolidation of power by the Supreme Council of the Armed Forces, with loyalist judges cooperating with the military-security apparatus in order to undermine the democratically-elected Morsi government and pave the way for General Sisi to overthrow the country's first democratically elected president; *see generally* Sahar F. Aziz, "(De) liberalizing judicial independence in Egypt." *Egypt and the Contradictions of Liberalism: Liberalism, Intelligentsia, and the Future of Egyptian Democracy* (2017): 17–11. In Iran, with western powers disgruntled by Mohammad Mossadegh's policies regarding Iranian ownership of its natural resources, the military lent support to the Shah of Iran in the coup – orchestrated by

the CIA – overthrowing Mossadegh; *see* 'CIA admits role in 1953 Iranian coup,' *The Guardian* (Aug 19, 2013), accessed on April 23, 2022 <https://www.theguardian.com/world/2013/aug/19/cia-admits-role-1953-iranian-coup>. This subversion of democracy prompted a subsequent populist response in the form of the Islamic revolution and the establishment of the Islamic Revolution Guard Corps (IRGC) to act as a counterbalance to the military, with all appointments to the IRGC now made by the Supreme Leader who is also the Commander in Chief; *see* 'Profile: Iran's Revolutionary Guards,' *BBC News* (Jan 3, 2020), accessed on April 23, 2022 <https://www.bbc.com/news/world-middle-east-47852262>. Lastly, events in Turkey also demonstrate how militaries rely on the judiciary in order to consolidate their own power. In response, having thwarted a coup attempt directed against his regime by calling upon civilian supporters and loyal army personnel, Turkish President Recep Erdogan clamped down on dissent in the country's military and judiciary, arresting over 2,800 soldiers, dismissing 2.700 judges, and issuing arrest warrants for 140 Supreme Court members. *See* 'Erdoğan clamps down after crushing attempted military coup,' *The Guardian* (Jul 16, 2016), accessed on April 23, 2022 <https://www.theguardian.com/world/2016/jul/16/erdogan-reprisals-turkey-attempted-military-coup>. With Khan's removal through a vote of no-confidence, and with support of the country's judiciary, the Pakistani military is now watching the reactions to these events unfold in the polity and is contemplating its next moves.

22. 'Imran Khan asks judiciary to explain why courts opened their doors at midnight prior to his ouster,' *DAWN* (Apr 13, 2022), accessed on April 19, 2022 <https://www.dawn.com/news/1684835>. ("The high court's decision to resume court activity at the unusual hour came after a pre-emptive petition was filed asking the court to restrain Khan from de-notifying Gen Qamar Javed Bajwa as chief of the army staff. The then government had denied having any such plans.").

23. There have also been reports, as early as December 2021, that the Pakistan Bar Council was already meeting with and rallying behind Nawaz Sharif, the leader of the PML-N, a move which seems to have had military support. 'Nawaz Sharif's rumored return to Pakistan sparks another debate,' *Geo News* (Dec 26, 2021), accessed on April 23, 2022 <https://www.geo.tv/latest/389823-nawaz-sharifs-rumored-return-sparks-another-debate>. Against this backdrop, it is unsurprising that even the national bar council, once given the green light by the military, pressured the courts to ensure that the vote of no-confidence proceeds as planned, urging the Chief Justice of Pakistan to take note of the matter as well; *see* 'No-trust motion: Pakistan Bar Council warns of negative impact of ongoing political rift,' *Geo News* (Apr 2, 2022), accessed on April 23, 2022 <https://www.geo.tv/latest/409010-pakistan-bar-council-warns-of-negative-impact-of-ongoing-political-rift

24. Furthermore, the Islamabad High Court has also directed the ECP to conclude the foreign funding case against Imran Khan's Pakistan Tehreek-e-Insaf within 30 days, a move that the PTI terms as political victimization, effectively disqualifying them from participating in upcoming elections. The case against the PTI has been pending before the court since November 2014, and was filed by one of PTI's founding members Akbar S. Babar who has alleged financial irregularities in funds received by the party. The PTI has challenged the Islamabad High Court's

single-bench decision directing the ECP to issue a ruling in 30 days. 'PTI challenges 30-day deadline in foreign funding case,' *DAWN* News (Apr 21, 2022), accessed on April 23, 2022 <https://www.dawn.com/news/1686064>.

25. 'In a veiled attack, Imran Khan blames Pak Army chief Bajwa for his ouster,' *Business Standard* (Apr 21, 2022), accessed on April 23, 2022 <https://www.business-standard.com/article/international/in-a-veiled-attack-imran-khan-blames-pak-army-chief-bajwa-for-his-ouster-122042100603_1.html>. *See also* 'Imran Khan warns those who ousted him to rectify their "mistake" by holding early elections,' *The Indian Express* (Apr 22, 2022), accessed on April 23, 2022 <https://indianexpress.com/article/pakistan/imran-khan-warns-those-who-ousted-him-to-rectify-their-mistake-by-holding-early-elections-7881542/>.

26. 'Sugar mafia hurled threats when probe began: PM,' *The News* (Jun 9, 2021), accessed on April 23, 2022 <https://www.thenews.com.pk/print/846573-sugar-mafia-hurled-threats-when-probe-began>.

27. *See*, for example, the Mutahida Qaumi Movement (MQM), which was established to represent the Mohajir ethnic community (i.e. Muslim emigrants from undivided British India to territories within Pakistan following the latter's independence), with its political base largely consolidated in the city of Karachi; the Pakistan Peoples Party (PPP), a party with an ostensibly socialist mandate, deriving its main political strength from Sindhi constituencies; the Pakistan Muslim League – Noon (PML-N), which principally draws its political strength and representation from the province of Punjab; or the Awami National Party (ANP), which is predominately based in the province of Khyber Pakhtunkhwa. None of these regional/ethnic parties have ever formed a majoritarian government on their own, and have in fact relied on negotiating coalitions with one another in order to form governments at the center. These parties also each have had their own fallings-out with the military establishment, even though a number of them have now opportunistically banded together as the PDM in order to regain control at the center, even if such comes at the cost of a mutually compromising power-sharing arrangement.

28. 'Ehsaas becomes a global model for reducing poverty,' *The News* (Dec 11, 2020), accessed on April 24, 2022 <https://www.thenews.com.pk/print/756755-ehsaas-becomes-a-global-model-for-reducing-poverty>.

29. 'Sehat Sahulat programme: A bonanza for private hospitals,' *The News* (Jul 14, 2021), accessed on April 24, 2022 <https://www.thenews.com.pk/print/863888-sehat-sahulat-programme-a-bonanza-for-private-hospitals>.

30. 'PM Imran Khan launches Naya Pakistan Housing Program,' *The News* (Oct 10, 2018), accessed on April 24, 2022 <https://www.thenews.com.pk/latest/379236-pm-inaugurate-naya-pakistan-housing-scheme>.

31. 'PM Imran praises NCOC after Pakistan ranked among top countries for handling Covid-19,' *DAWN News* (Jul 7, 2021), accessed on April 24, 2022 <https://www.dawn.com/news/1633713>.

32. 'Smart lockdowns ensured protection of downtrodden people: PM Imran,' *DAWN News* (Feb 12, 2022), accessed on April 12, 2022 <https://www.dawn.com/news/1674612>.

33. Essentially, local centripetalism champions a system of a strong federal government at the center, where all the federating units cooperate with one other over national issues, and where the enforcement and implementation of policy responses to these issues is executed through local governments. This leads to a system where pluralistic societies, such as Pakistan's, can accommodate ethnic diversity without experiencing inter-ethnic conflict. This is why the NCOC's response to COVID-19 management is a prime example of local centripetalist federalism in action in Pakistan.

34. The impact of three decades of rule in Pakistan by the two major ruling dynastic parties, the PML-N and PPP, mirrors Lijphart's consociationalist terminology, the "cartel of elites," where the continuous consolidation of power in a select group results in the further disenfranchisement of and discord between ethnic minorities, thereby undermining their autonomy. *See generally* Arend Lijphart. "Consociation Democracy," 2 *World Politics* 207 (1969); *see also* 'Pakistan dynasties unite against triumphant Imran Khan,' *Financial Times* (Aug 12, 2018), accessed on April 24, 2022 <https://www.ft.com/content/b3b159fa-9c92-11e8-9702-5946bae86e6d>.

35. Rohit, "Pakistan's Ruling Coalition Faces Split amid Row over Interim PM Candidate," *News18*, July 24, 2023, accessed January 22, 2024, https://www.news18.com/world/pakistans-ruling-coalition-faces-split-amid-row-over-interim-pm-candidate-8409715.html.

36. Naad-e-Ali Sulehria, "Pakistan's Interim Government: A Challenging Road Ahead," *Middle East Institute*, August 29, 2023, accessed January 22, 2024, https://www.mei.edu/publications/pakistans-interim-government-challenging-road-ahead.

37. 'PM Imran Khan decides in favour of direct party-based LG elections in Punjab,' *The News* (Nov 4, 2021), accessed on April 19, 2022 <https://www.thenews.com.pk/print/905833-ik-decides-in-favour-of-direct-party-based-lg-elections-in-punjab>.

38. 'Prime Minister Imran gives roadmap for local govt elections in Punjab,' *DAWN News* (May 6, 2019), accessed on April 23, 2022 <https://www.dawn.com/news/1480648>.

39. *Ibid.*

40. Khan's visit to Russia was to secure an important Gas Pipeline deal for Pakistan (see discussion below). Fahd Humayun. 'Why was Pakistan's PM in Russia amid the Ukraine invasion?,' *Al Jazeera* (Mar 3, 2022), accessed on April 24, 2022 <https://www.aljazeera.com/opinions/2022/3/3/why-was-pakistans-pm-in-russia-amid-ukraine-invasion>.

41. 'Imran Khan: What led to charismatic Pakistan PM's downfall,' *BBC News* (Apr 9, 2022), accessed on April 19, 2022 <https://www.bbc.com/news/world-asia-61047736>.

42. In a press conference conducted days after the successful vote of no confidence, the Director General Inter-Services Public Relations – the Pakistani army's "media wing," while claiming that the establishment is an "apolitical" institution, admitted that it was invited to play the role of a "mediator" following a deadlock between the political parties. This statement seems in itself to demonstrate that the army considers itself an – if not 'the' – authority on political matters, to the extent that it is admittedly willing to play the role of a political intercessor; 'COAS is neither seeking extension of tenure nor will he accept one, says DG ISPR,' *The News* (Apr

14, 2022), accessed on April 23, 2022 https://www.thenews.com.pk/latest/950237-dg-ispr-addresses-press-conference>.

In addition to this, COAS Gen. Bajwa, attended an iftar dinner hosted by a major textile and real estate tycoon, weeks after the successful vote of no confidence against Khan. This dinner was also attended by 20 other major business houses in Lahore. During this meeting Bajwa candidly discussed economic affairs, deeming economic salvation as being fundamentally linked to national security. As mentioned in Chapter 4, the army is so deeply economically invested in Pakistan that its own survival depends upon steering the direction of the country towards economic stability. The biggest problem with this, however, is that the institution of the army is not democratically elected, and thus has no legitimacy or mandate to drive state economic policy, or strategy, *see* 'Army draws strength from people: COAS,' *The News* (Apr 18, 2022), accessed on April 23, 2022 https://www.thenews.com.pk/print/951107-army-draws-strength-from-people-coas>.

43. This is perhaps why Khan found it easier to deal with the Trump administration in the US: although their reasons differed, both governments wanted an inward-looking foreign policy, with Trump pushing for less global involvement – a move welcomed by Khan as, for Pakistan, this translated into less pressure to "do more" in support of US vested interests, allowing Pakistan to focus instead on its own sovereign interests.

44. 'Why Pakistan's Imran Khan said no to American drones,' *TRT World* (Jun 16, 2021), accessed on April 24, 2022 <https://www.trtworld.com/magazine/why-pakistan-s-imran-khan-said-no-to-american-drones-47581>.

It can also be argued that as a result of this strong stance on the war in Afghanistan, and of disallowing the US from maintaining air bases on Pakistani soil, Pakistan was punished by its inclusion on the Paris-based Financial Action Task Force's (FATF) grey list.

45. 'Foreign loans imperil national security: PM Imran Khan,' *The News International* (Jan 15, 2022), accessed on April 24, 2022 <https://www.thenews.com.pk/print/925231-foreign-loans-put-national-security-at-risk-pm>.

This points to the discussion in preceding chapters on David Harvey's exposition of western neoliberalism as a hegemonic discourse that destroys institutional frameworks and perpetuates global inequality. Harvey specifically posits that: ("the rules of engagement now established through the WTO (governing international trade) and by the IMF (governing international finance) instantiate neoliberalism as a global set of rules. All states that sign on to the WTO and IMF . . . agree to abide . . . by these rules or face severe penalties".); *see* David Harvey. "Neo-liberalism as creative destruction." *Geografiska Annaler: Series B, Human Geography* 88.2 (2006): 145–158, p.146.

46. 18th Amendment to the 1973 Constitution barred presidents from being able to dissolve parliaments and impose emergency rule on his own.

47. *See* for example Gen. Ayub Khan's system of Basic Democracies, where the local government heads, called "Basic Democrats" were all answerable to the president, and were at once asked to endorse and legitimize Khan's presidency. Kunal

Mukherjee. "Ayub Khan's basic democracy and political continuity in contemporary Pakistan." *India Quarterly* 72.3 (2016): 268–277.

BIBLIOGRAPHY

"Army draws strength from people: COAS." *The News,* April 18, 2022. https://www.thenews.com.pk/print/951107-army-draws-strength-from-people-coas.

Aziz, Sahar F. "(De) liberalizing judicial independence in Egypt." *Egypt and the Contradictions of Liberalism: Liberalism, Intelligentsia, and the Future of Egyptian Democracy* (2017): 17–11.

Baloch, Shah Meer and Hannah Ellis-Peterson. "Pakistan internet cut as violence erupts after arrest of ex-PM Imran Khan." *The Guardian,* May 09. https://www.theguardian.com/world/2023/may/09/pakistan-former-pm-imran-khan-arrested-in-islamabad.

Begum Nusrat Bhutto v Chief of Army Staff PLD [1977] SC 657.

"CIA admits role in 1953 Iranian coup." *The Guardian,* August 19, 2013. https://www.theguardian.com/world/2013/aug/19/cia-admits-role-1953-iranian-coup>.

"COAS is neither seeking extension of tenure nor will he accept one, says DG ISPR." *The News,* April 14, 2022. https://www.thenews.com.pk/latest/950237-dg-ispr-addresses-press-conference.

CONST. of PAK. Art. 95.

"Day before Imran's no-trust vote, Pakistan army chief condemns Ukraine war, cosies up to West." *The Print,* April 2, 2022. https://theprint.in/world/day-before-imrans-no-trust-vote-pakistan-army-chief-condemns-ukraine-war-cosies-up-to-west/899570/.

"Ehsaas becomes a global model for reducing poverty." *The News International,* December 11, 2020. https://www.thenews.com.pk/print/756755-ehsaas-becomes-a-global-model-for-reducing-poverty.

"Erdoğan clamps down after crushing attempted military coup." *The Guardian,* July 16, 2016. https://www.theguardian.com/world/2016/jul/16/erdogan-reprisals-turkey-attempted-military-coup.

"Foreign loans imperil national security: PM Imran Khan." *The News International,* January 15, 2022. https://www.thenews.com.pk/print/925231-foreign-loans-put-national-security-at-risk-pm.

"General Assembly resolution demands end to Russian offensive in Ukraine." *UN News*, March 2, 2022. https://news.un.org/en/story/2022/03/1113152.

Grim, Ryan and Murtaza Hussain. "SECRET PAKISTAN CABLE DOCUMENTS U.S. PRESSURE TO REMOVE IMRAN KHAN." *The Intercept*, August 9, 2023. https://theintercept.com/2023/08/09/imran-khan-pakistan-cypher-ukraine-russia/.

Gul, Ayaz. "Ousted Pakistan PM Khan Sweeps Key By-Election." *Voice of America*, October 12, 2022. https://www.voanews.com/a/ousted-pakistan-pm-khan-sweeps-key-by-election/6793241.html.

Harvey, David. "Neo-liberalism as creative destruction." *Geografiska Annaler: Series B, Human Geography* 88, no. 2 (2006): 145–158.

Humayun, Fahd. "Why was Pakistan's PM in Russia amid the US invasion?." *Al Jazeera* March 3, 2022. https://www.aljazeera.com/opinions/2022/3/3/why-was-pakistans-pm-in-russia-amid-ukraine-invasion.

Hussain, Abid. "Another Khan party-led provincial assembly dissolved in Pakistan." *Al Jazeera,* January 18, 2023. https://www.aljazeera.com/news/2023/1/18/another-khan-party-led-provincial-assembly-dissolved-in-pakistan.

Hussain, Abid. "Pakistan's Supreme Court orders Punjab election on May 14." *Al Jazeera*, April 4, 2023. https://www.aljazeera.com/news/2023/4/4/pakistan-top-court-says-punjab-election-delay-unconstitutional.

"Imran Khan asks judiciary to explain why courts opened their doors at midnight prior to his ouster." *DAWN,* April 13, 2022. https://www.dawn.com/news/1684835.

"Imran Khan ousted as Pakistan's PM after vote." *BBC News*, April 10, 2022. https://www.bbc.com/news/world-asia-61055210.

"Imran Khan threatened to impose martial law, documents suggest." *The Guardian*, April 10, 2022. https://www.theguardian.com/world/2022/apr/10/imran-khan-threatened-to-impose-martial-law-documents-suggests-pakistan-elections-army.

"Imran Khan warns those who ousted him to rectify their 'mistake' by holding early elections." *The Indian Express,* April 22, 2022. https://indianexpress.com/article/pakistan/imran-khan-warns-those-who-ousted-him-to-rectify-their-mistake-by-holding-early-elections-7881542/.

"Imran Khan: Pakistan court rules no-confidence vote block is illegal." *BBC News,* April 8, 2022. https://www.bbc.com/news/world-asia-60978798.

"Imran Khan: What led to charismatic Pakistan PM's downfall." *BBC News*, April 9, 2022. https://www.bbc.com/news/world-asia-61047736.

"Imran terms May 9 mayhem bid to eliminate PTI." *The Express Tribune*, May 20, 2023. https://tribune.com.pk/story/2417736/imran-terms-may-9-mayhem-bid-to-eliminate-pti.

"In a veiled attack, Imran Khan blames Pak Army chief Bajwa for his ouster." *Business Standard,* April 21, 2022. https://www.business-standard.com/article/international/in-a-veiled-attack-imran-khan-blames-pak-army-chief-bajwa-for-his-ouster-122042100603_1.html.

"Is disloyalty to party not dishonesty? asks SC judge." *DAWN,* April 20, 2022. https://www.dawn.com/news/1685945.

"Jailed ex-premier Imran Khan barred from Pakistan politics for 5 years." Reuters, August 8, 2023. https://www.reuters.com/world/asia-pacific/pakistan-ex-pm-imran-khan-challenges-his-conviction-high-court-lawyer-2023-08-08/.

Lijphart, Arend."Consociational democracy." *World politics* 21, no. 2 (1969): 207–225.

Mukherjee, Kunal. "Ayub Khan's basic democracy and political continuity in contemporary Pakistan." *India Quarterly* 72, no. 3 (2016): 268–277.

"Nawaz Sharif's rumored return to Pakistan sparks another debate." *Geo News,* December 26, 2021. https://www.geo.tv/latest/389823-nawaz-sharifs-rumored-return-sparks-another-debate.

"No-trust motion: Pakistan Bar Council warns of negative impact of ongoing political rift." *Geo News,* April 2, 2022. https://www.geo.tv/latest/409010-pakistan-bar-council-warns-of-negative-impact-of-ongoing-political-rift.

"Pakistan abstains from voting against Russia at UNGA,' *The News* (Mar 3, 2022), accessed on April 25, 2022 https://www.thenews.com.pk/print/938140-pakistan-abstains-from-voting-against-russia-at-unga.

"Pakistan dynasties unite against triumphant Imran Khan." *Financial Times*, August 12, 2018. https://www.ft.com/content/b3b159fa-9c92-11e8-9702-5946bae86e6d.

"Pakistan's ex-PM Imran Khan was shot: What, where and why?." Al Jazeera, November 3, 2022. https://www.aljazeera.com/news/2022/11/3/pakistan-ex-pm-imran-khan-was-shot-what-where-and-why.

"Pakistan's Imran Khan sentenced to three years in prison, arrested." *Al Jazeera,* August 5, 2023. https://www.aljazeera.com/news/2023/8/5/pakistan-court-sentences-ex-pm-imran-khan-to-3-years-in-prison-state-tv.

"PM Imran Khan decides in favour of direct party-based LG elections in Punjab." *The News International,* November 4, 2021. https://www.thenews.com.pk/print/905833-ik-decides-in-favour-of-direct-party-based-lg-elections-in-punjab.

"PM Imran Khan launches Naya Pakistan Housing Program." *The News,* October 10, 2018. https://www.thenews.com.pk/latest/379236-pm-inaugurate-naya-pakistan-housing-scheme.

"PM Imran praises NCOC after Pakistan ranked among top countries for handling Covid-19." *DAWN,* July 7, 2021. https://www.dawn.com/news/1633713.

"PM Imran says 'foreign-funded conspiracy' out to topple his govt, claims to have evidence in writing." *DAWN,* March 27, 2022, https://www.dawn.com/news/1682104.

"President Alvi dissolves National Assembly on PM Imran's advice." *DAWN,* April 3, 2022. https://www.dawn.com/news/1683230.

"Prime Minister Imran gives roadmap for local govt elections in Punjab." *DAWN,* May 6, 2019. https://www.dawn.com/news/1480648.

"Profile: Iran's Revolutionary Guards." *BBC News*, January 3, 2020. https://www.bbc.com/news/world-middle-east-47852262.

"PTI challenges 30-day deadline in foreign funding case." *DAWN*, April 21, 2022. https://www.dawn.com/news/1686064.

"PTI would still be in power if ties with establishment weren't fragile: Fawad." *The Express Tribune*, April 21, 2022. https://tribune.com.pk/story/2353495/pti-would-still-be-in-power-if-ties-with-establishment-werent-fragile-fawad.

Rohit. "Pakistan's Ruling Coalition Faces Split amid Row over Interim PM Candidate." *News18*, July 24, 2023. Accessed January 22, 2024. https://www.news18.com/world/pakistans-ruling-coalition-faces-split-amid-row-over-interim-pm-candidate-8409715.html.

"Sehat Sahulat programme: a bonanza for private hospitals,' *The News International,* July 14, 2021. https://www.thenews.com.pk/print/863888-sehat-sahulat-programme-a-bonanza-for-private-hospitals.

"Smart lockdowns ensured protection of downtrodden people: PM Imran." *DAWN,* February 12, 2022. https://www.dawn.com/news/1674612.

State v Dosso PLD [1958] SC 533.

"Sugar mafia hurled threats when probe began: PM." *The News International*, June 9, 2021. https://www.thenews.com.pk/print/846573-sugar-mafia-hurled-threats-when-probe-began. *State v Dosso* PLD [1958] SC 533.

Sulehria, Naad-e-Ali. "Pakistan's Interim Government: A Challenging Road Ahead." *Middle East Institute*, August 29, 2023. Accessed January 22, 2024. https://www.mei.edu/publications/pakistans-interim-government-challenging-road-ahead.

"US reacts to PM Imran Khan's Russia visit amid Ukraine conflict." *Geo News*, February 24, 2022. https://www.geo.tv/latest/401195-us-reacts-to-pm-khans-visit-to-moscow.

"Why Pakistan's Imran Khan said no to American drones." *TRT World*, June 16, 2021. https://www.trtworld.com/magazine/why-pakistan-s-imran-khan-said-no-to-american-drones-47581.

"Why The Russian Invasion of Ukraine Has Galvanized the International Community." *Geopolitical Monitor*, March 1, 2022. https://www.geopoliticalmonitor.com/why-the-russian-invasion-of-ukraine-has-galvanized-the-international-community/.

Index

absolutism, 43
Acemoglu and Robinson, 162, 176, 179
Adeney, Katherine, 110
Afghanistan, 41, 60n84, 121n43, 159, 171, 181, 186, 190, 209, 268, 283n153, 310, 318n44
Ahmadi, 16n20, 42, 46, 47, 79, 86, 112, 188, 193, 210n178
Akhtar, Aasim Sajjad, 255–256, 261
Alam, Ahmad Rafay, 255
Algeria, 245, 280n130
Albo, Gregory, 228, 231, 272n23
Argentina, 167, 177, 275n70
Arusha Agreement, 80, 123n59
Asian Infrastructure Investment Bank (AIIB), 243
assimilation, 25, 29, 34, 41, 111, 235
atomization, 27, 29, 34, 40, 118
Azad Jammu and Kashmir, 9, 49, 61n99, 171, 171, 253, 257

Bagenstos, Samuel, 28
Bajwa, Qamar Javed, 7, 10, 216n246–247, 315n22, 318
Balochistan, 16n19, 44, 48, 86, 98, 100, 102, 143n285, 143n290, 216n242, 252, 256–258, 264, 284n161, 286n190, 290n229
Bangladesh, 1, 16, 89, 94, 105, 198, 110, 180, 188, 236, 275n74
Banai, Hussain, 50
Basit, Abdul, 260
Beijing Consensus, 243
Bekker, Simon, 56n31
Bentham, Jeremy, 25
bhasha andolon, 236. *See also* Bengal
Bosnia and Herzegovina, 80, 87, 122n58, 127n115
Britain, 28, 36, 37, 228, 260–261, 271n12, 288n208; Brexit, 80; British Raj, 3, 115, 145n145, 176
Brown, Wendy, 232
Bruneau, Thomas, 164
Burke, Edmund, 37
Burundi, 80, 87, 123n59

Cabinet, 17n31, 41, 121n47, 122n54, 301, 306–310
capitalism, 233, 234, 273n40–41, 277n105; Chinese, 276n87, 234, 241, 277n90
Canada, 29, 228; Quebec, 29, 53, 55n27
Christian, 36, 43, 47, 1212n47, 122n50, 126n103, 188; Catholicism, 43
Cheema, Moeen, 34
chief: of army, 5, 7, 10, 17n25, 44, 104, 183, 184, 185, 186, 209n166,

213n203, 303, 304, 315n21–23; minister, 100, 188, 286, 309; justice, 185, 208n154, 215, 315n23
Chile, 167
China-Pakistan Economic Corridor (CPEC), 3, 46, 47, 48–49, 73, 94–96, 102, 118, 130n156, 196, 200, 206n124, 251, 263, 310; Authority, 46, 49, 62n103, 137n224, 138nn229–232, 289n214, 290n229; Belt and Road Initiative (BRI), 2, 48, 216nn246–247, 243, 250–251, 257, 259; local communities 232, 240, 241, 247, 252, 254, 258, 262; One Belt One Road, OBOR, 243, 278n108; projects, 93, 104, 110, 116, 159, 160, 178, 181, 192, 199, 255, 258, 259, 261, 262, 264–270, 286n187, 289n220; Special Economic Zones, (SEZ) 49, 103, 248, 252, 253, 256
Chinese economic expansionism, 13, 15, 48, 227–243, 246, 248, 250, 268. *See also* neo-colonialism. *See also* Comprehensive Strategic Partnerships (CSPs)
Chomsky, Noam, 90, 128n131, 228, 230, 238, 270n5
Choudhry, Sujit, 78
civilian leaders: Bhutto, Benazir, 185, 186; Bhutto, Zulfiqar Ali, 17n31, 46, 101, 147n310, 184, 188, 206n123, 207n148, 282n145; Khan, Imran, 8, 9, 10, 11, 12, 41, 214n233, 253, 300–312, 312n4, 314n16, 315n22; 315n24; Sharif, Nawaz, 8, 17n31, 185, 250, 282n150, 302, 315n2; Zardari, Asif Ali, 185, 190
colonialism, 31, 36–37, 50, 230, 244–245
Cold War, 163, 168, 172, 207n150
collectivism, 24, 35
communalism, 23, 42, 72, 75, 89, 93, 119n18
communitarianism, 13, 14, 30–32, 37, 51, 54, 89, 119n18, 234, 309
conflict, 31, 53, 116, 127n115, 130n150, 141, 175, 229, 273n40; armed, 41, 43, 72, 74, 89, 125n94, 157, 162, 163, 167, 168, 184, 188, 195, 206n123, 239, 248, 261, 268, 275n75; ethnic, 13, 14, 23, 25, 34, 38, 43, 47, 54, 74, 78–82, 86, 88, 97, 100, 124nn81–86, 159, 179, 180, 236, 317n33; internecine, 8, 14, 28, 29, 74, 91, 101, 105, 107
Comprehensive Strategic Partnerships (CSPs), 245
conservatism, 160, 175
consociationalism, 3, 23, 32, 52, 54, 76–81, 89, 110, 111, 116, 121n47, 125nn94–95, 128n128, 190, 306, 307; ethnic, 35, 36, 39, 79, 130n148, 142n276; for Pakistan, 85–89; federal. *See* federalism
Constituent Assembly of Pakistan, 4, 5, 16n21, 33, 95, 122n58
Constitution of Pakistan, 2, 5, 43, 58n68, 64n126, 132n168, 159, 184, 209n167, 215n239; amendment procedure, 137n228; 2nd amendment to, 46; 4th amendment to, 147n310; 5th amendment to, 147n310; 17th amendment, 134nn188–189, 185; 18th amendment to, 39, 45, 52, 53, 63n124, 64n126, 134n190, 137n224, 144n295, 258, 267; 21st amendment to, 187; 25th amendment to, 132n171; rules and safeguards, 117, 302, 305
constitutionalism, 117, 305
cosmopolitanism, 24, 31, 54, 56n36, 272n35
Council of Common Interests, 137n224, 259, 286n189, 287n202, 137n224
Council of Islamic Ideology (CII), 104
COVID-19, 9, 113, 307, 317n33
Cyprus, 87, 127n115

Dar, Ishaq, 308
David, Pion-Berlin, 166
debt-trap diplomacy, 244
deep state, 171, 311, 314n21
Denord, Francois, 228
Descartes, Rene, 71
Desch, Michael, 163
devolution, 8, 9, 39, 52, 53–54, 64n126, 87, 92, 99, 100, 101, 107–111, 115, 123n60, 124n86, 136, 189, 191, 241, 258
discrimination/marginalization, 57; institutional, 28, 40, 42, 83, 93, 99, 109, 232, 266; cultural, 2, 14, 36, 38, 40, 52, 54, 103, 112, 180, 187, 244, 252, 258, 290n229
Dixit, 171
doctrine of necessity, 4, 183, 185, 208n162

East India Company, 105, 181, 288n207
Easton, David, 158
Ecuador, 246, 280n129
ecumenicism, 5, 28, 42, 43, 51, 111
egalitarianism, 25, 81
Egypt, 169–172, 245, 266, 304, 314n21; Nasserism, 169
Election Commission of Pakistan (ECP), 98, 302, 304, 305
Environmental Impact Assessment (EIA), 255, 267
ethnicity, 3, 13, 14, 30, 36, 42, 46, 61n99, 81, 91, 104, 112, 113, 127, 186, 198, 309, 312; Balochi, 24, 42, 44, 60n84, 98, 121, 193; Bengali, 4, 5, 6, 16n20, 61n100, 95, 143n6, 169, 177, 178, 180, 183, 193, 236. *See also* bhasha andolon; Hazara, 60n84, 86, 98, 121, 143; Mohajir, 44, 98, 182, 316n27; Pashtun, 3, 24, 44, 98, 102, 116, 143, 181, 182, 188, 192, 193, 210n173; Punjabi, 3, 4, 7, 24, 35, 39, 44, 78, 86, 97, 98, 101–103, 110–116, 180, 181, 188, 236, 247, 252, 258–259, 283n158, 309; Sindhi, 24, 44, 182, 316n27;
Europe, 28, 37, 43, 78, 167, 168, 172, 246
extrajudicial systems: panchayat, 9, 18n37, 39, 60n81, 113, 115, 138, 145n300, 146, 189, 210n182; jirga, 9, 39, 60n81, 113, 115, 128n129, 146n301
extremism, 102, 159, 186, 192, 196, 239, 250, 269, 276n79

factionalism, 11, 23, 53
federalism, 6, 8, 15, 31, 46, 71–156, 146n305, 159, 191, 195, 200, 248, 251, 252, 263–264, 287n202; centripetalist, 5, 14, 23, 24, 51, 81–85, 113, 116, 127n121, 267, 317; consociational, 8, 23, 76–81, 85; devolutionary, 98–101, 107, 112, 130n148, 141n266, 309; ethnic, 2, 3, 7, 12, 33–37, 52, 71–74, 86, 94–98, 100, 119n8, 124n86, 135n192, 159, 179, 180, 236, 259, 317n33
Federally Administered Tribal Areas (FATA), 100, 132n171, 264
federation, 6, 15, 24, 29, 77, 89, 109, 113, 117, 118, 132n170, 132n174, 132n190, 157, 159, 305; hegemony in, 44, 72, 74, 78, 81, 91, 96, 99, 100, 218; federating unit, 5, 24, 31, 35, 39–40, 52, 71, 72, 76, 81, 93, 95, 106, 107, 111, 137n224, 195, 206n121, 309, 312, 317n33; federal center, 5, 11, 24, 51
Feaver, Peter, 160–164, 177, 179
Feely and Rubin, 92
Finer, Herman, 26
Finer, Samuel, 176
First-Past-The-Post (FPTP), 97, 106, 113, 114, 134, 139n250
foreign direct investment, 242–243, 262, 277n90
France, 28, 167

fundamentalism, 2, 102, 188, 192, 233, 306

Gardezi, Hassan, 249
Germany, 167, 175, 289n217
Gilgit-Baltistan, 48, 49, 95, 104, 215, 253, 257, 258, 285n179, 286n186, 290n229
Ghana, 31, 56n36, 247
Ghosh, Ambar Kumar, 110
Global South, 56, 85, 166, 229, 232, 233, 234, 273n43
Gramsci, Antonio, 47; hegemony, 7, 39, 41, 44, 48, 88, 96, 111–114, 193, 235, 243, 244–245, 261, 263, 268
grassroots democracy, 5, 7, 13, 23–6, 34, 39, 45–49, 189, 247
Greece, 251
Green Revolution, 62n110
Grere, Frederick, 186
Guhavarthy, Ajay, 109
Gwadar, 48, 206nn123–124, 213n208, 245, 252, 254–255, 256, 257, 260

Hall, Stuart, 56n36
Haqqani, Hussain, 173
Harvey, David, 90, 230, 240, 318n45
Hayek, Frederick A., 229, 270n6, 129n136
Higher Education Commission, 264
Hindu, 3–5, 36, 42, 47, 51, 104, 107, 109, 110, 173, 188
historical asymmetry, 1, 45
Hobbes, Thomas, 71, 265
Horowitz, Donald, 76, 80, 82, 85–87, 112, 124nn76–77, 124n81, 124n86, 128n124, 216n244
Hume, David, 37
Huntington, Samuel P., 160–167, 173–177, 183, 194
Hussain, Ejaz, 181, 205n106

identitarianism, 54
Iftikhar Chaudry, 185
immobilism, 82
imperialism, 15, 36, 37 169, 227, 249, 273n44
India, 30, 94, 105, 105–111, 140n259, 142n272, 159, 169, 237, 238, 303; communalism in, 29, 33, 37, 42, 75, 105, 142n276, 143n290, 145n299; minority rights in, 42, 109, 181, 198; and Pak-relations, 170, 171, 173, 175, 177, 184, 190, 198, 207n150, 245, 280n122, 286n186, 316n27; subcontinent of, 4, 5, 37, 181, 182, 261, 288n208; Supreme Court. *See* Supreme Court; 73rd constitutional amendment, 145n299
individualism, 24, 37, 53, 71
Indonesia, 80
International Monetary Fund (IMF), 48, 101, 131n160, 191, 229, 236, 249, 282n145, 283n154, 288n207
interventionism, 8, 306
Iran, 37, 50, 170–172, 268, 304, 315n21; Iran Revolutionary Guard Corps (IRGC), 42, 170, 315n21
Inter-Services Public Relations, (ISPR), 179, 193
Iraq, 79, 80, 89, 127n115, 164, 166; 2005 Constitution, 80
Islam, 2, 5, 8, 17n24, 18n32, 29, 53, 79, 102, 150, 166, 171, 173, 175, 208; Islamic norms of social justice, 33, 51, 60n91, 95, 104, 134nn187–88, 170, 192; Islamic jurisprudence, 42, 43, 184; Islamist groups, 173, 175, 180, 283n153, 315; Islamization, 2, 33, 34, 94, 170, 173, 185, 208n161, 94, 170, 173, 185, 208, 250
Israel, 105, 170, 177
Ivison, Duncan, 36

Janowitz, 160, 162, 178, 179
Jinnah, Muhammad Ali, 4, 33
Joseph, Sarah, 238
judiciary in Pakistan: branches of government, 3, 12, 31, 117, 303; independence of, 2, 11, 12, 117,

216n242; judicial systems, 163, 181, 182, 184, 185, 186, 193, 194, 195, 196, 204n105, 208nn163–167, 215n235, 303; oversight, 2, 15n4, 46, 82, 107, 109, 112, 117, 124n77, 231, 147n309, 162

Kakar, Anwaar ul Haq, 308
Kant, Immanuel, 71
Karakoram Highway, 255
Kashghar, 254–255
Kaufman, Stuart, 76
Kayani, Ashfaq Pervez, 186
Kenya, 80, 244, 247, 266, 278n112, 279n115, 281n134, 282; Mambosa port, 244
Keskin, Tugrul, 230
Keynesianism, 129n138, 231
Khan, Danish, 8, 93
Khan, Liaquat Ali, 16n20, 183
Khyber Pakhtunkhwa, 1, 24, 48, 180, 183, 252, 253, 264
Kukreja, Veena, 171
Kymlicka, Will, 28, 32, 57n49, 78, 79, 234, 235, 274n53; cultural marketplace, 234, 235; legitimation crisis, 235; voluntary immigration, 41

Latin America, 166, 168, 233, 238, 273n44, 275n70
Lebanon, 79, 80, 89, 123n61
legislative interventions: Actions (in Aid of Civil Power) Regulations, 2011 (AACPR), 197; Elected Bodies Disqualification Order 1958 (EBDO), 189; Elections Act of 2017, 116; Government of India Act 1909, 106; Government of India Act 1935, 106; Land Acquisition Act, 1894, 253; Mutual Defence Assistance Agreement 1954, 171; Official Secrets Act, 1923, 45; Official Secrets (Amendment) Bill, 2023, 45; Pakistan Army (Amendment) Act 2023, 45; Pakistan Army Act, 1952, 253; Protection of Pakistan Act, 2014 (PPA), 197; Public Offices (Disqualification) Order 1959, 189; Special Economic Zones (Amendment) Act, 2016; Special Economic Zones Rules (2013), 253
legislature: National Assembly, 45, 96, 121n47, 145, 267, 302, 304; Provincial Assembly, 137n228, 144n295; Rajya Sabha, 106, 140n253; Senate, 40, 41, 45, 52, 88, 94, 95, 96, 106, 112, 114, 145, 187, 259, 267
Levitsky, Steven, 34
liberalism, 36, 37, 42, 50–51, 160; political, 71; Orthodox, 228; Pakistani, 33. *See also* Locke, John
Linz, Juan, 195
local democracy, 23, 43, 92, 130n148, 189, 193
local government, 8–10, 13, 26, 27, 31, 34, 39, 44, 45, 54, 64, 93, 99, 100, 108, 109, 112, 115, 135n201, 189, 193, 231, 253–254, 266, 270, 307, 309, 311, 312, 317
Locke, John, 71; laissez-faire, 90. *See also* liberalism
Lijphart, Arend, 76, 85, 86, 126n104, 317n34

madrassahs, 250, 251
majoritarianism, 94, 109, 110, 118, 127n120, 133n181, 142n276, 144n293, 234, 309, 311, 316
Malaysia, 30, 32, 83, 94, 146n305, 282n150
Mantena, Karuna, 36
Maoism, 240
Marantidou, Virginia and Glosserman, Brad, 246
Matei, Florina, 164
McCulloch, Alison, 84, 143n288
McGarry, John, 87, 143n288

Mehta, Uday Singh, 37
Meidner Plan, 228
Milbus, 199, 212n200, 213n208, 136n222
military: adventurism, 91, 104, 157, 163, 167, 174, 180, 305, 308, 310; civil-military relations, 13, 14, 23, 25, 33, 35, 43, 47, 49, 54, 82, 101–105, 112, 157–200, 200n13, 204nn102–107, 248, 251–252, 267–268, 303–305, 311, 314n19, 314nn21–23; courts, 4, 6, 11, 214n233, 316n27; dictatorship, 5, 6, 8, 17n31, 18n32, 33, 53, 64n126, 92, 99, 134n188, 135n201, 208n161, 250, 311; establishment, 2, 8, 10, 12, 45, 47, 269, 303, 305; influence, 2, 5, 7, 9, 10, 14, 15, 34, 44–46, 61nn100–103, 94, 97, 98, 110, 116, 117, 133n182, 210n173, 212nn200–208, 230, 245, 260, 263, 266, 283n158, 286n186, 306, 309, 310; institutionalism, 11, 20, 45, 166, 249; professionalism, 161–167, 173, 174, 213
military dictators: Khan, Ayub, 5, 6, 17nn25–26, 17n31, 44, 47, 64n126, 99, 138n240, 183, 184, 189, 211n184, 249, 318n47; Khan, Yahya, 7, 183, 184; Musharraf, Pervez, 17n27, 17n31, 18n33, 45, 52, 54, 64n126, 98, 134n188, 136n201, 147n310, 179, 185, 186, 189, 211n189, 214n220, 215n236, 249–250, 276n79; Zia-ul-Haque, 17n27, 17n31, 18n32, 33, 45, 47, 64n126, 99, 101, 102, 171, 178, 179, 184, 185, 188, 189, 191, 208n161, 208n163, 210n178, 211n189, 249, 282
military enterprises: Askari Bank, 172; Bahria Foundation, 172; Defence Housing Society, 172, 179; Fauji Foundation, 172, 179; Shaheen Foundation, 172
military operations, 161, 197; Radd-ul-Fasad, 179, 182; Zarb-e-Azab, 179, 188
Mill, John Stewart, 27, 28, 37; difference principle, 25
Ministry for Climate Change, 267
Ministry of Finance, 216n248
Ministry of Planning Development and Special Initiatives, 199, 216n248, 289n214, 290
Money Bill, 132n174
Morocco, 146n304, 245
multiculturalism, 6, 13, 14, 23, 24, 29–34, 37, 38–39, 42, 47, 53, 54, 79, 88, 93, 111, 115, 63n121, 159, 180, 186, 193, 235, 262
Muslim, 3–6, 29, 33, 38, 42, 51, 60n91, 84, 102–109, 122n50, 126n103, 144n295, 171, 180, 188, 194, 210n178, 250, 316n27; Sunni, 5, 36, 79, 193, 247; Shi'a, 43, 121n147, 170, 193; Ummah, 38, 42, 175, 183, 192

National Command and Operations Centre (NCOC), 9, 307, 317
National Finance Commission (NFC), 88, 98, 103, 109, 111, 114, 116, 131n160, 142n280
neo-colonialism, 243, 244, 260, 269
neoliberalism, 48, 90, 91–94, 113, 128n131, 129nn136–140, 131n157, 136n222, 142n272, 192, 227–249, 269, 270n5, 271n15, 272n23, 272n35, 273nn43–44, 274n53; in Pakistan 249–269, 282n150, 310, 312, 318n45; policies 87, 88, 101–105, 109, 111, 112, 116, 118, 159, 180, 191, 200, 282n145; scepticism, 230
Nepal, 37, 105, 107, 108, 110, 127n115
New Zealand, 75; Maori population, 75
Nigeria, 31, 83–85, 88, 113, 116, 126nn101–103, 143n288, 146n305, 212n202, 216n244, 247

norms: Constitutional, 31, 36, 39, 50; Democratic, 13, 14, 23, 24, 33, 34, 49, 51, 54, 73, 80, 88, 90, 91, 92, 94, 107, 111, 115, 159, 165, 171, 180, 192, 229, 230, 231, 232, 238, 239, 246, 247, 248, 250, 262, 267, 273n49, 304; Islamic, 33, 104; Multicultural, 5, 28, 34, 44, 162; Political, 1, 29, 45, 47, 162
Northern Ireland, 80, 87; Good Friday Accords, 80
Nunn, Frederick M., 167, 168
Nussbaum, Martha, 38, 59n69

Olaoluwa, Senayon, 56n36
O'Leary, Brendon, 85
Ong, Aihwa, 236, 237, 274n60

Pakistan Democratic Movement, 301, 302, 305, 307, 308, 316n27
Pakistan National Human Development Report 2020, 239
Parliamentary Committee on National Security 2019, 196
parochialism, 56n36, 84
participation: economic, 3, 48, 71, 90, 211n184; minority, 44–45, 52, 115, 116, 121n47, 123n62, 126n101, 145n300, 146n303, 232; political, 3, 13, 26, 27, 37, 39, 51, 77, 78, 80, 92, 124n78, 158, 168, 170, 234, 315n24
Pashtun Tahaffuz Movement (PTM), 182, 209n172
pluralism, 29, 53, 126n104, 172
Polanyi, Karl, 233, 234, 273n40; countermovement, 233, 273n40
political parties, 2, 7, 8, 11, 32, 80, 82, 84, 97, 99, 102, 114, 115, 130n156, 140n252, 163, 173, 179, 205n115, 206n127, 211n184, 250, 260, 282n150, 307; Awami League, 183; Bharati Janta Party (BJP), 107; MQM, 41, 316n27; PML-N, 17n31, 89, 133n178, 145, 185, 307, 308, 315n23, 316n27, 317n34; PML-Q, 17n31, 17n33; PNA, 18n32, 184; PPP, 89, 184–186, 207n148, 282n150, 307, 308, 316n27, 317n34; PTI, 8–11, 41, 131n160, 133n178, 253, 306, 314nn15–16, 315n24
polity, 2, 5, 9, 12, 13, 23–25, 27, 29, 30, 35, 42, 47, 51–52, 71, 74, 79, 83–89, 95, 97, 102, 104, 108–111, 157, 158, 160, 169, 175, 186–189, 191, 204n102, 231, 236, 238, 250, 256, 306, 307, 311; empowering the, 14, 28, 40, 46, 76, 78, 179, 184
populism, 231, 238, 310
postcolonial state, 1, 30, 50, 73, 83, 85, 92, 165, 166, 169, 176, 181, 183, 230, 231, 235
praetorian oligarchy, 181, 205n119
Provincially Administered Tribal Areas (PATA), 197
Prussia, 167. *See* Germany.
Punjab, 24, 47, 94–104, 136n214, 138n240, 180–184, 206nn120–121, 263, 264, 302, 308, 309; hegemony of, 35, 39, 40–41, 44, 48, 54n1, 60n81, 61n99, 78, 86, 88, 89, 110–118, 135n196, 143nn286–291, 192, 193, 215n242, 235, 243, 247–252, 258, 259, 283n158, 286n187, 290n229, 316n27

Ramo, Joshua Cooper, 243. *See also* Beijing Consensus
Rawls, John, 25; distributive justice, 9, 13, 15, 23–26, 34, 36, 39, 46–50, 54nn2–9, 111, 159, 180, 186, 192, 228, 247, 249, 269;
regionalism, 84
religio-political parties: Jamaat-e-Islami, 170; Tehreek-e-Labbaik, 170
Reynolds, Andrew, 74, 77
Ricardo, David, 37
Rouigier, Louis, 228
Russia, 255, 268, 275n70, 303, 310, 313n13, 317n40

Sandbrook, Richard, 233, 234, 238, 239, 273n41; development paradigm, 234, 273nn41–43
Saxena and Swenden, 107
Schiff, Rebecca L., 160, 162, 177, 178, 204n102, 204nn105–106
secessionism, 1, 2, 6, 14, 44, 74, 77, 80, 84, 89, 91, 95, 101, 103, 110, 111, 118, 123n62, 180, 183, 184, 188, 195, 235, 236
sectarianism, 170
secularism, 42
self-determination, 42, 57, 92, 111
self-governance, 24, 39, 54, 57n49, 115, 116, 248, 260, 267
Sen, Amartya, 38
Shah, Abrahim, 251
Shoup, Brian, 82
Sikh, 3, 36, 57n49, 188, 206n120
Sindh, 24, 44, 48, 61nn99–100, 98, 100, 111, 136n214, 143n290, 182, 183, 252, 258, 260, 264, 290n229, 316n27
Singapore, 80, 84
Sisk, Timothy, 71
Smith, Adam, 37
socialism: Chinese 240, 274n60
socio-cultural group, 14, 24, 35, 75, 235, 236, 247–248
socio-economic disenfranchisement, 1, 3, 12, 39, 94, 98, 102, 110, 178, 181, 238, 260, 317n34
sovereignty, 16n19, 29, 31, 38, 41, 56n37, 86, 106, 110, 167, 170, 171, 175, 176, 214n231, 245, 248, 260–261, 270, 301, 307, 310
Spain, 29, 30, 53, 56n37, 57n40
Spivak, Gayatri Chakravorty, 36
Springborg, Robert, 169
Sri Lanka, 105, 108–110, 141n266, 212n202, 244, 246, 251, 278n113, 280n122, 281n131; Hambantota port, 244, 251, 281n131; 1978 Constitution of Sri Lanka, 131n266
State-Owned Enterprises (SOEs), 47, 101, 241, 242, 248, 249, 277n90, 279n117
Supreme Court: India, 42, 107, 140n259; Pakistan, 4, 8, 63n116, 107, 117, 141n262, 183, 185, 208n154, 209n167, 215n235, 302, 304; United States, 130n155
Switzerland, 27, 126n108

Tariq, Hamna, 257
Taylor, Charles, 53, 235, 279n116
terrorism, 79, 179, 182, 186, 187, 195, 196, 197, 209n166, 214n231, 268
Thatcher-Regan political era, 228; Reaganomics, 229; trickle-down economics, 229
Third World Approaches to International Law (TWAIL), 227, 236
Toshakhana, 304
tribalism, 53
Turkey, 169–171, 275, 304, 314n21; Kemalism, 169
Two-nation theory, 170

Uganda, 116, 146n304, 247
Ukraine, 212n202, 303, 313n13
United Nations Development Fund (UNDP), 239
United States of America, 27, 42, 73, 169, 171, 172, 208n150, 255, 279n121, 285n182, 303; Agency for International Development, 169; Humphrey-Hawkins Full Employment Bill, 228; one drop policy, 78; Supreme Court. *See* Supreme Court; US Posse Comitatus Act, 197; war on terror, 182, 186, 197; Washington, 172, 233, 243, 273n41, 277n105

Vangeli, Anastas, 240; State Neoliberalism, 240

Washington Consensus, 233, 243, 277n105; Post-Washington Consensus, 273n41
Walter Lippman conference 1938, 228
Welfare initiatives: Ehsaas Program, 307; Kissan card, 9; Naya Pakistan Housing Development Authority, 9, 307; Sehat Sahulat Program, 9, 307
Western democratic theory, 24–28, 36–37, 50, 73, 160
Whalen, Hugh, 26
World Bank (WB), 141n266, 191, 229, 233, 236, 276n83
World War II, 172

Xinjiang, 256

Ziblatt, Daniel, 34

About the Author

Dr. Sikander Ahmed Shah is a distinguished faculty member and founding member of the Shaikh Ahmad Hassan School of Law at Lahore University of Management Sciences (LUMS). He holds an interdisciplinary academic background, having earned his Ph.D. from Indiana University Bloomington, accompanied by a B.A. in Economics and a Juris Doctorate (Cum Laude) from the University of Michigan, Ann Arbor. Currently serving as the Director of the Centre for Chinese Legal Studies at LUMS, Dr. Shah has received acclaim for his significant contributions to the field of law and policy.

Dr. Shah's academic influence extends beyond institutional boundaries, evidenced by his roles in visiting and adjunct faculty positions at various prestigious law schools nationally and internationally. During his sabbatical in 2012–2013, Dr. Shah served as the legal advisor to the Foreign Minister of Pakistan, showcasing his dedication to both academia and public service.

As a leading authority, Dr. Shah is recognized for his contributions to the understanding of constitutional theory, design, and practice in Asia, with a specific focus on Pakistan. His research elucidates the complexities of international law and constitutional dynamics in the region, establishing him as a preeminent scholar. In addition to his academic pursuits, Dr. Shah actively engages in public policy formulation in Pakistan. His teaching and research interests span a wide range of subjects, including foreign affairs, international relations, political theory, and constitutional rights.

Dr. Shah's expertise in international law is further demonstrated by his involvement with governmental and non-governmental organizations, where he delivers lectures and provides guidance on international legal matters. His academic contributions include a seminal book titled "International Law and Drone Strikes in Pakistan: The Legal and Socio-political Aspects" (published by Routledge Research in the Law of Armed Conflict), as well as numerous book chapters with leading publishers such as Edward Elgar Publishing and

Lexington Books. Additionally, he has authored articles in prestigious academic journals including the American Journal of International Law, Vermont Law Review, and the Hong Kong Law Journal.

www.ingramcontent.com/pod-product-compliance
Ingram Content Group UK Ltd.
Pitfield, Milton Keynes, MK11 3LW, UK
UKHW041832031026
15587UKWH00002B/710

9 781666 955453